THE CLASSICS OF WESTERN SPIRITUALITY

THE CLASSICS OF WESTERN SPIRITUALITY
A Library of the Great Spiritual Masters

President and Publisher
Kevin A. Lynch, C.S.P.

EDITORIAL BOARD

BÉRULLE
AND
THE
FRENCH SCHOOL
SELECTED WRITINGS

EDITED WITH AN INTRODUCTION BY
WILLIAM M. THOMPSON

TRANSLATION BY
LOWELL M. GLENDON, S.S.

PREFACE BY
SUSAN A. MUTO

PAULIST PRESS
NEW YORK • MAHWAH

Cover Art: Frank Sabatté, C.S.P., received his B.A. in art from U.C.L.A. in 1973, studying under James Valerio, Lee Mullican and others. He has been a campus minister since 1979 and an illustrator for Paulist Press since 1977. In 1986–87 he served as vice-president of the Liturgical Arts Guild of Ohio.

Scripture citations in the Introduction are from the *New American Bible* translation.

Library of Congress Cataloging-in-Publication Data

Bérulle and the French School: selected writings/edited with an
  introduction and notes by William M. Thompson; translated by Lowell
  M. Glendon; preface by Susan A. Muto.
      p.   cm.—(The Classics of Western spirituality)
    Texts translated from French and Latin.
    Bibliography: p.
    Includes index.
    ISBN 0-8091-0426-1: $19.95 (est.).—ISBN 0-8091-3080-7 (pbk.):
  $16.95 (est.)
      1. Spirituality—France—History.   2. Bérulle, Pierre de,
  1575–1629.   3. Spirituality—Catholic Church—History.   I. Bérulle,
  Pierre de, 1575–1629.   II. Thompson, William M.   III. Glendon,
  Lowell M.   IV. Series.
  BX1529.B46   1989
  248′.0944—dc20   89-3283
                                                                        CIP

Published by Paulist Press
997 Macarthur Boulevard
Mahwah, New Jersey 07430

Printed and bound in the United States of America

CONTENTS

CONTENTS

Editor and Author of the Introduction

WILLIAM M. THOMPSON is professor of theology at Duquesne University, Pittsburgh, Pennsylvania. A native of Boise, Idaho, he received the Ph.D. in theology from the University of St. Michael's College, Toronto, having written a dissertation on Karl Rahner's thought. He is an associate editor of HORIZONS, a member of The American Academy of Religion and on the board of directors of The Catholic Theological Society of America.

Professor Thompson specializes in the classical themes of systematics, especially Christology and soteriology, hermeneutics, and the contemplative-spiritual dimensions of theology. His major Christological-soteriological works are *Christ and Consciousness: Exploring Christ's Contribution to Human Consciousness, Jesus, Lord and Savior: A Theopathic Christology and Soteriology* and most recently *The Jesus Debate: A Survey and Synthesis*. His recent *Fire and Light: The Saints and Theology* represents his first sustained exploration of theology's roots in spiritual-mystical experience. The study of theology's and religion's foundations in human experience has also led him to a continual study of the works of Eric Voegelin. Dr. Thompson is active in the Eric Voegelin Society, and one of his more important studies on Voegelin, edited with John Kirby, is *Voegelin and the Theologian: Ten Studies in Interpretation*.

Professor Thompson's studies on the French School are directly linked to his stress upon the experiential-mystical foundations of theology. Among those studies are "The Christic Universe of Pierre de Bérulle and the French School" in *The American Benedictine Review*, "A Study of Bérulle's Christic Spirituality" in his *Jesus, Lord and Savior*, and "Olier's *La journée chrétienne* as a Guide for Today's Theology" in the *Bulletin de Saint-Sulpice*.

Translator of This Volume

LOWELL M. GLENDON, S.S., is a member of the American Province of the Society of Saint Sulpice and director of St. Mary's Spiritual Center in Baltimore. He has a long-standing interest in the French School. His doctoral dissertation from Fordham University (1983) studied Olier's theological and spiritual anthropology. He has also written "Jean-Jacques Olier's Shifting Attitude Toward the Human" for the *Bulletin de Saint-Sulpice* as well as *An Annotated and Descriptive Chronology of the Important Events in the Life of Jean-Jacques Olier (1608–1657)*. He has served as a resource person in French School Spirituality for his community in the United States, Canada and France. He is presently employed on the faculty of the Loyola Pastoral Counseling Program, Columbia, Maryland. Father Glendon is currently writing a book on spiritual direction.

Author of the Preface

DR. SUSAN A. MUTO, a native of Pittsburgh, Pennsylvania, is executive director of the Epiphany Association, an ecumenical lay formation center, and an adjunct professor of literature and spirituality at the Institute of Formative Spirituality, Duquesne University. She is also the author of six books exploring the art and discipline of formative reading and the related themes of silence, meditation, prayer, contemplation and action. Dr. Muto teaches courses at Duquesne that focus on the writings of the masters of Western spirituality and other great faith and formation traditions. Her books, fourteen in total, include *Blessings That Make Us Be: A Formative Approach to Living the Beatitudes* and *Meditation in Motion*. Her current projects entail co-authoring a book on adult Christian formation and readying a contemporary commentary on the collected works of St. John of the Cross to coincide with the four-hundredth anniversary of his death (1591–1991).

FOREWORD

One feels particularly blessed, but not quite worthy, to be a part of this project that introduces, in a somewhat new way, the French School of Spirituality to the readers of this series. One feels blessed, for surely here one finds rich and daring explorations of the movement of the spirit—"elevations," to use a term beloved to the School—which transport one into familiar and fascinatingly unfamiliar territory. One also feels not quite worthy, for this school pulsates with an ardor and passion—with a "fire," to use Father Olier's favored metaphor—that few would dare to claim as their normal possession. Illumination and passion, light and fire, insight united with heart—these are the ingredients of what the French School calls the "science of the saints."

In its own time—the exciting yet turbulent seventeenth century—the wedding of "science" with "sanctity" created by the mystics of the French School was an effective way to make the gospel contemporary. There is surely the element of science, in the French School's sense: the rich theological heritage, the awareness of new challenges from Reformers and Renaissance thinkers, an attempt at a new *apologia* of Roman Catholicism, a refusal to hide behind simplistic and overly pious slogans. But there is also the element of sanctity: an intense desire to ground theological science in living experience or in an experiential faith, which expresses itself most passionately on both the personal and the ecclesial-social levels. The reader of this volume, then, can expect to oscillate between daring, "metaphysical" speculations and glowing and "burning" outbursts of mystical love.

I suspect that the mixed genre, which the "science of the saints" is, will be the key characteristic that powerfully commends this School to our contemporary period. It seems that our very experiential age longs for a deep and renewed sense of adoration, reverence, God-centeredness, transcendence and the overcoming of narcissism, yet not without sensing how all of these great virtues are the deepest meaning of human experience. The rich explorations of human experience provided by the great mystics in this volume will, hopefully, confirm for the reader the belief that human experience opens out, in and through God, to a Mystery inviting adoration. This intersection between human experience and Divine Mystery is something of a master key in the French School, unlocking the meaning of humanity and indicating why our French mystics had such a concentrated fascination for the mystery of the Incarnation (for our mystics, the most intensive and unsurpassable expression of that intersection).

The French School as a term can be used rather loosely to embrace all those who have been deeply influenced by the founding mystics of that School. Even a sampling of texts from all such spirituals would be impossible in one volume, for this School's influence extends well into our own century. We have chosen to concentrate upon the glowing center of the School, the founders and foundress. By undisputed consensus Cardinal Pierre de Bérulle is the originating influence. Jean-Jacques Olier and John Eudes drink deeply from Bérulle's well, but they are never mere imitations; their creative adaptations also serve as sources for the later followers. Readers normally think of Charles de Condren as belonging to the founding circle too, and we would agree, but the paucity of writings by Father Condren has led us to emphasize the other "principals." If you will, Father Condren surfaces chiefly through those whom he influenced.

Somewhat new is the attention given Mother Madeleine de Saint-Joseph, the first French prioress of the Great Carmel in Paris. She was enormously influenced by Cardinal Bérulle, and also seems to have exercised considerable influence over the Cardinal. Something of Father Condren also radiates out from the Mother. Clearly she belongs to the foundational center and deserves to be more commonly recognized in this capacity. At the same time, she somewhat represents the very important contribution women have always made to the thought and vitality of the French School.

In the end, the French School is its own best introduction. The reader won't be into the text for very long before being transported into a world of daring, challenge and love. One suspects that Cardinal Bérulle was listening to his felt experience when he showed a special fondness for the metaphor of "elevation."

FOREWORD

Numerous people deserve to be thanked for their assistance in this project. I must especially thank Father Raymond Deville, the Superior General of St. Sulpice; Fathers Edward Frazer and Gerald Brown, former and current provincial of the U. S. Sulpicians, respectively; Sulpician Fathers Irénée Noye, Raymond E. Brown, Cale Crowley, Gerald Coleman, James Fredericks, William Lee, John Bowen, Joseph Bonadio, Frederick Cwiekowski, Gilles Chaillot, Vincent Eaton, Peter Chirico, William Morris, Raymond Hesler; Father Louis Levesque, Assistant Provincial of the Eudists in Quebec; Father John Sullivan, of the Institute of Carmelite Studies; Father Bonaventure Hayes, O.F.M.; Brothers Michael J. McGinniss, F.S.C., and Francis Huether, F.S.C.; Father Francis X. Malinowski, C.S.Sp., Chair of the theology department at Duquesne University, especially for his enthusiasm for the French School and for his meditative reading of the texts with me; and thanks, too, to my colleagues here at Duquesne University, for their encouragement. A very special thanks to Mary Ellen Lewis, Marybeth Hensberger, Father Jason DelVitto, Sister Margaret Ayers, O.S.B., Andrea Mallek, and Father William Rademacher for assistance with checking the texts and to Harry Hutchinson and Patricia O'Kane of the Duquesne University Library. And warm thanks, too, to the priests, staff and community of the Pittsburgh Oratory, for their support and encouragement, especially Father Drew Morgan, C.O.

The greater debt, however, is owed to my wife, Patricia Kobielus Thompson, for her encouragement, her helpful and also meditative reading of the texts with me, and her patience; to Susan A. Muto, for her inviting Preface to this volume, and to Father Lowell M. Glendon, S.S., the translator for this volume, for his perseverance, his stunning competency, his humor and support, and his love for the French School. Affection and competence are the characteristics of the scholarly method he has displayed throughout this project.

PREFACE

estern Catholicism boasts of a number of special schools of spirituality named after founders or associated with rules of religious life. A few of the most notable are the Augustinian, the Benedictine, the Franciscan, the Dominican, the Ignatian and the Carmelite. Special schools are also designated by location as, for example, the English School (Richard Rolle, Walter Hilton, the anonymous author of *The Cloud of Unknowing*, Julian of Norwich); the Rhineland School (John Ruusbroec, Henry Suso, John Tauler); and, of course, the French School, which is the focus of this edition of the Classics of Western Spirituality.

In the Roman Catholic tradition a special school represents and articulates the common ways of the faith—repentance, prayer, meditation on scripture, devotion to the sacraments—but its expression of these foundations includes a distinctive typology of styles and emphases. Special schools thus contain the essentials of a gospel, a Christian and a church-oriented spirituality, but they enable people so attracted to them to personalize these basics in a special, even intense manner that at once awakens them to God in a new way and facilitates their ongoing formation.

This book delineates the specific typology of the French School, revealing its place in the Catholic mainstream and disclosing its characteristic attitudes and applications. I would like to highlight a few key aspects of this spiritual doctrine and then encourage the reader to savor them more fully in the writings of the masters of this school: Pierre Cardinal de Bérulle, Jean-Jacques Olier, John Eudes and Mother Madeleine de Saint-Joseph.

It is the basic assumption of the French School of Spirituality that we are created by God and formed in God's image; we come from

PREFACE

him, as Augustinian exemplarism suggests, and it is to him that we must return. Thus our lives on earth ought to be pathways and pointers to what we shall be eternally in heaven.

The first emphasis of our journey has to be on *adoration,* a habitual state of soul that consists in acknowledging always and everywhere the greatness and divine goodness of God. This state of adoring love, proceeding from the core of one's being (one's heart of hearts) calls for an attitude of *abasement* before the supreme majesty, for a posture of deep humility as we creatures bow before our Creator in an act of unending oblation and surrender, expressing with our whole being the praise God alone ought to receive.

To live in this state of adoring and self-emptying love, the Christian must imitate in his or her everyday spiritual life three facets of Jesus' own love for the Father. We must *adhere* to Jesus, the Father's perfect adorer, whose attitudes, virtues and transcendent willing each disciple must reproduce by rejecting sin and remaining open to grace. Like Jesus, the Christian must also *annihilate* all traces of self-interest and act only and always to glorify God. We must, in Olier's words, "live entirely for God in Christ Jesus," becoming "annihilated" in regard to our own plans and committing ourselves as disciples to Jesus, who is in us in order for us to live wholly with the Father. As Jesus accepted God's will in everything, so must we say with unceasing faithfulness: Not my will but thine be done.

The most vivid exemplar of this profound surrender is Mary. She is the model of the third facet, *abnegation.* Jesus will live in us, as he dwelt in Mary's womb and in her heart, only to the degree that we joyfully "disappropriate" ourselves, that is, renounce proprietorship over ourselves and become God's servants. In so doing we let go gradually, with the help of grace, all that is contrary to the Christ-form of our soul. We submit our pride and every tentacle of sin to Christ's regenerating, redeeming renewal. Thus strengthened by grace and responsive to the call of the Spirit, we can accept and worthily fulfill our *apostolic* duty to teach all nations and to build up the body of Christ in his holy church.

Once we allow our frail, human hearts to become more and more like the adoring, adhering, annihilated, abnegated hearts of Jesus and Mary, we can carry out the work we are called to do "on earth as it is in heaven." In this way we become children of God, paradoxically liberated by renunciation, elevated by humility, and illumined by the night of faith. Purified thus in heart and mind, we cannot help but be pleasing to God.

PREFACE

This theme of spiritual childhood, taken up so powerfully by Saint
Thérèse of Lisieux, finds its seeds in the French School. Bérulle,
Olier, Eudes and Mother Madeleine capture in prose and poetic
prayers the soaring freedom of soul that can be ours if we willingly
let go of the egocentric gratification, greed and grandiosity that
separate us from God. Christ cautioned that unless we become as
little children, abandoned, trusting, joyful, we cannot enter into the
fullness of the reign of God. The founders and followers of the
French School would resonate, therefore, with these words of Olier:
"I feel that the Child Jesus has given me the grace to be like a small
child, without any will of my own. He has also given me the grace of
joyful abandonment and so abandoning myself to God, I place all my
trust in him. To put it . . . in a single sentence: I am as carefree as
a child."

This spirit of freedom, far from paralyzing productivity actually
enhances the depth and effectiveness of Christian commitment. It is
a tribute to the French School that it has made a lasting impact on
Catholic spirituality in the Modern Period. Its special emphases
serve as reminders of what is most essential to a Christian way of life:
openness to the inspirations of the Spirit and a willingness to incarnate these directives in daily life.

Abbreviations

C	*Le coeur admirable de la très sacrée mère de Dieu* (Eudes)
Cat	*Le catéchisme chrétien pour la vie intérieure* (Olier)
Coll	*Collationes* (Bérulle)
CB	*Correspondance du Bérulle*
DC	*Discours de controverse* (Bérulle)
DS	Dictionnaire de spiritualité
E	*Traité des energumènes* (Bérulle)
El	*Élévations* (Bérulle)
G	*Discours de l'estat et des grandeurs de Jésus* (Bérulle)
I	*Introduction à la vie et aux vertus chrétiennes* (Olier)
J	*La journée chrétienne* (Olier)
M233	Paris, Archives nationales, carton M. 233 (papiers Bérulle)
Ma	*Élévation sur saincte Magdelaine* (Bérulle)
Mars	Marseille, Bibliothèque municipale ms. 467 (microfilm) (Bérulle)
Mc	A later copy of *Mém* (Olier)
Mém	*Mémoires autographes* (Olier)
Mémor	*Mémorial* (Bérulle)
N	*Narré* (Bérulle)
OC	*Oeuvres complètes* (Eudes)
OP	*Oeuvres de piété* (Bérulle)
OR	Textes (Dupuy, *Bérulle et le sacerdoce*)
RHE	*Revue d'histoire ecclésiastique* 57 (1962): 813–62 (Bérulle)

ABBREVIATIONS

RJ   La vie et le royaume de Jésus dans les âmes chrétiennes (Eudes)

T   *Traité des saints ordres* (Olier)

V   *Vie de Jésus* (Bérulle)

Note: See Bibliography, under "Primary Sources," for all sources of the citations from Bérulle, Madeleine, Olier and Eudes. A reference to Lettres, *without any volume number being indicated, always refers to the Serouet edition of Madeleine de Saint-Joseph's letters. A reference to Olier's* Lettres *(Levesque edition, two volumes) will indicate the appropriate volume.*

AN INTRODUCTION TO THE FRENCH SCHOOL

I

Historical Aspects of The French School

The Larger Context: Some Dimensions

The period between Pierre de Bérulle's birth (1575) and John Eudes' death (1680) witnessed seismic transformations on the European continent in all the major areas of human concern: politics, economics, culture and religion. The phenomenon that was seventeenth-century France and the "child" it birthed—the French School of spirituality—needs to be set against this larger horizon of experience. If we begin with the political theater, this was the era of the newly emerging "middle-sized" sovereign monarchies/states. Power now was beginning to concentrate at relatively few urban centers, like Spain, or Sweden, or France. The crumbling of the earlier medieval jurisdictions set the stage for this. But the more immediate catalyst was the new military technology arising to meet the needs generated by the always-present feuding. That technology required an urban population sufficiently developed to offer the necessary artisan shops, manufactories, mining and metallurgical entrepreneurs, capitalists and bankers. Historian William McNeill suggests that this kind of technology was simply too complex for the smaller nobilities or principalities or cities. But it was also too delicate and sophisticated for the more "universal" sovereignties like Papacy and Empire.[1]

France clearly was able to supply the necessary powder and shot, the transportation for heavy artillery, and the military skills needed for the making of a new European power-center. So unnerving, in fact, was this new French power becoming that the Dutch and English, with the Hapsburgs, found it necessary if distasteful in 1689 to enter into an alliance to check Louis XIV's expanding power.[2]

A growing conflict with traditional powers like the Papacy and the Holy Roman Empire (the Hapsburgs) was a price to be paid by the new power centers. The period 1500–1648 (especially the years 1618–48, the Thirty Years War) is particularly illustrative of the new tensions. The Treaty of Westphalia in 1648 finally brought some easing of tensions by acknowledging the political and religious sovereignties beyond the Empire's borders. This kind of tension is a great theme in Cardinal Bérulle's career. He wanted France to remain loyal to Papacy, Catholicism and Empire. Richelieu, however, was more pragmatic and less principled, working for France's dominance, even if this meant coming to terms with Protestantism.

It might be well for us to take a closer look at this Bérulle-Richelieu conflict, for it is a very relevant illustration of the new kind of struggling emerging on the European scene. Richelieu, for example, had already criticized Bérulle and the "devout party" to which he belonged in 1620 through several anonymous pamphlets. The latter had backed the new Emperor Ferdinand in his struggle with the Protestant Elector Palatine Friedrich V and had even succeeded in convincing the Royal Council to oppose the Elector. Another conflict is especially revealing. Both Bérulle and Richelieu favored the marriage of Henriette of France to Charles I of England, but for quite different reasons. Bérulle hoped it might help salvage something of English Catholicism. Richelieu wanted to weaken Spain (the Empire) through an alliance with England. Both were disappointed in the end. Richelieu removed the aspects of the marriage contract favorable to Catholicism, which stung Bérulle, surely. But Richelieu had to turn toward Protestant Germany for his alliance.

Bérulle and his "devout party" continued to exercise important influence at court. The struggle with Richelieu intensified. And Bérulle's receiving the cardinalate in 1627 did not ease matters. The final blow came on 15 September 1629, when Bérulle refused to sanction the Treaty of Susa, a treaty that was ultimately harmful to France's alliance with England. Slightly earlier Richelieu, against Bérulle's recommendation, convinced the Royal Council to back the Duke of Mantua, Charles de Nevers, who was being attacked by the

INTRODUCTION

Spanish. The result of all of this was the famous political disgrace of Bérulle in 1629. Richelieu had hoped to remove his rival by making him the French Ambassador to Rome, but Bérulle's death cut off that possibility.[3]

But such political maneuverings, which the Bérulle-Richelieu conflict pointedly exemplify, were but one of the enormous transitions of the time. Surely the shock of the Protestant Reformation was another. As the Treaty of Westphalia illustrates, the older Catholic tradition, like it or not, had to arrive at some kind of settlement with the Reformers. In France that meant with Reformed or Huguenot theology and practice. Not a little of the French School of Spirituality is a response to the challenges of the Reformation. Echoes of the Reformers' thinking are quite evident in Bérulle, and still present in Olier and Eudes, but less intensively. There is a significant collection of "works of controversy" directed explicitly against especially Calvin's thought in Bérulle's collected works. Topics like the Eucharist, especially the sacrificial character of the Mass, the notion of heresy, the nature of justification, and even the infallibility of the church are taken up in response to the "new doctors," as Bérulle likes to call the Protestant Reformers. One can sense something of the pressures of the Reformation in Olier's stress on the sacrificial nature of the Eucharist, and rather more positively in his trying to work out criteria for discerning a true priestly vocation. John Eudes repeatedly had to deal with the Huguenot alternative on his many missions.[4]

To the Reformation we must add the Renaissance. Leonardo da Vinci, Michelangelo Buonarroti, Copernicus and Rabelais are only slightly earlier than our precise period of focus (from Bérulle's birth to Eudes' death). Many Renaissance "greats" fall precisely within the period. Cervantes (d. 1616), Shakespeare (d. 1616), Velázquez (d. 1660), Rembrandt (d. 1669), El Greco (d. 1614) and Rubens (d. 1640) were giving shape to a new kind of national literature and style of painting in the new urban centers. Nicholas Copernicus (d. 1543) and his heliocentric system of astronomy, arguing for a circular rather than an elliptical orbit for the planets, deserves special mention. As we will see, he caught the imagination of Bérulle, who imaginatively and hauntingly compares his new style of Christ-centered spirituality to a kind of "Copernican Revolution" in the second discourse of the *Grandeurs*.

There are many more scientific greats of the Renaissance falling within our precise period of focus. Galileo Galilei (1564–1642) defended the Copernican astronomy. William Harvey (d. 1657) studied the heart's role in the circulation of blood. The interest in the sacred heart may have something to do with this. In any case, John Eudes' theology and spirituality of the sacred hearts of Mary and Jesus were brilliant ways of rendering the gospel contemporary.[5] Johannes Kepler (d. 1630) discovered a mathematical formula exactly describing the elliptical motion of each separate planet, thus correcting Copernicus and removing an important objection to his views. Newton (1642–1727) formulated his law of universal gravitation, and Francis Bacon (d. 1626) formulated an "empirical" criterion of scientific knowledge. To all of this we might add the important inventions, still with us, of the telescope (c. 1608), microscope (c. 1590), pendulum clock (c. 1656), thermometer (c. 1654) and barometer (c. 1643). As we will see, one of the enduring debates is the precise nature of the influence of the Renaissance upon the French School. But that there was a definite influence can hardly be doubted.

McNeill sums up this entire period under the label "cultural pluralism."[6] Clearly Europe was experiencing a new kind of diversity and stretching of horizons. If we were to follow Karl Rahner's lead we could describe this as a qualitatively new kind of pluralism, for the new methods of inquiry, intellectual disciplines, and changing presuppositions about the nature of reality were making it almost impossible for any one person to truly master all the new discoveries.[7] It seems plausible to think that at least the beginnings of this kind of pluralism were making themselves felt. And as we well know from the intensified experience of our own pluralistic situation, the results can be ambiguous. Such richness of experience can lead to greater depth of insight. It can also lead to fear, insecurity, narrow-mindedness, totalitarianism (to restrain the new querying) and other simplistic solutions. In some ways it is all rather like a "dark night." Is it any wonder that sensitive souls like Bérulle, Olier and Eudes speak of *anéantissement* (abasement) so frequently? Surely the passage through all of this was something like an annihilation of former modes of thought and behavior. The times themselves were a superb analogy for the more difficult side of the spiritual ascent, and sensitive mystics like our three "greats" knew this quite well.

If we follow Yves Congar, theology at this time was on the way toward becoming rather arid, uncreative and "scholastic" in the rather pejorative sense.[8] The notion of a "dogmatic" theology, tied to an exposition of church doctrines and thus free of theological disputes, was coming into its own. Here the new pluralism seemed to foster a style of theology free from too much intellectual "insecurity." In illustration, Congar cites Noel Alexandre's definition of dogmatics (1693):

> [We understand as] dogmatic and moral, theology in which, having set aside all Scholastic questions and omitted questions of positive theology . . . only those things are treated which were defined or handed out as dogmas in the Council of Trent, or explained in the Catechism of this same council.[9]

The abandoning of the technique of the medieval *quaestio* and its replacement by a simple method of doctrinal exposition is a perfect illustration of this state of affairs. We all remember some of the great breakthrough thinkers like Aquinas and Scotus who put the *quaestio* to powerful use. But who can recall a great breakthrough systematician of the seventeenth century?

Louis Cognet, in his penetrating survey of systematic theology in the France of our period confirms Congar's more general assessment of Catholic theology as a whole. Theologians were, he says, "frequently influenced by the deteriorating Scholasticism of the waning Middle Ages."[10] Philippe de Gamaches (1568–1625), who held one of the two chairs at the Sorbonne established by Henry IV for "positive" theology, is a good example. He is also a quite relevant one, for he taught Bérulle and Condren (the next general of the Oratory founded by Bérulle) and had a profound influence on the former. Gamaches knew the *patres* and cited them frequently, but in the more "dogmatic" style coming into favor. The fathers were not part of a creative return to the sources but proofs and illustrations for a Catholic doctrine assailed by the Reformers. André Duval, the occupant of the other Henry IV chair, did show some originality in his creative use of Platonic themes and the mysticism coming from Ruusbroec and Harphius. But in the main he followed an ahistoric and deductive method. Cognet rather wittily says that even Bossuet didn't bother to keep his notes of the lectures from his days at the College de Navarre![11] Moral theology followed suit, growing ever more abstract (removed from people's experience) and even casuistic. Cognet comments: "To a certain extent this development was even demanded by the need to reform the clergy as well as by the necessity to educate sufficiently well-instructed confessors."[12]

The "regular" school theology did generate something of a reaction, which can partly explain the phenomenon that is the French School of Spirituality. Louis Bail (1610–69) issued, in four parts, his *Theologie affective ou saint Thomas en meditations* between 1638 and 1650. The Dominican Guillaume de Contenson (1641–74) surpassed this attempt to unite theology and spirituality with his *Theologia mentis et cordis,* issued between 1668 and 1687. Here speculative "scholastic" analyses of doctrine (*speculationes*) are followed by spiritual applications (*reflexiones*). This newer kind of "contemplative" scholasticism was in many ways a continuation of Gerhard Groote's attempt to wed mysticism to scholasticism in the fourteenth century. The Sorbonne had endorsed by official statute this kind of theology by 1600.[13]

We find much more creativity in the development of historical theology. This was partly a response to the Reformers, who would only listen to the scriptures and the *patres,* not the medieval scholastics. Thus the *Bibliotheca patrum* of Marguerin de la Bigne from 1575 on, as well as the editions of the patristic sources coming from the Benedictines of Saint-Maur, came into being. At first, as Cognet indicates, this *réssourcement* was more polemical, as Bérulle's controversial discourses with the Huguenots indicate. In time it would create the foundations for a new theological specialization in its own right.[14]

Some highpoints of this patristic renaissance are worth underscoring. The Dominican François Combefis published an impressive edition of St. Maximus Confessor in 1675. The reformed Benedictines of Saint-Maur (Maurists), of course, continued to issue their high-quality editions. For example, Dom Jean Mabillon gave us an edition of the works of St. Bernard in 1667, and Dom Thomas Blampin (1640–1710) directed the edition of St. Augustine. Comprehensive syntheses of the *patres* were contributed by the Jesuit Denis Petau in his *Dogmata theologica* (1644–50) and by the Oratorian Louis Thomassin's *Dogmata theologica* (1680–84).

Biblical studies, too, were undergoing something of a profound transformation and renewal, which would eventually bear fruit in today's historical-critical approaches to the scriptures. Richard Simon (1638–1712), a member of the Oratory founded by Cardinal Bérulle, is widely credited with being the originator of modern biblical criticism. He wrote works on both testaments, but unfortunately aroused the wrath of the likes of Bossuet. The Oratorians, despite their tradition of scholarship, were forced to expel him in 1678. But the Oratorians contributed other "proto-critics" of the scriptures: Jean Morin and Bernard Lamy. At the same time, as Cognet puts it, the "tradition of spiritual, moral, and even allegorical exegesis no doubt continued to be widespread."[15] Bossuet's *Apocalypse avec une explication* of 1689 might serve as an example of this kind of exegesis. The mystics of the French School, I might suggest, tend to be in the tradition of a more spiritual-contemplative exegesis. But more tenuous forms of allegory are missing, in the main. Perhaps something of the Renaissance critical spirit served as a modulating force in this regard.[16]

One of the greatest sources of renewal, and the one with the most direct importance for our study, must be, of course, the breakthroughs in mystical and spiritual thought and practice. On one level, surely, this mystical renaissance can be seen as a creative alternative to the dogmatic aridity of the prevailing school theology. It represents a deep effort to remain in tune with the experiential sources of faith and theology. On another level, too, it can be seen as a reaction against what is perceived to be an excessively humanistic trend in the Renaissance period. In other words, this mysticism is a tension-filled reality moving between two extremes. At times it fell into those extremes. The extent to which this creative tension is maintained rather than collapsed is one of the great debates among scholars of the French School, as we shall see.

In some sense, of course, the patristic and biblical renaissance rehearsed already forms a part of this renewal of mysticism and spirituality. The Johannine and Pauline texts, so beloved to the French School, are the biblical texts that easily lend themselves to a more inward, contemplative reading. The *patres,* too, practiced a form of theology wedded to spirituality and mysticism. The "theological" reappropriation of them was, then, a kind of reappropriation of spirituality.[17] The popularity of Dionysius the Areopagite meant the popularity of his brand of apophatic mysticism. The dissemination of Augustine's writings meant that the Augustinian inwardness and Christian-Platonic mysticism were making themselves felt, and both of these left a great impression upon Bérulle and the entire French School. Bishop Zamet, in approving Bérulle's *Grandeurs,* said that he found within it "the spirit of the great apostle of France, Saint Denis and his *Divine Hierarchy.*"[18] The historian Jean Dagens has this to say about Bérulle's Augustinianism:

It is beyond doubt that he receives the tone of his elevations, of his contemplative meditations, from Saint Augustine. . . . The powerful speculations on the Trinity and Incarnation, which form the beauty of the *Grandeurs de Jésus*, are of Augustinian inspiration; in the sweeping view of universal history which is that of the *Vie de Jésus*, one perceives the vestiges of the *City of God*.[19]

Alongside this, however, there was an increasingly appreciated literature of spirituality and mysticism penetrating France. After Dionysius must surely come the Rheno-Flemish writers: Harphius and Blosius in the late 1500s; and in the seventeenth century the greater writings: *The Pearl of the Gospel,* and Ruusbroec's *Ornament of the Spiritual Espousals,* translated into French by the Carthusian Dom Beaucousin. At about the same time appeared the translations of the Spanish and Italian mystics: Luis de Granada, Juan de Avila, the great St. Teresa of Avila, then St. John of the Cross and St. Catherine of Genoa. At the same time, of course, St. Francis de Sales and St. Jane Frances de Chantal were forging a uniquely Christian and French form of "everyday mysticism," which would have an effect upon Olier and John Eudes at a later time.

Bérulle probably absorbed much of this spirituality through frequenting Mme. Acarie's celebrated circle of friends, which included Dom Beaucousin, the Capuchin Benet of Canfield, the Sorbonne theologian Duval, the Jesuit Coton, the secular priest Gallemant and the Marquise de Maignelay. He was her cousin (she later became the Carmelite Marie de l'Incarnation at Pontoise, eventually receiving beatification), and one of his early works—*Bref Discours de l'abnégation intérieure*—reflects the kind of mysticism characteristic of the Rheno-Flemish writers and Catherine of Genoa. Often called abstract mysticism, it emphasized a transcending of all concepts and images as the sign of the deepest mystical union with the Divine. Oftentimes even Jesus' humanity was seen as one of the earthly realities needing to be transcended. In time, this "bypassing" of Jesus' humanity would find its corrective in the likes of Teresa of Avila and the later Bérulle. Somewhat earlier, even Canfield was pressured by his Capuchin superiors to add some chapters on the contemplation of Jesus' passion in the second edition of his *Rule of Perfection*. Bérulle's *Bref Discours* also has some references to Jesus' life and passion as an exemplar of the mystic's way.[20] As we will see, mysticism went through a number of modulations as it was received in France and as people began to explore the spiritual life and the kind of theology most congenial to that life. In many ways it seems to have been a self-correcting or self-enriching reality.[21]

Finally, in this brief overview of historical trends, mention should be made of the enormous pastoral renewal occurring. If you will, this was the praxis dimension of the various kinds of renewal and reaction coming into being. There was a kind of interchange among theology, spirituality and pastoral action that makes of this age a rather fascinating precursor of our own. For example, despite Richelieu's tendency to use the monasteries for monetary gain, abbeys like Cluny, Citeaux and Premontré did strive to be centers of spiritual renewal. What we today might call basic communities frequently gathered at the reformist convents of Port-Royal, Val-de-Grace, the Carmelites, the Visitation nuns and at the equally reformist monasteries of La Trappe and Rancé.[22]

A particularly active area of renewal, and one with profound consequences for the French School, was the embattled terrain of priestly reform. Quite clearly a crucial strategy for renewing the church, regardless of how one might define *renewing*—and we will see that that was a contested issue—is to concentrate on the transformation of the ecclesial leaders. In the seventeenth century, that meant the priests.[23] The Council of Trent had legislated the foundation of seminaries, but this never became law in France, despite the initiatives of people like La Rochefoucauld. The situation was quite desperate. Listen to St. Vincent de Paul's castigation:

> The Church has no worse enemies than her priests. Heresies have come from them . . . and it is through them that heresies have prevailed, that vice has reigned, and that ignorance has established its throne among the "poor" people; and this has happened because of their undisciplined way of life and refusal to oppose those three torrents now inundating the earth with all their might.[24]

Vincent clearly has in mind the Protestant Reformers when he speaks of heresies. When he speaks of vice, he has in mind the immorality of all kinds widely characteristic of the clergy. The large numbers ordained in the various sacred orders, despite their lack of training and the church's lack of need, as well as the piling up of benefices—these are what Vincent probably has in mind. After all, the life of the clergyman offered an easy career in a culture where

11

careers were hard to come by, especially for the less privileged. And the more privileged could gain quick income through the technique of piling up benefices. Cognet tells us that "virtually all monasteries and priories were benefices and many of their titulars were mere tonsured people less than twenty years of age." And he adds that the kings "used them unscrupulously for the purpose of rewarding loyal servants and supporting artists and literati."[25] When he speaks of ignorance, he has in mind the lack of preparation and training characteristic of the secular clergy. As we saw, seminary education had not yet taken hold.[26]

Adrien Bourdoise (1584–1665) is considered the pioneer in French seminary education. He formed a society for priestly candidates in 1612 at Paris, and by 1643 his seminary experiment, as Cognet calls it, was finally approved officially. Cognet continues,

> His example was emulated: between 1622 and 1680 there appeared in twenty French towns seminary societies of this type. . . . Initially Bourdoise's enterprise required true courage, for at that time even La Rochefoucauld did not dare open a seminary either in Clermont or in Senlis, the diocese he was given later on. Bourdoise's influence was to prove vital in connection with other foundings, such as the Oratory and Saint-Sulpice.[27]

Unfortunately he limited the preparation to practical matters for the most part. Little education in theology and spirituality transpired.

Learning from Bourdoise, partly building upon his labors but really creating an alternative style of seminary education, was Bérulle's Oratory, Olier's Company of Saint-Sulpice, and Eudes' Congregation of Jesus and Mary. Here the aim was to develop a secular clergy that might serve as a paradigm and example of what the priesthood should really be. Not a religious order in vows (although the French School adapted the religious orders to their own ends), but the "order" of priests of Jesus and the apostles, which could in turn educate aspirants coming to live with and learn from them. Perhaps one of the reasons Olier maintained cumulative benefices, a practice in violation of canon law, was precisely so that he would have an institutional-parochial basis from which to launch his program of priestly renewal.[28]

The Oratory had seventy-one houses by 1631. Obviously it met a real need. But under its second general, Charles de Condren (1588–1641), the Oratory ceased to make an effort to promote seminary education in its houses. The leadership in seminary education passed to Olier and his new Company of St. Sulpice, which became a veritable model of seminary training. John Eudes' new Congregation also took up the task of such training, as we will see. These efforts were profoundly lasting programs of ecclesial renewal, only really coming under serious question again around the time of the Second Vatican Council. When we add these breakthroughs in seminary education to the renewal among the aristocracy (as the *beata* Mme. Acarie and her circle partially illustrate) and to the extensive mission work of the time (think of St. Vincent de Paul, but also of the extensive missionary work of the Oratorians, Sulpicians and Eudists), we can begin to imagine the kind of irruption of pastoral praxis that was beginning to transform the French church.[29]

Bérulle, Olier and Eudes: A Brief Chronology

As we can see, the above forms the horizon of experience of our three founders of the French School. Each enters into it, contributes to it and significantly alters it in common yet unique ways—commonly enough to make it plausible to call them a school, I believe. But like all living schools, it is a commonality which preserves and even fosters creativity and uniqueness. There is something irreducible about Pierre de Bérulle, Jean-Jacques Olier and John Eudes. The Oratory, Saint-Sulpice and the Eudist Congregation are a kind of monument to this diversity-in-oneness.

The future Cardinal Bérulle was born at Cerilly (Yonne) in 1575 and studied philosophy and theology at the College of Clermont, being ordained a priest in 1599. He had already published his *Bref Discours* (1597), was participating in Mme. Acarie's mystically inclined circle, and perhaps had taken Dom Beaucousin for his spiritual director in 1596. In 1602 he made the Ignatian exercises under P. L. Maggio, which possibly sensitized him to the "Christological gaps" of the abstract mystics. His growing involvement with the Carmelites probably deepened this sensitivity. In 1603, by papal bull, he was named the third co-superior of the French Carmelite sisters (Mme. Acarie is usually considered their foundress) and helped escort Spanish Carmelite nuns to France for their founding of the Carmel of the Incarnation in Paris (1604). The following year Mother Anne of Jesus (one of the original Spanish nun-foundresses in Paris) denounced abstract forms of mysticism that ignore Jesus's humanity, and we know that Cardinal Bérulle grew decisively Christocentric about this time (1605–10) as evidenced in his writings of this period.

With the foundation of the Oratory by Bérulle (1611), its papal approbation two years later, and Bérulle's papal appointment as perpetual visitor of the Carmelite nuns in 1614 (there were not yet Carmelite priests in Paris), he became a more public, powerful, and also controversial figure. In the latter year he inaugurated the feast of Jesus' solemnity and proclaimed, against Dionysius the Areopagite, a "reversal of the hierarchies" that Dionysius had explored in Neoplatonic fashion in his writings. Henceforth, for Bérulle, all the hierarchies of angels will adore Jesus, the God-man. The Cardinal, as we shall see, never stopped drinking at the well of Dionysius, but he surely modified him in a Christocentric way.[30] For Bérulle, Jesus Christ is God's unique and highest revelation.

But it is Bérulle's role as Carmelite visitator that seems to have spawned the greatest controversy in his career to this point. We are referring to the delicate, complex issue of the vows of servitude to Mary and Jesus, vows he proposed both to his fellow Oratorians and then to the Carmelite nuns between 1615 and 1616. He actually "imposed" one to Mary upon the Carmelites of Chalons-sur-Saône in 1615. He could not know that these vows would thrust him into highly controversial waters for almost a decade. Why was he a partisan of these vows?

Bérulle, it seems, had encountered the tradition of professing vows to Mary, the perfect example of servitude, during a mission to Spain in 1604 for the Carmelites. Such vows can be dated back to Ildephonse of Toledo in 667. And, of course, such vows are a common Catholic tendency, perhaps especially in an anti-Protestant period. They were also congenial to the Dionysian horizon of thought: Reality was to be structured in various orders, the nature of one's vow expressing the order to which one belonged. The scholar Paul Cochois suggests that those professing the two vows of servitude to Mary and Jesus would, in Bérulle's plan, "form a choir and an order, capable of diffusing upon the inferior hierarchies the deifying light that they themselves received by means of the Virgin and the incarnate Word from the fontal deity of the Father."[31] Most important, these vows gave expression in an intensified way to the new Christocentric tone developing in Bérulle's experience.

In any case, Bérulle's desire to have the Carmelite nuns profess the vows—Marie of the Trinity professes one formulation of them in 1616—inaugurates a grand controversy of multiple dimensions. One suspects a certain jealousy in the attacks from the male Carmelites, perhaps displeased by Bérulle's influence with the nuns (his position had been reconfirmed by Pope Paul V in 1620). The Sorbonne professor Duval, also a co-superior of the nuns, viewed the vows as fourth, non-canonical vows. Meanwhile Mme. Acarie, now a sister, expressed disapproval of them. Bérulle began only to recommend them, but troubles continued. A defective copy of the vow found by the Carmelites in 1620 caused more misunderstanding. And some expressions in the vow were capable of receiving Nestorian or Monophysite interpretations. Bérulle's approach to Jesus' humanity led some to think that he was personalizing the human nature (in the School theology the human nature subsists in the Word's person; there is a human nature, not a human person). Others feared the monophysitic drowning of humanity in divinity.

It is possible that vowing servitude to a "deified humanity" or a "humanized divinity"—to use the expressions in question—can be bent in heretical directions. And sadly, the defective copy of the vow was indeed censured by the theological faculties of Douai and Louvain, and by P. Lessius.[32] But interestingly, Lessius himself writes that his action was uncharitable and unjust, and that the formula of the vow could be given an orthodox interpretation.[33] In any case, no further official action was taken, Bérulle did make clear that the vows were a prolongation of the baptismal vows (not uncanonical fourth vows), and most crucially, he wrote his great *Grandeurs* in 1623 at least partly as an apologetic defense of this entire episode. Let me end this chapter in Bérulle's life by citing his reformulation of the vows in the form of "elevations" from the Second Discourse of the *Grandeurs:*

I praise you [the holy humanity of Jesus] in the infinite dignity and in all the powers and offices which you receive in this quality; in the relation, rights, and appropriation which you maintain toward the Holy Trinity; toward the Father, in the filiation of the humanized Word proceeding from him; to the Son, in the subsistence which you receive from him; to the Holy Spirit in the operation by which he produces you and unites you to the Word! And finally I praise you in the supreme, wholly divine, and completely admirable state which you have entered through the hypostatic union, and in all the consequences, rights, and obligations owing to this divine state, according to the order of the

Power of Wisdom and the good will of the eternal Father towards a nature nearer and more intimate to him than any other, according to its essence, because it is intimate with and conjoined to his subsisting Son.[34]

Urban VIII was elected pope in 1623, and by personal decision (20 December) he put an end to the controversy associated with Carmel. Bérulle only had six more years to live, and he spent them working on both a theological-spiritual and more "political" front. He wrote his beautiful three elevations on the Trinity, Incarnation and Marian mystery (1625), which can be considered a concentrated summary of his thought. His meditative, less apologetic (than the *Grandeurs*) *Vie de Jésus* appeared in 1629, preceded two years earlier by the elevation on Mary Magdalene, and he devoted a number of important writings to the Oratory's work of spiritual direction and seminary renewal. This was also a particularly active period for Bérulle in the political sense, as we have already noted. It was between 1624, when Richelieu became chief of the Royal Council, and 1629, the year of Bérulle's "disgrace" by Richelieu, that the great struggles occurred. Bérulle's cardinalate (1627) was something of a consolation during this trying time. Pope Urban VIII was clearly a supporter of Bérulle, reportedly naming him "the apostle of the incarnate Word."[35]

Jean-Jacques Olier, like Bérulle, was born to the aristocracy; his father was a councillor of Parliament at Paris. The fourth of eight children, he was born in the year 1608. The first period of his life might be said to culminate in his attraction to the renewal work of St. Vincent de Paul and his priestly ordination in May of 1633. His parents did favor him with the usual kinds of ecclesiastical benefices: tonsured at eleven, and receiving the priory of Bazainville and the abbey of Pebrac. He also earned the bachelor's degree in theology at the Sorbonne (1630). The atmosphere of spiritual renewal greatly inspired him (not surprising for one who had known St. Vincent de Paul and St. Francis de Sales!) He was even thinking of joining the Carthusians. The year 1630 was important for another reason: Olier was healed from a condition of eye deterioration, a healing he attributed to his "first conversion" to a serious life of holiness through the Blessed Virgin's intercession.

A second period of Olier's life and work saw him exploring the consequences of his commitment to spiritual and churchly renewal.

INTRODUCTION

He collaborated with St. Vincent in a series of missionary endeavors (such endeavors were enormously important to the entire pastoral effort of the time): near his own abbey (1634), then in Auvergne (1636–37), near Nantes and at Montdidier (1638–39), and finally in the Diocese of Chartres (1639–41). Apparently Olier was becoming something of a star, for Bishop Zamet of Langres wanted to make him his successor (and Olier was only 26!). It was the advice of Charles de Condren, the Oratory's new superior general, which kept Olier from accepting the episcopacy. The following year Olier asked Condren to be his spiritual director. In this way the developing heritage of the French School began to shape Olier deeply.

The climax and even culmination of this second period must surely have been the "great trial" Olier underwent from 1639 to 1641. This is probably one of the more controversial aspects of Olierian scholarship, but the new critical work being done on Olier's *Mémoires* is bringing us to greater clarity on the matter.[36] Apparently this trial was a kind of total, somatic-spiritual ordeal and transformation. Nothing was spared! On a physical level basic bodily functions were lost:

> I cannot even move my arms, legs, head, eyes or tongue without this dependence which is within. That which I depend on is in the depth of my soul, and swallows up my natural powers. It is stronger than I am for it is the absolute master not only of this but capable of bestirring and moving the whole world as it does at each instant.[37]

And there was a psychological dimension:

> That which God's goodness brought about in my body he also caused in my soul. For he took away the strength from its natural faculties, leaving me languishing in foolishness, stupidities, and imbecilities which only those who have experienced it can understand[38]

Apparently even his mother began to wonder whether he were feeble-minded, and the leader of the mission he was on advised him to give up his benefices and to "hide [himself] in a hole."[39] Along with this went an experience of his profound sinfulness:

> After original sin, left to ourselves, we are only self-centeredness, incapable of raising ourselves to him. We are only dryness, restlessness, frivolity, blindness, in short, misery. And by misery, I mean

17

nothingness and sin. But on the other hand through his Spirit we are forever lifted up and attentive to God. He alone can accomplish this in us, beyond our capacity.[40]

It is unnecessary to view this entire episode simply as a neurotic breakdown, as Henri Bremond was inclined to do.[41] It is quite possible for a spiritual breakdown and breakthrough to occur through human experiences of suffering, tragedy and neurosis. The one explanation is not incompatible with the other, especially if one is persuaded of the plausibility of an incarnational notion of divine causality, whereby the Divine operates through the human. Bremond seems to create a dichotomy, whereas the *Mémoires* seem to give expression to a mystical experience of purgation and the dark night, an interchange between human suffering and Divine illumination.

Sometime in 1641 Olier experienced great peace. While praying to St. Anne at Chartres he experienced an "unparalleled peace" from her words in the "depths or *fond* of his soul." Earlier he had been given to understand that the Lord wanted him to learn to love with a kind of pure love: "Do it out of love, not only justice, for it is sweet to please one so beautiful."[42] Finally he wrote of a great deliverance from the ordeal, which he experienced on the Octave of Corpus Christi, 6 June 1641:

> O my God, I thank you for placing in my Jesus praises so worthy to be presented and offered to you. . . . O my God how pleased I am to know what he is; to know all he is for your glory, for it seems to me that nothing could be more lovable than to exist completely for your glory. O glory a thousand and a million times more cherished than my own glory. . . . In this way you delivered me from my ordeal, O my God, when you so grandly illumined my spirit . . . this light gave me an ardent desire for your great glory and my abasement [*anéantisse-ment*], and the abasement of all the world.[43]

Here we can see that the breakthrough to a deeper and purer love, and the peace it brings, is the brighter side of the breakdown caused by self-doubt and self-absorption expressing itself in the psychosomatic symptoms so powerfully experienced in Olier's spiritual itinerary.[44]

The experience at Chartres of 1641, which signals the beginnings of Olier's recovery from the dark night, occurred at the same time that a group of missionaries, led by Denis Amelote and including

INTRODUCTION

Olier, was attempting to found a seminary for the reform of the clergy. This work of ecclesial and priestly renewal and reform occupied the final period of Olier's life. Partly influenced by the pious widow Marie Rousseau, partly by Condren, and partly by his own interior movements, he founded a seminary near Paris at Vaugirard at the end of 1641, transferring it a year later to the parish of Saint-Sulpice, where he had become pastor. He served as pastor for the next ten years, profoundly influencing the well-meaning parishioners through his preaching and liturgical leadership as well as his spiritual direction. He experienced heavy opposition from the newly emerging Jansenists, from the Huguenots, and from the simply frivolous. He was able to influence the aristocracy in an especially deep way. As we have seen, the seminary work became quite successful too. Between 1649 and 1657 Olier founded, with his "Sulpician" companions (the Society of St. Sulpice was formally founded in 1645), seminaries at Nantes, Viviers, Saint-Flour, Magnac, Le Puy, Clermont and Amiens.

Before his death on 2 April 1657, Olier had successfully turned over his parish to Bretonvilliers, launched a mission to Montreal, co-founded a congregation of women religious (which did not endure), and written some of the masterpieces of the French School. Bremond suggested that Olier's "special grace and mission was, not exactly to popularize Bérullism, but to present it with such limpidity, richness of imagination and fervour that its apparently somewhat difficult metaphysics are placed invitingly in the reach of most readers."[45] The seventeenth-century scholar Louis Cognet did say, as if confirming Bremond's judgment, that Olier's *Journée chrétienne* "enjoyed rare success."[46] Olier's life and work comes home as hauntingly real and manifoldly rich.[47]

Saint John Eudes (1601–80) lived during most of Bérulle's life and during all of Olier's. He knew them both, and there can be little doubt that the growing spirituality of the French School reached something of a concentrated pitch in the heart symbolism, devotion and theology gradually explored and quite originally carved out by him. It is, says the Eudist scholar Paul Milcent, "a transcription of the more basic thinking of Bérulle and De Condren, and of the Pauline theme of life in Jesus Christ."[48]

We can conveniently speak of John Eudes' early period as that of his formation in the Oratory and its mission. Unlike Bérulle and

INTRODUCTION

Olier, John was born of a peasant family the first of seven children. He did some of his studies at the Jesuit College at Caen. Deciding to become a priest, he entered the Oratory, studying under both Cardinal Bérulle and Charles de Condren (1623–27). After priestly ordination (1625), he devoted his time to the kinds of missionary endeavors that the Oratorians engaged in, working in Normandy (his native area), Brittany, the Ile-de-France, Bourgogne, and even giving three missions in Paris at Louis XIV's court.

Toward the end of this period (1641) he also encountered Marie des Vallées (1590–1656). The bishop of Coutances wondered whether she might not be possessed and invited John Eudes to examine her case. John became convinced that she was a woman of profound holiness and derived much comfort from her.

It is the shift in attention to seminary work that enables us to speak of a second period in John's career. His missionary work had steadily convinced him of the need for the clergy's reform, if the seeds of renewal begun during the missions were to take hold. Like the other Oratorians, John found himself attracted to the formation of priests through seminary work. Unlike the model envisaged by the Council of Trent—namely, the training of adolescents—John, as some others (Sulpicians, the Vincentians, some Oratorians), developed the model of associating with themselves older candidates and even priests in an intensive period of spiritual and pastoral renewal. Such seminary work would almost define the future work of John Eudes.

Here we touch upon one of the more obscure and controversial areas of Eudist scholarship. Paul Milcent speaks of François Bourgoing's opposition to this work (Bourgoing was the superior general of the Oratory at the time) being based upon "reasons which are not clearly known." Was Bourgoing more comfortable with the Tridentine model, well-known to the Oratory?[49] Clément Guillon, another Eudist scholar, also speaks of the difficulty of clarifying the nature of Bourgoing's opposition.[50] In any case, on 25 March 1643, John Eudes founded, with some other like-minded priests, the Congregation of Jesus and Mary (the future Eudists), which took priestly formation and the missions as its work. This began at Caen, followed by the founding of seminaries at Coutances (1650), Lisieux (1653), Rouen (1659), Evreux (1667) and Rennes (1670). During this same period, he founded the Religious of Notre Dame of Charity to work with young girls experiencing serious difficulties. Eventually this group developed into two congregations: Our Lady of Charity of Refuge and Our Lady of Charity of the Good Shepherd.[51]

We can, perhaps, speak of two great climaxes in this second period of John's life and work. On the one hand, perhaps partly in response to the growing rigorism of Jansenism, his thought moved toward the developing of an impressive heart theology centered on the love of Mary and Jesus. As we will see, he worked out a mature synthesis of his own form of Bérullism around this metaphor of the heart. Coupled with this was his liturgical expression of this heart theology in feasts of Mary's (beginning in 1648) and Jesus' sacred hearts (about 1668). On the other hand John experienced his own form of the "great trial" through increasing opposition on a number of fronts. Jansenists smarted from John's opposition and disliked his supposedly insufficiently rigorous spirituality. Some of his former Oratorian colleagues opposed his new congregation. A mysterious "Letter to a Doctor of the Sorbonne" (circulating around 1674) attacked John's friend Marie des Vallées and the heart devotion as he had developed it. The dark night grew increasingly darker.

Particularly painful, to judge from John's letters, was his disgrace in the eyes of King Louis XIV, lasting from 1674 to 1679.[52] Apparently one of John's well-intentioned supporters in Rome expressed John's fidelity to the papal authority in such a way that King Louis interpreted it as a threat to John's fidelity to himself as John's monarch. By royal command John had to leave Paris, and the survival of his fragile congregation was in question for some time. This was a period of disintegrating relations between France and Rome, a period fertile for the emergence of Gallicanism. John finally had to appeal personally to the monarch for forgiveness. As we have indicated, the king did, in the end, receive John in audience and promise him the royal support he needed.

John Eudes wrote much throughout his career. His *The Life and the Kingdom of Jesus in Christian Souls*, written already by 1637, is widely recognized as his basic work. It manifests, with some Eudist touches we will examine later, the spirituality of Bérulle and his "school." Perhaps his most original and synthetic work is *The Admirable Heart of the Most Sacred Mother of God or the Devotion to the Most Sacred Heart of Mary*, finished only a few weeks before his death in 1680. The spirituality found here was both the cause of, and the greatest consolation in the midst of, the great trials. Upon his beatification in 1909 Pope Pius X called him the "father, doctor and apostle of the liturgical cult of the hearts of Jesus and Mary." Pius XI canonized him in 1925. Now perhaps we understand something of why Jean-Jacques Olier called him "this great preacher, the Père Eudes, the wonder of his time."[53]

A Woman's Perspective: Madeleine de Saint-Joseph

One cannot study the French School for long without being struck by the important, even critical role that women played throughout. The phenomenon of Cardinal Bérulle is very bound up with the Christocentric spirituality of the great St. Teresa of Avila, with the mystical aspirations of Mme. Acarie and her circle, with St. Catherine of Genoa's thought, with the work of the French Carmelite nuns in Paris, and especially with the Venerable Madeleine de Saint-Joseph, the first French prioress of Paris' Great Carmel. So, too, biographers of Olier stress the crucial role of women in his evolving spirituality. One thinks of Marie Rousseau's important role in helping Olier through his dark night and in his seminary reform work. One thinks, too, of the Mère de Bressand, Mère Agnes, and especially of Marguerite de Saint-Sacrement. All played important roles in Olier's life. John Eudes was also deeply impressed by Marguerite's holiness, particularly her devotion to Jesus' infancy. And who can forget the important bonds he had with Marie des Vallées?[54]

As feminist theological criticism is beginning to teach us, much of the contribution of women to theology and spirituality in general is only now beginning to receive the attention it has always deserved. As an aid in sensitizing us to this need and desire to surface more fully the critical role of women in the story of our French School, we will single out Mother Madeleine de Saint-Joseph. If you will, perhaps she can serve as a representative for us of the rich amount of theology and spirituality awaiting the critical scholar. Let us introduce her by a citation from Louis Cognet:

[Her] outstanding holiness irradiated the whole world of the devout. An intimate confidante of Bérulle, she no doubt influenced the evolution of the great spiritual master, who had the highest esteem for her revelations and mystical states. Warmly attached to Bérullian spirituality, she fought untiringly to defend it, to extend it in the Carmels and to

22

lessen the influence of the abstract school. But her Bérullism assumes a mystical form in many respects original and very attractive: it is a great pity that her writings, but for some very short fragments, have not yet been published.[55]

Venerable Madeleine du Bois de Fontaines was a contemporary of Bérulle, being born in 1578 at Tours, the sixth child in her family of fifteen children. She lived until 1637 (Bérulle died eight years earlier). She entered the Great Carmel at Paris only a few weeks after its founding and quickly became an important figure in the Carmel's development. She made her profession on 12 November 1605, and soon became a Mistress of Novices. She was elected prioress at the age of 30. Between 1615 and 1617 she assisted in the founding of Carmels at Tours and Lyon, returning to Paris to found a Second Carmel there, where she served as superior for another six years. Again, rather remarkably, she returned to the Great Carmel (at Paris), and found herself again the prioress for another eleven years (1624–35).

It is in this last period that Mère Madeleine became an intimate confidante of Bérulle. One can realistically speak of a kind of two-way spiritual direction, and the evidence is strong that she influenced the theological evolution of Bérulle's spirituality in important ways. She had apparently played a decisive role somewhat earlier in the founding of the Oratory, for Bérulle sought her counsel on the matter and was encouraged by her support.[56] She also supported Bérulle on the matter of the vows of servitude at the Great Carmel. At the time when Mme. Acarie and the theologian Duval were attacking his views on the vow, Madeleine wrote Bérulle (in 1616) that the thought of being in servitude to the Virgin in the Order had aided her immensely.[57] Cognet, basing himself on her correspondence of 1623–25, thinks she may have been the major influence behind Bérulle's great "Elevation on Mary Magdalene." She speaks of her own great troubles and promises him the help of the "great Saint Magdalene."[58]

Perhaps one of the most fascinating aspects of Mère Madeleine is her own theology of love, which Cognet suggests may have been quite influential on Bérulle. There does seem to be a tendency on Bérulle's part to stress love more fully at the very time that he is getting to know the Mother more intimately. Her letter 144 seems especially important in this regard. "Adoration not only cannot be perfect without love, but it doesn't even deserve the name of adoration . . . unless love is its soul and life," she tells us. Bérulle's *Vie de Jésus*, written in 1627, stresses an adoration always developing in love, unlike some of Bérulle's earlier thought, which seems to present love more as a gateway to adoration. Another text of Bérulle's distinguishes among three types of honoring the "uncreated, incarnate, and crucified life of Jesus: . . . first by adoration, which is an act of reverence, secondly by love, and then in a third way by an adoring love, that is to say, loving while adoring."[59]

After Bérulle's death, Mother Madeleine found herself having to clarify and even reject some aspects of the "abstract spirituality" that had been fashionable in Mme. Acarie's circle. Anti-mysticism was becoming more useful to the political forces opposed to the policies of the devout (namely, to Richelieu's camp). Further, the tendency to think that one can achieve sublime mystical states and revelations is always somewhat dangerous, both because it can be easily subject to illusion, and because it can be threatening to a religion like Catholicism, which stresses the mediation of revelation through Jesus and through the ecclesial structures. We should think, too, of Madeleine's Carmelite tradition: Teresa of Avila very strongly critiqued any bypassing of Jesus' humanity in the spiritual life.

There are ample letters from Madeleine's correspondence that illustrate this growing concern for the abstract school, at least in its extreme tendencies. At one point she criticizes Mère Agnes, a cherished confidante of Condren and Bishop Zamet, for being in "a profound illusion." At another point in her life she was very opposed to the notion of withdrawing (*désappliquer*) from Jesus' humanity in the spiritual journey, a term dear to Condren's austere spirituality of sacrifice. Some circles, after Bérulle's death, did try to associate his name with a kind of crusade against Benet of Canfield's abstract spirituality. Is this the source of the pressure that caused Mère Madeleine to say that Bérulle's zeal for an abstract spirituality caused her great pain? Did the Mother not understand the Cardinal's careful critique of this abstract spirituality in his later Jesus-centered theology and spirituality? Or was she simply pointing to a danger always in need of critique in the spiritual life? Bérulle, as we shall see, never completely abandoned the abstract spirituality stemming from Dionysius. He integrated it with a Christocentrism. Judging from the Mother's acceptance of the Bérullian theology of *anéantissement*, she, too, did not completely disown the "Dionysian moment" in Bérullian spirituality.[60]

The Mother died on 30 April 1637. During her life she had published a study of the mystic Sister Catherine of Jesus. But her letters are the particularly crucial sources for her developing thought and work. Given the critical role of the Great Carmel in the renewal taking place in France, and given her own contribution to the French School, she deserves to be considered one of the great initiators of the kind of spirituality we are studying here. The French School has a foundress as well as founders.

Alerting ourselves to the role of women in the history of the French School seems an appropriate place to say something about the theology of woman present there too. So far as I know, no studies exist on this issue, and we must rely upon educated guesses stimulated by the newly emerging feminist criticism of theology. If we borrow a clue from Rosemary Ruether and speak of three basic "types" of understanding of women—patriarchal, androgynous and liberationist/the-refusal-to-stereotype—then we might suggest that the French School seems predominantly influenced by the androgynous viewpoint.

By androgyny we mean the tendency to associate certain characteristics with either males or females. Both characteristics may be present in males and females in varying degrees, but the crucial facet of androgyny is to name a certain set of characteristics properly male or female. This is the source of the so-called masculine and feminine archetypes. Olier employs them frequently, it appears. God is like a mother who nourishes her son, and in imitation of this the church's prelates are like mothers who engender and nourish their babes. Spiritual directors are like fathers in their force, courage and ability to correct; like mothers in their tenderness, patience and compassion. They "enter into the two great qualities of Our Lord . . . [who] is truly father and mother."[61] Is this androgyny behind Bérulle's great elevation on Mary Magdalene, in which her founding of a school of love is contrasted with the Beloved Disciple's founding of a school of knowledge of the Lord? She has more fervor and love; he, more discernment and light.[62]

One senses that much of the Marian theology and piety characteristic of the French School particularly lends itself to an androgynous viewpoint. Mary is, after all, the great example of servitude to the

Lord through her maternity and virginity. "The great desire of the Mother of God is to see her son perfectly loved," says Mère Madeleine.[63] This Marian piety lends itself to a stress upon the mothering, nourishing aspects of woman. And yet Mary's servitude is her elevation, just as Jesus' servitude is his elevation. And, in line with this, Bérulle speaks of Mary Magdalene as the first to witness the Risen Jesus; indeed, as one who did not flee from the cross, but who was strong. "The first bull and patent" the Risen Jesus issued was to Mary Magdalene "making her an apostle, but one of life, of glory, and of love; and an apostle to the apostles."[64] Do these texts indicate that the French School was perhaps on the way to breaking out of the limiting, androgynous viewpoint? Androgyny seems too limiting a framework for this kind of experience and spirituality.

Could we perhaps sum up by saying that despite an occasional patriarchal text, misogynist in viewpoint, the French School leans more in the direction of androgyny, yet with indications of a move toward a more liberationist perspective? Much more research needs to be done, but for a first and tentative approach, this conclusion seems legitimate.[65]

NOTES

1. William H. McNeill, *A World History* (New York: Oxford, 1979), p. 311; cf. pp. 295–326, 359–76 for the basis of much of the following.

2. Ibid. p. 316. Some key dates and facts: Henri IV of France is assassinated in 1610, succeeded by Louis XIII (with Anne of Austria); 1624, Richelieu becomes chief minister; 1642, Mazarin succeeds Richelieu; 1643, Louis XIV succeeds under regency of his mother until Mazarin's death in 1661, and then he assumes full powers, ruling until 1715 (72-year reign). His wife was Marie Thérèse.

3. Cognet is the great church scholar on our period. See Louis Cognet, "Ecclesiastical Life in France," in *History of the Church* 6: *The Church in the Age of Absolutism and Enlightenment*, ed. Hubert Jedin and John Dolan, trans. Gunther J. Holst (New York: Crossroad, 1981), pp. 3–106 at p. 13.

4. Cf. Bérulle *Oeuvres complètes* 2 vols., ed. François Bourgoing (Villa Bethanie, Montsoult Seine-et-Oise: Maison D'Institution de L'Oratoire, 1960), Vol. 1, pp. 35–115; Vol. 2, pp. 679–743, esp. p. 742; see below on Olier and Eudes. Translations in the introduction are by me.

5. Cf. Paul Milcent, *S. Jean Eudes: un artisan de renouveau chrétien au XVIIe siècle, Semeurs* (Paris: Cerf, 1985), p. 450.

6. McNeill, pp. 325–26.

7. Pluralism involves complex ambiguities. Cf., for example, Karl Rahner's very suggestive "A Small Question Regarding the Contemporary Pluralism in the Intellectual Situation of Catholics and the Church," in *Theological Investigations* 6, trans. Karl-H. and Boniface Kruger (Baltimore: Helicon, 1969), pp. 21–30.

8. We lack a sustained study of seventeenth-century theology. See Yves Congar, *A History of Theology*, trans. and ed. Hunter Guthrie (Garden City, NY: Doubleday, 1968), pp. 177–81; the small amount of space Congar devotes to seventeenth-century theology says something about the era's (systematic) theological creativity.

9. Congar, p. 178, citing Alexandre's *Theologia dogmatica et moralis* (1693), 1, praef.

10. Cognet, p. 93.

11. See Cognet, pp. 94–101, for much of this detail.

12. Ibid. p. 95.

13. See Jean Dagens, *Bérulle et les origines de la restauration catholique*

(1575–1611) (Paris: Desclée de Brouwer, 1952), pp. 39–40; see pp. 16–103 for an overview of the times similar to Cognet.

14.   Cognet, p. 97; cf. pp. 97–101 for what follows.

15.   Ibid. p. 99.

16.   It is quite possible that the French School's "new" emphasis upon Jesus' humanity served as a kind of bridge toward a growing appreciation of the historical dimensions of scripture.

17.   See, for example, Harvey Egan, *Christian Mysticism: The Future of a Tradition* (New York: Pueblo, 1984), p. 375, and Hans Urs von Balthasar, "Theology and Sanctity," in *Word and Redemption, Essays in Theology* 2, trans. A. V. Littledale, in cooperation with Alexander Dru (New York: Herder and Herder, 1965), pp. 49–86.

18.   Dagens, p. 31.

19.   Ibid. p. 36.

20.   Bérulle, *Oeuvres complètes* 2, pp. 650, 657, 662–63.

21.   On all this see Dagens, pp. 103–32, 249–69, and Louis Cognet, *Post-Reformation-Spirituality*, trans. R. Hepburne Scott (New York: Hawthorn, 1959), pp. 56–68. Also see Henri Bremond, *A Literary History of Religious Thought in France* 2: *The Coming of Mysticism (1590–1620)*, trans. K. L. Montgomery (London: SPCK, 1930), pp. 145–94, for an engaging treatment of Mme. Acarie.

22.   Helpful here is Cognet, "Ecclesiastical Life in France," p. 20.

23.   Milcent has suggested that at least the nobility were regarded like priests, given their sacred character at the time (p. 257), and we have seen the spiritual renewal among them.

24.   André Dodin, ed., *Entrétiens spirituels aux missionaires* (Paris: Seuil, 1960), p. 502, my translation.

25.   Cognet, "Ecclesiastical Life in France," p. 8.

26.   Helpful here is Michel Dupuy, *Se laisser à l'Esprit: itinéraire spirituel de Jean-Jacques Olier* (Paris: Cerf, 1982), pp. 17–28.

27.   Cognet, "Ecclesiastical Life in France," pp. 20–21.

28.   Cognet, "Ecclesiastical Life in France," p. 8, mentions the cumulative benefices of Olier.

29.   Cf. Cognet, "Ecclesiastical Life in France," pp. 20–22, on much of this; also Dupuy.

30.   Cf. Jean Orcibal, *Le cardinal de Bérulle: évolution d'une spiritualité* (Paris: Cerf, 1965), p. 80, referring to Bérulle's *Coll* 245. For Bérulle's life, see the critical study by Dagens, especially pp. 13–245. Cf. Henri Bremond, *A Literary History of Religious Thought in France* 3: *The Triumph of Mysticism*, trans. K. L. Montgomery, (London: SPCK, 1936), pp. 1–222.

31.   Paul Cochois, *Bérulle et l'école française, Maîtres spirituels* Series (Paris: Seuil, 1963), p. 33; see pp. 30–43 for this entire controversy. Cf. Dagens, pp. 205–28.

32. Orcibal, p. 154, calls this *Formulaire III* of the vow.

33. See *CB* 2, P. 341, p. 245.

34. *G* 2, 4, p. 174. Cf. Bérulle's *N* for his own defense, appended to the *G.*

35. See Dagens, p. 291.

36. This remarkable document of around three thousand pages, written from 1642 to 1652, is available through important selections in Dupuy, which is the modern, critical study of Olier's life. See also Bremond 3, pp. 359–434.

37. Cf. Lowell M. Glendon, "Jean-Jacques Olier's View of the Spiritual Potential of Human Nature" (Ph.D. diss., Fordham, 1983), p. 82, for this and subsequent citations; this one is from *Mém* 1:117.

38. *Mém* 1:214–15; in Glendon, p. 83.

39. *Mém* 1:95; *Mc* 1:86 (a later copy of *Mém*); in Glendon, pp. 83–84.

40. *Mém* 1:128; in Glendon, p. 87.

41. Cf. Bremond 3, pp. 359–91. Interestingly, St. Thérèse of Lisieux suffered a remarkably similar illness in 1883, when she was ten. "I appeared to be almost always delirious, saying things that had no meaning. . . . I often appeared to be in a faint, not making the slightest movement." (*Story of a Soul*, trans. John Clarke [Washington, D.C.: Institute of Carmelite Studies, 1975], p. 62). Hans Urs von Balthasar, relying upon P. Roquette, who considers these illnesses mystical experiences, notes this similarity among Thérèse, Olier and Surin in his *Thérèse of Lisieux: The Story of a Mission*, trans. Donald Nicholl (New York: Sheed and Ward, 1954), p. 280.

42. *Mém* 1:192, in Dupuy, p. 112; *Lettre* 69, 1, p. 149; *Mém* 1:149; in Glendon, p. 90.

43. *Mc* 1:85; in Glendon, p. 91.

44. See Gilles Chaillot, "Les premières leçons de l'expérience mystique de Monsier Olier," *Bulletin du Comité des Etudes* 40 (1962): 501–43.

45. Bremond 3, p. 393.

46. Cognet, "Ecclesiastical Life in France," p. 78. The *Journée chrétienne* went through six editions in the seventeenth century, three in the nineteenth century, and three again in our own. The lack of eighteenth-century editions may have been owing to biases against mysticism in the church in general (information courtesy of Irénée Noye). Besides the major works of Olier referred to throughout these pages, mention should be made of his venture in "spiritual exegesis," *L'explication des cérémonies de la Grande Messe* (1657).

47. Besides Dupuy's critical life, see also Frédéric Monier, *Vie de Jean-Jacques Olier* (Paris: Poussièlgue, 1914).

48. Paul Milcent, "Jean Eudes (saint)," *Dictionnaire de Spiritualité* 8, ed. M. Viller, et al. (Paris: Beauchesne, 1972), cols. 488–501 at 498.

49. See Milcent's *Saint Jean Eudes: introduction et choix de textes,*

NOTES

Témoins de la foi Series (Paris: Bloud and Gay, 1964), pp. 15–16, for an explanation; the phrase "not clearly known" is my rough translation of "Pour les raisons qui restent mal connues . . . ," in Milcent's article on Eudes in *DS*, col. 489. See Bremond 3, pp. 133–92. Cf. Raymond Deville, *L'école française de spiritualité, Bibliothèque d'histoire du Christianisme* Series 11 (Paris: Desclée, 1987), pp. 92–94.

50.   Clément Guillon, *En tout la volonté de Dieu: S. Jean Eudes à travers ses lettres* (Paris: Cerf, 1981), p. 28. Eudist scholars manifest a quite understandable circumspection about the Oratory, the "mother," after all, of their own congregation.

51.   "Unlike attempts made elsewhere, Père Eudes did not admit the 'penitents' [young women] into the religious life; on the other hand he endowed this novel institute with solid constitutions" (Milcent, *Saint Jean Eudes: introduction*, p. 20, my translation).

52.   See the letters assembled and interpreted in Guillon, pp. 133–52, for a fine analysis of these trials by John Eudes himself, and by Guillon.

53.   Olier, *Mém* 2:221; for these details, see Milcent, "Jean Eudes," in *DS*, cols. 490–91.

54.   See above, in the text, for the role of most of the women mentioned in Bérulle's work. For Olier, Dupuy is especially sensitive to the place of the women mentioned in his *Se laisser à l'Esprit*, pp. 299–321. Also see Constant Bouchaud, "Le role de Mère Agnes dans la preparation spirituelle de Jean-Jacques Olier à la fondation du Seminaire de Saint-Sulpice," *Bulletin de Saint-Sulpice* 12 (1986): 160–70. On Eudes' appreciation for Marguerite, see Milcent, *S. Jean Eudes: un artisan*, pp. 228–30. This will surely become the critical study of the saint in our time. Also see Bremond 3, pp. 497–572.

55.   Cognet, *Post-Reformation Spirituality*, p. 104; see his *La spiritualité moderne* (*Histoire de spiritualité* 3/1) (Paris: Aubier, 1966), pp. 360–410, for Cognet's sensitivity to women.

56.   This was around 1611. See (Louise de Jésus), *La Vénérable Madeleine de Saint-Joseph* (Clamart: Carmel de l'Incarnation, 1935), p. 128. This is the key study of Madeleine; also cf. Dagens, pp. 191–228; and Bremond 2, pp. 227–67.

57.   See Lettre 3 in Madeleine de Saint-Joseph, *Lettres spirituelles*, ed. Pierre Serouet (Paris: Desclée de Brouwer, 1965), p. 17. Cf. Louise de Jésus, pp. 225; 500–02n10.

58.   Cognet, *La spiritualité moderne*, pp. 363–64; *Lettre* 14, p. 25.

59.   XXXI A in Michel Dupuy, "De nouveaux inédits de Bérulle," *Revue d'histoire de la spiritualité* 52 (1976): 363; for Cognet's view, *La spiritualité moderne*, p. 364; also see *Lettre* 144, p. 144; see below, pp. 200–03.

60.   See the appropriate texts in *Lettre* 39, pp. 46–47, and in Louise de Jésus, pp. 243–44n15. Orcibal, pp. 133–34n61, has an important analysis of the matter. For *anéantissement* see, for example, *Lettre* 159, pp. 166–67.

NOTES

61. Olier, *Projet de l'establissement d'un séminaire dans un diocese*, in *Traité des saints ordres*, ed. G. Chaillot, et al. (Paris: St.-Sulpice, 1984), p. 315; *L'esprit d'un directeur des âmes* [paraphrasing M. Olier] (Oeuvres complètes de M. Olier, ed. J.-P. Migne [Paris: Ateliers catholiques, 1956], col. 1219).

62. See Chapter 3 especially.

63. Serouet, *Lettre* 177, p. 181.

64. *Ma* 5, 5, 7; 7, 4. Mère Madeleine also speaks of the strength of women who followed Jesus: Lettre 174, pp. 179–80.

65. For these categories, see Rosemary Ruether, *Sexism and God-Talk: Toward a Feminist Theology* (Boston: Beacon, 1983). One apparently misogynist text in the French School: Bérulle speaks of "the vanity common to the fragile sex" in his *Observations sur le texte de Sainct Luc, en faveur de la Magdelaine*, I.

II

Theology and Spirituality in The French School

B ecause the French School forms part of the creative reaction against the separation of theology and spirituality, we will try our best to interrelate the two aspects throughout our overview. There is a continual *perichoresis* or interchange between the theological and the practical. "Some distinguish between a mystical and a practical theology, but this is a distinction which I do not wish to employ," says Bérulle. "All God's graces distributed upon earth are to enable us to act better."[1] In this respect Bérulle reminds one of the fathers, particularly Augustine. Like them, he is in quest of a "science of the saints."[2] The science dimension links it with the critical clarity of the scholastic tradition. The saints dimension attaches it to spiritual experience: a deep life of faith and even mystical experience. Not a small part of the fascination of the French School is the dynamic and sometimes surprising manner in which each of our four founding mystics enters into this tension-laden interchange.

The Basic Pattern

Two traditions intersect in the French School: the Neoplatonic and the Christian. Like the millennial tradition as a whole, Bérulle and his collaborators employ the Dionysian, Neoplatonic schema: We have come from God (*exitus*) and we find our being's fulfillment in returning to our origin (*reditus*). But the French School has thoroughly "Christianized" or "Christified" this pattern: Our emanation reflects Christ, our wounding it through sin deepens our need for Christ, and our return to God is through the mediation of Christ. Jesus Christ is God's unsurpassable revelation. This spirituality and theology is at once very Pauline and Paschal, and very Neoplatonic and Dionysian. Both of these aspects shine out in Bérulle in an almost perfectly balanced manner. In Madeleine, Olier and Eudes the Dionysian dimension constitutes a more or less deep context within which the Paschal or Pauline aspects are rather more heavily accented. But there is also a third element to be added: the unique modulations each of our mystics give to the millennial tradition. With Bérulle this can take the form of daring intuitions quite unheard of before, a kind of mining of new shafts within the tradition. With Madeleine, Olier and Eudes it more commonly takes the form of intensifications of aspects deserving greater stress.

Theocentric and Trinitarian

"So God who is unity leads everyone to unity, and through distinct degrees of unity comes and descends toward man that he might ascend toward God," says Bérulle.[3] Here we note the dynamic kind of unity, beloved of much Neoplatonism, that lies behind Bérulle's theocentric exemplarism: The divine unity is the example or form which creates in creatures the basic tendency toward unity. We come from divine unity and our being is a living dynamism of participating in that same unity. We should not think of intermediaries between humans and God, for the Divine grounds and permeates all: ". . . God, creating and forming all things, refers them and relates them all to himself . . . a movement more intimate to the creature than his own being itself."[4]

This divine "unity of essence" is also revealed to be a "unity of love" in the trinitarian mystery. At times Bérulle explores this in a more Augustinian, typically Western fashion: "All the divine persons are of the same essence." At other times he seems more typically Greek, stressing the persons more than the unity: "The divine society of persons subsisting eternally in the divinity." The Father is the "fontal deity," the source and even end of all, "like an admirable circle," who performs "the work of a father and mother simultaneously as regards his Son and eternal Word." The Son, "the image which the Father has formed of himself," is simply "a continual reference to his Father." The Holy Spirit, produced by the Father with the Word, is their "unity of love." In this sense, that the Spirit does not himself produce another person but is the loving fecundity of Father and Son, Bérulle will daringly speak of the "sterility of the Holy Spirit."[5]

This trinitarian theocentrism forms the background of Mère Madeleine's writings too. In her letters she usually dwells upon the inner life of the person and her relation to Jesus, but at times she will express the typically Bérullian trinitarian theology undergirding this. She knows that Father, Son and Spirit are "one in essence," but this unity is a rich one. She was known to have spoken of the "plenitude of God," from which emanates a "plenitude of grace." An especially fine formulation of her trinitarian thought, more reflective of the typically Greek approach and tinged with her own love theology, is the following:

> For, as in the eternal generation the Father is pleased in his Son and the Son in his Father, and this mutual contentedness happily finds its completion in the Holy Spirit who is love, so God, producing in the creature several different effects, finally wishes the creature to adore this contentedness of Father and Son in themselves and that love be the goal and fulfillment of all their work.[6]

Olier's commentators will say that some Platonic themes enter into his thought about God chiefly through Condren: God is the "All," for example. But the typically Dionysian stress on God's hiddenness finds only an echo in Olier. "God is transcendent by excess more than by difference."[7] Thus, Olier's God is very much a communicator, a fire, to use one of his favorite metaphors: "O my God, you have appeared like fire." Thus, he likes to stress the trinitarian (communicative) aspect of God, in whose image we are all made: God "has formed human society upon the model of the society of persons in the most holy Trinity." As the divine persons love one another, so "God wants each to love one's neighbor as oneself."[8]

John Eudes too, like Olier and Madeleine, developed a more biblical, less Dionysian formulation of the divine mystery. There is a well-known, Dionysian-like text in which Eudes counsels us to be detached from our own "attachments" to God, for God is truly so much more. But for Eudes, God is primarily love, perhaps through the influence of St. Francis de Sales and also attentiveness to his own inner experience. Thus he moves easily into meditations upon the trinitarian mystery, stressing the divine persons' sharing of love among themselves and imprinting that love upon us, especially through baptism. His great work on Mary's heart is really a prolonged meditation on how the Marian mystery is grounded upon the heart of Father, Son and Holy Spirit. "To adore the heart of Jesus," Eudes tells us, "is to adore the heart of the Son and the Holy Spirit; . . . a heart which is a furnace of love burning very intensively for us." Note the Eudist twist given the unity in Trinity: the "three persons in the adorable mystery of the Trinity . . . are but one heart."[9]

As we indicated earlier, the French School refused to separate theology from spirituality. Thus, the kind of theocentric trinitarianism essayed here goes along with a certain spiritual praxis. We will need to look at what the French School thinks about the reality of sin and the Christ event to fully appreciate its spiritual praxis, but even now we should mention that there is a spirituality corresponding to this theocentric trinitarianism. For each of our mystics, we are a reflection in some way of the inner mystery of the Trinity. Here the Platonic exemplarist and the biblical "image of God" tradition intersect: We are most ourselves when we reflect the loving relations of the divine reality itself.[10]

Christological and Soteriological

No scholar doubts that the French School is profoundly Christocentric. We have even seen that the early Bérulle, more deeply influenced by the abstract style of spirituality seeking to transcend everything finite and human (even Jesus' humanity), still saw in Jesus the exemplar of the life of ascent to the Divine Mystery. As he undergoes his so-called Christocentric conversion his Christology deepens. He never disowns his early acceptance of the abstract, Neoplatonic school of spirituality. But he rather creatively integrates it with a more biblical perspective.[11] This usually takes the form of viewing the Incarnation as a prolongation of the trinitarian mystery on earth. "For God produces all things by his Word," Bérulle tells us. "Now the first operation of God is the production of his Word, and the final, the incorporation of this same Word into the human nature."[12] In a passage unique in his writings, but which Cognet suggests sounds strikingly similar to Harphius, Bérulle calls the Incarnation a "second Trinity, a novel Trinity," for it unites Jesus' body, soul and Divinity. It is not a "Trinity of subsistence in the unity of essence" (as in the "First" Trinity), but a "Trinity of essence in the unity of subsistence."[13] Of course, all the trinitarian persons are involved in the Incarnation: the Father through his initiative; the Spirit, "infertile" within the Trinity becomes fecund outside of it in lovingly sharing the God-Man. But Bérulle especially underscores the role of the Word: the Image produces a perfect "image."[14]

What is this "novel state" of the Incarnation, as Bérulle likes to describe it? Bérulle particularly meditates upon the hypostatic union, combining insights from the fathers, the scholastics and the mystics. "The person of the Word . . . possesses an extraordinary and inexplicable relation to the human nature, which being deprived of its subsistence, must receive that subsistence from the Word," says Bérulle.[15] Bérulle here takes over the traditional notion that Jesus' human and divine natures subsist in the person of the Word (the so-called *enhypostasia* of the humanity in the Word). Jesus thus has no need of a human "person" (or act of subsistence). This establishes "an order and state . . . singularly divine and singularly proper to the eternal Word."[16]

If you will, the hypostatic union is what Bérulle elsewhere calls the substance of the mystery of the incarnation. He displays his originality in his meditations upon the economy of that same mystery, the way in which that mystery deifies the life of Jesus and of those who share in that life.[17] There exists a "commerce and communication . . . between [Jesus'] divinity and humanity." In more daring terms: "He who is, becomes: the Uncreated is created: . . . the One who enriches the world becomes poor."[18] Because of this, there can be no bypassing or surpassing of Jesus' humanity (against abstract mysticism). And yet Jesus' humanity is one of poverty, of subsisting not in itself but in the Word, of *dénuement* or self-emptying (with that abstract mysticism). Here we see how Bérulle unites the more Jesus-centered mysticism of the scriptures and the Teresian (Carmelite) tradition with the concerns of Dionysian, negative mysticism. Our goal is indeed the Transcendent One, but our means is Jesus, and our goal is Jesus too. He is God's highest revelation.[19]

Through this novel state, the God-Man Jesus now becomes a "Father" in the order of the economy. Bérulle can use the biblical notion of the "New Adam": Through Jesus' humanity, which is in solidarity with us, we enter into a new order. Bérulle can also use the Neoplatonic, exemplarist language: Humanity is deified through Jesus; "God becomes man in order to make us gods."[20] He will also use his complex and somewhat unique term *état* to develop this economy. At least as this term is used in the important *OP 77, On the Perpetuity of the Mysteries of Jesus Christ,* Bérulle sees in the mystery of the Incarnation some things "past" and others "present and perpetual." "They are over as regards their execution, but present as regards their power [*vertu*]." Or, Bérulle will say that the "love with which they have been accomplished will never pass away."[21] If you will, there is a power of deification perpetually at work in the events of the incarnation. In this sense, the "states" of Jesus are the archetype of "states" in the Christian:

> For the incarnation of the Word is the basis and foundation . . . of the deification of all the states and mysteries sharing in the life and earthly voyage of the Son of God upon earth. . . . Jesus . . . wishes that we have a unique share in these various states, according to the diversity of his will for us and our piety toward him.[22]

We find the main aspects of this Bérullian christology, with some unique modulations, among Madeleine, Olier, and Eudes. Madeleine sees the incarnation as the expression of the Trinity in the historical economy. Her own formulation of the God-Man mystery is to speak of it as the Son's abasement before the Father, whereby he enters into the "state of perpetual victimhood," a phrasing reminiscent of Condren's theology of sacrifice. Like Bérulle she uses the term *état* to refer to the inner dispositions within Jesus and within ourselves by which we are conformed to him. The Bérullian *état* often has a "permanency" about it: Our participation by state is deep and lasting. Her special charism was to emphasize the role of the humanity of Jesus as the never-to-be-bypassed mediator of union with God. "I know that not everyone can apply themselves through discourse to [Jesus'] mysteries; . . . I speak of an adherence of the will . . . ," she says, echoing the view of the French School as a whole. Whether verbally or not, we are always one with Jesus, through "state," adherence, in our depths. In this respect she was influenced by Bérulle, whose counsel on this issue she sought: "He gave me an explanation which filled me with great joy." She was also deeply influenced by the great St. Teresa of Avila, who regretted "having followed the advice . . . to bypass Jesus Christ's humanity, as if it were an impediment to the highest contemplation."[23] Again, Jesus Christ is God's unsurpassable revelation.

No one could doubt the Christ-centeredness of Olier's life and thought. He was deeply marked by his vow of servitude to Jesus (1641) and vow of host-victim two years later.[24] His writings are permeated by a Jesus-centeredness. We find the Bérullian view of the Incarnation as a prolongation of the Trinity, as the hypostatic mystery in which the human "person" is replaced by the person of the Word ("The holy humanity of Our Lord has been annihilated in its own personhood."), and as a "mystery" or "state" whose "dispositions" are "never interrupted," still working in "all his members." Under the influence of Condren he seems, again, to accent the host-victim nature of Jesus: "Our Lord, in his divine person, . . . is this altar of gold upon which is consumed the most perfect sacrifice."[25] Olier often spoke of the "heart" or "interior" of Jesus, rather than the *état,* something which Bérulle himself tended to do after the *Grandeurs:* "Thus the interior of Jesus Christ . . . filling his soul . . . must be always before our eyes as the source and model of our own soul's interiority."[26] Throughout his writings Olier treats us to an almost dizzying series of meditations and probings on various facets of the Jesus mystery, as we would expect from someone who knew that "it is necessary that Jesus' humanity flow through us that we might participate in his life." It is the summit of revelation.[27]

We can note in the later Bérulle of the *Vie,* in Madeleine's important Lettre 144, and in Olier's stress on Jesus' "interior" an increasing stress upon the loving heart of Jesus. It is as if the more the French School meditated upon the mystery of the Incarnation, the more it moved toward love as the "deep grammar" of it all. Perhaps the growing rigorism of the Jansenists had something to do with this. It is a fact that our mystics always opposed the Jansenists. Is their heart and love Christology their answer to Jansenistic rigorism? Perhaps, too, we can sense something of the Renaissance and Baroque humanism here: Jesus' "heart" is the kind of personalism capable of satisfying the new desire for a more human and personal existence. In any case, it is this heart Christology that erupts in the work of St. John Eudes.

INTRODUCTION

The great Bérullian Christological themes, of course, punctuate Eudes' works, particularly the early and foundational *Royaume*. One will find the Incarnation as the Trinity's supreme manifestation in history, and meditations upon the states and mysteries of Jesus and our participation in him.[28] However, even here there are noticeable shifts in accent: toward a more biblical language, especially Paul's. Milcent, for example, notes that the phrase "the formation of Jesus in us" (Gal 4:19) becomes almost a technical notion. The influence of St. Francis de Sales is probably also evident in the new stress on the heart, on love and on "devotion" instead of the Bérullian term "religion."[29] "To be a Christian," says Eudes, "this is but to be one with [Jesus] . . . to have but one life, one spirit, one heart . . . one devotion and disposition with you."[30]

John Eudes' theology of Jesus' sacred heart finds its consummate expression in the later *Coeur* and in the feast which he composed. It represents a truly great and appealing transposition into the register of charity of the Bérullian Christology. An interesting fact is that John Eudes followed historically the route "from Mary to Jesus," for it was only through meditation upon her loving heart that he slowly discovered Jesus' loving heart.[31] In any case, the Bérullian theme of the Incarnation as the prolongation of the Trinity finds expression in the Eudist theme of the divine heart present in the mystery of Jesus. Similarly, the Bérullian mystery of the hypostatic union is transposed into meditations upon Jesus' corporeal and his spiritual hearts as enfolded in that divine heart. These three—the divine, corporeal and spiritual hearts—embrace the total divine (divine heart) and human body and soul (corporeal and spiritual hearts) of Jesus. Even the Bérullian theme of the *état* of Jesus as a perpetual power of deification is transposed into the great heart of the mystical body. "My daughter," Eudes once wrote, "do you know that you possess two hearts, a great and a small?" And he explains: "The latter is your own, but the great one is that of our good Savior, which is also your own. . . ."[32]

Corresponding to these theocentric, trinitarian and Christological-soteriological accents is a view and practice of the Christian (spiritual) life as one of a struggle between attunement to our deepest being and the opposing failure to remain so attuned. The conflictual nature of this struggle is particularly accented by Bérulle and Olier. In Madeleine and Eudes we seem to encounter a somewhat greater stress upon our deliverance from this struggle through Jesus. But in all the founding mystics of the French School there is a refusal to slide into either a simplistic optimism, which would ignore human perversity, or a rather frightful pessimism, which would plunge us into a kind of miserable despair and spiritual impotence. Between these two extremes there seems to be room for varied and legitimate accents, depending upon the needs of the spiritual life at a given time and place.

Owing to his biblical and Neoplatonic horizon of thought, Bérulle possessed an emphatic sensitivity to the creature's fragility apart from God. If we are but "a tending toward him in the state of our lives and in all our actions," then the reverse side of this is our "nothingness," our "need," and our "impotency" *without God.*[33] Perhaps in the humanistic atmosphere of the Renaissance Bérulle felt a special pressure to think this way against tendencies to derail into an autonomous view of the human person. But the notion of the creature's "nothingness" (*néant*) seems directed at our being as separated from God. It is by no means an unqualified assertion, and some commentators have noted a tendency in the later Bérulle of the *Vie* to mollify the talk of *néant.*[34] Still, Bérulle seems to be an Augustinian "realist," in the sense that he recognizes our existence as fallen. We do not inhabit a state of pure nature. Far from it, as *OP* 29 gratingly puts it:

> The state to which we have been reduced by the sin of our first father . . . is deplorable. . . . For in this state we possess rights only to nothingness and to hell, and we can do nothing but sin, and we are but a nothingness opposed to God.[35]

Cognet thinks that Bérulle was even somewhat critical of St. Francis de Sales' optimism. He rather emphasizes the harsh judgments of the Council of Orange on human depravity, says Cognet. Bérulle also seems intrigued by Satan's captivity of humanity, a theme that surfaces in the early treatise on possession (1599). Our death, too, is in some way linked to our punishment for sin, according to the tradition upon which Bérulle draws: "This world is but a theater of death, and this life is but an obligation to die."[36]

But if Bérulle can accent our nothingness and sinfulness, he can also celebrate our grandeur. For as we have seen, we are a tending toward God and a reflection of the Trinity in our very being. "From the first," Bérulle tells us, "God has given us an instinct and movement toward himself . . . and this movement is inseparable from the creature and will endure forever."[37] Here, of course, Bérulle has in mind "theandric humanity," the person as related to the Divine, rather than the "nothingness" of a creature supposedly separated from God. Similarly God has acted through Jesus to restore us to our proper being after the ravages of sin. As we have already seen, there is a very developed soteriology in the French School. The permanent *vertu* operative in the "state" founded by the "economy of Jesus" graces us. Jesus, Bérulle will say, "gives us his heart, his grace and his spirit; he incorporates us into him."[38]

Bérulle's meditations upon the Incarnation, as substance and economy, lead him especially to emphasize the states of "adoration" and "servitude" as informing Jesus especially, and through him, other Christians. The Incarnation is, if you will, an irruption of adoration and servitude in history. Servitude, because God becomes one with a human nature whose being is to be God's servant. Because in becoming human, Christ lives out the painful life of a pilgrim during his human existence. But most especially, because

> This humanity . . . which is emptied of something so great and intimate to its own essence as is its subsistence, and according to the Angelic Doctor, of its existence, is much more under the power and possession of the eternal Word which receives and sustains its existence, which is but a slave within the power and possession of its master.[39]

And what is true of Christ, the archetype, becomes true of the Christian; our life, too, is marked by a radical servitude which in some way "Christiforms" our own existence. Christ's state of servitude "creates diverse states in souls" as it "operates in [Jesus] the dependence in which [he is]."[40] Through this servitude the Christian can become mystically passive and receptive to Christ in the depths of being and in all one's actions. This was the point of the Bérullian "vow of servitude," which more cautiously became an "elevation to servitude" in the *Grandeurs*. We deepen our creaturely dependence upon God through servitude. We also heal it, insofar as it has been ravaged by sin. It enables us to undergo the *anéantissement*, the "no-saying," to any attitude or action away from Christ. "The *anéantissement* of [Jesus]," says Bérulle, "is the basis and foundation of all our good actions."[41]

The Incarnation also renders us "adorers" in our actions and in our being. By now we should be getting used to Bérulle's penchant for moving to the deeper (metaphysical) level of being, the level from which springs our thoughts and actions. "You are now, O Jesus, [the] adorer" of a God who has been adorable from all eternity, but has only found an infinite adorer with the coming of Christ, Bérulle prayerfully exclaims.[42] This Jesus, who "alone adores by state the divine persons and emanations" has this state "imprinted into the *fond* [or "fount"] of his created being," and in turn we ourselves "must honor . . . the Son of God . . . first by adoration . . . secondly by love . . . and then thirdly by an adoring love, that is to say, loving while adoring."[43]

As Guillén Preckler puts it, Bérulle powerfully transforms the "essential introversion" of the soul's "fount," so dear to the mystics of the Rhineland, into a Christological adoration by state. His originality is in making the mystic's contemplation a sharing in Christ's exemplary adoration itself.[44] This state of adoration is the basis of our need for contemplation. As the Son is the "flower and fruit" of the Father's contemplation, so we are "called to contemplation, not only by inspiration but by state," Bérulle tells us.[45] Here the Bérullian contemplation becomes a Christological act of adoration itself. Servitude and adoration, then, or *anéantissement* and contemplation, are the two great movements within the spiritual life. They lead us to our end. They heal us from the sinful obstructions blocking our journey to our end.

We will find the main Bérullian themes sketched above in Mère Madeleine's writings. There seems less of a stress upon our nothingness and sin, but these themes do, of course, surface, as they must in any realistic exploration of the spiritual life. "Know that the truth of our *néant* is so great," she can say.[46] Her biographer, Louise of Jesus, records an especially strong awareness of sin that came to the Mother during her great dark night. "God made me see the malignity of the human being corrupted by sin; . . . I have seen with trembling what would become of me were God to leave me to my sinful being."[47]

We have already noted that the Mother told Cardinal Bérulle how helpful the vow of servitude was to her in her spiritual life. Like the Cardinal she can also commonly speak of abandonment, adherence, self-renunciation and *anéantissement*. Perhaps we might say that this complex of terms refers to one of the great movements of the spiritual life through which Christ acts to redeem us. In a somewhat more Carmelite-Teresian manner she will also speak of following the cross as the way to Christ.[48] But the Mother also knows the other, more positive movement of the spiritual life: honoring and adoring and loving. And we have seen that perhaps her great contribution to the French School is to have emphasized the love dimension of the moment of adoration.

Let's take a closer look at the Mother's teaching in this regard, especially as noted in her crucial Letter 144. Much of this letter seems to reflect the great second discourse of the *Grandeurs:* that adoration is what God has been seeking from his creatures; that our sinfulness has made it impossible for us to comply; that the Incarnation makes it possible for a God to adore God and for Jesus' humanity to enter into a state of adoration; and that inasmuch as we conform ourselves to this model and unite ourselves with his dispositions, we, too, can become adorers. Note, however, some unique Madeleineian accents. She tells her correspondent that she prefers "the act of adoration" to "thanksgiving." This will save one from self-preoccupation, and it might be a critique of the dangers of mystical "introversion." We remember the Mother's problems with abstract mysticism.

Particularly important is the great stress upon love: adoration "does not even merit its name . . . if love is not its soul and life," Madeleine says. And she adds a gloss: They are "but one duty called by two names because of their differing effects." Here, I think, she rejoins the biblical perspective of love as the foundation of the virtues, rather than simply one virtue among others. We have seen that Bérulle eventually seems to have come to this same position, when he speaks of an adoring love. In this same letter Madeleine also stresses the theme of Jesus' and the Christian's state of victimhood and host, probably under Condren's influence. It's perhaps not accidental that she senses the need to balance this through love. Of course, her own Teresian and Carmelite perspective must have a lot to do with this too. Along with this, she will also speak of prayer in more Teresian terms as a conversation with Jesus, and she counsels against too much attention to methods.[49]

In Olier we encounter an intensification of the "nothingness-sin-servitude-*anéantissement*" complex. Besides the already cited *Mémoires,* the early portions of the *Catéchisme* are the crucial witnesses here. "The entire mass of the flesh [of Adam's children] and all its substance is corrupt." Or, "Man is so depraved in his *fond* that he is nothing but an inclination to evil and sin." Olier even exclaims that "we are not only sinners, but sin [itself]."⁵⁰ The interpretations of these texts, and others like them, are controversial waters in Olierian scholarship. To help us make our way here, let us remember some points worth pondering.

First, the *Catéchisme*, from which the above citations come, is usually regarded as Olier's most severe account of human corruption. But of its little more than ninety pages, only approximately twenty-five are dedicated to the theme of sin. Second, it seems important to catch the nuances. Olier says that "man is only *néant* and sin *by himself* (*par lui-même*)." Or, "The old man . . . opposed to the spirit [is] in us *only inasmuch as we are not regenerated*." Or, finally, "without the grace of God" are we sinners.⁵¹ Third, I would suggest that Olier be interpreted against the horizon of the thinking of the French School, unless we can clearly prove otherwise. Given his nuances, it seems legitimate to see in him an intensification of Bérulle's spirituality, perhaps under the influence of Condren. That is, the human being inasmuch as it is considered as either separate from God or in sin is corrupt. Again, we aren't dealing with unqualified assertions. Fourth, I would suggest that Olier be read against the backdrop of the mystical tradition of the sort represented by the Rhineland and St. John of the Cross. Olier seems to accent the depth of our human evil and sin, thus calling for a profound and rigorous *anéantissement*. But this is not so different from the Sanjuanist *nada* and the Rhineland's self-renunciation. Finally, the larger portion of Olier's *Catéchisme* is dedicated to probing this statement: "We have recovered in Jesus Christ what we have lost, and many more graces and goods than the sin that has been removed."⁵² Perhaps what we need to do is to read Olier dialectically, as we read many of the other great mystics. We are both sinner and saved, in need of *anéantissement* and filled with grace, and the latter to the extent that we are "participating in all the mysteries of Jesus Christ."⁵³

Olier usually describes the two great movements of the spiritual life in the Pauline, Paschal categories of death and resurrection. As we die to our penchant for selfish autonomy and sin through Christ so we rise to new life.⁵⁴ He can even speak of our participation in the "state of the divine ascension," whereby, "as the saints say, [the soul] becomes perfectly deiform, that is, all burning with love and shining with the brightness of God!" And this "deification" reaches down to

the "fount of [one's] heart."[55] As Louis Cognet thought, Olier "was a
. . . very great mystic who experienced the highest unitive states,
and it was through his own interior atmosphere that he interpreted
the themes of Bérulle and Condren."[56] It is not surprising, then, that
we come upon profound explorations of the subtle depths of the
spiritual ascent in his works. Olier's piercing analysis of the Pauline
moment of "dying to the old self" extends to the highest stages of the
dark night. We are called to undergo the *anéantissement* beyond the
surface and up to the very *fond* of our being. We must, he says, aspire
for an "emptiness of everything," which is the kind of faith spoken
of by John of the Cross: "a completely empty faith and love alone."[57]

Olier is equally capable of profoundly moving explorations of the
other, positive movement of the spiritual life. He speaks, like Bérulle
and Madeleine, of our state of adoration. The deiform state in which
we find ourselves through participating in the resurrection-ascen-
sion states of Jesus enables us to pray with a prayer reaching down to
the depths. We are to have "our Lord before our eyes, in our heart,
and in our hands." And Olier glosses: "The first is called adoration;
the second, communion; the third, cooperation."[58] If you will, the
transformation of our depth (*fond*) bubbles up into a transformation
of our mind (eyes), our affections (heart), and our actions (hands).
Here we have hints of the profoundly moving unitive style of mysticism Olier experienced and fostered. Glendon has, in this regard,
spoken of the "remarkable statement" from the *Mémoires* in which
we find Olier speaking of Jesus as "more willingly [in us] than in a
ciborium."[59] We even find a nuptial mysticism: As God conquers
self-love in our soul, Olier explains, one is "placed into a true ecstasy" and "becomes a spouse of God."[60] And who can forget the
profoundly lyrical last pages of the *Journée*, where Olier chants the
praises of a God united with all of creation? His final meditation,
"Upon Hearing the Birds Sing," speaks of the birds' chant as but
"slight manifestations of the immense and unending jubilation which
God enjoys in his beatitude."[61]

St. John Eudes speaks a very biblical, Pauline language as he navi-
gates in these waters too. We must undergo the Pauline death to self,
because of the great triad of the world, sin, and our old selfish selves.
"For being members of our dead and crucified head," says Eudes,
"we must be crucified to the world, to sin, and to ourselves."[62]
Eudes, like all the members of the French School, is a realist aware of
the night-side of human existence. He can even use the familiar

language of Bérulle: We are "but nothing (*néant*), sin, and abomination; all that is in the world is but smoke, vanity, and illusion."[63]

Again, the two great movements of the spiritual life surface in Eudes. Of course, as an Oratorian he practiced the devotion to servitude and the states of "detachment" and *anéantissement* to which it gave rise. One of his most challenging pages is the section in the *Royaume* where he says that

> the perfection of Christian abnegation or detachment does not only consist in detachment from self and world; but it obliges us to even be detached from God in some way.

> . . . that is to say, from the delights and consolations ordinarily accompanying God's grace and love.[64]

This detachment is but a participation in the radical abnegation of Christ himself, for we are "like the image towards its archetype [Christ]."[65] Here we can sense something of the mystical dark night of the senses and spirit and a certain congeniality with Olier's own mystical experiences.

Few writers in the French School can surpass, however, the celebration of the positive movement of the spiritual life we encounter in John Eudes. In his *Royaume* he usually moves within the Pauline and biblical language of the covenant alliance and our baptismal obligations as a way of describing this. But, as we know, he developed his "heart" theology and spirituality, and came in time to prefer a language centered around this great metaphor. He was particularly fond of the phrase from the Latin translation of 2 Maccabees 1:3, *corde magno et animo volenti*, which he translated into *avec un grand coeur et un grand amour:* "with an immense heart and a huge love."[66] Somehow our participation in Christ becomes a participation in this great heart experience. Here Bérulle's late discovery of the primacy of love, perhaps through or at least with, Madeleine, breaks out. Our own "heart" is, widely viewed, "the whole interiority of the person," and, more narrowly, "the supreme part of the soul . . . , the place of the spirit from which emanates contemplation."[67] "God," Eudes tells us, places the soul "in the way of passive prayer" here through our heart. This is "contemplation," which is "a very unique regard and a very simple view of God, without discourse or reasoning, nor multiplicity of thoughts."[68]

INTRODUCTION

Here John Eudes, like all his colleagues in the French School, transposes the mystical introversion of the Rhineland-Flemish mystics into an experience of the heart and love. It is a very pure form of love, freed from all clinging and attachment. It is so pure, in fact, that he can say:

> I ask you to notice carefully that the practice of practices, the secret of secrets, the devotion of devotions, is to have no attachment to any practice or special exercise of devotion, but have a great concern to surrender yourself, in all your exercises and actions, to the Holy Spirit of Jesus.[69]

Mariological

There is a kind of natural passage from Christology to Mariology in the thinking and practice of the French School. Indeed, a sketch of this school would be woefully inadequate were it not to surface the enormous importance of Mary to all our founding mystics. The extremely intensive Mariological accents of a Louis-Marie Grignion de Montfort is in many ways a normal development of trends already well in place in Cardinal Bérulle.[70] Mary's "love and grace render her incomparable," said the Cardinal. "Her dignity brings her close to the Creator in the quality of motherhood."[71] But yet this intensified acclamation of Mary is closely linked to the Christological mystery for Bérulle: Note the stress on her motherhood (of Jesus, of course).

There are several Mariological accents found throughout Bérulle's writings, with a growing stress upon Mary's interiority in his later *Vie*, which could be called a kind of psychological biography of Mary in many ways. But all are agreed that the central Mariological principle for the Cardinal is her maternity of Jesus, thus rooting Mary's importance squarely in the event of the Incarnation itself. Her "grace and life as the Mother of God is the foundation and origin [of everything else]," says Bérulle. She "is born in order to be the Mother of God."[72] Bérulle loves to contemplate the multifaceted reality of this very special maternity. Unlike Aquinas, but like Scotus, he sees in it the basis of Mary's immaculate conception, a term he explicitly uses.[73] Mary's virginity is also founded therein, for the novel state of the Incarnation and her maternity gives her "a novel and perpetual primacy" over all others in the state of virginity. God has united, in Mary, "purity and fecundity, maternity and virginity." And God has done this in such a way that Mary's virginity is "not only preserved" but even "fulfilled . . . by her maternity; and her maternity is . . . divinely accomplished in her virginity."[74] Not surprisingly, then, although less commonly, Bérulle will celebrate the singularity of Mary and her grandeur: The eleventh discourse of the *Grandeurs* speaks of her occupying an order "distinct and separated from all the orders among the angels and saints."[75] And, in line with his penchant for daring intuitions, Bérulle even explores correspondences between Mary's maternity and God's paternity. The maternal relation to the child perhaps witnesses to the relational reality of the Trinity. The earthly maternity perhaps points to the heavenly paternity, for her earthly birthing of Jesus reflects the Father's eternal generation of the Word.[76]

Guillén Preckler, however, thinks that Bérulle reaches the summit of his Marian spirituality in the creative twist he gives to the abstract mysticism that he continually integrates into his Christological spirituality. Just as we find a Christological transposition of some of the themes dear to that abstract mysticism in Bérulle, so now we find a Bérullian "Marian transposition." "O inclination of Jesus towards Mary, of Mary towards Jesus emanating from the eternal inclination of the Father towards the Son, of the Son towards the Father," sings Bérulle.[77] This rooting of the Marian mystery in the trinitarian relations, this language of "inclination" (and many other terms dear to the Rhineland and Flemish mystics), is quite suggestive of Guillén's thesis. Notice, too, the following, typically mystical expressions: the body, heart and soul of the Virgin is said, by Bérulle, to be made for the Incarnation and the divine maternity, all of which has "imprinted in the Virgin a spirit of life, of grace, and of love toward Jesus."[78]

A second Marian accent of special import for Bérulle is that of "Marian servitude." We have already noted the great importance of this theme in Bérulle's Christology and in his struggle over the issue of the vow of servitude. Thus it is to be expected that we will find texts in which he surfaces the dimension of servitude in Mary. But here, as Guillén Preckler notes, we find something somewhat surprising. We do find the theme of Mary's own state of servitude, to be sure, for Bérulle does quite explicitly see in Mary's *Fiat* the "state of servitude" in which Mary was placed from the "moment of the Incarnation."[79] But Bérulle's normal tendency is to stress the Christian person's servitude toward Mary, much as he stressed our own servitude toward Jesus. Here, of course, he follows the lead of Dionysius the Areopagite: There is a Christological and Mariological hierarchy (this last is the Dionysian element), and the latter precedes the former, at least temporally. The state in which Mary exists is capable of founding an order, for the Virgin *dominium acquisivit in omnia opera filii sui:* Mary has acquired a dominion over all the works of her Son. She now, if you will, founds a "choir" of people in servitude to her, and through her, to Jesus. Through her maternity, Mary

> possesses a right and special power of giving Jesus to souls [. . . and . . .] a grace which forms a special choir in heaven. . . . She uses her power . . . giving a special place to Jesus who is her son, and to herself, she who is his mother.[80]

Here we can see again how spirituality and theology (Mariology) are united in Bérulle, for the varied states in which the soul in servitude to Mary finds itself correspond to the varied states of the soul of Mary herself.

We might say that the third and final Marian accent of Bérulle is his almost dizzying exploration of the varied states of Mary's soul, and of course the corresponding transformation these cause in the soul "in servitude" toward her. We also need to remember that, at least around the time of the *Vie,* he can move easily from a more ontological to a more psychological exploration of Mary's soul. Note the subtle shifts in this text:

> Contemplating the occupation of the most holy Virgin, I say that she is not in an action, but in a state: for her occupation is permanent and not passing. She is not in a state, but in an action: for what is occurring in her is powerful and penetrates the marrow of her soul. She is, in neither an action nor a state, but in a novel being.[81]

In any case, just as Bérulle contemplated the many-natured states of the Incarnation, so he did the same for Mary. His *Vie* is perhaps a major source for this, but one will also find moving elevations in his correspondence, in the archival materials and in his works of piety. The key principle here is that as Mary's soul corresponds to that of her Son, so that of the Marian *serviteur* corresponds to that of both the former. The infancy of Christ was, of course, a point of special intimacy between Jesus and Mary, and Bérulle has a special fascination for it. Thérèse of Lisieux, perhaps under the Cardinal's influence, will give this her own playful twist in her own life. It creates a special participation of Mary in Jesus' life, and begins the transformation of her throughout the depth of her being. During the infancy Mary becomes a contemplative mystic of the incarnate Word: She "is established . . . in a state of perpetual ravishment upon an object perpetually worthy of ravishment."[82] But Bérulle, in writings other than the *Vie*, can contemplate other states of Jesus penetrating Mary and the Christian "Marian *serviteur*." He particularly dwelt upon the paschal mysteries. Especially through her participation in these Mary became "attentive to the interior and spiritual life of her Son and a pure capacity of Jesus filled with Jesus."[83] The basic tendency of Bérulle is to present Mary's participation in Jesus in a mystical fashion. The Marian mystery is a mystical (gratuitous and "passive") transformation of Mary's deepest being through her participation in the life, death and resurrection of her Son. Through this emerges a "novel order of the cross and of heaven altogether! . . . an order of souls crucified with and by Jesus."[84]

The Mère Madeleine was, as a Carmelite, especially pledged to a spirituality deeply stamped by Mary. "It is one of my desires, of my greatest desires, that all the souls of this order, who have the privilege of having the Virgin for their patron and Mother, render her the honor which she deserves," she tells us.[85] There is, then, a strongly Carmelite and Teresian current within the waters of Madeleinian Mariology. At the same time, she quite explicitly mentions how Cardinal Bérulle thought that the Carmelite sisters' devotion to Mary's maternity would be one of their greater blessings and sources of influence.[86] And there is a strong Bérulle-like emphasis upon devotion to Mary's maternity in Madeleine's writings. And we do know that she was influential in causing the Oratorian theologian Guillaume Gibieuf to write his treatise on the life and grandeurs of the Blessed Virgin.[87]

I would single out *Lettre* 121 as particularly disclosive of the Mariological accents within Madeleine's spirituality. It is a letter in which she is commenting upon insights stimulated by Gibieuf's work on Mary's maternity. We find the grounding of all the Marian mysteries in the maternity. Madeleine celebrates, for example, the "privileges of the Mother of God" which "are rare and terribly holy." Hence she is venerated by a multitude of names, such as "Mother of divine grace, Gate of heaven, Seat of Wisdom, faithful

Virgin," and so on. But all of this happens to her "because she is the Mother of God." And like Bérulle, we can participate in her maternity: "She arranges matters for [us] so that we can fully receive the effects of her maternity." In this letter Madeleine also singles out the mystery of the infancy, in which Jesus shows not only "love and tenderness, but also the respect and submission of an infant towards the mother." We too, she says, "must honor this quality with her and as something which comes from her."[88] The typical Madeleinian stress on love seems conjoined here to the Bérullian and Condrennian stress upon submission or servitude and played in a Mariological register.

Jean-Jacques Olier presents us with an appealing and quite unique transposition of the Bérullian Mariology. To some extent it is also quite daring, because of the flexible and creative way in which Olier finds himself forced by his profound experience to invent new theologisms. Mary, he says in one of his beautiful letters, is an *abrégé de l'intérieur de Jésus-Christ,* a concentrated but less explosive expression of the depths of Jesus. He is not afraid to put this another way, which sounds terribly modern, by calling Mary a sacrament:

> Jesus-Christ is, in the sacrament [of the altar], risen and filled with glory; and even though he is in a sacrament of goodness and mercy, he also exercises judgments by his condemnations. . . . Thus we must go to a sacrament which is pure mercy, where Jesus-Christ exercises no judgment, and this sacrament is the most holy Virgin, through whom we can confidently have access to Jesus.[89]

It is clear from this that Olier roots the Mariological mystery in the Christological and soteriological mystery. She is what she is because of the mystery of Jesus, and her entire existence is a mediation of that, to herself and us. The common theme of Mary's submissiveness (the *Fiat*), expressed by Bérulle as servitude, becomes with Olier the virtue of humility: Her "poor little nothingness" is the "portrait" of the Word, the "Word's becoming 'tangible' " (*sensible*).[90] But like Bérulle and Madeleine, Olier loves to contemplate the many mysteries of Mary, emphasizing in a special manner the maternity, but in his own special way. In the *Introduction* he calls fecundity the greatest virtue, and maintains that because God has espoused himself to the Virgin, ennabling her to generate the Word in time, Mary herself possesses this, the highest virtue. This is an interesting Olierian spousal transposition of Mary's maternity. We have noted his use of spousal, marital mysticism before.[91] Related to this is his calling Mary the "Father's Spouse," echoing the Bérullian tendency to seek correspondences between Mary's maternity and God's paternity.[92] Perhaps the most celebrated expression of Mary's maternity is found in the following prayer from the *Journée chrétienne*, a prayer derived from Condren:

> O Jesus, living in Mary, come and live in me, in your spirit of holiness, in the fulness of your virtue, in the perfection of your ways, in the truth of your virtues, in the communion of your divine mysteries: overcome in me all the powerful enemies, the world, the devil, and the flesh, by the power of your Spirit and for the glory of your Father.[93]

Saint John Eudes composed his own slightly different version of this prayer, no doubt highly influenced by Charles de Condren, like Olier.[94] In fact, perhaps under pressure from the Huguenots, it has been suggested that he accents the Christological foundations of Mariology even more than his master Bérulle. For example, in his *Royaume*, his early, more Bérullian work, he rather daringly (for a Catholic of the Counter-Reformation) says that Mary, of herself, "is nothing, possesses nothing, can do nothing," for Jesus is "all to her: he is her being, her life, her holiness, her glory, her power and her grandeur."[95] In this early work, which is really a manual of devotion, we find varied meditations on the various states of Mary, all of them indicating the close link between Jesus and Mary:

> O Jesus, only Son of God, . . . you are in . . . your most holy Mother . . . imprinting a most perfect image of yourself, of all your states, mysteries and virtues, and rendering her so like yourself, that whoever sees Jesus, sees Mary, and whoever sees Mary, sees Jesus.[96]

Eudes never wavers; his fidelity to these fundamental Mariological principles remains constant. But it is clear that, under the surface, he was growing in an enormously deep devotion and commitment to Mary. How else can we explain, nearly forty years after the *Royaume*, the "explosion" of the three-volume *Le coeur admirable de la très sacrée mère de Dieu ou la devotion au très saint coeur de Marie* in the last few months before the saint's death? This remarkable work, comprising volumes 6–8 of the *Oeuvres complètes*, is an engaging theological-spiritual analysis of the history and meaning of devotion to Mary's sacred heart. And, on Eudist principles, because Mary is what she is because of Jesus, a study of her heart ultimately becomes a study of Jesus' heart. This *perichoresis* between Mary's heart and Jesus' heart is clear throughout, finally culminating in a more detailed exposition in volume 8/12. The three volumes, rather like a rosary, make up twelve books, to which are added devotions, rich liturgical feasts on the sacred hearts composed by John Eudes, and other documents relevant to this heart devotion.

The first nine books explore the foundations, rather similarly to what we have already seen in our treatment of Jesus' sacred heart. Like his treatment of Jesus, John Eudes employs the traditional faculty psychology of the time, finding in Mary the threefold differentiation of the corporeal, spiritual and divine heart. If you will, because of the union between God and Mary, the Divine (the divine heart) has transformed the complete being of Mary, bodily (the corporeal heart) and spiritually (the spiritual heart). "These three hearts of the Mother of God are but one, for, excepting the hypostatic union, there could never be a holier or closer union," says the saint.[97] This is a transposition, into the language of the heart, of the grounding of Mariology in Mary's divine maternity. John Eudes wants to show that Mary's heart is "admirable," because it is "an abyss of marvels."[98] And what makes it so is the mystery of the Divine Presence penetrating her being in a total way. Books 2–8 probe this mystery in a trinitarian manner: the Father, Son and Spirit are the first three foundations for the Marian mystery. Book 9 calls various "excellences" of Mary herself the fourth foundation of the entire treatise: her freedom from sin, her being a sea of grace, her love, charity, humility and mercy. Throughout these books, too, we find one of the more massive historical studies of this heart theology, in the scriptures, the Fathers and the great spiritual writers.[99]

The tenth book is perhaps the summit of the whole: a rather beautiful biblical meditation on the *Magnificat*, extending to about one hundred pages. Impossible to summarize, Eudes gives a kind of Bérullian-Eudist spiritual sense to the Marian canticle, which is still moving even today to a heart properly disposed. The canticle's "language," says the saint, "was not uttered until the very moment [Mary] received it from the [divine] heart." And continuing in a truly mystical mode:

INTRODUCTION

For the corporeal heart of this divine Virgin, filled with a sensible and extraordinary joy, caused her holy mouth to chant this *Magnificat* with a fervor and extraordinary jubilation. Her spiritual heart, completely ravished and transported in God, caused ecstatic words to arise from her sacred lips: And my spirit is exalted in God my Savior. . . . Her divine heart, that is, her divine child, residing in her blessed womb and remaining in her heart, and who is the soul of her soul, the spirit of her spirit, the heart of her heart, is the primary author of this Canticle.[100]

The eleventh book of the *Coeur* distills from the whole work twelve reasons for a special devotion to Mary, as well as twelve devotional means for doing so. To this is appended various meditations for the celebration of the feast of Mary's heart. And finally, arriving in a sense at the summit of the whole in a more didactic way, the twelfth book explores the sacred heart of Jesus, itself the ground of Mary's own heart. We have already spoken of this book's contents before in the section on John Eudes' heart Christology. This final book also contains numerous meditations on Jesus' heart, as well as the liturgical feasts (Masses and breviary offices) that the saint composed for these sacred hearts.

The feasts composed by John Eudes are in some sense a Eudist transposition of Cardinal Bérulle's own original feast of Jesus' solemnity, which the Cardinal composed for the Oratory as a celebration of the Incarnation (in all its facets, as distinct from particular mysteries of the Jesus event). Sulpicians had an Olierian feast to celebrate Jesus' interior life (or his heart: Olier uses the heart language too). We should not ignore Olier's influence in this regard.[101] In any case, it would seem that Eudes is especially original in giving liturgical expression to the heart devotion. The French School's notion of participating in or adhering to the states of Jesus and Mary finds in the saint a liturgical formulation.[102]

Ecclesial and Pastoral

The spirituality and theology of the French School is clearly interested in contributing to the spiritual and theological renewal of individuals. There is, clearly, an accent on the individual's own personal and intimate growth in interiority. All our great founding mystics are noted as profound spiritual directors, and were usually under a quite definite program of spiritual direction and discipline themselves.

Perhaps the most massive example of this would be Jean-Jacques Olier's two volumes of letters, most of which are concerned with spiritual direction in this individual sense. This sense of the individual person shouldn't be surprising in a spiritual tradition that stresses the interior or the inward or the heart. Partly this is a result of the personalism of the classical and Christian traditions. It is also probably a result of the deepening sense of the individual typical of a post-Renaissance world. The accent upon *anéantissement*, so common in this spiritual tradition, may result from an intuition that there were dangers toward narcissism that accompany this new sense of the self. On the other hand, the French School didn't only produce deeply holy individuals. We only need to think of Bérulle's founding of the Oratory, of Mère Madeleine's work for the success of the introduction of the Carmelite tradition (as influenced by Bérulle) into France, of Olier's Company of St. Sulpice (as well as his support for the Company of the Blessed Sacrament, open to lay participation), and of John Eudes' Congregation of Jesus and Mary and the female religious congregations he co-founded, to realize an equal accent upon the ecclesial and pastoral dimensions of the French School. These great institutional expressions of the school certainly imply a vision of the church and its pastoral practice. But our mystics do more than this for us. We find a fairly well developed explicit theology and spirituality of the church, and its ministries and pastoral practice (especially through missions and education), among the writings of our mystics.[103]

It is particularly in the period of his *Discours de controverse* (1609) that we find Cardinal Bérulle formulating more systematically his vision of the church. Clearly his debates with the Reformed (Calvinist/Huguenot) churches were the stimulus for this thinking. Again, we find here a Neoplatonic or Dionysian ecclesiology, integrated to some extent with the biblical vision. On the one hand, Bérulle seeks correspondences between nature and grace: the God who authored nature also formed "the church within the world, as a new earth, and as a new world." In a sense, the God of nature is an archetype of the church on earth. But Bérulle views the God of grace, the Trinity, as the church's archetypal foundation too: The church is "the living image of the divine essence, and the work of the most holy Trinity," says Bérulle. In a charming phrase, the Cardinal speaks of the "conclave of the holy Trinity" as the foundation of the church on earth. Of course the Cardinal, in line with this trinitarianism, will transpose his ecclesiology into a Christological register too. This is already true in the period of his controversial discourses, but it especially surfaces in the *Vie:* ". . . religion only tends to [Jesus], and only imprints upon us . . . his states and mysteries."[104] Bérulle's vision of the church is also quite practical, characteristically uniting the theoretical and the practical, theology and spirituality. For this church's deepest nature is one of mission, oriented to the

> salvation of people; the disciples' preaching of our Savior; in a word, the entire state and exercise of the Christian Religion. Thus it is as the basis and foundation of the house of God.[105]

Here we also note the characteristic term found in the French School of *religion*. Bérulle, and our other mystics, move back and forth between church and religion almost imperceptibly. *Religio,* of course, hearkens back to the Roman, Latin tradition; *Eglise,* to the biblical. The French School inherits both. One has the impression that the term *religion* carries a more philosophical resonance, intending to penetrate to the interior or depth dimension of the church. We will see later that M. Olier uses it in this sense, and Bérulle, for example, calls "the state of religion" an "alliance by grace of God with humanity, and of humanity with God for the service and honor they owe him."[106] Bérulle is a reformer, seeking to renew the church especially through a spiritual transformation. This word *religio* seems a good one for conjoining the institutional to the more mystical or interior dimensions of the church.

Guillén Preckler tells us that Bérulle gradually concentrated his attention upon the state of the priesthood, certainly after 1599, the year of his own ordination. In illustration of this, he refers to one of the Cardinal's letters in which he tells us that his "new priestly state . . . engages me in a desire and effort to aspire toward a very great purity, one better corresponding to the grandeur of my priestly state."[107] Of course, his controversies with the Calvinists also pressured him to turn his attention to a theology of ministry, and we find something of a beginning of this in his first controversial discourse on the mission of pastors referred to earlier. Bérulle always roots his vision and praxis of ministry in his vision of the church and of Jesus. His own biblical Dionysianism issues forth in a vision of the ecclesiastical state as "the first and the holiest state of the church of God," its origins being those of the church's holiness itself. When he puts this into Christological terms, he says that Jesus' "state of the Incarnation" is "the foundation and the origin of all the states to which God calls us." And among these callings or states within the church, the priesthood receives a special accent: The bond of the priestly state to Jesus is "greater and stronger than that of a solemn vow."[108] This is why, in the very Dionysian-sounding section on the priesthood in his *Narré*, appended to his *Grandeurs*, he calls bishops the archangels and princes of the church, and priests the church's angels. They "bear the character of the only Son of God imprinted upon their souls, and this doubly, through baptism and the sacrament of orders."[109]

Part of the Cardinal's genius and charism was to translate this vision of the priesthood into the reformist program of the Oratory itself. Bremond has a very moving chapter on Bérulle's foundation of the Oratory as in some way the summit of his work. And the renewal of the priesthood—always a crucial issue for any realistic renewal of the church—was clearly central in the Cardinal's vision of the work of the Oratory. The great motif sounding through Bérulle's program for priestly renewal—in one way or another—was to unite the great triad necessary for priestly ministry, a triad that had somehow splintered: "authority, holiness, and doctrine."[110] We might say today, priestly office, spirituality and learning. Perhaps with some exaggeration, the Cardinal believed that office had fallen to the prelates; holiness, to the religious; and learning, to the doctors. As a result, the ecclesiastical state was an unlearned, spiritless shell of authoritarian power. And he conceived the Oratory's charism as one of trying to reunite these great dimensions of priestly ministry. If you will, the spiritual or mystical dimension would free authority from derailing into naked power and manipulation. It would also free learning from the danger of egoism. Living out the *anéantissement* of Jesus in the concentrated way demanded by the priestly state is clearly a great and chief concern running through Bérulle's work. At the same time, it is interesting that his spirituality is very ecclesial, and thus also at least partly sacerdotal. Hence mysticism needs to be conjoined to ministry and ecclesiastical authority, lest it derail into a dreamy solipsism. And there is something rather modern in the stress on learning. In part this is a reaction to the Protestant Reformation, itself surely the result of the "doctors" of the day against the perceived abuses of the time. It may also be a reflection of the Renaissance and its new spirit of critical learning.

INTRODUCTION

Of course, other aspects of the church surface in the writings and work of Bérulle. Naturally the Eucharist was also a key concern, from the time of the controversial discourses on. The sixth discourse of the *Grandeurs* is an especially fine summary of his eucharistic teaching, in which he points out the correspondences between the mysteries of the Trinity, the Incarnation, and the Eucharist. If you will, the way the divine persons reside in one another is somehow reflected in God's residence in Jesus as incarnate and as eucharistically present.[111] And, despite his concentration upon the grandeur of the priestly state—a situation partly demanded by the ecclesiastical corruption of the time—Bérulle also held a high view of the lay state. For him, as for the entire French School of this period, all were called to perfection, each through his or her own unique manner of participating in the various states of Christ. "And we must regard every soul . . . as a hierarchy of heaven upon earth," says the Cardinal; or, again, "as a subject of [God's] holiness which should shine and operate [in him or her]."[112] We must not forget the importance of the lay aristocracy, especially in the renewal of the French church at this time. Mme. Acarie, we recall, was enormously important in Bérulle's work. Also, Bérulle was a profound spiritual director engaging in a direction which cut across all the "states" within the church, as his letters particularly exemplify. Direction was, for him, "the science of the saints" which "pertains to saints, makes saints, and directs saints."[113]

Mère Madeleine's vision of the church seems to remain rather more in the background as an implicit presupposition of her thought and work. Unlike the Cardinal, she did not have occasion—through, for example, debates with the Reformers—to explicitly fashion her unique thoughts on the matter. In her great letter on conjoining love with adoration, referred to so often, she does speak of the church in both Bérullian and Condrennian terms as the place where Christ "offers to remain in the state of adoration and immolation." Like Condren, the Mother says that Christ "has continually offered [the immolation of his blood] since the incarnation."[114] A survey of her letters leaves one with the impression that her focus is much more eucharistic, as the accent on Christ's sacrificial immolation just mentioned seems to indicate. The Eucharist, she says, is the "*abrégé* [concentrated expression] of [Jesus'] marvels and where he deigns to enclose himself for us . . . in order to associate us with all that he renders to his Father."[115] This focus upon the Eucharist is an interesting blend of the two traditions that converge in the Mother: the Teresian/Carmelite and the Bérullian/Condrennian.

As Bérulle focuses upon the priesthood and upon the Oratory as the instrument of the priesthood's revitalization, so Madeleine concentrates upon the religious life and the Carmel as the instrument of its effusion in France. Not only this, of course, for we recall that Bérulle sought her counsel on the matter of the founding of the Oratory. Still, it is only natural that her special charism should be that of being the first French prioress of the Carmelite tradition. Her letters are continually concerned with this, in one way or another. Note the Teresian and Bérullian tone of the following:

> You have asked me what the life of Carmelites should be like. I tell you that we must conform ourselves to the saints in heaven. The saints always contemplate the face of God and of his Son whom he has sent, Jesus Christ. This is what eternal life consists in, as the Son himself teaches us. We must seek to do the same on earth, insofar as we can.
> . . . Ceaselessly we must regard Our Lord Jesus Christ and, as we cannot see him in his glory and grandeurs like the saints in heaven do, we must contemplate and adore him in his abasement and in the mysteries of his holy humanity.[116]

In the service of this vision of the religious life the Mother, as occasion arises in her correspondence, advances various suggestions. A special charism of Carmel is to imitate the love of solitude characteristic of the fathers of the desert. Carmel is a kind of "perpetual novitiate" in which one learns the art, not only of leaving the world, but of leaving oneself too.[117] In line with this, she seems particularly concerned to develop criteria of the Carmelite vocation, as Olier will develop similar criteria for the priestly vocation. The abuses of the time made this imperative, of course. Letter 256 seems particularly important in this regard, pointing out some of the bodily (strength and health) and spiritual requirements (prudence, docility, capacity for repose, lack of agitation) of the religious vocation. But the Mother also indicates that one must have not only a vague religious vocation, but one especially suited to the charism(s) of the Carmelite tradition. "It is," she says, "necessary to see a particular attraction to recollection, solitude, silence, and the life of prayer which is the unique profession in our Order."[118] As this indicates, and as many of her letters also illustrate, the Mother was a highly respected and sought after spiritual director.

INTRODUCTION

The Mother tells us that "the direction of souls is a great matter." She especially emphasizes the need of the director to "submit to the power and conduct of Jesus Christ, who is the great Superior and common Father of souls." This liberates the director from her own "inclinations," enabling her to experience the kindness and charity required for direction. The Mother continually speaks of an oscillation between kindness and firmness in dealing with souls, dispositions which come to a director who is striving after self-renunciation and adherence to Jesus in her own life.[119] What comes through is a special concern to protect the unique path to which God may be calling a soul, a special concern that the director not project her own whims upon the directee. This is an accent that also characterizes Olier's abundant spiritual correspondence and his other writings on direction. In line with this, the Mother also manifests an appreciation for the lay state, like our other founding mystics of the French School. Her concentration upon the religious life does not needlessly narrow her ecclesial horizons. "This obligation of imitating by our life that of the Son of God is for all Christians, for they are pledged to it by baptism, but it is a stricter obligation for religious consecrated to it by vows."[120]

Jean-Jacques Olier's *Mémoires* indicate that the mystical dark night he endured during his terrible trial issued forth, at least in part, in an ecclesial "stretching of horizons." Perhaps he had already assimilated in a more surface way the general Dionysian perspective of Bérulle and the more sacrificial perspective of Condren, but his own dark night "burns" into his being a conviction of the church as "Jesus' extension," enabling him to develop his own unique perspective on the church and its mission:

> The Church is an awesome reality. After experiencing this, I am no longer astonished by the love one should have for the neighbor or for the least creature not yet a member of the Church. For myself, I fail to see how one could not die for the faithful insofar as they will one day form a part of the admirable body of the most holy Church.[121]

In general, this more simply Christological perspective on the church tends to dominate in Olier's thinking, and he explores it throughout his writings through striking symbolisms. It is a "mystical body" through which Jesus has willed to "dilate and expand . . . his Spirit." Or it has been "destined to honor Jesus' holy humanity

. . . accompanying [Jesus] in every mystery of the incarnation."[122] In his *Journée* and *Mémoires* we even find a strong "heart" language reminiscent of John Eudes employed to express the church's nature as the act of religion. The Spirit spreads, "in all the church," what "Jesus' heart" renders the Father. And our own "hearts and temples are but echoes . . . of the harmonies rendered to God by Jesus' heart."[123] Note the mention of the characteristic term *religion*. Olier begins his *Introduction* with a more systematic analysis of this, which interestingly blends Bérulle's Christocentrism, Condren's accent on sacrificial imagery, and Olier's own special sense of God's desire to enter into a deep mystical union with us through the church. Religion consists in "respect" and "love," we are told. And it is through "the inventions of [Jesus'] love" that the kingdom of Jesus brings about the state of religion. Ultimately Jesus' "intimate presence within us" is like a fire devouring us, transforming us into "consummated hosts" for sacrifice.[124]

Like Bérulle, Olier tends to concentrate upon the two realities of priesthood and Eucharist, on both a theological and pastoral front. Again, he is a reformer, and one of his special charisms is the renewal of the priesthood, and even the episcopacy. To this end, as we have seen, he founds his Company of Saint Sulpice, which works in pastoral reform and seminary education. In this regard, his *Projet de l'establissement d'un seminaire dans un diocese*, proposed to the Assembly of the Clergy of 1650–51, is a particularly fine document to study, and it is somewhat novel in its attention to the episcopal state.[125] It is clear that Olier is within the Oratorian tradition of the need to reunite authority, sanctity and learning in the ecclesiastical state, but with his own special modulations, as always.

To gain a perspective on Olier's complicated vision of the priesthood, together with the spiritual praxis it entails, modern scholarship should, I think, take its bearings from the critical analysis of the document traditionally ascribed to Olier, the *Traité des saints ordres*. This has recently been provided by the three Olierian scholars Gilles Chaillot, Paul Cochois and Irénée Noye. First published in 1676, this treatise underwent numerous editions up until even 1953, receiving eleven editions alone in the nineteenth century. It was, in other words, an enormously influential work, both in the formation of priests and in spreading a certain image of M. Olier himself. The general result of current scholarship, however, is to argue that the work is to some extent an anthology of some writings of the mystic, but also an expurgation and tailoring done by Louis Tronson (1622–1700), the Sulpicians' third superior general. The lack of any original autograph, as well as important inconsistencies with the "authentic" works of Olier, are the deciding criteria of evaluation.

Tronson apparently tends to stress the "cultic" side of religion, accenting the exercises to which the cleric is called; Olier, the interiority, as we have seen. This is related to a further tendency to transpose into a moral and obligatory register what Olier tends to put in a more voluntary, mystical register. The language of "obligation" and "exercises to perform" seems rather frequent in Tronson's touches to the Olierian texts. Tronson also likes to present the various ministries as so many moral preparations leading to the priesthood, moral steps along the way, so to speak. Olier, on the other hand, tends to see them as a dimension of the priesthood itself. Tronson speaks of the orders as *"only* the beginning," while Olier leaves out the "only" and sees them as the "commencement of the great powers" [of the priest].[126] Even more fundamentally, the *Treatise* shows no trace of Olier's Dionysian vision of the episcopacy as the sacramental sharing in the plenitude of the Spirit. We can only speculate on Tronson's ignoring of Olier's important texts on the epsicopacy. This enables Tronson to exalt the priest over all else. Was there also a growing fear of the bishops as instruments of the growing independence of the French church? A view of ministry that stresses the episcopal college, as Olier does in his *Projet,* is a view that gives more place to collegiality and territorial particularity. As Olier puts it in his *Mémoires,* in rather Bérullian language, "in the church the prelate and bishop imparting the Holy Spirit must live a heavenly life, [they] must be elevated to the divine life and to the conversation of heaven." And in a way somewhat unique to Olier, the episcopacy is "a communication and participation [in the] dispositions of our ascended Lord. . . ."[127] Finally, and highly problematically, Tronson omits Olier's avoidance of clericalism. Where Olier sees the priesthood as a special expression of the priesthood of all the faithful, Tronson omits any reference to the faithful.

The basic conclusion to which our scholars come is this: Olier does not make of priests, through the strong spirituality he demands of them, "super-Christians but rather—and this is something entirely different—they are experienced Christians and actual examples."[128] There seems to be an accent upon priests, to be sure, within the Olierian writings. But there is also an equilibrium between the faithful as a whole and the priest, which enables our mystic to avoid the abuses of clerical arrogance. "Priests are especially obliged to [a] continual sacrifice, because of their explicit and public profession," he tells us. But he continues: "At the same time, Christians are all priests in faith and in the secret of the life of the spirit."[129] Perhaps Olier's special contribution was to contribute to the forging of criteria of the marks of an authentic priestly vocation, given the abuses of the time. To this end he especially dwells upon the spirituality necessary for the priestly vocation. Particularly appealing in this regard is his application of the traditional triple way of the mystic ascent to the priestly vocation. In his *Mémoires* we are told that the church requires of its priests the ability to purify, to illuminate and to unify. One can see here the mystical dimensions of the purgation, illumination and union transposed into a priestly register.[130] One of the advantages of this way of thinking is that it nicely conjoins the spirituality of the priest with that of the Christian and mystical life in general. Searching for such a conjunction is quite typical of Olier's priestly theology and spirituality.

As we have mentioned, Olier also has a very developed eucharistic devotion and spirituality. And related to this is a particular emphasis upon a spirituality of devotion to the Blessed Sacrament. For example, much of his popular *Journée* is eucharistic, stressing the Eucharist as "a dilation of the holy mystery of the Incarnation." And we have earlier noted how he brings out the deeper meaning of eucharistic communion in mystical terms as a "marriage of Our Lord with the soul."[131] Of course, he will also accent the sacrifical nature of church and Eucharist, disciple of Condren as he is: Jesus "always offers himself to God in himself and in all his members . . . [he] is an altar upon which everyone is offered to God," Olier tells us.[132] And as we have mentioned several times, Olier was a noted and much sought after spiritual director, as his letters particularly manifest. In fact, his disciples Bretonvillier and Tronson also compiled a number of his thoughts on direction into *L'esprit d'un directeur des âmes* which we have already alluded to. Together with Olier's own *Regulae Artis Artium* this presents us with a mystic who devoted a substantial effort of reflection to the matter of spiritual guidance. The dominant note throughout is upon the motif of *anéantissement* necessary for both director and directed. This leads to a posture of openness to the one real director, who is Jesus. One becomes free to open oneself to the path desired by Jesus. Through self-abandonment the director will not project his or her own whims upon the directee, and the latter will have the freedom to move as the Spirit wishes. One will find, I think, a rather fine synthesis of the Olierian principles of guidance in the final chapter of the *Introduction*. In the end, as Olier indicates, the "interior of Jesus" becomes the "source and model of our own interior." We need not, he says, "feel" or "taste" Jesus' Spirit in us. It is enough "to unite ourselves to [this Spirit] in faith."[133]

John Eudes, of course, inherited the Oratorian tradition through his years of membership within Bérulle's Oratory. He also knew M. Olier very well, having given a mission for him at St. Sulpice. It is interesting that St. John Eudes directed that Olier's writings be among the important works used by new members of his Congregation, along with Condren's letters and Eudes' own *Royaume*.[134] It is not surprising, then, that we find the ecclesial and pastoral accents typical of our French School with the saint.

Eudes is very much a practical, pastoral person. His writings, other than perhaps the great *Coeur*, bear all the characteristics of *ad hoc* practical works. It is from them that we can discern the lines of a rather full ecclesiology and pastoral theology.

Perhaps the key accents of the saint's thought can be found already in his *Royaume* in the "Exercise for Holy Mass." "Jesus Christ," we read, is the "supreme Priest." We, clergy and laity, are "participating in his priesthood," and this means that we should not only assist at Mass but actually "do it with the priest." Eudes' ecclesiology is very Christological and biblical: "Christians . . . are but one with Jesus Christ, as members with their head, . . . sharing all his qualities." Notice the equilibrium between priest and laity, characteristic of the French School: clericalism is avoided. Like Condren and Olier, we also find some sacrifical accents: We are "but one victim [with Jesus the victim] . . . to be immolated and sacrificed with [him] to God's glory." We even at this early date find the beginnings of Eudes' heart theology: Our sacramental communion is the result of Jesus' "very burning desire to make his dwelling in our heart."[135]

In the service of this ecclesial vision Eudes founded his Congregation of Jesus and Mary to carry on the work of pastoral and priestly reform. He also contributed a significant number of pastoral works for the same end: on baptism, on priestly piety, on the art of being a good confessor, on preaching, and on the theology and spirituality of the priesthood in general.[136] There is clearly an accent on the priesthood, as with Bérulle and Olier. In fact, some statements can seem exaggerated if they are not balanced with his wider ecclesial vision and usual estimate of the lay state.[137] At the same time, there is a fine emphasis upon the pastoral dimension: the "salvation of souls" is "the first and the greatest obligation of the ecclesiastic." This is why one becomes a priest.[138] We also find, as with Olier, an emphasis upon developing criteria of the priestly vocation, as well as the need to unite priestly office with the pursuit of sanctity. Priests, we are told, "must be animated [by the Spirit] in order to preach the gospel and work for the salvation of souls."[139]

We are especially in John Eudes' debt for his appealing transposition of ecclesiology and ministry into the language and conceptuality of a theology of the heart and love. Here his ecclesiology seems even more directly rooted in Christology and Mariology, and the accent on sacrificial love avoids any hint of ecclesial clericalism and elitism. As the great Eudist scholar Paul Milcent illustrates, the symbolism of the heart functions for Eudes as a master metaphor, enabling him to expose the reader to the multiple dimensions of theology and spirituality at once. We have already seen its Christological and Mariological dimensions. To this should be added the ecclesial and pastoral. As the heart signifies interiority, we might suggest that a heart ecclesiology surfaces the depth dimension of the church. This depth is Jesus' heart, which loves us and attracts us to him and to one another. It also, of course, makes us think of immolation and sacrifice, thus bringing out this facet of the Condrennian and Olierian aspects behind Eudes' thought. In Milcent's terms, "We rediscover here the theme of the mystical body."[140] We perhaps catch much of this in the saint's suggestive transposition of Ezechiel 36:26: "I will place within you my Spirit and my heart so that you will love God with a great heart, with much love, *Corde magno et animo volenti* ["with a giant heart and a burning spirit"].[141] This notion of the giant heart—embracing Jesus, his mystical body, our call to sacrificial mysticism, our union with Mary's burning heart, and the heights of mystical love—is clearly one of those primal metaphors that at once attracts us with its power of integration and yet even somehow invites into this mystery. Perhaps we can see why John Eudes, like our other founding mystics, was also noted as a great spiritual director, with a tremendous gift of spiritual fecundity. His published letters of spiritual guidance number, like theirs, in the hundreds.[142]

With this we come to the conclusion of our survey of the theology and spirituality of our founding mystics. There are other aspects that would deserve to be treated in a more complete analysis. The numerous and moving elevations or contemplations of the states and mysteries of the events of Jesus, earthly and risen, and of Mary and even Mary Magdalene particularly deserve more attention. The devotional and liturgical creativity of the French School is also impressive. I might fittingly conclude with a mention of the eschatological dimension. Although our mystics lived and wrote chiefly in the "grand century," they basically seem to preserve their critical balance, avoiding too easy a synthesis between the times and the Christian revelation. This theology and spirituality, especially in Bérulle, is one of grandeur, but it is also one of servitude, kenosis, *anéantissement*, and the cross. I would say that it is mainly through these Christological and Mariological accents that our mystics preserve the eschatological reserve of an authentic faith. But we also find other ways of expressing this, perhaps more direct ways.

With Bérulle, one might look particularly to his elevations on Jesus' resurrection and ascension for much of this. He also emphasizes, as a special mark of the Oratory, the devotion to the saints. Because we ourselves do not yet know the state of glory, we must have "a bond with the holy souls who converse with the Son of God," says the Cardinal. For we must "in some manner conform ourselves to the impassibility of the Son of God in his glorious state."[143] In her own charming way Mère Madeleine speaks of the disproportionate experience of "our baseness and smallness," which we experience now, and thinks it is "just" that we will have an eternity in which to have a place for our capacity to revere the mystery of Jesus' love.[144] Olier holds out the image of the "church in heaven," and tells us in a meditation on Jesus' resurrection "to aspire continually to heaven."[145] John Eudes, too, knows of the mystery of eternal life. His prayers to be united in eternity to the hearts of Mary and Jesus are quite expressive of this. But we perhaps catch a more interesting sense of his eschatological sensitivity in the way he begins a famous prayer of the French School: "Come, O Lord Jesus, come into me."[146]

NOTES

1. *OP* 118 col. 1143.
2. *Mémor* 11, p. 625. Cf. Dagens, pp. 249–69, and François Bourgoing's *Préface* to the *Oeuvres complètes*, pp. vi–vii.
3. *G* 7, 4, p. 267. On exemplarism see Julien-Eymard D'Angers, "L'exemplarisme bérullien," *Revue des sciences réligieuses* 31 (1957): 122–39. Dupuy offers a succinct explanation of Neoplatonic (Dionysian) exemplarism: "Resemblance is the fundamental relation between beings thanks to which they become intelligible. To explain . . . to know causes . . . is to discern similarities. A creature is situated in the hierarchy of beings when one knows what it imitates. To be a cause of a category of beings, this is to be the archetype upon which they are molded." (*Bérulle et le sacerdoce: étude historique et doctrinale* [Paris: Bibliothèque d'histoire et d'archéologie chrétiennes, 1968], p. 151).
4. *Coll* 1151.
5. The citations and references are, in order: *G* 3, 8, p. 205; 7, 6, p. 271; 5, 3, p. 232; 4, 10, p. 228; 10, 2, p. 323; 5, 2, p. 231; 5, 8, p. 237; *OP* 33, col. 968; *G* 4, 2, pp. 212–14. See Cognet, *La spiritualité moderne*, pp. 328–34, for helpful commentary. The distinction between Western and Eastern emphases in trinitarian theology is not as rigid as one sometimes think. One can find Westerners who stress the persons, and Easterners who stress the unity. Cf. Walter Kasper, *The God of Jesus Christ*, trans. V. Green (New York: Crossroad, 1986) pp. 296–98. See below, pp. 131–34.
6. Madeleine de Saint-Joseph, *Lettre* 129 ("one in essence"), p. 124; Louise de Jésus, p. 416 (God's plentitude); *Lettre* 130, p. 125 (this citation).
7. Irénée Noye and Michel Dupuy, "Olier (Jean-Jacques)," *DS* 11 (1982), col. 741. Cf. Dupuy, *Se laisser*, p. 61.
8. *J*, p. 209 (the fire metaphor: see pp. 208–13); I, p. 148.
9. *RJ* 2, 10: *OC* 1, pp. 187–91 (on detachment from God; see below, pp. 310–12); *C* 12, 11: *OC* 8, pp. 262–63. Cf. Milcent, *Saint Jean Eudes: introduction*, p. 33, for the influence of De Sales.
10. A breakthrough work on the relational view of God and corresponding relational view of humanity in Bérulle is R. Bellemare, *Le sens de la créature dans la doctrine de Bérulle* (Paris: Desclée de Brouwer, 1959). This is now a standard view; see Fernando Guillén Preckler, *"état" chez le Cardinal de Bérulle: Théologie et spiritualité des "états" bérulliens, Analecta Gregoriana* Series, 197 (Rome: Gregorian University, 1974), p. 71.

11. See Orcibal, p. 134: "Thus he renders possible the reconciliation of dionysian apophaticism with union to the divine will, this latter being revealed by the incarnate Word, and, since the Man-God realizes the ideal of *anéantissement* and of adoration by being, there is no need of any other 'supereminent way' than his own."

12. *G* 4, 10, pp. 227–28.

13. *G* 3, 8, p. 207. See Cognet, *La spiritualité moderne,* p. 336, referring to Harphius' *Théologie mystique,* trans. J. B. de Machault (Paris, 1617), p. 16. Also see below, pp. 126–30.

14. See *G* 5, 11, pp. 241–42, and 5, 2, pp. 230–32.

15. *G* 4, 5, p. 218. For the "novelty" of the incarnation, see *G* 11, 6, pp. 348–49.

16. *G* 8, 4, p. 284. See Cognet, *La spiritualité moderne,* p. 340, for the sources: Cajetan, St. Thomas Aquinas, Harphius. The crucial source is the Second Council of Constantinople (553). Cf. Kasper, *Jesus the Christ* (New York: Paulist, 1976), p. 239.

17. See *OP* 16–18, cols. 937–42.

18. *G* 4, 6, p. 220.

19. *G* 11, 4, pp. 344–46. Bérulle uses the term *dénuement* in one of his formulations of the vow of servitude: cf. Guillén Preckler, p. 88. On the issue of the humanity of Jesus in spiritual theology, see William M. Thompson, *The Jesus Debate: A Survey and Synthesis* (New York: Paulist, 1985), pp. 312–15; Dagens, pp. 301–21; Karl Rahner, "The Eternal Significance of the Humanity of Jesus for Our Relationship with God," *Theological Investigations* 3, trans. Karl-H. and Boniface Kruger (Baltimore: Helicon, 1967), pp. 35–46. Helpful here is also Louis Cognet, "Bérulle et la théologie de l'Incarnation," *XVIIe Siècle* 29 (1955): 330–52.

20. See *G* 5, 9, pp. 238–39 (on Jesus' paternity); 9, 3, pp. 312–15 (on the New Adam); *OP* 73, col. 1049, and *G* 5, 12, p. 242 (on deification). Cognet, *La spiritualité moderne,* pp. 343–44, suggests that Bérulle was both a Thomist and a Scotist when it comes to the motive of the incarnation: God wants to be in union with us (Scotus), and in the only world in which we live that means God must redeem us from sin (Thomas). See *G* 11, 7, pp. 350–52 and 9, 3, pp. 312–15. Also 5, 25, pp. 500–4.

21. *OP* 77, col. 1052. Guillén Preckler is the important study here: He traces the origins of the notion in canon law, theology and mysticism, suggesting that Bérulle does not create the term, but uses it more frequently between 1611–15 and gives it novel and creative Christological nuances: see pp. 250–63. Also see below, pp. 153–54.

22. *OP* 17, col. 940.

23. *Lettre* 142, pp. 138–39; 144, pp. 142–46 (the state of victim); 49, pp. 57–59 at 58 (adherence to Jesus); 139, pp. 133–35 (advice from Bérulle); 238, pp. 253–55 (on St. Teresa of Avila). Cf. Louise de Jésus, pp. 479–88.

Charles de Condren (1588–1641), second superior of the Oratory, developed an accent upon the sacrificial aspects of Christology, seeing Jesus' state of victimhood (or host) as the consummation of his life. We have only his letters and posthumously published conference notes to rely upon. See Cognet, *La spiritualité moderne,* pp. 382–89. Bremond 3, pp. 243–358, offers the English reader an extensive selection of Condrennian texts and commentary. See Charles de Condren, *Lettres du Père Charles de Condren (1588–1641),* ed. Paul Auvray and André Jouffrey (Paris: Cerf, 1943), the most "secure" source of our knowledge of Condren's thought.

24. See Dupuy, *Se laisser,* pp. 391–93.

25. Cf. *Cat,* pp. 45–47, for these citations and a good summary.

26. *I,* pp. 156–57; Cf. Dupuy, *Se laisser,* pp. 127–28, for evidence from the *Mem.*

27. *J,* p. 155; cf. pp. 153–57. Cf. Dupuy, *Se laisser,* pp. 323–31, for Olier's approach to abstract mysticism: He stresses in his itinerary a later fascination for Jesus' divinity, but through the humanity, not by bypassing it.

28. See *RJ* 2, 1–21: *OC* 1, pp. 161–204, on the foundations of the Christian life; and 5, 3–11: *OC* 1, pp. 419–40, meditations on the states of Jesus' life; and passim.

29. Milcent, *S. Jean Eudes: Introduction,* pp. 32–34.

30. *RJ* 7, 13: *OC* 1, p. 515.

31. Cf. Milcent, *S. Jean Eudes: un artisan,* pp. 449–58, for the major sources behind Eudes. Cf. also Jacques Arragain, "Evolution de la pensée de saint Jean Eudes sur le Coeur de Jesus," Charles du Chesnay, "Place de Saint Jean Eudes dans l'histoire de la dévotion au coeur de Jésus," and Louis Cognet, "Le coeur de Jésus et la Trinité d'après Saint Jean Eudes," in Jacques Arragain, et al., *Le coeur du Seigneur: études sur les écrits et l'influence de saint Jean Eudes dans sa devotion au coeur de Jésus* (Paris: La Colombe, 1955), pp. 43–68, 19–42, 108–119. Cognet interestingly argues that Eudes applies Bérulle's theme of Jesus' paternity to the theme of Jesus' heart [*C* 12: *OC* 7], although one does not find the central theme of the Cardinal of "the privation of the personal subsistence in the humanity of Jesus": pp. 116, 115.

32. Cited in Milcent, *S. Jean Eudes: un artisan,* p. 452. For the theme of the "great heart," see *C* 3, 3: *OC* 6, pp. 264–65; for the three hearts (divine, corporeal and spiritual), see the entire *Coeur* and Cognet, in Arragain, for a good commentary; also see below, pp. 331–34.

33. *OP* 1, col. 911; 172, col. 1222; 181, col. 1234. Cf. Dagens, pp. 335–66.

34. See Cognet, *La spiritualité moderne,* p. 349.

35. *OP* 29, col. 958.

36. See Cognet, *La spiritualité moderne,* pp. 349–50. The texts are: *OP* 137, col. 1172; 29, 1, col. 959; *E,* esp. 2 (the study of possession); and *OP* 60, col. 1035 (this citation).

37. *OP* 111, col. 1131.

38. *OP* 17, col. 941. Bérulle knows our being is gifted by both "created grace," the Scholastic term for the modification of our being through Christ, and "uncreated grace." See Cognet, *La spiritualité moderne*, pp. 350–51, for texts and commentary.

39. *G* 2, 10, p. 185 (a crucial text on the enhypostasis of the humanity in the Word [see below, pp. 122–26]); for the other reasons for Christ's servitude: *OP* 15, 3, col. 935 and *El*, n. 12, pp. 536–37. Guillén Preckler, pp. 103–45, is superb on the background in Thomism and the mystics of the Rhineland. I follow him throughout this section.

40. See *CB* 3, P. 686, pp. 333–34. Bérulle speaks of our general (universal) participation in Jesus' states and mysteries as well as more specific participations in special states of Jesus, depending upon our own unique response to Christ's offer. See Guillén Preckler, pp. 159–67, and *OP* 17, cols. 940–41.

41. *Mars.* fol. 12 *RHE* 133 D. Many of the themes of abstract, Rhineland mysticism surface here: abandonment, denial, nothingness, etc. See Guillén Preckler, esp. p. 119.

42. *G* 2, 13, pp. 190–91; see below, p. 126 (a famous text) and p. 109.

43. *G* 11, 6, pp. 348–49 (this entire section is a key text on adoration); "De nouveaux inédits de Bérulle," XXXI A. See below, pp. 153–54.

44. Guillén Preckler, p. 143; esp. cf. Michel Dupuy, *Bérulle: une spiritualité de l'adoration* (Paris: Desclée de Brouwer, 1964).

45. *OP* 7, cols. 917–18. Cf. *OP* 8, cols. 918–20. Bérulle never offers us an analysis of prayer, unlike some of his followers. His teaching on these movements of purgation (*anéantissement*) and contemplation are the closest he comes to such a thing. Of course, his writings are filled with prayers (or "elevations"). Cf. Guillén Preckler, pp. 27–28.

46. *Lettre* 159, p. 167. This letter, pp. 166–67, is an especially rich source for the Mother's view of nothingness and sin.

47. Louise de Jésus, p. 508.

48. See *Lettres* 159 (esp.), pp. 166–67; 28, p. 39; 49, pp. 57–59; 157, pp. 164–65, for representative examples.

49. *Lettre* 144, pp. 142–46; see below, pp. 200–03; cf. *Lettres* 137, pp. 131–33; 149, pp. 155–57, and 150, pp. 157–58 (on prayer). Cf. Louise de Jésus, pp. 488–94 (on adoration in her life). On the issue of love in Bérulle, see *OP* 164, cols. 1207–10, fully devoted to love; note esp. col. 1210: [love] "is the greatest action of nature and grace . . . yet up to now I have thought about it so little . . ."; cf. Karl Rahner, "The 'Commandment' of Love in Relation to the Other Commandments," *Theological Investigations* 5, trans. Karl-H. Kruger (Baltimore: Helicon, 1966), pp. 439–59.

50. *Cat*, pp. 19, 36, 34.

51. *Cat*, pp. 24, 17, 38.

52. *Cat*, p. 44.

53. *Cat*, p. 45.

54. *I*, p. 18, referring to Rom 6.

55. *Cat*, p. 52; *J*, p. 100.

56. Cognet, *Post-Reformation Spirituality*, p. 96.

57. *J*, p. 148; *Cat*, p. 82. Helpful here is Noye, et al., cols. 742–45, and Dupuy, *Se laisser*, on the influence of St. John of the Cross, pp. 288–89. We know from his *Mém* that he read and studied John.

58. *I*, pp. 228–32; see below, pp. 228–32; cf. *Cat*, pp. 71–74. Here we have a bit more of an exploration of methods of prayer than we find in Bérulle. See G. Letourneau, *La méthode d'oraison mentale du séminaire de Saint-Sulpice* (Paris: Victor Lecoffre, 1903), who traces this form of prayer as far back as Ambrose (pp. 286–87, 304–5).

59. *Mém* 3:49 (July 1642), in Glendon, p. 215.

60. *I*, p. 81. Cf. *Cat*, p. 63, where Olier speaks of the "marriage of our Lord with the soul" through holy communion.

61. *J*, p. 247; see below, pp. 285–87; cf. *J*, pp. 234–47. Dupuy, *Se laisser*, pp. 354–57, likes to underline the notion of complete abandonment to the Spirit and of "being lost in God," pp. 361–81, as major themes in Olier. They are further expressions of his unitive mysticism, employed especially in the *Mém*. For a challenging interpretation of Olier's view of human corruption, see Glendon, pp. 128–261. Also note the Olierian use of the Pauline notion of the "flesh." Olier is not a metaphysical dualist, but more Augustinian and Pauline. Cf. Dupuy, *Se laisser*, pp. 131–32. Olier employs the traditional tripartite anthropology (body, soul, spirit) in a number of places (viz., *I*, pp. 88–89, 159). This is corrupted by sin, but not destroyed.

62. *OC* 2, p. 182. Eudes' view of the "world" is Johannine: see *RJ* 2, 7: *OC* 1, p. 178.

63. *RJ* 2, 4: *OC* 1, pp. 170–71.

64. *RJ* 2, 10: *OC* 1, pp. 187–88; see below, pp. 310–12.

65. *RJ* 1, 3: *OC* 1, p. 101.

66. See *Letter* 10 in Guillon, pp. 38–41, esp. the commentary in note 2.

67. *C* 1, 2: *OC* 6, p. 35. Cf., on this, Milcent, "Jean Eudes," col. 498.

68. *Lettres*, *OC* 10, p. 439; *C* 1, 2 and 4: *OC* 6, pp. 35, 87.

69. *RJ* 6, 18: *OC* 1, p. 452.

70. See Deville, pp. 139–55.

71. *Ma* 2, p. 558.

72. *OP* 9, 1, cols. 920–21.

73. See *M* 233 *RHE* 98 D.

74. For these texts on Mary's virginity see *V* 12, pp. 470–71; 15, p. 481.

75. *G* 11, 11, p. 360.

76. See *OP* 119, col. 1144, and *M* 233 *RHE* 94 B, for example. A key work on the correspondences between divine paternity and Marian mater-

nity is M. de Vidal, *Le cardinal de Bérulle théologien marial. La doctrine de Marie Epouse* (Nicolet Quebec Centre marial canadien, 1957).

77. *M* 233 *RHE* 94 B. See Guillén Preckler, pp. 231–34.

78. Guillén Preckler, pp. 231–34. See, for example, John Ruusbroec, *The Spiritual Espousals and Other Works*, Classics of Western Spirituality Series, intro. and trans. James A. Wiseman, (New York: Paulist, 1985), for an example of the kind of Flemish mystical language Guillén Preckler has in mind.

79. *OP* 162, col. 1206 *RHE*. Cf. Guillén Preckler, pp. 234–37; I have been greatly aided by Guillén Preckler, pp. 221–49, for this entire section on Bérullian Mariology. Guillén Preckler provides us with perhaps the best synthesis available.

80. *Coll* 1615, p. 70; *CB* 2, P. 409, pp. 344–45 (January 1623).

81. *V* 17, p. 484. The term *state* would indicate a more ontological concern; that of *action*, a more psychological one. Of course, this way of analyzing the matter, common among Bérullian commentators, is based on a view of ontology that is static. Bérulle himself, in the final line of this citation, seems to want to break free of this way of thinking, I suspect.

82. *V* 28, p. 517. This work actually ends before Jesus' actual birth. It is greatly a meditation upon Mary's singular intimacy with Jesus in the conception stage (*infancy* is meant in this extended sense). Bremond 3, pp. 435–96, has a very suggestive treatment of this theme in the French School. For Thérèse, see Von Balthasar, *St. Thérèse of Lisieux*, pp. 215–24.

83. *V* 29, p. 520 (perhaps the most famous line of the work!).

84. *Ma* 5, 6, p. 574.

85. *Lettre* 179, p. 183.

86. *Lettre* 96, p. 91.

87. Cf. Louise de Jésus, pp. 533–37, esp. p. 537; Guillaume Gibieuf: *La vie et les grandeurs de la très saincte Vierge Marie Mère de Dieu* (Paris, 1637).

88. *Lettre* 121, pp. 113–14. Louise de Jésus, p. 536, notes that the Mother had a special devotion to the mystery of Mary's Assumption among all the Marian mysteries. This seems reflected in *Lettre* 177, p. 181 (and note the Bérullian tone): "We owe a special application of ourselves [to the Assumption]. And we must desire in our eternity to participate in the glory of our great Patron and our Mother, and to believe that there is no greater service we could render the Son than that of honoring his Mother, because her own greatest desire is to see her Son perfectly loved; and in this way we would become his daughters if we were to love Jesus Christ and have his actions, his words and his mysteries continually present."

89. *Cat*, p. 59; *Lettre* 340, 2, p. 234.

90. *I*, p. 44.

91. *I*, p. 153. A related notion here is Mary's mediatorship of participation in Jesus; cf. *Cat*, p. 88.

92. *Lettre* 408, 2, pp. 389–90.

93. *J*, p. 178. On this see Irénée Noye, "Sur la prière 'O Jesu vivens in Maria,' " *Bulletin du Comité des études* 7 (1954): 8–17, and Dupuy, *Se laisser*, pp. 181 and 267.

The Latin version is the more common one, handed down traditionally in Sulpician seminaries, and it differs slightly from the one in the *J*: the second line has "your servants" rather than "me"; it omits mention of the world, devil and flesh; and there is some paraphrasing:

> *O Jesu vivens in Maria,*
> *Veni et vive in famulis tuis,*
> *In spiritu sanctitatis tuae,*
> *In plenitudine virtutis tuae,*
> *In perfectione viarum tuarum,*
> *In veritate virtutum tuarum*
> *In communione mysteriorum tuorum,*
> *Dominare omni adversae potestati,*
> *In Spiritu tuo, ad gloriam Patris, Amen.*

Condren's prayer, as Eudes' in n. 94, lacks the Marian accent of Olier's; there is another version of Olier's prayer that is even more Marian. See Deville, p. 68, for texts of Condren's and Olier's prayers.

94. See Milcent, *S. Jean Eudes: un artisan*, p. 303: "Come, Lord Jesus, come in me, with the fullness of your power, with the holiness of your Spirit, with the perfection of your mysteries, and the purity of your ways. Come, Lord Jesus!"

95. *RJ* 3, 11: *OC* 1, p. 338. Cf. Milcent, "Jean Eudes," *DS*, col. 494, for the suggestion about the Protestant influence.

96. *RJ* 5, 9: *OC* 1, pp. 432–33.

97. *C* 1, 2: *OC* 6, p. 38; see below, pp. 326–31.

98. *C* 1, 1: *OC* 6, p. 17. Vol. 6 contains Books 1 through 4; 7, Books 5 through 9; 8, Books 10 through 12, as well as the remaining appended feasts and documents.

99. Jean Eudes explicitly shows the foundations of his heart theology in Bérulle at *C* 8, 1: *OC* 7, pp. 344–49. See Milcent, *S. Jean Eudes: un artisan*, pp. 406–21, 449–58, for historical background, as well as Bremond's exciting pages, 536–72 in vol. 3.

100. *C* 10, 2: *OC* 8, p. 10. Note, too, the typical stress on the divine child/infancy in this citation.

101. Cf. Bremond 3, pp. 549–72 (on Bérulle's feast and its role in Eudes' thought), and Michel Dupuy, "Intérieur de Jésus," *DS* 7/2 (1971) col. 1877. See Bérulle's *V* 26, p. 507; 27, p. 510, for similar heart language. Arragain, pp. 56–59, is helpful.

102. John Eudes spoke of the novelty of his devotion to the sacred

hearts, but felt that development was allowed in the area of piety. He apparently did not believe in historical development in the area of dogma. Cf. *Lettre* 46: *OC* 11, pp. 104–5, and Milcent, *S. Jean Eudes: un artisan*, p. 456. Olier, in his *Cat*, p. 86, has an even more emphatic denial of the historical sense in theology: "God would not be pleased that I propose anything new in matters religious!" Still, the French School is actually quite novel, and were John Eudes to reflect on the relationship between piety and dogma, he would have to nuance his views. But as we know, the notion of doctrinal development was still in the future.

103. See Bremond 2, pp. 227–67, on the founding of the French Carmel, and 3, pp. 133–92, on the Oratory, Sulpicians and Eudists. The Oratory is Bérulle's unique adaptation of the earlier Italian Oratory of the sixteenth century, founded by St. Philip Neri. It has some spiritual connections with Catherine of Genoa too. For The Company of the Blessed Sacrament, see Edward Healy Thompson, *The Life of Jean-Jacques Olier: Founder of the Seminary of St. Sulpice* (London: Burns and Oates, 1885), p. 103; and Henri Daniel-Rops, *The Church in the Seventeenth Century* (*History of the Church of Christ* 6), trans. J. J. Buckingham (London: J. M. Dent & Sons/N.Y.: E. P. Dutton & Co., 1963), pp. 98–104.

104. *V*, Préamble 14, p. 445; *DC* 2, 4, pp. 75–76; 1, 22, p. 63; 1, 23–24, pp. 65–66. Cf. Dagens, pp. 322–34, 367–76, for a basic overview. Pages 229–45 of Dagens offer a valuable commentary on the controversial discourses, so important for Bérulle's views on these issues.

105. *DC* 1, 27, p. 71; cf. Dagens, pp. 238–39.

106. *DC* 2, 10, p. 86.

107. Guillén Preckler, p. 41; *CB* 1, P. 1, p. 2.

108. *CB* 1, P. 89, p. 166; *OR* 1, p. 260; *OP* 141, cols. 1177–78; *OR* 18, p. 297. Cf. Dupuy, *Bérulle et le sacerdoce* and Bourgoing's Préface, *OC* 1, pp. xxiv–xxv.

109. *N* 19–20, pp. 393–94.

110. Bremond 3, pp. 133–92. See *CB* 3, P. 891, pp. 617–18. See below, pp. 183–85.

111. *G* 6, 3, p. 247. Cf. *DC* 3. See below, pp. 138–40.

112. *Mémor* 3, pp. 618–19.

113. *Mémor* 11, pp. 624–25.

114. *Lettre* 144, p. 143.

115. *Lettre* 142, p. 139; cf. Louise de Jésus, chapter 21.

116. *Lettre* 142, p. 138.

117. *Lettre* 205, pp. 212–13; 229, p. 184; 312, pp. 290–91.

118. *Lettre* 256, p. 280.

119. *Lettre* 219, p. 232; 236, p. 250; 11, pp. 22–23; 22, pp. 33–34; 214, p. 225; Louise de Jésus, pp. 363–87.

120. *Lettre* 260, p. 287.

121. *Mém* 3: 336, 275.

122. *I*, p. 69; Cat, p. 91.

123. *J*, p. 123; Mém 1:310. Cf. *I*, p. 7, on the Olerian notion of religion.

124. *I*, pp. 7–10; see below, pp. 217–20.

125. Appendix 10 in *T*, pp. 311–17; full text in Etienne-Michel Faillon, *Vie de M. Olier* 3 (Paris: Poussièlgue, Frères, and F. Wattelier et Cie, 1873), pp. 555–71.

126. *T*, p. xxxvi.

127. *Mém* 2:163; cf. *T*, p. xxxix. For Olier, the episcopal state is a special sharing in Jesus' ascension, the state of Jesus' plenitude. Yet all people share in it: *Cat*, pp. 51–53. So, too, the priest specially shares in Jesus' resurrection, yet all share in it: *Cat*, p. 50; Mém 4:21–47.

128. *T*, p. xiv.

129. *J*, p. 193; cf. *I*, p. 108; *Cat*, pp. 14, 45; *Lettre* 443, 1, pp. 479–83 (on the resurrection state).

130. *Mém* 3: 321–42, in Appendix *J*, *T*, p. 269; *Lettre* 441, 2, pp. 473–75 (on vocational criteria). On the priesthood in Olier, also cf. Gilles Chaillot, "Criteria for the Spiritual Formation of Pastors: The Pedagogical Tradition Inherited from M. Olier," *Bulletin de Saint-Sulpice* 4 (1978): 24–32; Stanislaw Nowak, "J.-J. Olier 'Docteur du sacerdoce' dans l'école française," *Bulletin de Saint-Sulpice* 10 (1984): 25–62; and Eugene A. Walsh, *The Priesthood in the Writings of the French School: Bérulle, De Condren, Olier*, S.T.D. diss. (Washington, D.C.: Catholic University of America, 1949).

131. *J*, p. 153; see pp. 152–64; *Cat*, p. 63.

132. *Cat*, p. 47. Cf. Gilles Chaillot, "L'expérience eucharistique de J.-J. Olier: le témoignage des *Mémoires*," *Bulletin de Saint-Sulpice* 10 (1984): 63–106.

133. *I*, pp. 156–59. Cf. especially Timothy K. Johnson, "Jean-Jacques Olier: Spiritual Director," *Bulletin de Saint-Sulpice* 6 (1980): 287–310; and, for some selections and helpful commentary on Bérulle and Olier, among other great directors, see Jerome M. Neufelder and Mary C. Coelho, eds., *Writings on Spiritual Direction by Great Christian Writers* (New York: Seabury, 1982).

134. Milcent, *S. Jean Eudes: un artisan*, pp. 284, 121. See *Constitutions* 6, 3: *OC* 9, p. 302.

135. *RJ* 24: *OC* 1, pp. 459–64; see below pp. 322–25.

136. On baptism, see *Contrat de l'homme avec Dieu par le saint Baptême* (1654), *OC* 2, pp. 204–70 (cf. Milcent, *S. Jean Eudes: un artisan*, pp. 254–57); *Manuel* (1668), *OC* 3, pp. 235–92; *Le bon confesseur* (1654), *OC* 4, pp. 143–369; *Le prédicateur apostolique* (1681), *OC* 4, pp. 1–115; *Le mémorial de la vie ecclésiastique* (1681), *OC* 3, pp. 1–233 (on all these latter see Milcent, *S. Jean Eudes: un artisan*, pp. 423–33).

137. *Mémorial* 5, 14 and 16: *OC* 3, pp. 207 and 212.

NOTES

138. *Le bon confesseur* 2: *OC* 4, pp. 165, 182.
139. *Mémorial* 2: *OC* 3, p. 48.
140. Milcent, *S. Jean Eudes: un artisan*, p. 452; cf. pp. 449–58.
141. Office of Matins, Second Response: *OC* 11, p. 471. The phrase is from a Latin rendering of parts of 2 Maccabees 1:3; see p. 46 of this text.
142. See Milcent, *S. Jean Eudes: un artisan*, ch. 23, pp. 367–80, on Eudes as a spiritual director, especially of women. Guillon is also helpful, as well as *OC* 10 and 11, which contain much of the saint's correspondence.
143. *M* 233, *RHE* 73 E and A; cf. Guillén Preckler, pp. 197–206.
144. *Lettre* 65, p. 69.
145. *I*, p. 155; *Cat*, p. 50; cf. *J*, pp. 119–20, and *Cat*, p. 89.
146. *RJ* 5, 11: *OC* 1, p. 439; cf. *Exercice de piété: OC* 2, p. 363.

III

The French School:
Retrospect and Prospect

In this chapter I would like to touch upon a number of rather more speculative questions. Among those of a more retrospective character would be, first, how scholarship might evaluate the French School's relationship to its own times. We have already mentioned that this is a somewhat controversial matter. Is our French School[1] to be seen as a conservative, restorationist reaction to the unsettling events of the time, especially the Renaissance and the Protestant Reformation? Or is it rather a more positive affirmation of the forces unleashed by those two great movements? I have waited until now to raise the question in a more sustained way, because now that we have surveyed the key tendencies of our writers the reader will be in a position to make a tentative judgment for himself or herself.

One can receive the strong impression from today's scholarship that Bérulle and his colleagues/heirs are mounting a rather powerful restorationist assault upon the forces of both the Reformation and the Renaissance. This seems rather clear with respect to the Reformation, for one must search in vain for positive statements about the Reformers. With respect to the Renaissance, there is a general agreement that an excessively humanistic reductionism was being opposed by Bérulle. Recall his great "Copernican Revolution," announced in the second discourse of his *Grandeurs*. Bérulle's stress upon the relational nature of the human being, as always referred to God and Jesus, and as nothingness and sin when severed from that reference, seems the key assault upon any excessive humanism. And although these Dionysian, Neoplatonic accents may be somewhat toned down in Madeleine, Olier and John Eudes, still the creature's "reference to God" is there as the crucial fact about us.[2]

And yet there is another side to the matter, especially if one entertains the hermeneutical notion that a writer's work is in some way distanced from the author's intention, becoming a world of meaning in itself, bearing a catalytic power of its own. Let us take the concerns of the Reformers first. Much of what they wanted finds its echo in our school, despite the mutually unecumenical atmosphere of the times. The emphatic Augustinianism of the French School is surely significant in this regard, with its emphasis upon the priority of God over all. When Olier prefers the term *cooperation* to *resolution* as a moment in prayer, because it "indicates more explicitly the power of the Holy Spirit,"[3] he is but exemplifying what we have in mind for our School as a whole. And our mystics surely share, at least broadly, the concerns for ecclesial reform that motivated a Luther and a Calvin. How else explain their view of the need to reform the ministry, rejoining the great triad of learning, authority and sanctity?

Bremond felt, in the great study often referred to, that the French School was not opposed to a Christian kind of humanism, but united it to its theocentric and Christological concerns. In this sense it was not, at least for Bremond, a simple rejection of the Renaissance. I would prefer to speak of our School's integrating some Renaissance concerns, for integrating introduces a critical element: tendencies incompatible with theocentrism and Christocentrism are rejected. We have already noted that Bérulle did not simply reject the abstract mysticism so favorable to (the young) Mme. Acarie and her circle. This more intellectual, Neoplatonic tradition was rather critically integrated into a Christological piety and theology. So, too, our School favorably received and used the new biblical and patristic "sciences" then developing, albeit within certain limits. And the new accent on Jesus' humanity, while traditional, seems also quite modern in the Renaissance. Jesus' humanity, and the transformation devotion to it works in Mary, Magdalene, and the saints and mystics, is a kind of Christian humanism, the French School's alternative to the possible reductionism of the time. This seems particularly clear in the heart theology of John Eudes. But it is also there in the stress upon Jesus' love and interiority in Bérulle, Madeleine and Olier. The heightened stress upon the interior depth dimension of the states of

Jesus, and our own interior appropriation of them, also strikes a contemporary chord. This was surely not a modern narcissism or introspectionism. At the same time, it was a deepened probing of our human depth in the light of Jesus.[4]

In the light of all of this, perhaps we need to move beyond the simple alternatives of restorationism or Renaissance liberalism. Again we seem compelled to think dialectically: not either/or, but both/and. We seem to be in the presence of various creative tendencies, which can go now this way, now that. In the main, these tendencies are integrated in a kind of creative friction. The best of the past is kept current, but critically so. Interestingly, Karl Rahner, when evaluating the theology of the devotion to the sacred heart as practiced by Margaret Mary Alacoque (the Paray-le-Monial devotion), a near contemporary of John Eudes (and probably influenced by him), spoke of this devotion as avoiding the extremes of Jansenistic rigorism, on the one hand, and Renaissance secularism on the other. It was in between, in a way rather like the French School as a whole, I would suggest. As we have seen, even the harshly rigorous negativity and sense of sin of the French School keeps its balance, even when vigorously accented. It is a critique, surely, of Renaissance secularism to employ the Rahnerian vocabulary; but a critique that needs to be set against other tendencies, as we have already suggested. In this regard, it is interesting that the Jansenists always regarded Olier and Eudes as enemies.[5]

This in-between posture of our French School, avoiding both excessive rigorism and faddish novelty, probably explains its creativity and endurance. For this in-between space seems to be a creative and tension-filled one. Excessive rigorism usually means an inability to remain contemporary or relevant. Faddish novelty usually means one is at the whim of every new gust of wind that's blowing, with no discriminating sense. The fecundity and generativity of the French School, however, indicates that it has maintained its critical balance and perspective. And yet in an exceedingly lively and non-boring way, for our great mystics, with their unique modulations, avoid a banal kind of balance. We have balance, to be sure, but a creative and tension-filled balance.

This brings us to a second issue, which could be said to be both retrospective and prospective; namely, the generativity of the French School. What did it birth in the past, and what has it birthed today? Tracing lines of historical causality is exceedingly difficult, however.

INTRODUCTION

What do the scholars suggest? If we keep in mind the practical and theoretical sides of the French School, its refusal to separate ecclesial practice and personal development from theology and reflective spirituality, then we need to measure its fecundity on these two fronts. It is an irruption in the spheres of both practice and meaning.

On the practical level, first place must surely go to the great ecclesial foundations birthed by our mystics, as well as others greatly influenced by them. Of course, the Oratory of France, the Company of Priests of Saint Sulpice (with a presence beyond France in Canada, the United States, South America and Asia), and the Congregation of Jesus and Mary, or Eudists (with a presence beyond France in North and South America) are the capital foundations. Tightly linked with Bérulle, surely, although also with Mme. Acarie and her "devout circle," is the foundation and flourishing of the female branch of Carmel in France. The request for the relic of Bérulle's heart by Mother Madeleine stands as a powerful expression of this relationship between Bérulle and Carmel. Also rather closely linked with St. John Eudes and his Congregation are a surprisingly large number of female congregations. Well-known in this country are perhaps the "Good Shepherd Sisters" (the Congregation of Our Lady of Charity of the Good Shepherd), founded by Saint Marie-Euphrasie (Rose-Virginie Pelletier). The saint also co-founded the Institute of Our Lady of Charity. Various Eudist priests have also played an important part in founding a number of female congregations, some quite recently.[6]

It is somewhat more difficult to trace the lineage in the area of theology and spirituality. We can, I think, meaningfully speak of the French School when the master images and fundamental horizon of thought are shared in common, even allowing for and wanting original modulations of the master metaphors. This seems true of our founding mystics and perhaps of some few others. Cognet, in the important study often referred to here, speaks of the "Bérullian Current," and includes some of the following. Two Carmelites of the same name, Marguerite du Saint-Sacrement (1619–48) of Beaune, who greatly furthered devotion to Jesus' infancy, and the other Marguerite du Saint-Sacrement (1590–1660), who was a daughter of Mme. Acarie, of the Carmel of rue Chapon, are clearly forceful Bérullians. François Bourgoing (1585–1662), third general of the Oratory, wrote the *Vérités et excellences de Jésus-Christ*, which went into numerous editions. We have already mentioned the importance of Condren. Of less importance, but still heavily Bérullian, were the Oratorians Guillaume Gibieuf (1591–1650), who wrote an important work on the grandeurs of Mary, and Paul Métézeau (1583–1632), whose *De sancto sacerdotio* of 1631 is the sole Oratorian work on the priesthood alone, heavily Dionysian in tone. The Oratorian Claude Seguenot (1596–1676) authored the *Conduite d'oraison* in 1634, thus somewhat systematizing the Bérullian views on prayer.

St. Vincent de Paul (1581–1660) goes his own way, according to Cognet, although Cognet thinks he was more influenced by Bérulle than anyone else. He seems to have transposed Bérulle into more simple, pastoral terms, stressing especially the Bérullian accent on interiority and personal commitment to Jesus. Still roughly within the seventeenth century, Cognet hesitates to attribute much Bérullian influence to a number of Jesuit mystics (Bremond tends to be more affirmative of this influence). Cognet suggests that Louis Lallemant (1587–1635) has very diverse influences and is chiefly Ignatian, although some Bérullian terminology may have influenced some of his successors: Jean-Joseph Surin and François Guilloré.[7]

Among later members of the French School special place must surely go to St. Louis-Marie Grignion de Montfort (1673–1716) and St. John-Baptist de la Salle (1651–1719). Both were formed at the Seminary of St. Sulpice in Paris and were decisively influenced by the later "Sulpician" transmission of the School. The Sulpician Superior General Louis Tronson (1622–1700) directed Montfort and suggested to him the devotion of servitude to Mary and to Jesus in Mary. One thinks of him especially as a propagator of Marian devotion, as we have already noted. But he also developed a rather more total spiritual theology, especially developing Bérulle's meditations on the Wisdom writings. La Salle, of course, founded the Christian Brothers. He, too, was directed by the Sulpicians Tronson and François Leschassier. He was clearly Bérullian, but uniquely blended a number of dimensions present in the French School into his new community: the apostolate, the importance of education, a sense of the needy, the element of service, and so on. As the French School, among its male representatives, had stressed the priesthood as the experienced example of commitment to Jesus, so now La Salle stressed the apostolate of teaching as an expression of Jesus.[8]

Beyond this, I think we would have to say that the French School usually became, not the major influence, but an important formative influence over some religious "families," theologians, and those in quest of a spiritual life in general (excepting those who perhaps choose to allow this school the major voice). Here I have in mind those who explicitly refer to the School and/or its representatives, although one could make the case that in some instances the influence is rather more subtle and unnamed.[9] For example, the Congregation of the Holy Ghost, formed through the union of an earlier society of priests of the Holy Spirit (founded by Claude-François Poullart des Places) and the Congregation of the Immaculate Heart of Mary (founded by François-Marie-Paul Libermann in 1841), was influenced by the Sulpician and Eudist transmission of the French School through Libermann (1802–50), who was trained at St. Sulpice and was formed by the Olierian and Eudist spiritualities. Libermann is representative of this wider, more diffuse transmission of the French School, I think. His independence from it is great, and his charism quite original, stressing especially the active apostolate, but still he drinks from the Christocentrism and Marian piety of our founding mystics.[10] This more diffuse "Bérullianism" could be applied to the numerous priests, nuns, brothers, seminarians, students, and so forth, who have come under the influence of the religious families we have mentioned above. Viewed in this perspective, the French School has been enormously fecund in France and indeed throughout the Western world, with some beachheads in Asia and Africa.

Bérulle and his disciples commonly receive acknowledgment as crucial forces in spirituality in the standard studies on spirituality. Although, as I have tried to indicate, tracing historical causality is exceedingly difficult, what Jordan Aumann says in his recent history of spirituality is standard: "The Christocentric spirituality of the French School was diffused so widely that for all practical purposes Catholic spirituality in modern times could be characterized as French spirituality."[11] Among speculative theologians, the French School occasionally surfaces as a source of theological renewal in our times. For example, already in the early part of our century, Emile Mersch believed that the mystics of our School

> have been more successful than others in effecting the synthesis between Christology and spirituality, and in proposing the truth of our incorporation in Christ as a code of perfection; they have also been more successful than anyone else in the Latin Church, in bringing out

INTRODUCTION

the divine and transcendent aspect of the life that is given us in Christ, and the elevation of soul that is demanded of us in consequence.[12]

What was true for Mersch remains true for a number of significant speculative theologians today. Hans Urs von Balthasar has long pointed to the need to unite spirituality and theology, stressing the importance of the saints as theological sources. And in a central essay he has pointed to the saints of the *grand siècle,* among whom he numbers Bérulle and Condren, as important sources. In his multi-volumed theological aesthetics he has also, as is well-known, devoted important studies to Pascal and to the influence of the French School, especially Condren, upon him, as well as to Bérulle and Condren in their own right. Von Balthasar especially sees in them an expression of the precisely theological and Christological moment in theology: the transcendent grace through Jesus shattering the human being with its beauty.[13]

Karl Rahner has a number of times (which is significant in a theologian who rarely indicates sources) mentioned Bérulle as an important figure for the theologian. In an important study in which he is indicating the need of the theologian to "consult" spirituality and saints and mystics, Rahner says that the "true theologian ought to prove his education also by planning within five or ten years to acquire an idea of the history of spirituality by reading Gregory of Nyssa, Augustine, the great medieval mystics, Francis de Sales or Bérulle and Charles de Foucauld, to mention only a few names." The company Bérulle keeps, in Rahner's mind, is surely significant, is it not? And Rahner has especially pointed to Bérulle as a key source for a theology and spirituality centered on the Incarnation, even citing from one of the Cardinal's works. There has always been a Christo-centric dimension to Rahner's thought (he is, after all, a son of St. Ignatius Loyola), but the Christocentrism deepened and became more emphatic as time went on. Surely his own deepening medita-tion on Ignatius Loyola played a key role in this—the key role, Rahner has said. But Rahner has also singled out two others for their Christocentrism: St. Teresa of Avila and Cardinal Bérulle.[14]

This "consultation" of Bérulle and the French School in contem-porary theology provides us with a smooth transition to our final, "prospective" issue, that of the role of this School in today's spiri-tuality and theology. This seems an appropriate issue to end with since the French School always practiced theology with a practical intent, hoping to contribute to the ongoing revitalization of church and faith. In a general sense, I think we can say that our School has proven its worth as an ongoing and valuable source of the Christian heritage. Its generativity—through the religious families it has birthed, through the spiritual and theological literature it has contributed to us—attests to this. The fact that the hierarchy has canonized John Eudes, La Salle and Montfort, and declared Madeleine venerable, as well as granting official recognition to the religious families coming into being through this School, also witnesses to this worth. The constant reputation of profound mysticism attributed to our principals also provides important attestation. To borrow David Tracy's categories, the French School's spirituality and theology is a classic instead of a period piece, a proven source of continual human and Christian enrichment, theoretically and practically.[15]

Many would agree, I think, that the task today is to bring the tradition of the French School into an appreciative but critical dialogue with the concerns of our contemporary experience. A to-and-fro conversation between both stands the best chance of preserving the best of the "Bérullian current" in our contemporary period. Along these lines I would suggest that this School might serve as one model or paradigm of a theology firmly grounded in experience or in a lived spirituality and ecclesial praxis. It is experiential, on the whole, presenting us with a "translation" of the Christian message that is far from extrinsic and alienated from our experience, personally and socially. Of course, this is a somewhat grand statement. Like everything else human, our French School has known its derailments and corruptions, at times through an excessive rigorism (quasi-Jansenism), or clericalism, or moralism, and so forth. But on the whole, especially when appropriated at its glowing center in Bérulle, Madeleine, Olier and John Eudes, it is a powerful paradigm of the kind of experiential theology and spirituality that the Christian Faith is meant to be and that our experientially-oriented age seeks.[16] If you will, it is highly experiential without succumbing to reductionism.

In the main our founding mystics present us with a critical integration between the classical inheritance (through its Neoplatonic, especially Dionysian transmission) and the biblical-patristic. Much of the enduring relevancy of the French School finally turns on the enduring relevancy of these sources, for in many ways the genius of the School was to surface the spiritual and practical dimensions of these great traditions. I would suggest that it was relatively successful in revising the non-biblical accents of Dionysianism by bringing out the Jesus-centered nature of Christianity and its ecclesial nature. We are involved, not in a flight to the Transcendent One, but in an ecclesial movement to the interpersonal life of the Trinity through the mediation of Jesus Christ. The biblical accent on the historical and dynamic is present in our School; we are a reference, a relation, a tendency, a dynamism, and so forth. It is not as historically conscious as our modern period, to be sure, and perhaps too much of the static seeps through the Dionysianism: the notion of states or castes, for example.

A good case can be made that our School surfaces the crucial elements in its theocentric trinitarianism. With the biblical heritage God remains the transcendent Creator, but with the Neoplatonic heritage this transcendent One also "births" through emanations reflections of the divine life upon earth. Biblical creationism and Neoplatonic emanationism (purged of pantheism) are nicely integrated: God is the Holy One, but not too distantly so. The School's trinitarianism brings out the loving, interpersonal reality of God, a love that ecstatically spills out into the world through Christ. The Holy One is a plenitude of sociableness, we might say, deifying us with an analogous sociableness. The emanation of God in history is a loving, Christic sharing in the inner life of love of the Trinity. Today's heightened stress upon the social could find here a rich source of theological renewal.[17]

A particularly appealing facet of our School is the way it sought to bring out the *unsurpassable* centrality of the Jesus event for its own time. It was very creative, yet appropriated the tradition. Notice the "translation" of the Chalcedonian *enhypostasis* of the human nature in the person of the Word into a theology of servitude and adoration, or of selfless sacrifice, or of the great heart of love. Guillén Preckler has recently suggested *service* or the more biblical *kenosis* as a more contemporary expression of the Bérullian insight.[18] If you will, the Jesus event is an *unequalled* explosion in history of service to humanity on behalf of God. The person of Jesus is a total pouring out of himself into that service (an *anéantissement* or surrendering, we might say today). But Guillén Preckler's stress on service can be fruitfully complemented by a renewed stress upon adoration, which is the other side of the Bérullian servitude. The Incarnation is also an explosion of adoration, and because it is, Jesus is able to be the utterly selfless servitor. Adoration keeps our service open and really utterly at God's disposal, creating a space for our neighbors and for God especially. This is perhaps what Madeleine and Olier, under Condren's influence, were trying to surface in the notion of the perpetual sacrifice or immolation to God in the Jesus event. Perhaps in our own time, when we run the danger of instrumentalizing and manipulating everyone and everything, even our service, this kind of adoration (or reverence) is crucially needed.[19] John Eudes' great metaphor of the heart still has the power to surface this note of non-manipulative love at the center of the Jesus event.

Entering into or participating in this great heart, this movement of service and adoration, is the French School's insight into the soteriological drama unleashed by the Incarnation. This is our being, through our graced nature, and it is only in its light that our great mystics "attack" the reality of human depravity and sin, which are what happen to us as we fail to participate in this great movement. They are a kind of *Restbegriff*, to use a Rahnerian term: Evil and sin are what is left over when we stay aloof from the dialectic of service and adoration.

There is no question that the French School is rigorous in its phenomenology of human depravity. It moves beyond the surface to the *fond*, from a symptomatology of evil and sin to its roots. Rather like the Jesus of the gospel: "Wicked designs come from the deep recesses of the heart" (Mk 7:21). But this seems to be standard mystical fare. True, Olier perhaps especially, and Bérulle somewhat less, accent our depravity. But an accent is not an exaggeration, and when one is describing the dynamic movement of the Christian life, at times an accent is what is called for. Perhaps as we move out of an era marked by a kind of Enlightenment utopianism and naivete, at least in the West, we will be able to reappropriate in our own way the rich exploration of evil and sin found in the French School. We might even want to develop it, by surfacing rather more fully the social aspects of sin and evil known somewhat, surely, in the biblical notion of the evil of the world and the devil. But the "somewhat" can be enhanced.

We surely have a "high Mariology" in the French School, but it seems centered and balanced, I suggest. The fundamental Mariological principle for our mystics is Mary's maternity; that is, at the core of her being, the root of it all, is that same Jesus-like mystery of service and adoration, that great heart nourishing our small heart. In this sense, Mariology bridges trinitarianism, Christology and ecclesiology; her being witnesses to these realities. The God of loving sociability, through her, makes a beachhead in history and "dilates" that loving sociability into the community of believers. To be Mariological, for our School, is to believe that one is rooted in this same dilation of love, to believe that one is a part of this great movement in history. The accent in Mariology, at least in this tradition, is on Mary's maternity. Appreciating that requires transcending an individualism that ignores our bondedness with one another, our interwovenness in the "great heart," to use John Eudes' terms.[20]

I suspect that we can still find much that is helpful in the French School in our attempts to revitalize church and ministry today. Reuniting the great triad of authority, learning and holiness seems, still now, an effective formula for the renewal of the ministry. And a formula very congenial to the Christology of service and adoration of our mystics. This is perhaps their greatest contribution: to wed a deep spirituality to ecclesiology and ministry. The church and ministry is the "soul writ large," if I might borrow a famous phrase. Many of us today will feel that this ministry of service and adoration gets along somewhat uneasily with the Dionysian stratification of holy orders, which is also found in our school in varying shades of accent. Bérulle began a critique of Dionysius on the issue of Christology. We might want today, faithful to Bérulle's instincts, to carry through the critique into the area of ecclesiology/ministry.

Perhaps what we need to accent is Olier's notion of the priest as the experienced Christian in service to all, helping them to move toward the perfection to which all are called. This preserves the place of the priest without denigrating the other members of the faithful. As we have seen, there is an attempted balance between ministry and other faithful in the French School that stays clear of clericalism without lapsing into anticlericalism. Interestingly, Bernard Cooke's recent great study of ministry would seem to share our misgivings about the Dionysian accents of the French School, yet wanting to retain the great spiritual renewal it contributed. Edward Schillebeeckx seems harsher, arguing that despite some attractive things the French School dangerously roots the priesthood in Jesus' divinity, making the priest a very cultic, other-worldly and unchangeable reality. This is perhaps truer of the later alteration of Olier's thinking, for example. But in the main the French School stresses the humanity of Jesus as the unsurpassable revelation of the divine presence. Few schools are as centered on Jesus' humanity as this one. We come to divinity through humanity, and the priesthood is rooted in this incarnational principle. Our own call to perfection is rooted in it too. This is, we recall, the whole point of Bérulle's Christological critique of the abstract mysticism and theology.[21]

Of course, there are other limitations of the French School our age will need to consider, issues raised in our own time that these mystics could not consider. We can draw inspiration from them for these new issues too, surely, but we cannot expect them to give us answers with respect to the feminist critique of religion (which we have but alluded to), the place of liberation theology, and so on. Like everything else, the French School is limited. We have already seen that it was largely a renewal confined to the aristocracy.[22] Although it radically critiqued the aristocracy by its mystical renewal, still it accepted other aspects of the culture: the class structure, the role of women by and large, the inherited assumptions about the poor, and others. We do find a stress upon charity and almsgiving in our mystics and the founding of congregations to care for the poor and outcast,[23] but not a radical critique of social structures such as the contemporary political theologies and the papal teachings variously have in mind. Still, the rooting of all genuine renewal in the contemplative transformation of the heart seems as fresh today as it must have seemed back then.

NOTES

1. The name French School seems to have been first used by the Sulpician G. Letourneau around 1913, being taken over by Bremond in his great volume 3, and receiving its currency there. I hope that, by now, our continuing to use this title seems justified. It seems preferable to Bérullian, bringing out the non-Bérullian character of each of the founding mystics (that is, his or her own unique modulation of the tradition). Cf. Louis Cognet, "Mysticism: E. École Française," in *Sacramentum Mundi* 4, ed. Karl Rahner, et al. (New York: Herder and Herder, 1969), pp. 151–52. Whether reserving this title to our principals does justice to other spiritual families in France needs nuancing. "French spirituality" embraces more than the "French School."

2. Dagens can give the impression of proposing a simply restorationist perspective. But a careful reading reveals a Bérulle who critically assesses the Renaissance, accepting congenial elements; see pp. 16–27, 49–68 esp., for this subtle view. Bellemare's great work, referred to earlier, is the breakthrough one on the relational self of the French School. Anne M. Minton, "Pierre de Bérulle: The Search for Unity," ed. E. Rozanne Elder, *The Spirituality of Western Christendom* 2: *The Roots of the Modern Christian Tradition* (Kalamazoo, MI: Cistercian Publications, 1984), pp. 105–23, stresses this unifying facet of Bérulle over against the deterioration of the unified, Christian West prior to the twin forces we are discussing. It is important to keep in mind the unecumenical atmosphere of the times. St. Teresa of Avila, for example, in *The Way of Perfection* 1, makes a typical comment which surely inspired the Carmelite nuns to come to France: "News reached me of the harm being done in France and of the havoc the Lutherans had caused and how much this miserable sect was growing. The news distressed me greatly, and . . . I cried to the Lord and begged Him that I might remedy so much evil" (*The Collected Works of St. Teresa of Avila* 2, trans. Otilio Rodriguez and Kieran Kavanaugh [Washington, DC: Institute of Carmelite Studies, 1980], p. 41).

3. *Cat*, p. 73. For the notion that a text undergoes a distancing from its author, see David Tracy, *Blessed Rage for Order: The New Pluralism in Theology* (New York: Seabury, 1975), pp. 49–52.

4. For Bremond's suggestions, see vol. 3, esp. p. 15, and vol. 1, *Devout Humanism*, trans. K. L. Montgomery (London: SPCK, 1928), esp. pp. 397–405. Karl Rahner has written suggestively on the Renaissance horizon

of St. Ignatius Loyola, albeit an horizon somewhat unthematic. I have been stimulated by his work: "Modern Piety and the Experience of Retreats," *Theological Investigations* 16, trans. David Morland (New York: Seabury, 1979), pp. 135–55.

5. Cf. Karl Rahner, "Some Theses for a Theology of Devotion to the Sacred Heart," *Theological Investigations* 3, trans. Karl-H. and Boniface Kruger (Baltimore: Helicon, 1967), pp. 331–52 at 339; C. Annice Callahan, *Karl Rahner's Spirituality of the Pierced Heart: A Reinterpretation of Devotion to the Sacred Heart* (Lanham, MD: University Press of America, 1985); and Bremond's still suggestive comments comparing Eudes (and the French School) with Paray-le-Monial, Bremond 3, pp. 567–72.

We have mentioned Jansenism several times throughout these pages; perhaps a further word should be said about it. It takes its name, of course, from Cornelius Jansen (d. 1638), theologian and bishop of Ypres, whose *Augustinus* was published in 1640. It is usually described as an extreme form of Augustinianism, with its notion of a rigorous divine election. It tends to pit the human (free will) dimension against divine grace, and in the area of morality stresses a rigorism against a so-called Jesuit probabilism. Only actions above all moral doubt can be performed; contrition demands love of God, not simply fear of hell; communion should be rare, since it is enormously great; the priesthood was a vocation of great heroism; and so on. Clearly Jansenism opposes grace to human freedom, rejecting the more incarnational view that grace is the ground and basis of human freedom. I think it should be clear from our treatment of the French School that our mystics are more within the incarnational perspective.

From an historical perspective, the Jansenistic reaction to the dawn of modernity spread into France chiefly through the convent of Cistercian nuns of Port-Royal under the Abbess Angelique Arnauld (d. 1661). There was considerable influence from the Abbot of Saint-Cyran, Jean-Ambroise Duvergier de Hauranne (d. 1643), who was a friend of Jansen while a student at Paris. From a sociological perspective, Jansenism seems to have been favored by the upper-middle class, which felt increasingly impotent under the weight of the absolute monarchy (perhaps this experience of human impotency made this class ripe for the anti-humanism of Jansenism?). The controversy over Jansenism was a long one in the church, leading to a number of papal condemnations (the latest in 1713) and the eventual suppression of Port-Royal (1707–12). Bérulle himself knew some of the leading figures involved here: He learned from Saint-Cyran, drawing upon his patristic scholarship, and sent him a copy of the *Vie* to study and correct; Jansen approved a formulation of his vow of servitude too. The extreme tendencies of Jansenism did not surface, however, until after Bérulle. Cf. Orcibal, pp. 154–56; Bremond 3, pp. 277–87 (on Condren, Olier and

NOTES

Saint-Cyran); Konrad Hecker, "Jansenism," *Sacramentum Mundi* 3, pp. 171–74.

6. The Congregation of the Sacred Heart of Coutances (1674); that of the Sisters of Providence of Evreux (1705), and of the Good Savior (1712), united after the Second Vatican Council; the contemplative Holy Family of Sees (1805) and the secular institute of the Faithful Servants of Jesus (1941–84, in Colombia). Several members of John Eudes' "third order" of the Society of the Heart of the Admirable Mother founded further female congregations: that of the Daughters of the Sacred Hearts of Jesus and Mary (1821) founded by Marie-Thérèse Auffray; that of the Congregation of the Little Sisters of the Poor (1852) founded by the recently beatified Jeanne Jugan; and that of the Congregation of the Sacred Hearts of Jesus and Mary (1853) founded by the Venerable Amelie Fristel. On all this, see Milcent, S. *Jean Eudes: un artisan*, pp. 561–64. Helpful information on the Oratorians, the Sulpicians and the Eudists can be found in Raymond Hostie, *Vie et mort des ordres religieux* (Paris: Desclée de Brouwer, 1972), pp. 191–221.

We might note, too, that Bérulle can be regarded at least as a co-founder of the Carmelite nuns in France, and of course there are strong spiritual bonds between the Ursulines of France and the Oratory, all forming a part of the same renewal movement. J. B. Romaillon, who eventually joined the Oratory, is regarded as one of the founders of the French Ursulines. See Bremond 2, throughout, and W. H. Principe, "Bus, César de, Ven.," *New Catholic Encyclopedia* 2 (New York: McGraw-Hill, 1967), p. 908. M. Olier, as noted, tried to establish the Daughters of the Interior of the Blessed Virgin (to help in retreat work); it was actually established only after his death, and it did not endure. Sulpicians have been somewhat active in promoting religious foundations over the centuries, either as co-founders or as catalysts. A recent letter to me from the Sulpician Irénée Noye lists the following: in France, (1) seventeenth century: Charles De Lantages: Daughters of Instruction; (2) eighteenth century: Louis Normant du Faradon: Gray Sisters; (3) nineteenth-twentieth centuries: E.-M. Faillon: the *"Petite oeuvre,"* which later fused with the Daughters of Mary; Marius Lepin: Servants of Jesus the High Priest (extinct); Claude Animé: Trinitarians of St.-Marin-en-Haut; Paul Laurain: Benedictines of Jesus the Priest (extinct); in Canada, Antoine Mercier: Little Sisters of St. Joseph, and Onil Lesieur: Servants of Mary Immaculate. Americans may be especially interested to note that Sulpicians played a very formative role in the spiritual life of (St.) Mother Elizabeth Seton, as well as in the earliest formation of the American hierarchy. The Sulpician James H. Joubert co-founded, with Elizabeth Lange, the first community of black sisters in the United States in 1829 (Oblate Sisters of Providence), and the Sulpician Bishop Jean-Baptiste David co-founded what eventually became the Sisters of Charity of Nazar-

NOTES

eth in the early 1800s with Mother Catherine Spalding. Interestingly, this community's name derives from Bishop David's very Olierian devotion to Jesus' "hidden, interior life." Cf., for Olier's Daughters, *Lettre* 221, 1, pp. 550–52, esp. the explanatory comment. For the American (U.S.A.) materials, see Christopher J. Kauffman, *Tradition and Transformation in Catholic Culture: The Priests of St. Sulpice in the United States from 1791 to the Present* (New York: Macmillan, 1988), esp. pp. 75–82, 89–90, 113–16.

7. See Cognet, *La spiritualité moderne*, pp. 360–452, and "Mysticism E. École Française," p. 152. Also, on the "Bérullian" Jesuits, see Bremond's views in vol. 3, pp. 223–42.

8. See Deville, chaps. 8 and 9, pp. 125–55. Cf., among others, Th. Rey-Mermet, *Louis-Marie Grignion de Montfort* (Paris: Nouvelle Cité, 1984); and Michel Sauvage and Miguel Campos, *St. John Baptist de La Salle: Announcing the Gospel to the Poor*, trans. Matthew J. O'Connell (Romeoville, IL: Christian Brothers National Office, 1981).

9. For example, Alain Gouhier, "Néant," *DS* 11, cols. 64–80 at 73 argues for a connection between Bérulle's stress upon kenosis and the same as found in St. Thérèse of Lisieux. Ida Friederike Görres traces Thérèse of Lisieux' devotion of the child Jesus to Bérulle, Condren and the French School in *The Hidden Face: A Study of St. Thérèse of Lisieux*, trans. Richard and Clara Winston (New York: Pantheon, 1959), pp. 344–48.

10. See Hostie, p. 201; Bernard Tenailleau, "Father Libermann's Spirituality," *Spiritans Today* 4 (1985): 49–76 at 58 and 65; and J. M. R. Tillard, "Father Libermann's Missionary Intuition," *Spiritans Today* 4 (1985): 77–94. This "diffuse" French School plausibly is found in, for example, Pascal, Bossuet, Fénelon, Malebranche, among the "earlier" representatives.

11. Jordan Aumann, *Christian Spirituality in the Catholic Tradition* (San Francisco: Ignatius, 1985), p. 218.

12. Emile Mersch, *The Whole Christ: The Historical Development of the Doctrine of the Mystical Body in Scripture and Tradition*, trans. John R. Kelly (London: Dennis Dobson, 1938), pp. 531–55 (on the French School) at 542. To be fair, he does think the School is too rigorous in its estimate of human nature (p. 552). He does not read the School in the dialectical manner proposed by us.

13. Hans Urs von Balthasar, "Spirituality," *Word and Redemption*, pp. 87–108 at 92–93; cf. idem, "Theology and Sanctity," pp. 49–86; idem, "Pascal," in *The Glory of the Lord: A Theological Aesthetics* 3: *Studies in Theological Style: Lay Styles*, ed. John Riches, trans. John Saward, Martin Simon and Rowan Williams (San Francisco: Ignatius, 1986), pp. 172–238, esp. 173, 175, 238; idem, "Die Metaphysik des Oratoriums," *Herrlichkeit: Eine Theologische Ästhetik* 3/1, *Im Raum der Metaphysik* (Einsiedeln: Johannes Verlag, 1965), pp. 471–79.

14. Karl Rahner, *The Practice of Faith: A Handbook of Contemporary*

Spirituality, ed. Karl Lehmann and Albert Raffelt (New York: Crossroad, 1984), p. 56; idem, *On Prayer* (New York: Paulist, 1958), pp. 20–21: "The Incarnation is our great source of inspiration in prayer. 'In stooping without defiling Himself,' wrote the famous seventeenth century mystic, Cardinal Bérulle, 'God the Son raises us; in His union with the Father, He purifies us; in Incarnating Himself, He deifies us." (Rahner does not reference this; it might come from *G* 4, 6 or 5, 12); *Karl Rahner in Dialogue,* ed. Paul Imhof and Hubert Biallowons, trans. Harvey D. Egan, (New York: Crossroad, 1986), p. 191 (on the importance of Loyola for him); idem, "Teresa of Avila Doctor of the Church," *Opportunities for Faith,* trans. Edward Quinn (New York: Seabury, 1974), pp. 123–26.

15. See David Tracy, *The Analogical Imagination: Christian Theology and the Culture of Pluralism* (New York: Crossroad, 1981), pp. 99–338, esp. 107–15: "Certain expressions of the human spirit so disclose a compelling truth about our lives that we cannot deny them some kind of normative status. Thus do we name these expressions, and these alone, 'classics' " (p. 108).

Perhaps this is the appropriate place to say something on the beatification processes of our principals. Pope Innocent X, at the request of Bourgoing, introduced the beatification process for Cardinal Bérulle in 1648; forty-five miracles were actually attributed to him. So far as I can tell, the process was halted mainly because Jansenists put the Cardinal on their calendar (something they also did with St. Francis de Sales, for example) and thus Bérulle, quite wrongly, was suspected of Jansenistic leanings. See A. Molien, "Bérulle (Cardinal Pierre de)," *DS* 1 (1937), cols. 1539–82 at 1580, and A. Liuima, "Bérulle, Pierre de," *New Catholic Encyclopedia* 3, pp. 362–63 at 363.

Mother Madeleine's beatification process was introduced in 1645, and the heroic nature of her virtues was proclaimed by Pope Pius VI on 16 July 1789 (hence her title of "Venerable"). See Serouet, "Madeleine de Saint-Joseph," *DS* 10 (1980), cols. 57–60 at 58.

M. Olier's beatification process was introduced in June of 1867 with the support of the bishops of Canada, 230 priests of the diocese of Montreal, and forty of the bishops of the Second Plenary Council of Baltimore. Various factors, it seems, have delayed the process: (1) perhaps a tendency to link Olier with Jansenist rigorism (which is quite inaccurate) as in Bérulle's case; (2) a certain anti-mystical tendency in the Roman Curia, wrongly suspecting Olier of quietism (a book by the Sulpician Etienne-Michel Faillon on Mary's interior life [*La vie intérieure de la t. s. Vierge*] based on fragments from Olier and published in 1866 was so suspected, even though it obtained a Roman imprimatur; a different work by Faillon, a life of Olier, was intended to aid in the beatification process); and (3) the charge that Sulpician seminary professors taught Gallicanism (of course this would not apply to Olier himself). Actually, they sometimes favored a moderate Gallicanism, which avoids ultramontanism and extreme Gallicanism, a position very close to the current, acceptable one among many theologians today. See Kauffman, pp. 158–60; an important defense of St. Sulpice is H.-J. Icard, *Doctrine de M. Olier* (Paris: Victor Lecoffre, 1891).

The late canonization of St. John Eudes (1925), too, may have been partly caused by Jansenistic pressures, as well as by his relationship with Marie des Valleés. Jansenism's influence may also have caused St. Margaret Mary Alacoque's canonization to be delayed (until 1920). See Daniel-Rops, pp. 76 and 249n.1.

16. Recall Tronson's later "clericalizing" and "moralizing" of Olier's views on the priesthood; recall, too, the powerful influence of the Jansenistic current up to Vatican II. We know, for example, that the ex-Oratorian P. Quesnel was the primary target of the bull *Unigenitus* of 1713 condemning Jansenism. Cf. A. J. Krailsheimer, "Jansenism," *The Westminster Dictionary of Christian Spirituality,* ed. Gordon S. Wakefield (Philadelphia: Westminster, 1983), pp. 219–20 at 220. For a theological hermeneutics such as the one proposed in the text, see Tracy, *Blessed Rage for Order.*

17. Bertrand de Margerie, *The Christian Trinity in History,* trans. Edmund J. Fortman, (Still River, MA: St. Bede's, 1975), p. 349, appreciatively mentions Bérulle's emphasis upon Jesus and the Eucharist as "icons" of the Trinity.

18. Fernando Guillén Preckler, *Bérulle aujourd'hui 1575–1975: pour une spiritualité de l'humanite du Christ, Le point théologique* Series, 25 (Paris: Beauchesne, 1978). He particularly sees in the theology of von Balthasar a theology and spirituality congenial to Bérulle (pp. 64–65n. 39, for example). This may be so, although it is interesting that von Balthasar has spoken of the "proclivity to empirical and psychological considerations" characteristic of the mystics of the *grand siècle,* like Bérulle, Teresa, Ignatius, John of the Cross, and so on! See his "Spirituality," p. 92. Interestingly, Bérullian scholars, even Bremond (throughout vol. 3), stress the objectivity (as distinct from a modern subjectivity) of Bérulle: Guillén Preckler, *"Etat,"* p. 27n71; Dupuy, *Bérulle: une spiritualité de l'adoration,* pp. 51–52, distinguishing him from Loyola in this respect. I would tend to see an integration of both dimensions in Bérulle, as argued above.

19. Dupuy, *Bérulle: une spiritualité de l'adoration,* is very helpful here. Friedrich Von Hügel, himself formed by the French School through the Sulpician-Fénelonian-Huvelinian transmission, nicely stresses the import of adoration. See, for example, *The Reality of God and Religion and Agnosticism* (London: J. M. Dent and Sons, 1931), p. 71: "Religion, at least among the mystics (and I believe that, on this point at least, the mystics merely dive deeper into and bring out more explicitly the sap or the central core of the religious passion), consists centrally in the sense of Presence—the sense of

an overflowing Existence distinct from our own and in the Adoration of the same." For the influence of the French School upon Von Hügel, see Joseph P. Whelan, *The Spirituality of Friedrich von Hügel* (New York: Newman, 1971), pp. 15–32. Recall Von Hügel's great work on Catherine of Genoa, *The Mystical Element of Religion as Studied in Saint Catherine of Genoa and Her Friends*, 2 vols. (London: J. M. Dent and Sons, 1961), and recall also that Bérulle always carried "her image upon him," according to Madeleine's *Lettre* 284, p. 314.

20. Cf. Vincent R. Vasey, "Mary in the Doctrine of Bérulle on the Mysteries of Christ," *Marian Studies* 36 (1985): 60–80.

21. See Bernard Cooke, *Ministry to Word and Sacraments* (Philadelphia: Fortress, 1976), pp. 147–48, 152, 293, 301, 382, 388, 487–88, 495, 610–11, 622–23; Edward Schillebeeckx, *The Church With a Human Face: A New and Expanded Theology of Ministry* (New York: Crossroad, 1985), pp. 3, 202–3. The critical work on Olier's *T* was, of course, not yet available to these authors.

There is an interesting tradition in the French School of closely associating the Virgin Mary with the presbyteral priesthood. Bérulle, Olier and Eudes see analogies between them: Mary, like presbyters, brings the Word into history; both sacrifice; and so forth. But M. Olier also calls Mary a priest in a seemingly presbyteral sense, and Eudes gives her the title, but then qualifies it (and in some texts M. Olier also seems to say that Mary doesn't express her presbyteral priesthood like other priests). See, for the sources, Bérulle, *OR* 4, p. 426, and Guillén Preckler, "État," p. 247; Olier, *T*, pp. 177–250, and H.-J. Icard, pp. 344–45; and René Laurentin, *Maria Ecclesia Sacerdotium* 1 (Paris: Nouvelles Editions Latines, 1952), esp. pp. 370–73 (see 278–82 and 341–85 for texts on the entire French School, with historical antecedents); Eudes, *C* 9, 11: *OC* 7, pp. 563–73, 676; cf. Louise de Jésus, p. 533, for Madeleine.

Of course, this is a controversial issue, and despite the calling of the Virgin a priest by Popes Pius IX and X (the latter indulgencing a prayer to Mary as priest and virgin), still the Holy Office has issued a warning against "incorrect" inferences and practices in this area. See Michael O'Carroll, "Priesthood of Mary," *Theotokos: A Theological Encyclopedia of the Blessed Virgin Mary* (Wilmington, DE: Michael Glazier, 1986), pp. 793–96. Is it possible that this presbyteral-Marian devotion may open up some new perspectives on the question of the (presbyteral) ordination of women?

22. For helpful comments on this, see Dagens, p. 181.

23. One would have to look through what our mystics say about *charité* or almsgiving, or to their support of religious foundations (like the Good Shepherd Sisters), for their understanding of what we might call the commitment to the poor and the oppressed. It is there in subdued tones, but we need to develop this in our own way. See, for example, Olier's great chapter

on *charité* in the *I*, pp. 148–55, esp. 153, where we are told that Jesus is a "mystery. . . known only to the little ones . . . [which] overturns all states (*États*), monarchies and empires." This is surely a fine beginning of a social, political critique of modern society, is it not? See below, pp. 267–73. Cf., in Bérulle, *CB* 3, P. 855, p. 573; P. 904, p. 628; for Madeleine's sense for the poor, see Louise de Jésus, pp. 476–78; for Eudes, see Milcent, *S. Jean Eudes: un artisan*, pp. 73–76, 430–33, 456–58 (for his custom of inviting twelve poor people to the refectory for the Feast of Jesus' Sacred Heart), 562 (the Good Shepherd Sisters). Cf. Raymond Deville, *"Actualité de l'école française?" Bulletin de Saint-Sulpice* 8 (1982): 42–54, and chap. 10 of his *L'école française de spiritualité*, pp. 157–69.

IV

Comments on the Texts

I n our choice of selections, we have used the best critical editions
available, hoping for a proportional sampling of texts. In the case
of Bérulle, this means we have worked from the *editio princeps* of
his *Oeuvres complètes,* which originally appeared in 1644, through the
work of Gibieuf and under the Oratorian generalate of Bourgoing.
This edition was reissued by the Oratory in 1960, in two volumes.
Migne also reissued the complete works in 1856, but the texts are
inferior in some cases to the *editio princeps;* hence our choice of the
1960 reissue, at least for our selections from the *Grandeurs,* the *Vie*
and the *Elévations.* Our selections by no means represent the full
range of Bérulle's works, whose pages number in the thousands. But
most would agree that the *Grandeurs* and the *Vie* are the masterworks
of the Cardinal, and that the "Elevation on Mary Magdalene" is a
work of enormous mystical depth and literary power. We have included a celebrated letter on the priesthood too.

The case of Mother Madeleine de Saint-Joseph is similar. Her
writings too are extensive. We are fortunate to possess a truly critical edition of about three hundred of her letters produced by Pierre
Serouet in 1964, and so far as I know, this is the only truly critical
edition of her works in existence. With every letter Père Serouet
indicates the sources he works from (usually copies dating to the
seventeenth and eighteenth centuries), and his comparative analysis
of "more suspicious letters" against the "more authentic" renders his
work the crucial one in Madeleinian studies. Unfortunately a collection of original autographs of her letters, numbering over three

hundred, was sent to Rome for her beatification process but remains lost. A decree signed by Pope Pius VI in 1785 confirms that these originals were received. Père Serouet has not yet been able to find them.

Deciding what to choose from the published writings of Olier was more complex because scholars do not agree upon a particular work as his masterwork. We have already seen that Louis Cognet found evidence for the high popularity of the *La Journée,* and if one reads through Bremond's selections from Olier, one will note his predilection for this work too. It is a remarkable work, a kind of guide for the Christian day, with deeply moving meditations on just about everything likely to confront the serious Christian in the daily struggle. But the work is too long to translate in this introductory volume, and perhaps does not range as fully as we would want through most of the major Olierian spiritual and theological themes. For this reason we have chosen mainly from the *Introduction à la vie et aux vertus chrétiennes,* which also has its lyrical power, albeit in a somewhat more didactic framework, and ranges through a good representation of Olierian themes. We have included a few pieces from the *La Journée* too, which are incontestably praiseworthy for their spiritual and lyrical power. These might give the reader a first feel for this fascinating work. We have worked from the most recent 1954 critical edition of these works prepared by François Amiot, who worked from the original 1655 and 1657 editions respectively. Again, these are but a small part of Olier's complete works, especially if we keep in mind the *Mémoires,* which alone are around three-thousand pages. Still, there is a basic unity amid the diversity of M. Olier's works, and we remain confident that the reader will sense that unity-in-diversity in the selections presented here.

The reader will recall our speaking of St. John Eudes' enormous output, much of it found in the twelve-volume *Oeuvres complètes,* edited with notes by J. Dauphin and C. Lebrun between 1905–11. We have worked from this in every case. Here our selections were easier to come by. The *Royaume,* first published in 1637, is usually considered the expression of the saint's basic theological and spiritual framework, from which he never really departed. We have chosen passages that range through the key Eudist themes in this work, aiming for selections that combine theological depth with literary power of expression. The *Coeur* of 1681 is also represented, since it shows how John Eudes eventually placed the decisive accent upon the metaphor of the heart, summing up his entire work through this rich theme. This work ranges through three of the volumes of the collected works, and so we have had to be very selective, choosing passages that might enable the reader to glimpse the overall movement of the *Coeur.*

In our selections we have tried to be sensitive to the subtle relationship between thought and expression, idea and form. The two often cannot be detached, as if the form or literary style were accidental to the content struggling to come forth. In many ways the French School has generated its own symbolic form, its own cluster of images and metaphors, which it has structured through certain genres that seem to correspond to the kind of spiritual and theological disclosure it has been its charism to give to the rest of us. It would be well for the reader to pay attention to this dimension of our selections, I think. As some literary critics and philosophers put it, we naturally move from the texts to the world of meaning opened up by the text, from the sense encoded in the text to the references of a historical and theological nature expressed through that sense. The medium is, often, an essential dimension of the message.[1]

Bérulle's *Grandeurs,* for example, seems a kind of mixed genre. It is a theological treatise, a kind of grand synthesis of twelve discourses (and the number may have a symbolic impact foreign to us). And yet it continually breaks into "elevations" or aspirations to the Divine and the God-Man Jesus. Here theology becomes prayer and prayer becomes theology; learning slides into adoration, and adoration slides into the "servitude" of theological analysis. The genre itself expresses the science of the saints, the new style of theology wedded to mystical experience, which Bérulle wants to develop in his times. The elevations, if you will, keep the theology humble, open to a stance of adoration and transcendence. They break the theologian out of himself or herself, as it were. The master metaphors found throughout—adoration, servitude, *anéantissement,* reference, capacity, adherence—are all structured in the *Grandeurs* as in the service of this great theological movement into mystical contemplation and depth. And yet somehow an elevation is not an absorption into divinity, which Bérulle may have feared was true of some forms of abstract mysticism. Elevations keep us aware of the Divine distance: We must be on earth before we can stretch upward. And so the *Grandeurs* does not forget about earthly things: the world, the church, the priesthood, our call to holiness. I would suggest that this genre also expresses something of that critical balance between the Classical/Christian Heritage and the new Renaissance stress upon human interiority. The movement between elevation and analysis is the aspect I have in mind. Rather like the early beginnings of the Baroque, with its mixture of classical themes and the new Renaissance probings of nature and human existence.[2]

Madeleine's letter form, like all letter forms, expresses the dialogical nature of the Christian life and brings out the potential of the French School to move us into the dialogue with God. The message of the French School, and of Carmel, becomes a personal address, a Thou summoning a you. In this sense it expresses beautifully Madeleine's love theology and also gives added meaning to the letter output of all the principals in this book. Olier's *Journée* and *Introduction* are again that mixed genre so typical of the French School, theological analysis wedded to elevation and prayer. Reading them is to enter into that great movement from the self and its daily concerns to the Divine Mystery through Jesus. Only in Olier the texts are much less grand than Bérulle's: less of Neoplatonic Dionysianism and more of the evangelical poverty and humility seems to shine through. Bérulle's vastness becomes rather scaled down to size in Olier: It is not so much the universe as a whole on the way to God but the humble person, or at most the churched community of those struggling for perfection. And John Eudes continues this mixed genre too. He wants to reflect upon the Christian life in a theological way, but more like a preacher. And he always weds this to prayer. The mixed genre generates the same mixed movement from self to God. But John, preacher and missionary that he is, seems in a hurry in his writings, moving now here, now there. The *Coeur* is like a summary, but it seems loaded with incomplete beginnings. The text makes us hurry, filling us with eagerness. What should we expect, if we really believe we are moving toward the great heart of God?[3]

In the end, all our principals of the French School could have said of them what was said by Father Amelote of Bérulle: "[Bérulle] is the one to have raised up this buried virtue [of respect]. . . . it is certain that, in this century in which so much sanctity appears, we see in souls more familiarity with God than reverence, and we find many Christians who love God, but few who respect him . . . but should one penetrate to the depth of spirits, he will doubtlessly confess that respect for God is hardly known, and that children aren't raised with a profound adoration of his grandeur, but only with a freedom toward him. This is the source of the neglect of the Holy Sacrifices, the esteem for apparent austerity, and the scorn of priests."[4]

NOTES

1. Helpful information on the texts, which I have drawn upon, can be found in Guillén Preckler, *"Etats"*, pp. 1–5; Serouet, *Lettres,* pp. 9–11; Glendon, pp. 5–6; Noye and Dupuy, "Olier," cols. 739–40; Milcent, "Jean Eudes," cols. 490–92. Louise de Jésus, p. 523, notes Madeleine's destroying her letters to Bérulle.

For a sensitivity to the kind of literary analysis I have in mind, see especially Tracy, *The Analogical Imagination,* on the nature of genres and their meaning. The notion of "symbolic form" is taken from Eric Voegelin; see Eugene Webb, *Eric Voegelin: Philosopher of History* (Seattle: University of Washington, 1981), pp. 52–88, for an introduction and bibliography. Paul Ricoeur is also enormously helpful here; see his *Essays on Biblical Interpretation,* ed. Lewis S. Mudge (Philadelphia: Fortress, 1980).

2. Dagens, pp. 37 and 249, suggests that Bérulle was greatly influenced by Augustine in his literary form. The *De Trinitate* does continually move between analysis and prayer/aspiration (elevation?), and this is typical of Augustine. Dagens sees Eph 3:18–19 as an important biblical elevation that may have influenced Bérulle. And, of course, Bérulle's influence can be felt in the Oratorian Malebranche's elevations, as well as in Bossuet's. On his classical or Baroque tendencies, Dagens wavers: pp. 165, 208. See "Baroque," *The Oxford Companion to Art,* ed. Harold Osborn (Oxford: Clarendon, 1970), pp. 108–111, for helpful comments. Bérulle seems to bridge a more classical and later Baroque era in France, but apparently classical influences remained powerful in France until quite late. Bremond 3, pp. 93–132, has insightful comments on Bérulle's literary style.

3. See Bremond 3, pp. 393 (on Olier) and 536–45 (on Eudes) for insightful literary comments that have helped me. Bremond is a very helpful source for sensitizing one to these kinds of concerns. See also Émile Bertaud, "Elévations spirituelles," *DS* IV/1 (1960), cols. 553–558, for helpful historical and liturgical sources of the Bérullian elevations. As the preface of the Mass invites us to lift ourselves up to God, so does Bérulle. The lyrical Bérullian "O's" might, I think, be partially rooted in the "O" antiphons.

4. Denis Amelote, *La vie du père Charles de Condren,* 2 (Paris: Henry Sara, 1643), pp. 80–81.

THE TEXTS

Translator's Foreword

This is the first English translation for most of the selections in this volume. I have attempted to present these texts in contemporary American English. At the same time I have tried to respect, as much as possible, the original "feel" of their poetic, flowing and passionate style. I hope this will allow an English-speaking public to understand what these remarkable spiritual authors wished to convey without losing a sense of their enthusiasm, creativity and originality.

Since this volume does not pretend to be a critical edition I have taken two general liberties. First, I have placed the references to the scripture quotations in parentheses immediately following each text. In the original works this varies; sometimes the references are in the text, sometimes in the margins, sometimes in footnotes and at times there is no reference at all. My choice was motivated by a desire for simplicity and accessibility.

Second, I have translated all scripture quotations, whether in French or Latin, into English without identifying the original language. Most texts were in French, but a substantial number were in Latin, following the practice of the period. I followed the same procedure for the few non-scriptural Latin quotations. On those few occasions where the authors furnished a translation for a Latin quotation in the text, I left the original version as well.

All the translations of the scripture quotations are mine. Since the writers did not always cite the texts exactly and at times took slight liberties because of the context, it seemed more in keeping with the purpose of a translation to present their version in these instances. The few accommodations they do make with the scriptural texts are innocent enough and will be obvious to the reader who is at all familiar with the Bible. For example, on page 139 (*G* 6, 4, p. 247) Bérulle changes the verses around and omits a phrase that he probably thinks is not necessary to the point he is making.

Furthermore, the writers worked mainly from the Vulgate, but often utilized the Hebrew and Greek editions of their period. Therefore it makes more sense to translate what they wrote rather than to insert references from a contemporary edition of the Bible, which would frequently be based, at least in part, on other sources and on contemporary scholarship.

The question of exclusive/inclusive language was a real struggle for me. For many years I have been committed to the use of non-sexist references to God and humankind. After some experimentation, as well as consultation with a number of people, I decided to leave the exclusive language. It is in fact part of the writers' world. It reflects how they saw reality. It is the way they wrote. Just as I would not think, as a translator, of altering those theological or spiritual points with which I might disagree, or try to update some of their anthropology, in the same way I chose not to change a language that reflects a different sensitivity to the interplay of masculine and feminine reality than many of us have today.

I am greatly indebted to Joanne Bierl, M.M.M., Virginia Brown, Barbara Glendon, O.S.U., Margaret Glendon and Anthony Lobo, S.S., for their gracious assistance in the revision of the manuscript. I am also very grateful to William Thompson, the editor of this volume, whose understanding, support and guidance were crucial to the completion of this work of love.

PIERRE DE BÉRULLE

Discourse on the State and Grandeurs of Jesus[1]

*First Discourse on the Excellence and Singularity
of the Sacred Mystery of the Incarnation*

[1, 2, p. 162]

One of the first and most important lessons that we are taught in this school of wisdom and salvation,[2] which was founded and made available to the world, is the holy mystery of the Incarnation. This mystery is so exalted that it surpasses the loftiest thoughts of men and angels. It is so excellent that it contains and includes both God and the world in itself. This mystery is so deep that it is hidden from all eternity in the most secret thoughts of the Ancient of Days and in the very bosom of the eternal Father, in such an exalted and ineffable manner that the Apostle speaks rightly of it in various places as: *the mysterious design which for all ages was hidden in God, the Creator of all* (Eph 3:9).

Nevertheless this mystery, which is so exalted and excellent, so deep and so hidden, is at the same time quite public. It is realized in the fullness of time, in the center of the earth, so as to be seen by both earth and heaven. Its purpose here is to become the object of faith for all people, the anchor of their hope, the cause of their salvation and the fulfillment of the glory of God in the universe. For it is through this mystery that heaven is opened, earth is made holy and God is adored. This adoration is new. It is ineffable and was unknown to earth and heaven even in former times. For although heaven previously had adoring spirits and an adored God, it had not as yet an adoring God.

109

PIERRE DE BÉRULLE

It is through this mystery that God is on earth hiding his greatness in humility. He is covered with our weaknesses and clothed with our mortality. He himself accomplishes the salvation of the world in our midst just as if he were one of us. Through this mystery earth is a heaven. It is a new heaven where God dwells in a manner that is loftier and more august, holier and more divine than the way in which he dwelt previously in the highest heavens. It is with faith, love and homage toward this sacred mystery that God himself, rather than through angels and servants, established a religion on earth.[3] This religion will never be changed or removed from the earth. He saved it for the end times since this mystery also bears within it the final manifestations of his power, his love and his eternal wisdom.

The church should be caught up in this mystery in a holy and divine way. It should be the focus for the devotion of the most advanced souls, transfixed with wonder and admiration as they contemplate this object where they discover and perceive in an unspeakable fashion the majesty of the divine essence, the distinction of its persons and the depth of its designs as well as the exalted, rare and unheard of way in which God chose to exist in this masterwork. For everything that is great, holy and worthy of admiration is there. It is like a résumé and a summary of all that the oracles of faith reveal and teach us about God and his works. This divine mystery is like the center of the created and uncreated world. It is the only place where God chose once and for all to contain and reduce to our level both the world and himself, that is, his own infiniteness and the immensity of the whole universe.

[1, 6, pp. 165–68]

After an eternity of dwelling, being absorbed and operating within himself, God wanted to move outside, as it were, in a new type of operation. That is to say that in addition to the internal emanations, which in a blessed and divine way occupy him in his essence and in his eternity and which constitute the divine persons in the holy Trinity, he wished to become active outside himself. He wanted to produce creatures capable of knowing, serving and loving him. He decided to create the world that we see. Even though he was able to bring forth many worlds from the treasures of his power and wisdom, he wanted to create only one to represent the unity of his essence by the unity of his work.

PIERRE DE BÉRULLE

Also as this same God contemplated himself, he loved his own unity and wanted to paint it more vividly and dedicate it in a more holy fashion within this same world. And since he had created a world in his honor, in this very world he wanted to choose a subject to be a work of his own, which was unique, singular and unlike any other; rare and surpassing all the other works of his hands; a work that, because of its own excellence, would have a perfect relationship with its maker; because of its unity, a perfect relationship with his own unity. This is the divine mystery of the Incarnation, the finest work of the divinity; the masterpiece of his power, his goodness and his wisdom. It is God's very own work, as his prophet calls it in this word, *God, your work* (Hab 3:2). It is a work beyond all understanding, which contains God himself. It is the work and the triumph of uncreated love, in which fortunately love triumphs over God himself. This work, this mystery is unique and unlike any other in the world. Eternal wisdom produced it as its work of works and its mystery of mysteries. Heaven and earth are blessed by its presence, filled with its grandeur, ruled by its power and sanctified by the effects of this power.

We see God's unity imprinted in the unity of this mystery and engraved in this work, as in a precious diamond. In this world where there are several natures capable of receiving his greatness, God only chose one. Leaving aside angelic nature, he chose to unite himself to human nature. We see that in the whole of the human race, where there are many possible subjects, he chose only one and that there is only one Son of Man who is Son of God among the children of the world. We see that in God himself, where there is a plurality of persons in an essential unity, only one person became incarnate, although the Father and Holy Spirit are both powerful enough to communicate their divine substance in this way.

Thus the unity of God is honored not only as before through creation, but also by the very unity of a divine and uncreated person in this masterwork of the Incarnation. Let us speak more simply and let us offer more clarity and breadth to this thought. Let us say that it is no longer the unity of the elemental and earthly world, the material and tangible world that proclaims, praises and worships the unity of God, but rather the unity of a new work and a new world; a world of grace, of glory, and of greatness; a world that is in all ways heavenly, glorious and divine. It is a world that is the equal of God himself, containing God himself as if he were a part of it (if we can speak this way).

For Jesus is a world, a splendid world, according to authentic theology, and this is true for many more reasons than philosophy ever knew when referring to the human person as a world in miniature, as we will say later. Furthermore, we adore in Jesus the unity of a divine person, subsisting in two different natures, who, divinely and unspeakably, proclaims, honors and serves the supreme unity of the divine essence. O supreme unity, how lovable and admirable you are in the divinity and in the most divine of its works! How adorable you are, because God himself honors you through the unity of his Word in two related natures! He honors you forever because you are eternal and everlasting!

How guilty are those mortals who think so little of you, preserve you so neglectfully and violate you so freely in your works. They do not realize that God is unity and that he creates everything for unity and creates everything through unity itself. For it is the unity of his power, his essence and his intelligence that is the source of all he accomplishes outside himself in all his works. He intends to draw everything to himself and to his holy unity through the unity of his Spirit in grace and through the unity of his Word in the Incarnation, using this mystery and through it, even one of the divine Persons to honor the unity of the divine essence. O unity of essence, how adorable you are in the holy Trinity! O unity of person, how adorable and lovable you are in the Incarnation; unity of divine Essence and divine Persons in these two mysteries, uniquely adorable and lovable, you wish to draw us to God and to his unity!

There are reckless spirits who, motivated by inadequate reasons and strong passions, rupture so easily the unity of minds in faith through heresies and the unity of hearts in obedience through rebellions! But let us leave these thoughts behind to return to our discussions and mysteries.

Let us say that God has established in the universe three distinct orders; the orders of nature, of grace and of glory. In each of these there are many subjects, which fill heaven and earth with practically an infinite variety of creatures, admirable in their diversity. In the midst of this he wanted to found a new order with only one subject who would be alone and without prototype. For when we contemplate the order of nature, how many stars do we see in the sky, how many plants on the earth, how many birds in the air, how many fish in

112

the waterways, how many animals in the forests, how many millions of people, and how many thousands of angels? If we then look at the order of grace, how many just men and women do we see, how many prophets and patriarchs, how many martyrs and confessors, how many virgins and how many souls who serve God either in innocence or in repentance? And if we raise our sights to the state of glory, how many varieties of saints do we see? How many seraphim, cherubim, thrones, virtues, dominations, powers, principalities and how many other names that are unknown in this world, but recognized in the other?

However, in the order of the hypostatic union, which is the highest of all the orders, the light of faith tells us that there is only one subject. Just as our faith tells us that there is only one God, it also tells us that there is only one Man-God and one God-Man. For just as there is only one begotten Son in the bosom of the Father, so also did God desire that there be only one Son of Man who was Son of God. He wished this Son of Man, born of the Virgin Mary to be unique and singular, not in his human existence, but in his divine state; not in his nature, but in his dignity. He wished that he alone be included in that ineffable order of personal union with the divinity, the only subject of that admirable order. God wished that each of the orders of nature, grace and glory be shared and communicated with an infinite number of subjects. However Jesus was the only one to take part in this ineffable order, with which no other human being or angel could be associated.

In the heavenly orders and hierarchies each angel fulfills adequately his species without the need for any other individuals. In the same way the only son of the Virgin, the angel of good counsel, fulfills in himself this great order and no one else can ever be there with him. God wished to bring his creation to a close with him as his masterwork. In him God wished to express and bring to fulfillment his greatness, his power, his goodness and the unspeakable communication of himself. He could never make anything greater, holier or more divine than Jesus. He would never want to make anything like him.

Let me say that although there are many who possess grace and glory, Jesus is the only on earth or in heaven, in time or in eternity, to possess uncreated and infinite being. Jesus is the only one who has the divine Essence as one of his own essences and the divine Person as his own person. Jesus is the only one seated at the right hand of the

Father, the only one placed on the throne of the Godhead. He alone is worthy to be adored by all creatures. He alone is worthy to possess our hearts and minds, our sentiments and our thoughts, just as he alone, through the holy mystery of the Incarnation, possesses the divine Essence and divine Person in a way that is ineffable and quite unique to him.

Second Discourse in the Form of an Elevation to God Upon the Mystery of the Incarnation

[2, 1, p. 170]

Those who contemplate a rare and excellent object are pleasantly surprised by the astonishment and admiration they experience at the first sight of that object, even before they recognize in detail the particularities of the subject they are contemplating. Furthermore, this astonishment, which appears to cause a weakness in the soul, gives it strength and vigor. For the soul draws strength from its weakness, elevating itself to a greater light and to a higher and more perfect knowledge. This same thing happens to us when we first behold and think of the excellence, the rarity and uniqueness of our Lord Jesus Christ and of the sacred mystery of the Incarnation. Because we are deeply and tenderly touched by the grandeur of this rare object, which was presented in the preceding discourse, we believe we should lift ourselves to God and praise him in this unique work of his, waiting until later to reflect more on the state and grandeurs of Jesus and to penetrate the secrets and the depth of this most exalted mystery.

Thus we are like one who emerges from a deep, dark cave, finds himself on a high mountain and beholds the sun for the first time. He sees this sun as a serene, beautiful day breaks over our hemisphere, decorating and embellishing the universe and enlivening it with its light and rays. Touched by the sight of such a beautiful object, no doubt he would be surprised and delighted by this view. He would feel the need to honor God in this work of his, without taking the time to measure, by the rules and principles of astronomy, the size and dimensions of this great star. He would not stop to study and observe with curiosity the properties of its light, the power of its influence, the phases of its movements and the other perfections of this great heavenly body.

In the same way, we leave the obscurity of earthly things and we come to contemplate the true Sun of the world, the Sun of this sun that enlightens us, the Sun of justice who enlightens everyone coming into the world. We are taken aback in astonishment and infatuated with love and admiration at the first brightness, the first sight of this splendor. For at the beginning of this work and as we first begin thinking about so worthy a subject, we need to interrupt our discourse in order to approach God and contemplate the greatness of his only begotten Son and the state of this most holy mystery. Let us contemplate God made man and let us approach this sanctuary with a spirit of humility and devotion. Let us try to enter with reverence and love into his clarity, rather than enter by clarity into his love. Of course we desire to receive from him both of these qualities and impressions as we direct our stirrings and affections toward an object and a mystery that is one of love and clarity at the same time.

[2, 2, pp. 170–72]

The Egyptians adored the sun and inappropriately referred to it as the visible son of the invisible God. But Jesus is the true sun who looks upon us with the rays of his light, who blesses us with his countenance and who rules us by his movements. He is the sun we should always behold and adore. Jesus is truly the only begotten Son of God and neither the sun nor any other created thing, whether in heaven or on earth, is his equal. Jesus is the only begotten Son and the visible Son of the invisible Father, as we shall say later. Let us say for now that he is not the sun of the Egyptians, who were deceived by their myths, but the Sun of Christians, who have been instructed in the school of truth, in the light of this sun, who is the light of the supernatural world. He is a sun who chose to depict and represent himself by the natural sun, which is only his shadow and symbol.

For the sun is the image of God, the Father of nature, the universal source of life. And Jesus is the true and living image of the eternal Father. He is his image both in his divine person and in his sacred humanity, which is united to the Godhead. He is the author of the world, the father of human nature both by his power, which created it, and his love, which redeemed it. He is the source of grace and the principle of true life on earth and in heaven, in time and in eternity, in men and in angels, in grace and in glory. The sun was formed in the middle of the days set aside for the creation of the world. It was placed in the middle of all creatures, some higher and some lower, that it might illumine them all. And Jesus, the splendor of the Father, reveals himself in the world and enters the world of grace in the middle of the ages; at the end of the old law and the beginning of the new. By the light of his grace he illumines the Fathers who preceded him and those who came after him. All of them were, according to scripture, like stars, shining with the clarity of this sun and in the middle of them he emerged and appeared to the world.

Created light, which subsisted from the first day of the world, was united to the body of the sun on the fourth day in order to be, in and through the sun, a body and source of light for earth and heaven. In the same way the eternal light, the totally uncreated light, subsisting in the Godhead, was during the fourth millennium united and incarnated in the humanity of Jesus in order to become, in and through him, a source of life, grace, glory and light for all eternity.

One of the most renowned astronomers of antiquity was so infatuated with the sun, which is the principal object of his science, that he wanted to look at it and contemplate it at close range.[4] He was burned and consumed as he looked at it. Jesus is the object of the science of salvation, the science of Christians. The teacher and the Apostle of the world proclaimed openly that his science was to know Jesus (1 Cor 2:2). Should not Christians then be touched by the love and desire to see and contemplate the principal object of their belief, their science and their religion? Should they not have more affection for the Sun of their souls than this philosopher had for the sun of the earth, which is commonly exposed to the sight and usage of both humans and animals? And should they not be burning to come near to this Sun of justice, not in order to be consumed, but rather to be set afire by love and charity as they look upon it?

An excellent mind of this age[5] claimed that the sun and not the earth is at the center of the world. He maintained that it is stationary and that the earth, in conformity with its round shape, moves in relation to the sun. This position goes against all appearances, which constrain our senses to believe that the sun is in continuous movement around the earth. This new opinion, which has little following in the science of the stars, is useful and should be followed in the science of salvation.

For Jesus is the sun that is immovable in his greatness and that

116

moves all other things. Jesus is like his Father. Seated at his right hand, he is immovable like him and moves all things. Jesus is the true center of the world and the world should be in continuous movement toward him. Jesus is the Sun of our souls and from him we receive every grace, every light and every effect of his power. The earth of our hearts should be in continuous movement toward him, so that we might welcome, with all its powers and components, the favorable aspects and benign influences of this great star. Let us bring, then, the movements and affections of our soul to Jesus. Let us raise our spirits and praise God for his only begotten Son and for the mystery of his Incarnation with the following thought and words.[6]

[2, 5, pp. 174–77]

In this state[7] and subsistence you are an abyss of marvels, a world of greatness, an abundance of eminent, rare and singular realities. You are the Center, the Circle, the Circumference of all the outer emanations of God![8] You are the masterpiece of God. As he moved outside himself you became the work in which he exhausted his greatness, power and goodness and in which he enclosed himself so as to become part of his own handiwork and to exalt you over all the other works of his hands, thus dignifing and deifying you through his very being. You are the throne of glory and greatness where the fullness of the divinity dwells in a unique, divine and bodily fashion, according to St. Paul, that worthy herald of the glory of this sublime mystery (Col 1:15–23)!

In the holy Trinity, the Son of God is united to the Father in a unity of essence. Here he is joined to his humanity in a unity of Person. In the Godhead, this same Son of God is one with the Father. They are a single source, which produces the third Person of the Trinity. Here he is united to his humanity, in a unity of Person, to be a co-principle with it, and through it, of the whole order of grace and all the holiness of earth and heaven. The being and order of nature is attributed to the Father through the Son. The being and order of grace and glory is attributed to the Son through his humanity. He carries this out and accomplishes it through his humanity, which he has elevated and chosen to be an instrument united to the Godhead. The divine essence is a substantial grace and you, O most holy humanity, united with the Word, you are another type of substantial grace, subsisting personally in divine and uncreated holiness. Just as the accidents and properties flow from the substance, existing and depending on it, in the same way the effects of grace have their root and their subsistence in you, O deified humanity, O humanized divinity! This is so true that this Man-God, this Word Incarnate, this unique Son of the eternal Father in heaven and of Mary on earth, is in the order of grace what substance is to accidents and what the sun is to light. He has an excellence, an influence, a power; a supreme excellence, a universal influence, a singular and absolute power over the whole state of grace and all the effects that flow from it! In eternity, through the essence that he receives from his Father, he is the source of the holy, eternal and uncreated Spirit. In the same way in the temporal order, through the essence he receives from Mary, that is through the instrumentality of our humanity, he is a new, living and powerful source of all created holiness, of all infused graces, of all divine assistance, of all the holy operations of earth and heaven, in time and eternity.

Oh, abundance! Oh, abyss! No one can count the stars in the sky, the leaves on earth or the sand in the sea, even though these things have limited value and are finite in number. But who could count the number or estimate the value and the uniqueness of all the effects of grace? I am speaking of all those effects in every saint in heaven, in all the just of the earth or even in those sinners who resist the grace that is offered to them? Who could adequately examine all that is contained in the unfolding of the centuries until the end of time or in the infinite length of eternity? I mean an eternity which has no other life than that of grace and which is nothing but holiness with all its possibilities, being totally filled and absorbed by the effects of grace and of glory.

All these effects of grace, both of God with men and men with God, are related to you and will be related to you forever, as to their source. Furthermore, they find their support, their sustenance and their foundation in you as in their substance. Oh, substance, oh, source of grace! What a wonderful thing this says about Jesus concerning grace!

The order of nature and all the universe, which we see so lavishly spread out in admirable diversity, is divided in two different categories, substance and accident, which contain all the varieties of creation. In the same way, the order of grace has its accidents and substance. Its substance is in the Incarnate Son of God. Its accidents are found in his saints and in his servants. However, there is this difference. The Man-God is the singular and unique substance of all the order of grace, while the order of nature is divided and diversified in various types of substances. Thus the order of grace, being more excellent and closer to the Godhead, is also closer to unity, which is so celebrated in the divinity. Thus this order has only one deified substance, as there is only one divine essence and substance.

This Jesus, in whom we contemplate this rare, excellent and unique substance of the order of grace, does not only support it as a substance supports its accidents. He is also the substance that is the origin of the whole order and state of grace. For the grace of earth and of heaven flows and emanates continually from Jesus, just as accidents flow from their substance or as the light of earth and heaven originates from the sun.

Now let us raise our sights to an even worthier object and more divine exemplar. For this emanation of grace is a sort of created divinity, of which God said, *I said, you are Gods* (Ps 82:6). It is an excellent imitation of that great, noble and primary emanation of the Son in the Godhead, which looks to God the Father as to its Father and origin. In the same way, we are called to recognize and honor two distinct emanations in Jesus, one derived from the other: his own personal emanation from his Father and the emanation grace has drawn from Jesus in honor and imitation of the one he has himself from his Father.

This second emanation uncovers and manifests for us an admirable and perpetual state of Jesus. This state is one of the greatest secrets and is founded on the most sublime mysteries of the Christian religion. It should serve as the norm and guide of our devotion toward him. For in the Holy Trinity the divine persons have a relation and a rapport to their principle of origin. They only subsist through his attributes and relations and are happy to live in this relatedness, rapport and mutual love. It is the same way in the order of grace, which is a perfect imitation, a living portrait and a formal participation in the divinity. All created holiness has an excellent relationship to the Son of God and a singular rapport with the Incarnate Word. It has life in Jesus, as in him who is and calls himself the life, since he is its origin and exemplar.

Those souls who are endowed with this created holiness, contemplate and adore Jesus in this way. They adore and imitate the divine and uncreated holiness, the rapport and eternal relationship of the Holy Spirit toward the Father and Son and that of the Son toward the

Father, who is the origin. Therefore, just as uncreated holiness sub-sists in the mutual relations of Persons who process toward those from whom they proceed, in the same way created holiness subsists in the rapport and singular relation to Jesus and his holy humanity, from which it flows. Thus we will contemplate Jesus, love Jesus and live in Jesus. For he is life. He wants to be our life, both now and through eternity.

Oh, humanity, divinely subsistent, divinely living, divinely active! You are worthy in this divine and infinite attribute that you possess. You are infinitely, most infinitely worthy of ruling all that has been created or could be created. Endowed with superior power, you are worthy of commanding all that can be commanded. For even brute nature is sensitive to your commands. We see this in tempests, winds and storms and other raging elements, which have obeyed you. As we read in the holy words of a great saint and doctor of the church: *The majesty of the Creator.*[9] This expresses worthily the homage and submission that even unintelligent things rendered to the powerful authority and august majesty of the creator, made visible and tangible in you, oh, sacred humanity! You are worthy of acquiring and merit-ing everything that can be acquired and merited; of sanctifying every-thing that can be sanctified; and of abolishing and wiping away all that should be wiped away and pardoned. For you are holy with the very holiness of the divine essence. You are the meeting point of uncreated and created reality. For like the first, you have a divine person and like the second, you have a finite and limited nature. You are the new and unique focus for both God and humanity. For the Eternal Father sees you united to his Son, the Son united to himself and the Holy Spirit united to him who is his origin and the source of his eternal emanation. All of us see you as the spouse of our God, as the Ark of our covenant, as the temple of our Divinity and as the source of our salvation.

[2, 6, pp. 177–78]

I wish to honor your greatness, your power and your blessings; the greatness within yourself, your power over us, and your great bless-ings toward us. Furthermore, I wish to honor all the divine objects we have contemplated and all the mysteries that relate to you: the Holy Trinity, Father, Son and Holy Spirit, decreeing and bringing about the ineffable union of human nature with the divine Word; the blessed Virgin, in whom that divine union was accomplished and consummated. Thus I lift my spirit and address myself to you, O Jesus my Lord. I say to you the words of one of your apostles in ecstasy. I want to say them to you with his spirit and his affection: *Dominus meus et Deus meus,* My Lord and my God (Jn 20:28).

Contemplating and thinking of your grandeurs I offer and present myself to you in the humble, blessed state and condition of servitude.[10] I propose and make a constant, certain and inviolable promise of perpetual servitude to you, O Jesus Christ, my Lord and my God, my life and my Savior! It is an offer of servitude to you, to your sacred, deified humanity and to your humanized divinity. For your humanity is deified not only through the infusion and deification of grace, but through a much nobler infusion and imprint, that is to say, through the infusion and imprint of the Word himself, who communicates his own person to this humanity. In a reciprocal fashion, your divinity is made human, that is to say, clothed with our humanity, as a new substance, which is joined to it and adheres to it, through the support and communication it receives from the existence and very subsistence of the Divinity. O grandeur, O beauty, O love, O ineffable link between Divinity and humanity! I join myself to you by the bond of perpetual servitude, in honor of the holy and sacred bond that you have with us on earth and in heaven, in the life of grace and glory. I enter this holy union with all my strength, begging you to give me more grace and power so that I might unite myself to you in a greater, holier and closer bond.

Our being is linked to you, O my God, through your grandeur and its poverty, that is, by its need to be sustained by you so as not to fall into the nothingness from which your powerful hand has drawn it. Our being is also linked to you through your goodness and its powerlessness, since it is unable to accomplish any work of salvation if it is not joined to you through grace. This bond belongs only to those who are good, separating them from those who unfortunately are separated from you. However, beyond these two bonds, it pleased you to have a third one, which is yours alone and which can belong only to you. It is a bond of love, a rare and singular love. It is a holy and sacred bond, which joins your person to our nature; a bond that forms a new being, a new state, a new order; a bond that makes a new man and a new Adam. When I say a new man, I mean not simply a just man, or a holy man; not an angelic or divine man, but a Man-God who sustains, rules and delights heaven and earth.

PIERRE DE BÉRULLE

I adore your being, O my God, supporting all being through the first bond, which is universally necessary to every created being, whether good or bad. I implore your goodness and mercy that I may be linked to you forever in the second way through the bonds of your love, through the effect of your grace and through the infusion of your Spirit. But beyond all that, I long for you, O my Lord Jesus. I want to partake of you and, through you, have a share in the new grace of your new mystery of the Incarnation! In honor of the admirable union of your humanity with the Divinity itself, I want to unite myself to you, to exist in you, to live in you and to bear fruit in you, like the branch on the vine!

[2, 10, pp. 183–86]

Thus the secret of this new mystery, the source of this great work, the work of the works of God and the unique means divine wisdom has found in order to join earth to heaven as in its point and center, the invisible with the visible in the same subject, created being with uncreated being in the same person and this without any mixture or confusion of the two beings and the two natures, which are so distant and so united at the same time. This secret, as I was saying, this source, this means unknown to heavenly intelligences, this divine invention is to strip the humanity of Jesus of its own ordinary subsistence, so that it could be clothed with a subsistence, foreign and out of the ordinary for his nature, divided and separated from its own subsistence, which it had the right to possess and from which it finds itself happily deprived at the moment of its production.

Thus, for example, in grafting we divide and open up the trunk, which will receive the graft. Now the fruit of this graft, selected by the gardener, is not the ordinary fruit of the tree to be grafted. In a similar fashion, the eternal Father whom the gospel mentions as the divine cultivator of the gospel, chose a wild plant from the earth (if we consider it in its origin and nature), which is humanity bearing the likeness of sinful flesh. God separated the nature from the person that would have been proper and connatural to it and that would have flowed out of its essence once it was actuated and existing. He substituted the heavenly graft, the divine subsistence, the very person of his Son in place of the human subsistence, which had been negated. Therefore this plant, divided in this way and wounded in what is most intimate, most appropriate and most connatural to its being, bears fruits that are different and do not belong to it, but rather to what was grafted onto it.

This nature, which has been stripped and subsequently clothed in this way, possesses henceforth a being that is different not in its essence, but in its existence and subsistence. So much so that its life, its movements and its actions no longer flow from it nor belong to it, but rather belong to the one who divinely sustains it. For we should notice this difference between the gardener's graft and this divine graft of the eternal Father, the celestial gardener. Instead of the graft being sustained by the wild trunk onto which it has been grafted, in this case the Word, which is like a divine graft on human nature, a wild plant because of its resemblance to sin, this Word is the subsistence of this very nature. The one who with three fingers sustains the world, sustains this humanity in a more powerful and unique way by appropriating it, sanctifying it and deifying it in his person. Thus it follows that the life and actions of this human nature do not belong to it. It is not that they do not proceed from it as from their source, but rather it can not claim ownership, neither from a logical perspective, nor from the standpoint of law or morality.

I apologize for prolonging this topic and for using words that would be more fitting in theses and in academic settings than in pulpits and in discussions of faith. However, the reader will be kind enough to forgive me since I am constrained by the need to ward off those difficulties some people create. I graciously beg those people either to keep quiet for modesty's sake or please make the effort to consider attentively and to study more deeply the truths that the faith teaches in order to assure that we all share the same opinion and are united in love regarding the realities of faith the apostle commanded (Rom 12:6; Phil 2:2). For they do not understand that by contesting this truth, they are implicating the basis of Christianity, whose treasure and foundation are the actions and the sufferings of this humanity, not simply as humanity, but as the humanity of the Word. In other words, it is a humanity that in its nature, its actions and its attributes belongs to a divine, uncreated and infinite being, which elevates the essence, status and merit of this human nature to an uncreated existence and subsistence, to a divine condition and dignity, to an inestimable worth and value.

Therefore, let us say to them that the actions of this humanity cannot be thought to belong to it from a logical point of view. For they are not proper to this humanity in itself, and this is necessary if a thing is judged to belong perfectly according to the rules of logicians. The truth is that these actions are proper to a substance that is foreign to this humanity, when considered simply within the state and limits of nature. Let us say to them, furthermore, that from the perspective of the law, whether it be common and natural, or divine and supernatural, the actions of this nature belong properly to the Word and not to itself. For the eternal Word, as an uncreated and divine Person, preempting the right of human nature through infinite power and love, takes possession of this humanity. It unites it to itself, and through infinite power and love, makes it its own, rests and dwells in it as in its own nature, draws it beyond common and natural limits, anointing and consecrating it with the unction of the divinity. It exercises right and authority over this nature, its actions and in general over all that belongs to this humanity. For everything in Jesus Christ has its foundation in the hypostasis of his divinity. The eternal Word, as the substance and divine suppositum of this human nature, is the proprietor of all its actions and sufferings. He sustains them, elevates them, deifies them in his own person, by sustaining, elevating and deifying the substance of this humanity, through which they adhere to the divinity in a common bond of hypostatic communion. Therefore it is evident from this perspective that the Word has the right and the legitimate authority to use and dispose of the state, the life, the actions and the sufferings of his humanity, as something that belongs to him and is truly, blessedly and divinely his because of his admirable power and because he deigned to take such unusual possession of this nature and everything proper to this nature, which has been thoroughly emptied of itself and so worthily clothed in the Word.

A slave, after having given up or losing his liberty, loses the right and authority over his actions and the use of his own life that our common birth gives him. This right is legitimately transferred from the person of the slave to the person of the one who holds him in captivity. How much more is this humanity stripped of this right and this power to dispose of itself and its actions. This right is legitimately transferred from the human nature to the divine Person who sustains it. For seeing itself stripped of its natural subsistence in order to be mightily elevated to the very eminent subsistence of the eternal Word, not only does this nature willingly hand over its freedom and liberty so as to be the fortunate slave of his power, greatness and love, but it gives over to him as well its natural right to subsist in itself, so as to subsist only in the divine Person; and to be in his power and possession, not only morally, voluntarily and temporarily, as is the case of a slave who is under the control of his master, but also in a personal, perpetual and even natural way, if we can speak thus. For it is clear that the stripping of the human subsistence from human nature is a privation of something much more bound and inseparable, much more intimate and intrinsic to nature, than is the freedom and liberty of a person who enters servitude and slavery. For a nature can only be separated from personal existence by the very author of nature, whereas a free person can lose his freedom and liberty through a thousand occurrences. Personal existence is intrinsic to nature. It is its term, bringing it to fulfillment, making it in a way part of the very substance of things. Whereas freedom and liberty are simple accidents and qualities, which are temporary and disappear without implicating the subject. They only enter into the conditions of a given state, not the person. Thus this humanity is stripped of such a great reality, as intimate to its essence as its subsistence; and according to the Angelic Doctor, it is stripped of its existence as well. This humanity then is much more under the power and possession of the eternal Word, which receives it and sustains it in its being, than the slave is under his master's power and possession. Furthermore, according to the law, a tree transplanted from one place to another, once it has taken root, no longer belongs to the lord of the original plantation, but rather to the master of the second, because through the nourishment received from the new earth, it has become in some way a different tree, even though it is the same stalk, the same substance and the same vegetative soul both in gender and species and even in its individual nature, bearing the same fruits and leaves. How much more could we say the same thing of that human nature, which is a heavenly plant, which in its species is an inverted tree, as Plato calls it, and in this individual is even more truly an inverted tree in a more exalted sense unknown to the great philosopher but known only to Christians?[11] This humanity has been lifted out of the sterile soil of the common and ordinary existence of its specific nature and happily transplanted into the very soil of divine and personal existence, in order to subsist and live forever in this new existence of the divine Word. How much more then, I ask, should we say that this humanity is no longer subject to the power and possession of nature, which is the soil and the state from which it is separated, but to the power and possession of divine and uncreated grace, which is the new soil. . . .

[2, 13, pp. 190–91]

. . . You are still this chosen servant, who alone serves God as he ought to be served; that is, with an infinite service. And you alone adore him with an infinite adoration, as he is infinitely worthy of being served and adored. For previously, neither men nor angels could serve and adore this supreme majesty with this kind of service by which it is cherished and adored according to its infinite grandeur, the divinity of its essence, and the majesty of its persons. From all eternity there had been a God infinitely adorable, but still there had not been an infinite adorer. There had been a God infinitely worthy of being loved and served, but no man nor infinite servant able to render an infinite service and love. You are now, O Jesus, this adorer, this man, this servant, infinite in power, in being, in dignity, so that you can fully satisfy this need and render this divine homage. You are this person, loving, adoring and serving the supreme majesty as he deserves to be loved, served and honored. And just as there is a God worthy of being adored, served and loved, so there is also in you, O Jesus my Lord, a God adoring, loving and serving him eternally, in the nature which was united to your person in the fulness of time. . . . from now on we have a God served and adored without any defect in this adoration, and a God who adores, without detracting from his divinity!

Third Discourse on the
Unity of God in This Mystery

[3, 8, pp. 205–07]

In order to better understand this truth, we must look at it from a loftier perspective and affirm that there are three holy, divine and adorable unities. The excellence of our mysteries helps us to know them and the sublimity of our faith proposes them. The Son of God on the earth contemplated, loved and adored them. They are the unity of essence, the unity of love and the unity of subsistence; the unity of essence in the Divinity, which we adore, the unity of love in the Trinity, which we admire, and the unity of subsistence in the Incarnation, which we profess. They are the unity of essence, which the Son receives from his Father, the unity of love, which he produces with his Father and the unity of subsistence, which he communicates to our humanity through the will of his Father.

According to Saint Paul, the first function of the soul of Jesus was, without doubt, the adoration of his God as well as the vision and contemplation of his unities. This is his first duty and his first exercise. It is his first duty to adore him and his first exercise to behold him, that is to behold his essence and his glory. This man called Jesus is God through this mystery and he saw with the light of glory (which no one denies him) that he was God. Because of this, undoubtedly, his first duty and his first operation, given this vision and blessed life, was to adore through his human nature the supreme unity of the divine Essence. And following the order of the eternal origins and emanations, within which he is the only Son of God and the second after the Father, he devoted himself at once to the admiration and adoration of his Father's power in begetting him, as well as his own birth, his subsistence and his unique and eternal filiation in the bosom of his Father. The first activity of Jesus in his divinity is the production of the Holy Spirit, of which, with the Father, he is the source. Thus, following this same order of divine processions, he saw and adored also in the same instant this divine emanation, this eternal Spirit, this personal love of which he is the source and the origin in the Divinity. It is an uncreated and ineffable bond uniting the Father to the Son, and the Son with the Father through an eternal unity of Spirit and unspeakable love.

As he beholds these two natures, one human and the other divine, joined in the unity of a subsistence that is divine and uncreated, in the same instant he beholds, loves and adores this new unity, which makes him the new man, that is to say, which makes him Man-God through a type of new unity, which constitutes his being, his state and his greatness. After the divine Essence (according to Saint John) our happiness resides in the vision of our Lord Jesus Christ and in the unspeakable unity that unites two such distinct natures in him. Therefore the second object of the happiness of Jesus' soul is the vision of himself subsisting within uncreated being and in the vision of this same unity, which by uniting these two natures, constitutes the divine composite and makes God man. From that moment on it establishes the new mystery of the Incarnation and gives the world a new object, an eternal object, an object of grandeur and love, an object of life and happiness. He conceals such grandeurs with his humility, frequently calling himself Son of Man in the scriptures. Yet even though he does this, he does not underestimate them, nor ignore or forget them, because he has known and seen from the first moment that in being Son of Man, he was Son of God.

For as he is Son of God, in his divinity, through an eternal generation, so similarly in his humanity, where he is Son of Man, he is also Son of God by a temporal communication of the divine Essence to human nature. And thus the Son of Man, who is Son of God, sees and contemplates continuously this excellent state, always offering himself and this new unity, which makes him the new man, in homage to the adorable and divine unities of the supreme, uncreated being. O new unity! O holy unity! O unity of subsistence, how precious, lovable and honorable you are to Jesus. For in you, that is in this unity of personal subsistence, consists all his being and his grandeur. O soul of Jesus, when you were brought forth from nothingness and united to God, you beheld his glory, you saw this new mystery of the Incarnation. In seeing it, you have seen how it brings about a holy and incomprehensible unity, a new unity between two such distinct realities, which is also real, divine and adorable. You beheld that your consistency and divine subsistence exist in that unity. What contemplation, what love, what homage did you offer at that moment to this divine being that is your being, to that divine unity that establishes this new, supreme and divine mystery of the Incarnation?

And since you are the only one, O Jesus, to receive it and the first mortal to have seen this unity of subsistence in your two natures, you were as well, even before the virgin who conceived you and before the angels who announced you, the first of all to have recognized and honored this new, divine unity in the fullness of its wonders! You were the first to contemplate this holy unity and who prayed to diffuse its grace, its power and its effects in order to bring about the reuniting of our souls with God, as Saint John said. You are the first to have offered undying gratitude to the eternal Father for having established in you and in this unity the center and the source of the unity of grace and the Spirit, which was to be shared with angels and men and was to govern earth and heaven forever.

Thus, O Jesus, my Lord, in a holy and divine manner you began and you ended your life in the womb of the Virgin, in this Cenacle of

Zion, reflecting, loving and adoring the divine unities. You continued in the same way on the earth in Bethlehem, Jerusalem, Nazareth, Egypt, Judea and in all the places you honored and sanctified by your holy presence. And this interior exercise was part of the spiritual and contemplative life you wished to practice in order to accomplish our salvation, to give an example to your children, as well as to serve and honor the majesty of God on earth. And now that you are in heaven and are established in the Father's glory, you still reflect on and contemplate this same object. Your triumphant, heavenly and immortal life has the same occupation you had during your humble, suffering and pilgrim life. For you are true life. You are the model of our life. You are the exemplar revealed to us and to Moses on the mountain, according to which we are commanded to live. Thus may our interior life be devoted to the contemplation, adoration and imitation of your interior life. May our spiritual life contemplate and imitate the exercises and activities of your divine love and your sacred life.

Following your example let us all contemplate and adore, after you and through you, this divine object. May we see that because of these admirable unities, we have two holy, divine and adorable Trinities in our mysteries. The first is the Trinity of subsistence in a unity of essence. It is the first, most exalted and most august mystery of faith in the Person of the Father, of the Son and of the Holy Spirit. The second is a Trinity of essence in a unity of subsistence through the mystery of the Incarnation, essence of the soul, of the body and of the divinity of Jesus.

One of these two Trinities exists from all eternity. The other exists for all eternity. One is uniquely divine and uncreated in both its Persons and its Essence. The other is divine and human at the same time; divine in the Person and human in two of its essences. One of them is adored but never adores. The other is humbly adored and also divinely adores the most exalted, ineffable and incomprehensible mystery of the Trinity, which is the loving source, the perfect exemplar and the final cause of the Incarnation.

In the Incarnation, the first Trinity, the eternal Trinity, the Trinity of Persons is sublimely, uniquely, majestically and divinely recognized, served and adored on earth and in heaven by the second Trinity. This new Trinity of essences, which constitutes the new Man and is contained in this new mystery of the Incarnation, also renders this new mystery and this new Man, with the diversity of his natures, worthy and capable of humbly and divinely adoring the supreme mystery of the most holy Trinity.

[3, 10, pp. 209–10]

Thus God lives eternally in the unity of his essence. Thus God operates powerfully as a unified source and rules blessedly through the unity of his love. And thus, in a new way, God introduces his Son and his greatness to the unity of the divine subsistence and grounds his state and reign in the unity of that subsistence. O divine unities; O unity of essence, unity of principle, unity of love and unity of subsistence. How admirable you are, how lovable you are, how adorable you are in yourself, in your emanations and in your works! How much we should search for you in your very self, seek you in your designs, respect you in your counsels, glorify you in your works and include you carefully in all those things your spirit and your grace bring us to undertake in your honor! How much we should adhere to the secret and powerful activity of your wisdom, which leads everything back to unity, just as everything flows from unity!

For, according to Saint Denis, *all things are brought forth from unity by nature* and they seek this unity by a secret instinct of nature. They return to it through grace; they lose themselves in it through glory. But above all created things, this humanity that we adore in Jesus returns and loses itself in another type of totally divine unity through a path which is equally divine and incomprehensible. This humanity is introduced by the Spirit of love, through the new mystery of the Incarnation, into the new unity of a divine Person and into this supreme state that contains in itself such uncreated and infinite unity and dignity. Through this mystery Jesus is forever the center, the source and the foundation of the unity of spirit, grace and love to which he calls us and leads us, strengthening us by the divine state of his subsistence, by the unfolding of his life, by the merit of his death, by the efficacy of his prayers. For this is what he desires, and he insists that it be this way. And there were three solemn and significant prayers, which he wished to offer on the last day of his life, on the day of sorrow and suffering, as the scripture said, *In the days when he was in the flesh* (Heb 5:7). One of them was in the Cenacle of Zion, according to Saint John (chap. 17); another in the Garden of Olives, according to Saint Luke (chap. 22); and the third on the cross, according to Saint Paul (Heb 5). In the first one he begged for the grace that we might all be consumed in the supreme unity, which he has in himself, and which he shares eternally with the Father, according to the sacred words recorded by the most intimate of his servants, the most faithful of his apostles, the greatest of his evangelists and the most loving and beloved of his disciples: *O my Father, may all who believe in me be one, as we are one; as you are in me, O my Father, and I am in you, may they be one also in us, so that the world may know that you have sent me. I have given them of the glory you have given me* (that is, I have given them my divinity through my humanity) *so that they may be one, as we are one. I am in them and you are in me, that they may be consumed in unity and that the world may know that it is you who have sent me and that you love them as you have loved me* (Jn 17:20–33).

Fourth Discourse on the
Unity of God in This Mystery

[4, 2, pp. 212–14]

These two aspects together have a natural and perfect relationship. For love tends naturally to unity, and it is clear that a love that is supreme and divine should be unity itself. But what is most strange in the contemplation of the Holy Spirit, is that although he is love in the divinity, he is sterile in that divinity (if such a common word can be used to speak of something so exalted and so great), instead of love and fertility being naturally joined together. It is one of the most hidden and impenetrable aspects of the depth of the mystery of the most holy Trinity, where each aspect is an abyss in which the human spirit loses itself and is engulfed, when it wishes to understand rather than reverence that which surpasses the limits of our intelligence.

Thus with a humble spirit, poised in adoration of the wonders of our belief and the secrets of the Godhead, guided by the light of the faith, let us proceed from depth into greater depth, from secrets into deeper secrets, from wonder into greater wonder. With a loving and reverent spirit let us say, drawing on a secret that is equally strange and wonderful, that this sterility of the Holy Spirit is as divine and adorable as the fertility which produces it. It is a sterility flowing from the power and fecundity of its production, which divinely through its person, exhausts and brings to term divine fertility. It is a sterility founded in greatness, in the dignity and reality of its very Person, which is happily produced as the termination and divine repose of the emanations within the Trinity. It is a sterility, which because it flows from the fertility of God, ends in the fertility of God; in other words, in the fecundity of a divine Person, operating outside itself. For just as it is unique to the eternal Word to be both origin and originated at the same time, so it is unique to the Holy Spirit to be sterile and fertile at the same time. It is sterile in itself and fertile outside itself. It is the uniqueness of its Person that it is the termination that terminates divinely and brings to a close, in itself, the divine fecundity within the holy Trinity. However, it is the termination that receives, contains and brings to an end within itself the fullness of that fertile nature, so that in receiving, conserving and terminating that fecundity, it may pour it forth powerfully and divinely outside itself.

This is why in the works of God, just as power is attributed to the Father, and wisdom to the Son, so also fecundity is appropriated to the Holy Spirit. As soon as God begins to speak in the scriptures and to operate outside himself, this fertility of the Holy Spirit is activated and celebrated. For in the opening words of Genesis, at the beginning of the creation of the world, during the first of God's works and before the first day of the world, it is said that the Holy Spirit moved and hovered over the waters: *Incubabat aquis* (Gn 1:2), in the words of the Septuagint. This was to impregnate them with his fertility and to assure that subsequently many excellent creatures would emerge from the waters and fill heaven and earth, thus forming this universe. This is what God revealed to his servant Moses, so that we might know that everything that was produced in the universe and differentiated afterward during the six days of Genesis, owes its relatedness and its origin to the fecundity of the Holy Spirit.

However, to stop with the creation of the visible and material world would not be a worthy termination point for the fertility of the Holy Spirit. It should produce a more exalted being and create a more excellent world. Its power requires a greater object and its activity needs a more worthy and exalted outcome. Since it is sterile in the divinity by the very nature of the mystery of the Trinity, it is necessary that, in some other ineffable manner, it be fertile through a new mystery: by giving a new being to one of the Persons subsisting in the fullness of the most holy Trinity. In this way just as the fertility of God, in God himself, comes to term in a divine Person, so also the fertility of the Holy Spirit, outside itself, leads to the production of a God, preexisting (O strange wonder!) and from now on existing in a new nature.

We see this in the renewal of the world, when the architect of heaven and earth, the eternal Word, is clothed with human nature and comes to take on this new being in order to give a new being to the world. For this same Holy Spirit, who became active in the material world and in the natural order, according to Genesis, becomes active in the invisible world and in the order of grace, according to the testimony of Saint Luke, by forming the head of this order of grace and the new source of supernatural existence, who creates a new heaven and a new earth and constitutes a new world, to use the language of God himself in the holy scriptures, and who himself is, in his own Person and in his two divinely united natures, an incomparable universe.

Thus we see how the Holy Spirit does not exercise his fertility within himself but rather outside himself, not within the world of archetypes but within the world that is understandable to us; not in eternity but in the fullness of time. For he impregnates the blessed womb of the most holy Virgin with his fecundity. He produces a God-Man and gives a new birth to the eternal Word within human nature. He produces nothing within himself, but happily and blessedly he produces outside himself this divine mystery of the Incarnation as the greatest of his works in which he realizes a life-like portrait of himself, creating a perfect image of himself, applying to it his finest brush strokes and the most vivid and ultimate colors of his likeness.

Now let us summarize in a few words what we have explained. Since he is the personal love and unity within the holy Trinity, he accomplishes this undertaking as a work and mystery of love and unity. He is love produced but does not produce love within the Godhead, where he is the only one who does not reproduce his equal. Therefore Jesus is the work of the Holy Spirit, who creates him in the womb of the blessed Virgin, bringing him forth as the love of heaven and earth. Jesus is also love produced, who does not produce anything equal to the being, order and state of the hypostatic union. Just as the Holy Spirit is the termination and the resting place for the love of Father and Son, bringing to term the incomprehensible movement of the divine emanations within the divinity and pouring the fecundity of God outside into his works, in the same way Jesus is the termination and divine resting place for divine love operating outside the Godhead, pouring forth outside himself, into his creatures, the fecundity of his Spirit in the order of grace and glory.

Thus the sacred mystery of the Incarnation is a work, a state and a mystery of love and unity. It is a masterpiece of the Holy Spirit, reflecting his two divine qualities. On the one hand, it is a masterpiece that adores the distinct unities existing in the eternal Persons, who produce and are produced. On the other hand, it is a masterpiece that contemplates the Spirit of love and unity as its source and relates to him as its prototype, since he has divinely expressed himself and vividly represented himself in this mystery of love and unity. This is a unique aspect, which should be noted, for it contains an excellent exercise that we must perform and underlines the adorable relationship this work has with the Holy Spirit and the divine unities, which are most worthily contemplated in the singular state of this divine mystery of the Incarnation.

Fifth Discourse on the Communication of God in This Mystery

[5, 4, p. 233]

Let us develop this line of thought more and see in this work how the Son of God wished to reflect further about himself, that is, about his unique and intimate eternal activity, which is the production of the Holy Spirit. For just as he saw that this person who is produced is the bond between the divine Persons, he also wanted his own person, as producer, to be the bond between human and divine being. This Holy Spirit, this person proceeding from him in the Holy Trinity, is the bond that creates such a unity among the divine Persons that they are perfectly united in the unity of the Holy Spirit and yet they remain distinct in their personal separateness. In the same way, he wished that his own person be the sacred bond creating such a unity between the two natures that they retain their distinctness and what is naturally proper to them, while being perfectly united in the unity of person, without confusion or any division, as expressed in the Holy Councils.

Thus, in our first mystery we have a divine Person, whom we adore, uniting two Persons. Similarly in the second mystery, we have a divine Person, whom we adore, uniting two natures, one divine, the other human. He contemplates, adores and imitates the unity of the Holy Spirit, who is the third Person in the order of the Holy Trinity and who, by his very nature, is the eternal bond between the two Persons from whom he proceeds. He is their personal love and sacred unity. Let us conclude then and say that as we contemplate the divine Word in his emanation, in his Person and in his eternal production, in other words, in all the ways in which we can contemplate him in the Godhead, we see that he is uniquely expressed and vividly represented by the state and qualities of this divine mystery, which is in a perfect relationship with what is ineffable in eternity, as well as being a living portrait of God.

[5, 9, pp. 237–40]

As we contemplate thus the birth, the grandeur and the function of the eternal Word, we adore his being, his life, his state in God his Father and also his power, which produces within eternity itself a divine and uncreated person. We admire his birth and his primacy in the order of the divine emanations, by which he refers eternally to God his Father both himself and the Spirit, who emanates from him. Furthermore, we recognize the right he has, by virtue of his own birth, to establish himself through a divine mystery where he divinely, substantially and personally offers all created reality in homage to God; just as in the Godhead, he offers to God his Father all that proceeds and is uncreated at the same time. Therefore, in this way, he is guided and invited by his very self, that is, by his personal qualities and perfections, to enter into a new state for the glory of his Father and to bring about this new mystery.

For he is the first to emanate from God, and he wishes to be in a state and condition through human nature so that he can be offered to God as the first fruits in thanksgiving for all that universally proceeds from him. He is the only one emanating from the Father alone. He wishes to be the only one constituting, in himself, this new mystery; the only one adoring personally and divinely, in his humanity, the unique source without origin of all reality, that is his eternal Father, whom Saint Denis calls the origin and source of all divinity. He is the vivid image the Father produces in contemplating himself. He wishes to be, in a new way, a living and eloquent image of the grandeurs of God. Through the power of God he wishes to repair in us the image and likeness of the divinity imprinted in our nature and erased through sin.

He is the stamp of the substance of the Father, who offers and communicates to him the impression of his own substance. He wishes to be the seal and stamp, imprinting his own essence and subsistence in human nature. And in honor of his Father, who gives and imprints in him eternal being, he wants to give us this being, and he wishes to commit himself and imprint himself in created nature, much like a divine stamp. He is the uncreated Word by which all things were formed. He wishes to be the incarnate Word, by which all things will be reformed and elevated to a higher dignity. He is the only Son of the Father, and he wishes to create for him by his power, beget for him by his love, acquire for him by his merits and give him by his Spirit many children to manifest his glory. He wants to transform his own natural filiation into a living source of adoptive filiation. This makes him Father and source in the order of grace and glory. It confers on him some beautiful titles, rights and privileges and gives us some beautiful teachings.

We need to collect them before going any further and learn through the state of the Son of God before his Father what should be our state before him. We need to contemplate in the exalted and sublime life of the only Son before his Father the life we should begin on earth and bring to completion in heaven: tracing the preliminary lines and sketches of our perfection based on such an accomplished model; forming ourselves in the life of the Spirit and in all that is virtuous by imitating such a divine life and such a rare and excellent exemplar. For as the eternal Word proceeds in his divine being and has God for Father, so also we proceed in our supernatural being (though in a different manner) and we should recognize the Son of God as our Father, from whom we all draw existence and the life of grace. This gives him, among those titles and attributes announced in the prophecies of his coming, the name of Father of the world to come.

As the Word and eternal Son of God always contemplates his Father, because he is his Father, so we should constantly contemplate the Son, because he has been established as our Father. Our gaze toward him should be a gaze of the greatest honor, the most powerful love and total and absolute dependence. We should wish that our beings were nothing but vision and spirit so that we could be completely occupied and given over to this spiritual and divine contemplation of the new source and principle of our being. The only Son of God continually refers all that he is to his Father. His being and his life consist in this relationship. Even strictly speaking, his life is nothing but a life that substantially and personally refers all that he is to his sole source. In the same way our being and our life should be totally dedicated to a perfect and absolute referral of all that we are, in the order of nature and grace, because of his eternal mercy.

In profane literature fabled loves often transform people into strange substances. How much more should we desire that the power of him, who truly transforms the nature of things, be brought to bear on us, so that by the strength of his powerful love the substance of our being might change its state and condition to become happily a pure relation toward him to honor, love and imitate his substance, life and personal subsistence, which is totally related to the eternal Father.

The Son of God truly proceeds from the Father, contemplates the Father and refers all that he is to the Father in such a way that he is very intimate to his Father and dwells in him: *He flows forth from the source without leaving it,* as the learned Tertullian said.[12] In the same way, we should be inseparably joined to the Son of God as the branch to the vine, just as he himself is inseparably united to his Father. We should exist and dwell perpetually in him, just as he exists and dwells in his Father. We should always live and act through him and for him, just as he lives and acts through his Father. For he is both the source and goal of our existence and our life.

Finally the only Son of God, seeing himself immutable in his being, wishes to change his condition for the glory of his Father and become human in order to live the kind of life in which he can suffer and accomplish what he could not do in the Godhead. He even wishes to retain forever this new being to honor God his Father, not only through his works and his sufferings during his pilgrimage on earth, but also through a new permanent state in heaven and eternity. In the same way, by imitating his example, we should change our life and condition. For the glory of him who struggles so with his greatness, we should struggle with ourselves, our habits and our passions. There are two ways of serving him. One by actions alone, and the other by a stable state of being. We should choose the way that is constant, solid and permanent by embracing a way of life that by its nature honors the majesty of God and becomes the source of many holy, virtuous actions. We should do this in honor of the state and the life into which the Son of God entered through the sacred mystery of the Incarnation and in which he perseveres eternally in heaven.

All of these aspects and unique relationships are quite worthy of inspiring Christian enlightenment and piety. All of them are solid foundations, which establish the relation we should have and claim to have with the Son of God through the humble state of servitude that we vow to him in honor of his relationship to his Father, through the admirable state of his divine and eternal filiation. It is enough to mention it here in passing. The practice and implications of it will be dealt with elsewhere.

Sixth Discourse on the
Communication of God in This Mystery

[6, 1, p. 245]

There are three mysteries that serve as the principle object and exercise of our faith. They distinguish and separate it from those academies and religions introduced and proclaimed to the world. They demonstrate that it is truly divine, unique and superior, exceeding the light and capacity of nature. The first is the mystery of the most holy Trinity, through whose power we have been created and fashioned, in whose belief we have been already baptized and justified, and in whose beatitude we will one day be glorified.

The second is that of the Incarnation, in which human nature has been singularly exalted and united with its original source, being joined to it in a new, holy and admirable way which, as it is mentioned elsewhere, has never been known before in its state on earth or in heaven. Through this new and supreme life and holiness, which has been established in the center of the earth, the empire of death has been destroyed on earth, sin has been annihilated and mortals have been declared to be the children of God, capable of eternal life, heirs of heaven and co-heirs of Jesus Christ, receiving from him his grace and his glory in exchange for our nature, which he deigned to assume from our midst.

The third is the Eucharist, in which God gives us and returns to us the very nature he deigned to take from us, like a sacred deposit. Having received it from us and dignified it in himself, he returns it to us with interest. For it is in this nature that he gives us his grace, his Spirit and his divinity, and imprints in our bodies by his divine and sacred touch, as the Fathers say, a power that disposes us to the glorious resurrection and heavenly life and communicates to all human substance a new and supernatural privilege, a secret and admirable power, a vital and seminal quality of rebirth, incorruptibility, resurrection and immortality.

[6, 4, pp. 247–48]

In order to better understand these sublime truths, we need to consider that in the holy Trinity, there is a substantial and essential indwelling of the Father's divinity in the person of the Son by means of the eternal generation, according to these sacred words of this very Son of God: *Ego in Patre et Pater in me,* I am in the Father and my Father is in me (Jn 14:10). There is subsequently a substantial and personal indwelling of the same divinity of the Son of God in his humanity through the Incarnation. Thus the one in whom the Father dwells, dwells also in this sacred humanity, which is united to the Son of God in the unity of Person, just as the Son is united to his Father in the unity of Essence. Third, there is a substantial and bodily indwelling of the living and glorious body of the Son of God in our earthly and mortal bodies through the Eucharist, in which we receive the living Son of God. Through him we live a holy and divine life, just as he lives through his Father, as he says himself in Saint John, chapter 6.

In this manner we enter into excellent communication with the Divinity. From this very moment and in this lowly world we are united substantially, in a certain measure and degree, with God. This is what the Son of God, at the end of his days, in his holy prayer, expressed to his Father in these sacred words: *I have given them of the glory you have given me, so that they may be one as we are one. I am in them, you are in me, so that their unity may be complete.* And in the preceding verse: *I pray for them, so that they may be one, just as you are in me, O my Father, and I am in you, so that they may be one in us* (Jn 17:20–23 *passim*). Sacred words and utterances of the eternal Word, worthy to be engraved in heaven and on earth by the hands of angels and men. Words and utterances that express these three mysteries and express, in this trinity of mysteries, the bonds, the divine links, bound and intertwined divinely one with the other, by which God the Father, beginning in this lifetime through the humanity of his Son, joins substantially the body and nature of mortal, earthly men to the supreme Essence of the divinity!

It is as if we have in these divine mysteries, not the false and mythic power of a profane love, which links gods and men, lowering false gods to earth and falsely elevating men to heaven in order to situate them as shining stars in the firmament. Rather we have the true and holy power of an inexpressible and incomprehensible love, which joins God and men, bringing about a real and veritable self-emptying of the Son of God, who is God himself, and making him human in order to make us gods.

Furthermore, through him, as if with a strong and powerful chain, the eternal Father exalts us and draws us up to heaven, even to the heaven of the Godhead. It is a chain of love, for he speaks of it in that way himself; a chain that draws us and keeps us united to the Father through the Son and to the Son through himself and his holy mysteries. It is a precious chain, exceeding all price and value; a sacred chain, made up, in a holy and religious way, of the principle mysteries of the Christian religion. It is a divine and inviolable chain of unity and charity; the charity of the Father and the Son toward humanity and the unity of the Father with the Son in the Trinity; the unity of the Son with human nature in the Incarnation and the unity of the Body of Jesus Christ with us in the Eucharist. It is a precious, sacred and divine chain in which is contained the greatest secret, the strongest bond and the principle source of the designs, counsels and works of the true God toward humanity. It is a chain made up of the three mysteries, like sacred and divine bonds, like admirable and strong links by which the eternal Father, drawing us to himself, lifts us up forever into the heavenly reign whose king is Trinity, whose law is charity and whose measure is eternity.

Seventh Discourse on the
Communication of God in This Mystery

[7, 9, pp. 275-78]

Let us say that God's presence in human nature, through this mystery, should not be conceived and thought of as a simple, naked presence, simply a lack of distance between things without any relationship to each other. Nor should it be understood as the purely natural presence of God, flowing simply from the use of his creative power, conserving the nature of those things in which he dwells. Nor is it the presence of God, followed and accompanied by his friendship, his privacy and familiarity with the soul, as it is with grace; nor even his fulfilled love and perfect beatitude as in glory. Rather, it should be understood as a presence that is special and particular to the unique and singular state of this new mystery.

It is a presence that imitates the eternal indwelling, repose and communication of God in himself. It is a presence that operates and activates this humanity with a new being, a divine and uncreated being (without any intrusion or confusion between them). In other words, it is a presence of God, imbuing this humanity with the divinity of his essence, the infinity of his power, the uniqueness of his love, the fullness of his subsistence, the reality of his existence, as well as the intimacy, depth and fullness of his divine, supreme, uncreated being.

In short, this sort of presence is such that this humanity receives from it a communication of God so vivid, so exalted, so perfect, so secret, so intimate and so unique, that it is penetrated by his Essence, enlivened by his Spirit, exists with his existence, is sustained by his subsistence and is divinized by his Word. For God the Father dwells and reposes in himself, in such a way that through this indwelling and repose he communicates his Essence continually to the divine Persons, and in the same way, the Son of God dwells in this humanity and reposes in it, unceasingly communicating to it his own subsistence. Furthermore, the Word, which dwells in his Father, inasmuch as he is his Father, wishes to dwell also in this humanity as in his own Essence. For he makes it his very own by this subsistence. Therefore, just as he dwells and reposes in the Godhead, as in his eternal Essence, he also wishes to make his repose and make his dwelling in this humanity as in his new Essence, and he wishes to dwell there forevermore.

It is only in the Godhead itself and in this humanity that God is present, dwelling, residing in this way, bringing about an unspeakable and substantial communication of himself. For on earth he pours forth his grace, and in heaven he gives his glory. However, it is only in the Trinity and in the Incarnation that there is an appropriate, immediate and substantial communication of the Divinity; whether by Essence as in the Trinity, or through subsistence as in the Incarnation. These are two mysteries and two distinct communications. Both are unique, adorable and proper to the Godhead. For, in the one God communicates his Essence, and in the other he communicates his subsistence, which is the same as his Essence. In the one God is Father as he gives his substance to his Son, and in the other God is a human being giving his subsistence to humanity.

In such a unique fashion, through such a powerful and divine communication, God is man and man is God. God is man, clothing himself with our humanity. Man is God, subsisting and living in the Godhead. In the world there is a mediator between God and man, who is man in order to undergo the death men have merited. He is God to overcome death, which men could not defeat, and to offer them his life and his eternity. It is the only Son of God who is this mediator, who became man for men and who, through a wondrous love and power, exalted us by humbling himself, glorified us by suffering, divinized us by becoming human and rendered us eternal by dying.

This is how the long desired work of redemption is prepared. Thus the very great mystery of the Incarnation, which will bring it about, is established and introduced into the world. Saint Paul exalts and glorifies this mystery in these splendid words: *Manifeste magnum est pietatis sacramentum, quod manifestatum est in carne, justificatum est in spiritu, apparuit Angelis, praedicatum est gentibus, creditum est in mundo, assumptum est in gloria!* How undeniably great is the mystery of piety, which was manifested in the flesh, vindicated in spirit, seen by the angels, preached to the Gentiles, believed in throughout the world and taken up in glory (1 Tm 3:16).

How great is this mystery, which begins on earth and ends in heaven where Jesus is at the right hand of the Father! How great is this mystery, which joins for all eternity earth with heaven and God with man! How great is this mystery with a greatness and an attribute opposed to that of the mystery of the Trinity. For the one is great in sublimity; the other is great in humility! The one is natural and necessary; the other is free and voluntary! It is a great mystery, truly great in dignity, love and piety, worthy of bearing the beautiful name and the lovely praise that the Apostle gives it: *Great is the mystery of piety!*

In keeping with the nature of the sacraments, this mystery and sacrament is composed of two natures, one external, the other internal; one divine, the other human; one visible, the other invisible. It is like the foundation, the source and the exemplar for the other sacraments, which, following its example, are all composed of two natures in relation to the incarnate Word, who wished to depict and represent in his works and in the sacraments of his church the mystery of the Incarnation, which is the sacrament of sacraments and also a means of grace more divine and august than the other individual sacraments. It is a sacrament and mystery full of God, full of grace, full of light, which contains and manifests the invisible God in the visible flesh of man and sanctifies humanity through the Spirit of the divinity, as these beautiful words say: *Manifested in the flesh, vindicated in spirit.*

It is a powerful and universal mystery, which diffuses its rays and effects everywhere, giving light to the angels and salvation to the world! *Seen by the angels, preached to the Gentiles, believed in throughout the world.* It is a mystery, which is totally divine and celestial, lifted up from earth to heaven, establishing there its permanent dwelling, drawing us and calling us all into glory: *Taken up in glory;* a worthy goal and crown for such a great mystery! May God be blessed forever in himself and in his only son Jesus Christ our Lord, whom the Father wished to give us through a unique love and gift in this mystery. Also he calls himself the gift of God in these beautiful words, which he spoke to the Samaritan woman: *Si scires donum Dei,* If you knew, O woman, the gift of God (Jn 4:10).

Let us give ourselves to him, for he is the gift of the Father and gives himself to us. Let us belong to him, for he belongs to us. He is totally ours, in his divinity, *given for us,* in his humanity, *born for us,* as his prophet and his church say. Let us go to him, for he comes to us, and he has the words of eternal life. Let us adhere to him for through him, our humanity adheres to his divinity. Let us love him, for he is our life, our glory and our love! Let us adore him, for he is God. He is our God; God and man forever. As we love him, praise him, and bless him in his greatness and wonderful works, let us lift ourselves to him, manifesting his glory. Let us desire that he bless us and that he be known, served and adored throughout the whole world. Let us conclude with this wish from the words of his prophet: *Benedicat nos Deus, Deus Noster, benedicat nos Deus; et metuant eum omnes fines terrae,* May God, our God, bless us. May God bless us and may the whole world, even its farthest reaches, revere and glorify the greatness and power of his majesty.

Eighth Discourse on the
Communication of God in This Mystery

[8, 10, pp. 297–99]

For notwithstanding this supreme and divine state, he experienced swaddling clothes, the crèche, childhood and the powerlessness of childhood, flight and persecution. In other words, he experienced the lowliness of human nature, the thorns of the cross, the darkness of death. Even though in all these states he was truly God-Man, he was God the infant, powerless in a stable. He was God fleeing and hidden in Egypt. He was God living and unknown in a corner of Judea. He was God suffering and dying on a cross. He was God dead and buried in a tomb. In this humble state of abasement, the Divinity of the Father was in him, the love of the Father was in him, and the Father said of him, *In whom I am well pleased* (Mt 17:5). However, the glory of the Father had not yet been established in him. He was in the Divinity of the Father. He was in the love of the Father, but not yet in the glory of the Father.

This glory was deferred by the plan of the Father for his Son, by the love of the Son for his Father, and by the respect that the Father and the Son had for human necessity and need. In giving his Divinity to humanity and in giving it the Person of his Son, the Father suspended the gift of the full and perfect state of glory. As we see from the account of his life, he left him for a while in infancy and powerlessness, in swaddling clothes and the crèche, in persecution and flight, in a life both known and unknown, on the cross, in death and in the tomb.

Oh, what a strange division and wondrous separation, even between the Divinity and the glory of the Divinity! A division that existed in Jesus alone and in him for the sole purpose of representing, expiating and erasing the separation that occurs between God and his creatures through sin! Is Jesus less adorable and less lovable because he possessed less glory during his lifetime, given that it was love and only love that separated him from it and that it was for us that he was thus deprived?

Because he was separated from glory through love, let us love Jesus in his love, the love that deprived him of his glory. Let us adore Jesus in his Divinity, the Divinity through which he humbled himself to take on our misery. O love, strong love, powerful love, love exercising its power and its discipline on the very Person of God in his new nature, which he unites to himself and which he causes to live and subsist in himself! O love, stopping the flow of divine emanations in the exercise of the very emanation of his love; in other words in the exercise and the infinite outpouring of himself, as he gave himself to humanity!

It was because of love that he gave his divinity to this humanity. And yet glory was suspended and interrupted for a while due to the excesses of this emanation. He is worthy, even infinitely worthy, to receive this glory and in his time he will possess it as something naturally due to him. However, he will be deprived of it for quite a long time, that is, for his whole life, by the power and fullness of his love. I am speaking of the love of Jesus for his Father. For if the love is so powerful as to deprive and strip Jesus himself of something as great as his glory, will it not have a powerful effect on our hearts? Will it not deprive and strip our spirits of their perverse inclinations, their disordered pleasures and their illicit affections?

If love is exercising its power and discipline over Jesus, setting him amid thorns, placing him on the cross and leading him into death, will it not lead us to the thorns of penance, to the cross of the Christian life and to the death of our vices and earthly affections? Indeed! There is this crucifying love, which crucifies a God. Let it not be less powerful toward men. Let it crucify us in Jesus and with Jesus. For while it is humbling and ignominious for Jesus to be crucified and even crucified for sinners, it is glory, grandeur and happiness to be crucified for Jesus and with Jesus, being able to say with the Apostle, *Christo confixus sum cruci*, I have been crucified with Christ (Gal 2:20).

On that cross, thus attached with Jesus, let us be exalted like him and separated from the earth. For he himself has depicted his crucifixion as an exaltation separating him from the earth. Let us then be exalted and lifted up above earthly, temporary and passing realities. Let us be fastened in heart and spirit with Jesus and to Jesus, despising everything for his love and for his glory. Let us utter in spirit and in truth this word of the Apostle: *I consider everything to be loss, because of the surpassing knowledge of Jesus Christ my Lord* (Phil 3:8).

[8, 11, pp. 299–300]

A writer of old once said that as God created the world, he was so enraptured with what he saw and so pleased with the beauty of the universe, that he was transformed into love.[13] However, he never saw this mystery and, among the works of God, he only knew the material world. We have been given a higher knowledge. We have appeared at a better time, in the fullness of time, which bears the fullness of God and the fullness of the love of God in this work of his, the greatest of his works. We are delighted as we contemplate this mystery. So let us say that as God created a new world, and the world of worlds, that is Jesus, he was transformed into love. For God is love and is nothing but love in this work of his, where his power, goodness, greatness and majesty have changed and transformed themselves into love.

This mystery is love and only love. For since in it love has united God to man, then also the greatness of God and the lowliness of man are transformed into love by the power of love accomplishing this mystery and triumphing in this mystery, where God brought, in a special way, both his love and the triumph of his love together. Can we not see how the power of God is transformed into love, and how by making himself powerless, God reveals himself most powerful in his loving? Can we not see that the greatness of God is transformed into love and that God only reveals his greatness through loving? Can we not see even that power and greatness are captured by love in the powerlessness and in the lowliness of childhood? Can we not see here that majesty is also transformed into love and changed into the benevolence and humanity of a child?

Thus God is love and is nothing but love in this mystery. Since the state and the grandeur of God are transformed here into love, then also the state and the lowliness of man are transformed by the exercise and the power of love. God is man, but it is not his nature, rather it is his love that makes him man. For the divine nature is infinitely distant from human nature. It would remain forever distant if love, which is as powerful and infinite as nature, had not united divine nature so intimately to human nature; unifying them in the unity of subsistence, existence and Person. God is a child, but he is a child through love and not through the necessity of his condition as is the case with human children. He is a God-Child. His power and his Divinity are united powerfully, personally and lovingly with childhood and powerlessness.

This is so true that we can say with surprise and wonder, *Lowliness was taken on by majesty, weakness by power and mortality by the eternal*.[14] For we also see God suffering, God dying, God dead on a cross and in the tomb. But it is love and not nature that reduces him to that state. His life, his cross, his death are love, and each of them is nothing but love, life and power. Jesus lives, loves and rejoices in death and suffering, as he gives us and merits for us life, love and joy. O love of God existing in this mystery! O love triumphing over both God and the love of God at the same time! O love, exercise your power over us and over our love! Triumph over us! Triumph over us in Jesus, according to the truth of this word, *In Christ he led us in triumph* (2 Cor 2:14)!

Let us live in Jesus, let us love in Jesus, let us triumph in Jesus, and may Jesus live in us, love in us and triumph in us forever! And since love triumphs over God himself, may it triumph over us who are his subjects and his creatures. And since only love triumphs over God, may the love of God be the one thing that captures us and not our passions and disorders. May the love of God alone lead us triumphantly into his captivity! Since love wishes to triumph over both God and the love of God in this mystery, may the power of both this triumphant love and this mystery, in which it triumphs, hold sway over us and over our wills forever.

Ninth Discourse on the Love and Communication of God in This Mystery

[9, 1, pp. 309–10]

We notice that one of the ways in which understanding is superior to the will is that understanding transforms its object into itself, whereas the will transforms itself into its object. It is also one of the aspects that make knowledge different from love. For knowledge draws the object to itself and does not lower the knowing subject to the known objects. Rather it elevates and adjusts the known objects to the proportion and dignity of the knowing subject. Love on the other hand transports the soul to the object it loves and, through a gentle power, lowers and inclines the lover to the beloved reality.

This general difference between love and knowledge is quite considerable, especially because it produces a specific difference between the knowledge and the love of God we can acquire here on earth. Now knowledge places the object in us and does not place us in the object, while love, on the other hand, places us in the object and so powerfully transports us into it that, according to this sacred saying supported by various philosophies, the soul exists more in what it loves than in what it animates. It has more life, more presence, more involvement and affection in the one than in the other.

It follows then that, through knowledge, the soul possesses God on earth, not as he is in himself, but as he is in the soul. However, through love, the soul possesses God on earth, as he is in himself and not as he is in the soul. For love transports us out of ourselves into him and, what is more, it makes us like he is in himself, by divinizing and transforming us into God. Blessed is the state of the soul, which is trained in the school of the love of its God, provided it has learned how to know and serve him. What a strange condition (if we can say this in passing) found even among the most eminent and knowledgeable Christians, who can never know God as he is in himself, but can love him as he is in himself, and yet they work much harder to know him than to love him.

This is why there are so many schools and academies that train souls in this obscure, uncertain and imperfect knowledge, and so few, and so little attended, which train and perfect the soul in love and in the exalted and eminent possession of its God through love. While in this mortal life we cannot know God as much as we would wish, yet we can love him as much as we wish, lifting ourselves up from one level to the next by his grace and love. The condition and the level of knowledge, which we will have of God in heaven eternally, depends on the level of this love on earth. For we will know God to the degree that we will have loved him, and not to the degree that we will have known him on earth.

However, let us leave until later this fundamental point of mystical theology. Let us save this secret for the school of love and for its disciples. Let us return to the preceding point, for it will serve as a base and foundation for this discussion and our mystery. Let us add once more that from the general difference that exists between love and knowledge, we have gathered that there is a special difference between the love and the knowledge of God. From that special difference we realize, furthermore, that for good reason and cause in the school of Christians, happiness on earth is primarily attributed to love and charity and, in heaven, it is primarily attributed to the knowledge and vision of God.

For, already on earth, love joins us to God as he is in himself, transporting us out of ourselves into God. The knowledge we have of God on earth does not unite us to God as he is in himself, but as he is in us; in other words, as he is in our spirit and in the understanding we fashion of him, which we only know in enigma and shadow. *In enigma* (1 Cor 13:12) says he who knew him in the third heaven. The knowledge of God we have in heaven has this advantage and power over the knowledge and light of God available on earth in that it unites us and joins us to God as he is in himself. For in heaven his very Essence unites itself to our spirit and activates it much more nobly with its light than a transparent body is activated by the ray that penetrates it; thus elevating it to know God as he is in himself. It establishes us in a state of life that is proper to God himself, because it is the life of God, whose being and nature are intellectual, to know himself and to behold himself, who is the primary, the noblest and the most worthy object of all knowledge.

Since angels and men possess only the shadow of being and light compared to the being and light of God, then they are naturally capable of only receiving the shadow and the image of the knowledge that God has of himself. He does not raise them up any higher during their time of pilgrimage and merit, being happy to enable them to love him through grace and to love him as he is in himself, according to the nature and the reality of love. This is why love on earth offers the greatest happiness. This is why in heaven knowledge claims this prerogative, which it does not possess on earth.

For since love possesses God already on earth, as he is in himself, so also in heaven the knowledge of God brings us to behold and possess him as he is in himself; a God who through love imprints and unites himself to both our essence and our faculties so that we might behold him as he is, in keeping with the power of this apostolic word and promise, *We will see him as he is* (1 Jn 3:2). For happiness consists in possessing God and possessing him as he is in himself. This is realized by love on earth and by knowledge in heaven.

PIERRE DE BÉRULLE

[9, 2, p. 310]

For as the happiness of man has its roots and origin in the love of man toward God, so also does this love originate in the love of God toward man and in the excess of this love of God, who gives both his Son and his love to the world. It is this love that astonishes the Son of God in this sacred text, as he says with admiration, *God so loved the world* (Jn 3:16).

Tenth Discourse on the
Three Births of Jesus

[10, 1, pp. 321-23]

We find in the book of life three wondrous births of Jesus, who is the life of God and men. They are his birth in the womb of his Father in eternity, his birth in the womb of the Virgin in time, and his birth in the tomb to immortality. These three births are accompanied by wonders, worthy of Jesus and worthy of his source and origin in these three different lives.

For in his birth in divine and uncreated life, there is a twofold wonder: that God engenders and that God is engendered. In his birth in the human and incarnate life, there is a twofold wonder: that a Virgin gives birth and that God becomes incarnate. In his birth or rather his rebirth to the heavenly and glorious life, it is marvelous that a tomb becomes the source of life and that a place of death becomes the source of life without end. Thus God, who is admirable in himself, his works and his saints, is also admirable in his only Son, who is another self; and in his masterwork, which is the Incarnation; and in the holy of holies, who is Jesus Christ, our Lord, foretold and given this name by one of the prophets.[15]

These three births of Jesus, by which he lives these three types of holy, distinct and adorable lives, are expressed in the Word of life and in the Word expressed by the eternal Father, saying to himself and to his Son, *Today I have begotten you* (Heb 1:5 and Ps 2:7). For these are the words which Saint Paul, in the first chapter of the Hebrews, applies to the eternal generation, proving by the power and authority of that text that Jesus Christ belongs to God the Father, through a distinct sort of belonging and emanation from him that the

150

angels do not possess. For he engendered him according to that explicit word, *Today I have begotten you.* This applies only to the Son of God and not to the angelic nature.

Now this proof would be thoroughly unconvincing if this text, which the great Apostle presented and produced, did not signify truly and literally the eternal generation, which is divinely presented in these terms, where through a clever use of words, the present is joined to the past, *Today I have begotten you.* This expresses him who is forever born and is forever being born and whose procession is such that it is without end or beginning. By an impenetrable secret this procession is so fully realized according to the term denoting the past that it is forever being fulfilled according to the term signifying the present.

Again Saint Paul, guided by the same Spirit of God, speaking to the same Hebrews in Acts, chapter 13, presents the same text and applies it to the resurrection of the Son of God, which is a type of new birth for Jesus into immortality. In the church resurrection is commonly called rebirth and regeneration. Furthermore, the Son of God himself is its author. Since he is the eternal Word of the Father, his word possesses a special grace and appropriateness, and he names it thus with his own lips, speaking of the day of judgment when the universal resurrection will come to pass: *In the new age, when the Son of Man will take a seat on a throne of glory* (Mt 19:28).

Third, the same Holy Spirit, who dictated this word to the prophet David and who applied it through his spokesman, Saint Paul, one of his greatest apostles, to the eternal generation and to the resurrection of Jesus, explains it and applies it, through the voice of the church in the office for Christmas day, to the temporal birth of Jesus in the world. God, who is fecund and fertile in his works and in his words, wished that this same memorable word be applied in the same spirit to these three different meanings, to these three states and mysteries of the eternal Word: to the mystery of his birth from his Father, to the mystery of his birth from his mother, and to the birth from the tomb, from which he is reborn like a phoenix to a new life.

These three births are truly wondrous. The first has no time or day, for it never begins or finishes, rather from it flow days, times and centuries, all of which have a beginning and an end. Even our eternity of grace and glory draws its origin from there. For it is through his Son that the Father created the centuries, as the Apostle says to the Hebrews: *Through whom he created the world* (Heb 1:2). It

PIERRE DE BÉRULLE

is through his Son that the Father introduces us into his grace and his glory, as all scripture testifies. We should worship him who, through his first and divine birth, is the Orient to which every Orient owes tribute and homage.[16]

As I say, we should adore him as an Orient, but an eternal Orient; an Orient that exists always at midday by the fullness of its light and always in its Orient by the state and perfection of its birth, which continues forever and never finishes, just as it never has a beginning. He is so fully begotten that he is always being born in eternity. Oh, wonder! Oh, prodigious nature of this birth, by which Jesus is an Orient, by which Jesus is an eternal Orient, by which Jesus is eternally Orient; Orient to which our Orient and our birth in nature, in grace, and in an eternity in his glory owe homage!

This is why, in former days, catechumens entered the church on the day of their baptism with a solemn and remarkable ceremony, in which they turned toward the Orient as a sign of their homage and communion with the eternal Orient, who is Jesus Christ, our Lord. It is equally evident that we are all reborn through baptism in the name and in memory of this divine birth and filiation; being baptized in the name of the Father as Father, in the name of the Son as Son. Through this powerful and precious name we enter into the church and into grace.

Thus our own Christian condition and our status as believers underline this truth and oblige us to preserve the honor and memory due the divine and eternal birth of Jesus, which is the source of our rebirth in the church. If there is no day in the year set aside by the church to celebrate and commemorate it, this is because of its greatness. It is because it has no moment on earth. It is because its feast day is the eternal day, in which it is adored unceasingly in the abode and the state of glory.

Eleventh Discourse on the
Second Birth of Jesus

[11, 4, pp. 344–45]

From these grandeurs flow others. As we contemplate the birth of Jesus we proceed from grandeur to grandeur. For this human birth is a mystery of life. For the one who has life from the Father, and who

152

is begotten as living by the very nature of his emanation; the one who is true life and who gives himself without reservation the name of life; the one who is life and source of life within himself and outside himself wishes to take on life in this mystery in order to be our life eternally.

It is a mystery of light. For the one who is light of light, who comes forth from the Father of lights, who emanates from him as light and who, in the very nature of his Person, is the splendor of the Father, being light in his Essence and in his Person, comes into the world through this mystery to be the light of the world. He says it himself: *As light I have come into the world. . . . I am the light of the world* (Jn 12:46; 9:5). Moreover, he is born with light in the very midst of the night. He comes to the earth with a light from heaven, illuminating the shadows of night and giving a double light to the shepherds. Just as in his death the light of the world was blocked out and changed into darkness, also in his birth a new and extraordinary light appeared, illuminating the Magi, the Orient and Judea. In this way the heavens manifested and revered the birth of Jesus as the birth of a new light in the world.

This birth is a mystery of holiness, according to the angelic words, *your offspring will be holy* (Lk 1:35). It is a mystery of holiness, superior even to the other mysteries of Jesus. For it contains and produces in the universe the greatest holiness and the most eminent sanctification that exists or that could exist. On it are founded every other holiness and sanctification worthy of note on earth and in heaven. It is the birth of the Holy of Holies. It is the birth of a God-Man and of a Man-God. It is the birth of the order and the state of the hypotastic union, which produces outside of God the most exalted and most eminent holiness possible, that which is closest to the superessential holiness of God himself, which this order and supreme state encloses and contains in itself as its form and source. For this holiness, new to heaven and earth, this wondrous grace of the hypostatic union has its birth in the birth of Jesus. It has its source in this mystery, flowing forth from it and diffusing itself in all the other mysteries of Jesus, in all his states and in all his works.

[11, 6, pp. 348–9]

Jesus . . . bears in himself a state which contemplates and adores his eternal state. Before him, nothing, on earth or in heaven, properly contemplated, perfectly expressed or divinely honored the Father as

Father, and the Son as Son, in the state of his divine birth and eternal filiation. And Jesus alone adores through his state the persons and divine emanations which the angels adore well in heaven by the actions of their understanding and will; but not with the sort of adoration we are speaking of here, which is a very different kind of adoration. For we are speaking of an adoration by state, not by action; an adoration not simply coming from the faculties of the spirit or depending on thoughts. Rather it is solid, permanent, and independent of powers and actions, deeply imprinted in the depths of the created being, and in the condition of its state. And so we say that before this totally new birth, nothing, in itself or in its natural or personal condition, adored and rendered homage to these divine realities nor carried in its origin, being or state the affinity, mark and impression of something so great and exalted.

Twelfth Discourse on the Third Birth of Jesus

[12, 2, pp. 373-75]

But I discover here a new effort and a new surprise of your love, which desires to manifest its power and its effects in the beginning of your new and immortal life, as it manifested it during the whole time of your pilgrim and mortal life. For in abandoning your body to his glory, he suspends again the place of this glory and Jesus lives between heaven and earth, dwelling on earth for forty days. O love, love without end, forever victorious, triumphing over exalted and divine realities such as the life and glory of Jesus! O triumphant love, victorious over Jesus, even in the triumph of his glory!

For in the birth from the Virgin to mortal life you are born on earth, which is the place that must receive you in this humble birth. In the same way, in the birth from the tomb into immortal life you are born into heaven, which is the place that should rightfully receive you in this blessed birth into the state of glory. However, the love you have for your apostles, your disciples and your church interrupts for a while the final result of this final birth. Your entrance into heaven is deferred and suspended by a miracle. It is a miracle of love, performed by yourself on yourself, suspending not the state of glory, as previously, but the rightful place of glory. For this powerful love, capable of drawing you from heaven to earth, from the bosom of the Father into the womb of the Virgin, holds you back and suspends you between earth and heaven. Thus, while you have been reborn into the state of glory, you are not however in the place of glory.

By dividing a mystery in two in order to unite us with you, you placed an interval of forty days between the resurrection and the ascension, so that we could be with you all that time, thus dividing, through your love, that which the nature of reality and ultimate reality should be joining together, that is to say, the state of glory and the place of glory. O love whose nature and effects in Jesus are so unusual! For the nature of love itself is to unite, and the nature of divine love is to lift up to heaven. On the contrary, the nature of love in Jesus is to divide and draw Jesus to earth.

O Jesus, love draws you out of the bosom of the Father and leads you outside, as you yourself state, to live in a foreign nature and land. You express it this way: *I came forth from the Father and I came into the world* (Jn 16:28). Love separates your human nature from the human person to offer it to another Person, who is infinitely removed from its rightful nature and condition. During your earthly life love separates glory from the state of glory and the glory of the soul from the glory of the body. Through a peculiar exercise, love separates this divinized soul from this divinized body. Nevertheless, they were joined together not only by a natural relationship, as in us, but much more powerfully by their Divinity, in which they remain united in their state of separation. And now that God reunites this divinized soul and body by the mystery of the resurrection and gives the body the glory that is its due, love separates the essence and state of glory from the place of glory, and so on.

O love that divides and no longer unites! What a separation you cause between such worthy and powerful subjects! In a clearly excellent way you separate the Son from the Father, by a foreign nature, even though their own nature joins them in a unity of essence! You separate human nature from human subsistence, and yet it is in itself and in all other instances the normal term and substantial fulfillment of that nature! You separate glory from the state of glory, the state of glory from the place of glory. Yet these realities are supreme, divine and supernatural. They are divinely united and in every other instance, except in you alone, they are inseparably joined together!

This is the remarkable difference between love in God and love in Jesus. For love in God unifies, but love in Jesus separates. Love in

155

God goes so far as to create an essential unity. Love in Jesus creates an essential separation, dividing the human essence from the human person; the glorified essence from the place of glory; the divinized soul from the divinized body, which are two essences joined together by nature, grace and glory! O Jesus, may this love that is in you, be in us! May this love that acts in you, act in us. May this love that triumphs over you, triumph over us. May this love that creates separation and division in you, divide and separate in us. May it separate us from sin, the earth and ourselves so that we may live for you. May this love absorb us in you, draw us to you and fill us with you.

I see that this separating love creates, establishes and accompanies three sorts of life in you. Allow me to contemplate and adore you in these three lives and in the three moments when you enter these three lives. They are the three lives to which all human and angelic life should be dedicated. They are the three precious moments to which every moment of our mortality and our eternity should be consecrated.

There is the moment of the Incarnation, when Jesus begins to be Jesus and to live with an uncreated life. The Word begins a new and incarnate life, a divine and human life, a divinely human and humanly divine life. There is the moment of his pilgrimage and life of merit, when the soul of Jesus is united to a body capable of suffering and to the life of glory at the same time. Through this arrangement Jesus possesses a new type of life. It is a life that is his alone, a life that is the origin of our eternal life! It is a life of glory and suffering! It is a life that unites and joins two very distinct states in the same soul, through a miracle performed in Jesus Christ by Jesus Christ himself. It is accomplished in him alone and continues for thirty-four years on earth![17]

There is the moment of his celestial and fully glorious life when Jesus is victorious in life, glory, and immortality. It is a life without suffering and without mortality! It is life that is nothing but life and nothing but glory! It is a life that will last eternally! From these three moments originate three lives. These three lives have three distinct dwelling places, in which we must adore the sacred humanity of Jesus. O moment! O dwelling places! O adorable life! This should occupy our thoughts and be the center of our activities. It will be the object of our eternity.

Allow me to behold you, O Jesus, in these three moments! Allow me to adore you in these three lives! Allow me to contemplate you in these three dwelling places! For God is your abode and your retreat in these three lives. God receives you in his bosom, his love and his glory. You are in the bosom of the Father by your eternal birth. It is there in the fullness of time that your divine Person brings forth and lifts up your humanity. It is there that the mystery of the Incarnation is discussed, is resolved and is established.

There God is man and man is God. There the soul and the humanity of Jesus subsist with the Divinity. There the only Son of God, who dwells in the bosom of the Father, also dwells in this humanity. There this humanity possesses its being only in uncreated being and possesses its life, its subsistence and its state in a Person produced in the bosom of the Father and who dwells in the bosom of the Father, inseparable from the bosom of the Father. There this man called Jesus is at the right hand of the Father by his power; in the bosom of the Father through his subsistence; and lives and dwells forever in the Divinity.

In truth, the Word spent an eternity without this humanity, but will also spend an eternity with it. There was never a moment when the Word did not behold in his divine essence, as in a perfect mirror, that human nature; beholding it as a nature that would be his for an eternity. There was never a moment when he did not behold it in this way. For his contemplation and his love of our humanity is an eternal contemplation and love. From all eternity, he beholds it as his own essence, which will be one day and forever one of his essences, and as the being which he wishes to perfect and fulfill with his own subsistence.

O divine gaze! O eternal gaze! O gaze full of love and honor! O gaze that should draw our gaze, our love and our homage toward that humanity, which God beholds eternally and unceasingly as his own, and which we should look upon as our own. It is ours through a gift of the Father, through the activity of the Holy Spirit, through the subsistence of the Son, which was given him so that he might accomplish our salvation. Finally it is ours through the power of the cross and his death, which consumed him for us in sacrifice and holocaust.

[SECOND PART OF THE DISCOURSE ON THE STATE AND GRANDEURS OF JESUS IN WHICH BEGINS]

The Life of Jesus

The Rare Conduct of God
Toward the Virgin

[6, 1, p. 456]

To consider his conduct toward the most exalted and rarest person who will ever live in dependence on him is to give homage to the Most High. Also to consider the condition of the one whom heaven ordains to be his mother is to honor Jesus. To speak of Mary is to speak of Jesus, for they are closely united together and she is the grandest object of his grace and the rarest effect of his power. Therefore, let us spend time reflecting on such a splendid subject.

When God held his first deliberations in the world after the creation of man and his sin, he spoke of Mary and set her in opposition to the serpent, the source of the curse of the universe. From then on God and the world have considered her the source of blessing for the world. At the time decreed by divine wisdom, she entered the world through a miracle, like a work of grace, not of nature; like a result of prayer, not of sin; like a special subject of God's power, not of human power. She receives from God more graces, more favors, more privileges than all the saints together.

While on earth she already bore in her soul a higher grace and a

159

nobler grace than that which triumphs in heaven. God had but one temple on earth, and he hid her in it from her childhood. And he does more. God exalts, guides, cherishes and hides her in himself. He himself, O most holy Virgin, is your temple and your sanctuary (just as he is in the heavenly Jerusalem, of which it is written that the Lamb is its temple). For you were to be also one day his temple, the living temple of a God living in the world. Therefore God conceals this chosen person in himself, like a treasure that he keeps for himself through the mystery and uniqueness of her election; for he destined her to be his mother.

The Virgin's Occupation With Jesus Is Ravishing and Perpetual

[28, 1, pp. 512-16]

. . . Let us see what [the Son of God] is and what he does in his Blessed Mother. For she is the one who is the closest and the most united to him by the state of this new mystery accomplished in her and through her. This is the first period of Jesus' stay in the Virgin. These are two subjects important enough to be considered. Therefore let us say that strictly speaking, after the divine Persons, there is no other person to whom the Son of God is more closely bound than to the Virgin.

Moreover this bond imitates and adores the bond he has with the divine Persons. He is united to his Father through birth and nature, and he is united to the Virgin through nature and birth. He is joined to the Holy Spirit as to its origin since he is its source in eternity. He is united to the Virgin through production and the infusion of a Spirit in her spirit, which is the life of her life and the soul of her soul. He is the source of her grace. For all grace in the Virgin originates from the highest grace and the mysteries of Jesus. Thus he is joined to her through both nature and grace.

The bond that he has with the divine Persons is eternal. The one he has with the Virgin is new and quite recent. However, it will be for all eternity. This holy Virgin is and will be always the Mother of Jesus. She will possess that attribute in heaven as well as on earth, and he will honor her eternally in her condition as Mother of God. However, we see tangibly that in this present state she is closer and more united to him while he is in her and is a part of her; while she lives for him and he lives through her; while he is in a constant state of dependence and even neediness toward her.

He is in her in a variety of ways according to his various attributes. It is pleasant to consider them more than once. The period of this mystery invites us to reflect carefully on it often. For it is the period when he is and will be nine months in the Virgin. He is in her as a son is in his mother, drawing his life from her. He is in her as her son and her God, giving life to her as he receives life from her. He is in her as in his earthly paradise. For everything in the Virgin is holy and delightful. Even the darkness of sin is not there and never was.

Jesus finds in her his peace and his delight. Outside of her he meets only sinners and sin. Being in her is like being in heaven. For he experiences life and glory, seeing God and enjoying his divine Essence. He is in her as in a temple where he praises and adores God; where he offers his respects to the eternal Father, not only for himself but for every creature. It is a holy and sacred temple where Jesus dwells, the true ark of the true covenant.

It is the first and holiest temple of Jesus. The heart of the Virgin is the first altar on which Jesus offered his heart, body and spirit as a host of perpetual praise; and where Jesus offers his first sacrifice, making the first and perpetual oblation of himself, through which, as we have said, we are all made holy. Thus Jesus is in the Virgin. In her he finds his peace, his paradise, his highest heaven, his temple, his mother.

In this state and during this period the Virgin is a sanctuary where there are more wonders than have existed in heaven up to that time; a Man-God, a Word-Child, a Child-God, a suffering body united to a glorified soul, a humanly divine life and a divinely human life, a Spirit regulating all the bodies and spirits of the universe; a unique order, the order of the hypostatic union, an order superior to every order of nature, of grace and of glory. These are the wonders that are in the Virgin, not in heaven, and that make her particularly venerable to us.

Let us think of her and think of what she is. Let us contemplate Jesus in this state, fully in the Virgin as her center and her heart, or rather like a rising sun. According to the prophets, a sun covered with a light cloud, that is with the blessed Virgin, who hides him still from the earth and will hide him for nine months.

Mathematicians claim that there are stars surrounding the sun, which is their center. They revolve around it, just as the sun revolves around the earth. May it please God that we might be one of those stars revolving around Jesus, rather than around ourselves, as we do on a daily basis. We must forget ourselves in this so that we might remember only Jesus and the Virgin. Thus he is a sun and the Virgin is a planet that revolves around Jesus, around this glorious sun. She revolves only around him. He is her center. He is her circumference. It seems that she encloses and brings to perfection his greatness and his power. He looks at her unceasingly from every angle. She is directed only toward him.

He draws her to himself. He enraptures her with himself. These two hearts of Jesus and Mary, so closely united by nature, are even much more united and more intimate through grace. They live in one another. But who could proclaim this life? It is described in heaven. We must wait until this book is opened for us to behold the favors and tendernesses, the raptures and wonders that are narrated there. While we await this grace, we will stammer rather than speak of these great realities: that Jesus, being so united to his Mother, attracts and enraptures her in himself continuously; that just as he is being born, is living and is producing in his Father an uncreated love who is the third Person of the Trinity, in the same way, as he is being born and living in his Mother, he produces in her a Spirit and a love that indeed is created, yet does not and never will have an equal after his own.

Just as Jesus' first involvement was with his Father, his second involvement is with his Blessed Mother. He chose her. He prepared her for such great things, so united to him. She is the most worthy object of his thoughts after the divine Persons. She is the subject most amenable to his influence and activity. She is closest to his holy presence. Yet he is joined to her in a state of dependence, since he is her Son and she is his Mother and since he is now living in her and living through her. He wished to share the mystery of the Incarnation with her, by drawing forth from her this body with which he is clothed and by willing that, as his Mother, she was involved through her cooperation in this work, which is incomparably greater than the creation of the world.

He still shares his ongoing nascent life with her. For the life of Jesus is needy and begs for life from the Virgin. He is in this condition and shares in this blessed way with her for nine months without reneging for a single moment. And after this he will offer her a share in his greatest works on earth and in souls. Such a great and blessed sharing between Jesus and Mary! For the time being he is not involved with anyone other than his Father and the Virgin. Saint John will have his opportunity for a while and Saint Joseph after, but now it is the Father alone and the Virgin alone who belong to Jesus, who is devoted to them, delights in them and communes with them.

He does great things in her, which are worthy of him and worthy of her. We have no way of measuring their extent. We are not as fortunate as the angel of the Apocalypse who has a rod of gold in his hand to measure the temple (Rv 21:15). The Virgin is a greater and more august temple. Only her Son has in hand the measure to take the dimensions. We have only to admire, not to judge and speak of things that surpass so mightily our intelligence. All we can say is that he is her Son and she is his Mother.

Now is the time when this human filiation begins for the Son of God and this divine motherhood begins for the Virgin. The Son of God treats her, contemplates her, cherishes her and honors her as the Mother of God, as his Mother. This divine motherhood is such a holy attribute that she approaches God, that she attains, according to the great doctors of the School, *the very boundaries of the Godhead,* that she reaches into infinity itself, that she is counted among those incomprehensible realities and we cannot fathom what is hers because of this attribute.

May Jesus, who knows this infinite dignity and whose greatness is the cause and the source of this infiniteness, honor her motherhood as it deserves. He honors himself in honoring his Mother, because she is his Mother. He honors her to the extent of his wisdom and power. He employs his sublime thoughts and heavenly creativity on a subject so worthy of him and close to him, in which he has so large a part and so great an interest.

With these thoughts, dispositions and foundations, let us undertake the study of this first involvement of Jesus with the Virgin and of the Virgin with Jesus.

[28, 2, pp. 516–17]

Let us say then that for four-thousand years there has never been an undertaking like the Incarnation. Furthermore, since the world has been in existence there has never been a more remarkable time than this, when the Son of God becomes the Son of Man and a Virgin becomes the Mother of God. It is the time of delights promised by the prophets, when heaven sends down dew, when the clouds rain down the just one and the earth, watered from heaven, opens to sprout the Savior (Is 45:8). It is the time of the greatest, most blessed and most helpful production of all time.

It is the time when heaven and earth cooperate together to generate the wondrous effort of presenting the Holy of Holies to the world, which is in such great need of it. It is the fullness of time, according to the apostles. It is the time of universal salvation and of heavenly delight on earth, when we can behold and adore the marvels that are on earth and are not in heaven. This moment, which is so blessed, so remarkable and so delightful, takes place in Nazareth and involves only Jesus and the Virgin. The rest of the earth has no part in it. The more alone they are, the more this solitude is splendid and noteworthy, the more the subject of their solitude engages them given its importance, and the more their mutual involvement is profound and fills them with delight.

Thus Jesus is involved with the Virgin and only with the Virgin at this time. The Virgin is involved with Jesus and she is the only one in the whole world involved with Jesus. Thus she is the only one in the whole world adoring the mystery of the Incarnation, which was brought about on earth for the earth but unknown to the earth. She is the only one adoring Jesus. The more that she is the only one captivated by such a great subject, the greater is her involvement. She is devoted to it with all her faculties. All her senses are brought to bear on it, for it is a tangible mystery and tangible within her. All her senses should pay homage to her God made tangible for human nature. Her whole mind is concentrated on it. And the Spirit of Jesus, which enlivens this little divinized body, enlivens the spirit and body of the Virgin as well, through grace, love and a holy, gentle influence.

This Spirit of Jesus is more powerful and more active in the spirit and body of the Virgin than the Virgin's own spirit. The most eminent and exalted grace, infused in the Virgin, captivates and absorbs all the senses, all the faculties and the entire spirit of the Virgin for this great object; an object intimately present and well-proportioned to this same grace. For the Virgin's grace is not like our own. It is a grace that is quite unique and belongs to her alone. It is a grace that from its beginning reached out toward the mystery of the Incarnation as toward its goal, its origin and its exemplar.

It is a newly infused grace, now attaining its fulfillment, its principal outcome in the Virgin and its present fulfillment in this mystery of the Incarnation. It is a grace totally binding Jesus to the Virgin and the Virgin to Jesus. In the same way that ordinary grace binds us to God, so this type of special grace also binds the incarnate God to the Virgin and the Virgin to the incarnate God. This grace which is so unique to this mystery produces a unique result in the Virgin, and she is absorbed in such a great, exalted and powerful way in Jesus, living in her, that we cannot express it. Thus grace and nature conspire in her to create an eminent disposition by which her heart and mind are totally enraptured by her Son and her God.

Besides this movement, a very powerful movement of nature and grace, Jesus himself is present and active. Without any intermediary he draws her mind and heart into this involvement. He is present in her. He is powerful in her. He is active in her. She is perfectly disposed to welcome his holy activity and to welcome it in all its power and fullness. These are the first fruits of Jesus' activity in Mary his Mother. Thus as Jesus produces his first works on earth and his first effects in the Virgin Mary, he draws her to himself and totally enraptures her.

What tenderness! What love! What favors from this Son to this Mother and from this Mother to this Son at the very beginning of their love and their mutual enjoyment! It is a perpetual rapture. For the object is always there and the power of attraction is always operative. It is like heaven where rapture is perpetual, for the object is always present and always perceived. In this state, also, the object is always present, always tangible, always active. Besides the Virgin is rooted not in some accidental reality, but in a state of perpetual rapture toward a subject perpetually worthy of such rapture.

We do not have the capacity for this state on earth. However the Virgin does, and we should not judge her by ourselves. The type of unique grace conferred upon her disposes her to this state and to something even greater, since it disposes her to be the worthy Mother of God. Her life is exalted and freed from the weakness of the senses and the human spirit in her relationship to holy and heavenly things. She is liberated from the disproportion between nature and grace, which is the cause of the weakness and the loss of consciousness that happens during the raptures of the holiest souls on earth. She is even rooted in the strength and power of celestial grace, which is capable of great effort without being weakened in the least. Thus she is living an earthly life. She is rapt with heavenly delights. Her rapture is without end and what is more, her human life is not weakened by divine contemplation.

Jesus' Occupations in the Virgin
Regarding the Virgin

[29, 1, pp. 517–19]

Such is the Virgin's state of rapture. It is in keeping with her grandeur and her permanent and ordinary state of contemplation. Jesus is the object of this rapture. He is the source of it, as we have just said, for he is the one who creates it. However, he is the object as well. Do we need proof to persuade Christians of this truth? Is it not enough simply to present it to noble souls in order to persuade them of it? Is not Jesus, newly dwelling in and through the Virgin, a worthy and reasonable object for the Virgin, especially in this holy moment as he begins to draw life from her and in her? Thus during this blessed time Jesus occupies and converses with the Virgin; converses about himself and delights her with himself.

In Jesus there are several aspects worthy of causing his Blessed Mother to delight in him. However, in my opinion, what holds her attention now and enraptures her is this new work brought about on earth and in her, the mystery of the Incarnation. It is the natural or rather supernatural state of her Son in her. This is the first object of this first rapture, which Jesus causes on earth in the Virgin's heart. Oh, how she recognized this state! Oh, how she fathomed this mystery! Oh, how she lived and was absorbed in it! It was her life and in a way, she lost her own life and personal subsistence in order to live in him who is life itself and her life as well.

However this type of life and rapture, which the Virgin experienced in her Son, is almost as hidden from us as is the life of the Word in this very humanity. Faced with such splendid things we possess only darkness, not light. Some think that from that moment the Virgin was elevated to the clear vision of the divine Essence and the Person of the incarnate Word within her. Certainly if this grace was granted to some others on earth (there are some doctors who ascribe it to Moses and Saint Paul), then there would be no doubt about giving it to the Virgin and even to give it to her in this blessed moment when God humbles himself in her and exalts her in himself, uniting her to him so intimately through this great mystery.

Even if this grace were not given to Moses or Saint Paul, the Virgin certainly has many privileges that are reserved for her alone. Furthermore, the moment of this new mystery deserves such great, singular and new privileges that the Virgin can be given what is given to no one else. In this moment of the Virgin's life she could be given what was not given during another period of her life on earth.

There are reasons for pursuing this line of thought this far. However to go further and to inquire whether these favors and privileges included even the enjoyment of the Divinity, this is a secret of Jesus' activity in his Blessed Mother that is not revealed to us. I would prefer to reverence it rather than fathom it. I should prefer to remain unaware of it rather than confirm it.

Therefore, humbly ignorant of this specific aspect, we can say that whatever she might have seen, even if she did not see the Person of the incarnate Word in her, this divine Person possesses the Virgin and the Virgin possesses this divine Person incarnate in her with such a rare and singular possession, proper to her alone, that we have no pen to write about it, no tongue to speak about it, no heart to sense it and no mind to understand it. It is too much grace for us to dare think about it and to reverence it. It is such a great and perfect possession. It is such a powerful and intimate communication. It is such an exalted and elevated joy, even in the order of miraculous and special grace, that if it does not go any further and does not allow the Virgin to see this divine Person who has just become flesh within her, at least it abundantly fills her soul and occupies such an exalted place among the divine operations and such a rare privilege among the favors of the incarnate Word that there has never been and never will be anything like it.

Stuttering rather than speaking, this is what we can say about things that so greatly surpass the human mind and even the angelic mind. These are the first thoughts of the incarnate Word. This is the first conversation of Jesus in the Virgin. This is the Virgin's first contemplation, or better yet, this is the Virgin's first ecstasy before the Son of God made Son of Man in her.

PIERRE DE BÉRULLE

[29, 2, pp. 519-22]

However, she has in this same instant yet another reason to be captivated, to be rapt in Jesus who is alive and active within her. It is the first movement of the interior life of Jesus toward his Father. This object is different from the one we have just described. This contemplation is different from the one in which the Virgin was totally focused on the state of Jesus in himself and on the depths of the mystery of the Incarnation. For in this instance, she is not rapt and captivated by the state, but by the actions of Jesus himself and by the first interior, spiritual actions of Jesus' soul dealing with God his Father.

For this divine child, who is without a name as yet, is not inactive. He is not idle. He is not prevented from acting interiorly by his infancy, which limits his body, but does not limit and impede his spirit. He sees. He is alert and active. This is the interior and spiritual life of Jesus. And this life is worthy of enrapturing heaven and earth. For now it enraptures the Virgin, who is captivated in a holy way by her Son and by the states and activities of her Son. The life of her Son is her life. And Jesus' contemplation is her original and principal contemplation.

For if the Virgin did not possess the divine light, which reveals the divine Essence, at least she possessed the angelic light, which reveals to her the soul of Jesus and its sacred activities. This was her light, her grandeur and her happiness on earth. It was one of her principal activities and she began to experience in this moment a very holy knowledge and a very exalted contemplation. Thus she contemplates the life and activity of Jesus within her. This is the Virgin's book, which her Son opens for her, just as he opens it in heaven, according to the Apocalypse (Rv 5 and 6).

In this book, she sees the dealings of Jesus with his Father. She sees the praise, the adoration, the gifts, the offering that he makes of himself to God his Father and all the dimensions of this splendid reality; the life and the dealings of the Son with the Father and the Father with the Son, who is incarnate in the world for the glory of his Father. Thus the Virgin comes to know his secrets, since they take place within her. She is the living royal council where the Son deals secretly with the eternal Father.

Happily, she leaves behind her own thoughts and her interior spiritual life to enter into the thoughts of Jesus, into the interior life of Jesus. She enters the love and adoration Jesus offers his Father. She enters the obligations and actions of Jesus. She surrenders the use of her own interior life into the profound depth of the new interior life of her Son. Up to this point, the spiritual life of the Virgin had been most splendid. The Holy Spirit had trained her in a good school, but now it is something quite different. She enters a new school where the Son of God draws her into himself and the knowledge of his activities toward God his Father.

She bears the impression of and a share in his divine actions. She exists not through her own light and love, but through the light, love and activity of Jesus who draws her into union with himself. He also draws her out of herself and her own interior actions so that she might live in him and be the bearer of his holy activities through a sort of gentle, exalted and powerful impression by which the Mother is enraptured by her Son, the Virgin by Jesus. Thus Jesus is living in the Virgin and hers is the first soul in which he established his life. The Virgin's proper role is to be attentive to the interior and spiritual life of her Son and to be a pure capacity for Jesus, filled with Jesus.

The Virgin was so careful, as the gospel teaches us on two occasions, to gather up the actions and words of other people regarding her Son and to preserve them in her heart, not allowing a single word about such a great reality to fall to earth: *Mary kept every word* (*every*, it says), *reflecting on them in her heart* (Lk 2:19). How much more then should she be attentive to the interior and divine actions of her Son, which, although the world cannot see them, her insight made known to her? They are so much more excellent because their source is of greater worth. They can be imprinted only in the sacred heart and the divinized spirit of Jesus. Therefore the Virgin is enraptured by Jesus and doubly delighted by him; delighted, I say, by his state within her and by the interior exercises of his Spirit, while he lives in her. For this is the most worthy object that exists after the Godhead itself.

Nevertheless, it is necessary that I discover some humiliation in the midst of these grandeurs, bitterness among the sweetness. I would wrong the author of these mysteries and the truth of this story if I did not present it as it is; if I did not describe truthfully what is happening, either in the state of the Son or in the state of the Blessed Mother. I must not omit, therefore, that in the midst of these grandeurs to which the Virgin is exalted, that in these raptures where she is established, I discover there the cross and humiliation. For our mysteries are for God himself both cross and humiliation.

It is reasonable that these two realities, which are appropriated to the Creator, be attributed to this creature and be spread through all the states of her life on earth. Thus the Virgin shares in the cross and humiliation. What is most remarkable is that she shares in them even on the day of her grandeurs and her greatest exaltation.

Since she is the first to share in Jesus, she is the first as well to share in the cross and the humiliation of Jesus. Her participation is unique and is suitable only to her, as we shall see later. The blessed Virgin's participation in this cross and humiliation does not flow from the requirement of sin like us, nor from its claim on her Son who bears our sins, for he is the only one to carry this burden, but from a law of love and union with her son. For one of the effects of love is this mutual sharing of attributes with one another.

Thus the Virgin is too united with her Son not to conform to and resemble him. She is too close to him and too intimate to be ignorant of his state and his secrets. She knows what goes on between his Father and him. She knows he has taken on the condition of host-victim[18] and that he already bears the marks and effects within her. Because of this condition, Jesus experiences a state of humiliation within his divine state. This humiliation pierces the heart of Mary and humbles her as well. And as a result of the state of her Son, she bears similarly a type of abasement and humiliation within the very state of her divine Motherhood.

Jesus, being the Son of God, is treated as the Son of Man, and even as God's victim for men. He is conceived, will be born and will live according to that humble state, exposed to suffering. Thus just as the Son of God is humbled in this state of his new human filiation, so also the Virgin experiences a condition of humiliation in the sublime state of divine Motherhood. The privileges due to both the Son and the Mother are reserved for heaven. Earth is not worthy to experience them.

She should have begot him as immortal. She begot him as mortal. He should have been born from her as he was born from the tomb, full of glory and splendor. She begot him vulnerable to our lowliness and misery. She should have begot him in paradise, in heaven, in the bosom of the Father. For he is his Son and will be one day elevated to the throne at the right hand, in the bosom of the Godhead. She begot him in Nazareth and gave birth to him in Bethlehem, in a stable on hay and straw.

She recognizes the greatness of her Son and her own as well in relationship to her Son. She knows the Father's plan to humble his Son and the Son's plan to humble himself. She embraces these plans and agrees to be the humiliated Mother of the humiliated Son. Now this is the place and the time where she becomes aware of these truths and begins to accept the humiliation destined for her Son and for herself, for her Son's human filiation and for her divine Motherhood.

For it is in Nazareth, in this birth of Jesus in her, in this moment that these things are accomplished. They are known to her, born in her and experienced by her according to the splendor of her knowledge, the strength of her love and the vitality of her sensitivity toward divine reality and the things of her Son and her God.

Elevation to Jesus Christ our Lord Concerning the Conduct of His Spirit and His Grace Toward Saint Magdalene[19]

[1, 1, p. 554]

During your time on earth, O Jesus, my Lord, during your blessed association with the world for three years as Messiah of Judah and Savior of the world, you performed many miracles, you conferred a number of graces and you chose to attract many souls to you! However the rarest choice of your love, the worthiest object of your favor, the masterpiece of your grace is Magdalene and you performed the greatest of your miracles for her.

[1, 2, p. 554]

It was for her that you raised Lazarus, granting the greatest of your wondrous works to her tears. It was as if you wished that the most brilliant moment of your power be at the service of your greatest love and that her brother receive in his body your most miraculous deed just as she herself was your greatest miracle in souls and the rarest result of your favors.

PIERRE DE BÉRULLE

[1, 3, p. 554]

On earth you were a hidden God, as your prophets said, *Truly God is hidden, God the Savior of Israel* (Is 45:15). As such, you had two natures, one invisible and divine and the other human and visible. And just as man created in your image is composed of two substances, one spiritual and the other corporal, so you also, O Man-God, you are composed of two beings, one divine and the other human; one created, the other uncreated; one visible to our mortal eyes, the other invisible even to the angels unless they have been raised up into glory. In that state you are a rare object, totally divine, totally miraculous, revealed to men and adored by angels. Being an excellent craftsman, you wished to perform two types of miracles as well. Some are interior and visible to the angels. Others are exterior and visible to men. In his body Lazarus bore the greatest of your exterior and tangible miracles. In her soul Magdalene bore one of the greatest of your interior and invisible miracles through the hidden operation of your Spirit in her heart and soul. One of these miracles delights men, and the other delights the angels.

[1, 4, pp. 554–55]

During your pilgrimage on earth, working wonders, O Lord, you noticed many souls, but your gentlest gaze, O Sun of Justice, and your most powerful rays fell on this soul! You lifted her from death to life, from vanity to truth, from the creature to the Creator, from herself to yourself. You poured out your Spirit in her spirit and in an instant you loosed in her soul a torrent of tears, which flowed onto your feet, watered them and created a salvific bath, which washed, in a holy and unctuous way, the sinful soul who was shedding them. In an instant you gave her such an abundant grace that she began where others hardly finish. From the first step of her conversion she was at the height of perfection, experiencing such an exalted love that she deserved to receive praise from your sacred lips, when you chose to protect her from her opponents and complete her defense with this lovely word, *She has loved much* (Lk 7:47).

[1, 5, pp. 555–56]

Such a great and remarkable word on the lips of the eternal Word! Tell us, Lord! Is love the lot of this soul from the first moment of her conversion? And your love, that is to say the sacred love of Jesus, is it the lot of this sinful woman? A unique and new love; a love that begins on earth and not in heaven, but begins here for both earth and heaven; love that is shaped at your feet and creates from then on a new difference in the order of grace and in the order of love; a love that is more than seraphic. There is in you a new being that establishes a new state in the realm of created and even uncreated reality. You are a new life in the universe, and you are as well a new source of grace and a new object of love. You are most worthy to be a new subject of a new order of love in the universe.

This new order begins on earth, not like the angelic orders, which began in heaven. For this order is related to the Incarnation, which also begins on earth, not in heaven. This order is linked to the time of this sacred mystery and to the presence of Jesus on earth. This new order is reserved for Magdalene, and you wish to give her the primacy in this order and in this love. This is the moment when you ignite its flames in her heart. The sacred fire of this love is born in the waters that flow from the eyes of this humble sinner and most blessed penitent, whom I see glued to your feet and enraptured by you.

How is it that this new love is not yet in heaven, but it is on earth? It is not in the Seraphim, but it is in the heart of this humble and prostrate penitent? It is because she is at your feet and these feet are nobler than the highest heavens. It is right that this new order of grace and love begins to take shape in such a worthy place, which I revere and adore, for I should not even adore the highest heavens, since they are so inferior to the feet of the Son of God on earth. But does this soul need to be raised up for this love? She is a sinful woman, Lord, but she is at your feet. In such a holy and adorable place there is nothing but great dignity and holiness in her. Also you do not at all mention her sins. You only speak of her love. For love has already covered her offenses. You only mention her tears, her fragrances, her love and her care in kissing, washing and wiping your feet.

If the petty thoughts of the Pharisee require that you bring up her past life, you cover it with a word that simply pays honor to her love, attributing to it the remission of her faults: *Many sins,* you say, *are forgiven her, for she has loved much.* Even the counsel to sin no more, given elsewhere, is not given to her here, as if that would be superfluous, given the strength and power of her love. This soul is so covered with her tears and her heart so dissolved in love that nothing but love is visible there, except to the disdainful Pharisee who can neither see the love nor the soul.

Thus love, the love of Jesus is the lot of Magdalene. From that moment on it is the lot of this holy, blessed and glorious soul. From then on she even exists in that love. For Lord, you do not simply say *that she loves,* but *that she has loved and that she has loved much.* O wonder! O grandeur! O uniqueness of the love that dwells in the heart and spirit of this despised penitent woman. The Pharisee disdained her and it seemed, Lord, that you did not notice her. Nevertheless, her love was great. It was great from the first moment of her soul's birth into your grace and love. She has just arrived at your feet, and at these divine feet she makes such great progress that her love deserves to be called great even by him who is love and greatness itself. It was the first moment of her life in grace.

Nevertheless, O Jesus, my Lord, you weigh all things and hold in your hand the weight of the sanctuary as you weigh this soul and her love. You do not say *that she loves,* but *that she has loved and that she has loved much,* as if she had been doing it for many days, months or years. But an instant of this soul is worth a century, because she is so alive and powerful in grace and fervent in love. In her abasement at your feet, she experiences such exalted and powerful prayer that in very little time she makes remarkable progress in the sacred school of your love.

May God grant that the whole of my life be equal to one of these moments, and that after all the years of a long and strenuous life, I might share somewhat in this level of love with which she began and about which you chose to state *that she has loved much.* O soul! O love! O sinner! O penitent! O Jesus, the source of repentance, grace and love!

The Blessed Time Spent by the Son of God on Earth

[2, 1, p. 557]

How blessed is the time of Jesus' life and sojourn on earth! It is a time of mystery and wonders. It is a desirable and salvific time. It is the springtime of grace and salvation. It is the fullness of time, as the

scriptures say. It is during this time that the greatest and most wondrous things were to be accomplished, in honor of the presence of a
God, nascent and alive, a God walking and communing, a God
speaking and acting on the earth. Let earth rise and rejoice and let
heaven humble itself in amazement before the vision and nobility of
this truth. There are greater wonders on earth than in heaven. For
you are on earth, O Jesus, my Lord, and you are not yet in heaven,
and still you are the God of heaven and earth. In heaven I behold
angels. I admire both their grace and their glory. However, I behold a
Man-God on earth and in him I see a grace that is the source of grace
and a glory that is the living source of glory.

The angels, dwelling in heaven, possess an existence that is excellent, but nevertheless created. This new man, dwelling on earth, is a
new living reality, author of life and life itself. He is a divine composite of created and uncreated being, composed of two very different
beings, yet very much joined together. One is divinized by the other,
and the other cannot be defiled by the created, human and abject
being that we see. In that lowliness there is an incomparable grandeur
and in that poverty an inestimable treasure, a treasure that earth alone
possessed at that time and that heaven itself sought and adored on
earth. If we need to value the earth, let us value and love it only
because the Son of God became incarnate on earth and not in heaven.

It is earth that beholds and carries this Man-God. Heaven does not
yet hold him. Earth is honored by his presence, bears the imprint of
his steps, is taught by his word, sprinkled by his blood and honored
by his mysteries; a worthy reason for valuing earth more than heaven.
Thus this Man-God, this new citizen of the earth honors the earth in
which he was born, gives it privileges worthy of his birth and desires
to perform greater works on earth than had been previously accomplished in heaven. He even chooses to repair on earth what was lost
in heaven and to repair it in a more excellent way, which is worthy of
the incarnate Word, worthy of the noble thoughts of eternal wisdom
clothed with our humanity, worthy of the eminent ways of him who
is the way, the life and the truth.

[2, 2, pp. 557-58]

In heaven the greatest degree of love that had been created was lost
through the loss of the first angel to whom it had been given. And it is
on earth that this love lost in heaven must be restored. It is at the feet

of Jesus that this love must be restored. It must be restored to a higher degree and in a more excellent manner, so as to honor the mystery of love, which is the Incarnation, and to give honor to the triumph of love, who is Jesus. For he is the love of heaven and of earth, the love of angels and of men, the love of the eternal Father. He is his beloved Son in whom he takes the greatest pleasure.

I welcome gladly this thought, which honors Jesus and the sacred mystery of the Incarnation. It is the mystery of mysteries. Its splendor and dignity easily convince us that the grace that flows from it surpasses that which existed before it took effect, whether in the earthly paradise or in the heavenly paradise. Neither man nor angels have received anything similar to the great and precious realities (thus the first of the apostles calls them) that have been prepared for us in Jesus Christ our Lord. It is an incomparable grace. The angels in their glory admire and revere it, and they seek no other rank than as servants of this grace. The love based in this new grace, which depends on the Man-God, surpasses the infused love of the angels in heaven and rekindles on earth a greater fire of love than the one which was extinguished in heaven.

I am not speaking here of the Virgin. Her love and her grace suffer no comparison. Her dignity as Mother makes her too close to the Creator to be compared to that angel or to all the angels together. She is their ruler and not their companion. She holds a superior position over all the creatures of both heaven and earth. This excess of love, splendor and dignity that belongs to her and that surpasses the thoughts of both men and angels must never be understood in the categories of sin and grace. In all this she is the exception, even if she is not expressly named. In all this her privileges remain. Thus without prejudice to the Virgin, and even with homage to the Son and the Mother of God, let us continue our thoughts and pursue our discussion of the love lost in heaven and restored on earth.

This love is dignified in being restored by Jesus. Jesus is honored in that it is restored by himself on earth, during his humiliation rather than at the time of his power and glory. It is easy for me to believe that this heavenly love should be restored by Jesus on earth, that this divine handiwork should be accomplished at his feet, in order to honor the love and humiliation of Jesus on earth. But to whom should fall this blessed lot? The gospel notes and portrays for us that Magdalene was frequently and devotedly at the feet of Jesus.

She begins that way in the home of the Pharisee. She continues in the same way in the home of Martha, her sister, and in the home of Simeon the Leper in Bethany. She ends that way at the foot of the cross and later at the tomb in the presence of Jesus appearing as the gardener. Everywhere we see her at the sacred feet of Jesus. It is her dwelling place and her lot. It is her love and her constant occupation. It is what identifies her and distinguishes her in grace. Furthermore, she is the one who collects at his sacred feet the celestial dew and the divine love lost in heaven. Jesus is the one who restores it and pours it into her heart while she is at his feet.

The Words of the Angels and Jesus, at the Tomb, to Magdalene

[7, 4, pp. 582–83]

There [in the scriptures] I discover that the first person you visited in your new life and in your state of glory was the Magdalene. There I discover that the first word you uttered in that blessed state was addressed to her and concerned her tears and her grief. *Woman, why are you weeping?* (Jn 20:15). There I find that the first name your sacred lips pronounced in your glory was her name, that sweet name of Mary, which enlightens her, which makes her recognize her Lord, which makes her fall at his feet, which restores life to her and fills her with joy and with new love.

When you were born in Bethlehem, Lord, indeed it was your holy Mother whom your mortal eyes first beheld. However, you did not speak to her. You did not at all utter her name, which is the same name, Mary, even though this name, in her, was dedicated to innocence, to divine Motherhood and to an eminent grace that has never had any equal. Nevertheless, you did not utter it, and you remained in the sacred silence and powerlessness of your infancy.

When you were reborn, Lord, from the tomb into your life of glory, the first gaze and the first view of your immortal eyes, glorious and as brilliant as the sun, was of the Magdalene. Your first words were to Magdalene. The first name you pronounced was her name, the name Mary, the name dedicated, in her, to love and penance. The first commission you gave and, if I can speak this way, the first Bull and Patent that you officially issued in your state of glory and power, was to her, making her an apostle, but an apostle of life, glory and

178

love, and an apostle to your apostles. You had made them apostles some time before, but it was during your mortal life. You made them twelve in number but you made them your apostles to the world to proclaim your Cross and your death. In this case, you make Magdalene your apostle in your state of glory. In this new state you make her alone an apostle, an apostle of your life only, for she will proclaim and make public only your life, power and glory. You make her an apostle not to the world, but to the very apostles of the world and to the universal pastors of your church because you are so pleased to highlight the honor and the love of her soul.

The Spirit in Which Magdalene
Enters Into Her Desert

[12, pp. 594-95]

It is Magdalene's desert. She enters it in honor of Jesus and his hidden life. She enters it by the decree of God, who wishes to take her aside in this place to speak to her heart. She enters it by the secret urging of a surpassing love, which draws her and leads there moreso than the urging of penance does. Without detracting from the honor due such penance, may I be allowed to say that her blessed penance is no longer anything but love. Love has acquired such power and possession of her and has converted all that she has and all that she is into love! Her penance is love, her desert is love, her life is love, her solitude is love, her cross is love, her languish is love and her death is love. I see only love in Magdalene. I see only Jesus in her love. I see only Jesus and love in her desert.

She is more alive and hidden in Jesus, in the unknown life of Jesus and in the hidden proofs of Jesus' love, than she is alive and hidden in the desert where she is dwelling. O desert! O Magdalene! O Jesus! O mountain, you are much more useful to Magdalene than was to Saint Peter the one where he said to Jesus, *Let us erect three tabernacles, one for you, one for Moses and one for Elijah.* For I see three tabernacles also on this remote and elevated mountain where Jesus is drawing and leading Magdalene. However, all three belong to Jesus and to no one else. All three were erected by the Spirit of God and not by human hands, and all three offer Magdalene a place of retreat, a holy retreat, sacred tabernacles where she dwells for such a long time, where she is alive and hidden, where she is unknown to all, except for her love.

We can say that the first of these tabernacles is Jesus himself in his very person, for he is her life and dwelling place. She dwells in him more than her soul dwells in her body and more than her body lives in this desert. The second one is again Jesus in the state of his hidden and unknown life. For she has withdrawn and is hidden in this state and she adheres to this life and shares in it in a very rare and divine way. The third is still Jesus. For Jesus alone is the dwelling place and the retreat for her soul. She dwells in him in a variety of ways, according to the various states he possesses and chooses to communicate to her.

In Magdalene's third tabernacle on this holy mountain is Jesus with the fullness of his Spirit and love. For the Spirit and love of Jesus is distinct and superior to others in heaven and on earth. It is one of those sacred orders and names, that are pronounced, according to Saint Paul, both in this world and in the world to come. In this holy tabernacle Jesus wishes to initiate this soul into the hidden proofs of his love. She bears within her constantly the most excellent activities of the Spirit of Jesus, who wishes to accomplish things worthy of himself in a soul so pure, so holy, so sublime, so separated from all and so united to him.

Blessed are those who know this soul and are aware of her thoughts. Blessed are those who share in her secrets. They are incomparably more blessed than if they shared in the secrets of all the great and learned people of the universe. Blessed are they who have access to these three tabernacles and are prepared to enter deeply into this desert, into this Spirit and into this sanctuary.

Elevation to Saint Magdalene

[15, pp. 599–600]

O soul, blessed are you living, dying and suffering this way in this desert! O desert, blessed are you to hold and possess such a soul for so long a time! This desert is a school of love and for Magdalene a school of various sorts of love. I see there a separating love, for Jesus is in heaven and Magdalene is on earth. I see there a crucifying love, for Jesus unites himself to her, but as crucified. Moreover he unites himself to her as crucifying. For it is the very nature of the Spirit and love of Jesus to crucify and to crucify in this way his most cherished souls.

Magdalene welcomes him in both ways, that is, both as crucified and crucifying. She embraces him with all the faculties of her soul, as if she were more loving than that soul in the Canticle, when for the least reason she delays welcoming her beloved. However, I see there as well a third sort of love, an incomparable love, a love that surpasses and crowns the two preceding loves, a love that brings her desert and her life to fulfillment. It is a love that is enraptured at the sight of Jesus, who is no longer crucified but glorified. A love that consumes her, enraptures her and lifts her from the desert to heaven and from the cross to glory. O soul! O desert! O life! O cross! O love! O glory!

What will that glory be like, which responds to such a love? What will that love be like, which carries such a cross and responds to such a life? What kind of life is it that is filled with so many exercises, that is filled with so much love, and that has spent so many years in such a holy, meaningful and divine way? I reverence every moment of this life, singularly spent in your unique love. I admire all that was accomplished in her, all her states and all the progress she made. I am lost in the thought of the supreme height to which she has been elevated. If one hour of your time spent at the feet of the Son of God in the Pharisee's house has produced and formed such a great love in your heart that the love of heaven and earth himself, that is, Jesus, values it, proclaims it and admires it, what should we think and say about so many hours spent on earth with the Son of God, who is the honor, love and delight of heaven and earth?

If two or three years in the school of the Son of God exalted you so greatly in love and adorned you with graces, favors and privileges beyond the apostles and even beyond the beloved of the apostles (who nevertheless are primary in the school and state of the Son of God), what degree, what love, what status in the midst of the angels, the Seraphim and above the Seraphim themselves would you have attained in thirty years of a life where you would have lived and died only for love, where you would have lived only to love and suffer for love, where you would have lived such a long and unique life; quite long even compared to the passage and moment that we attribute to the angels, a life in which each moment is admirable and inimitable?

O life, always either accomplishing or suffering such great things on love's path! O life, constantly lively and unique through the love of Jesus; constantly lively and sublime, whether longing for or possessing Jesus! A life that astonishes and enraptures the angels, who behold such an object on earth. They see a Seraph in a desert, continually discerning, forever alive, constantly fervent; having no other purpose for her life than living, loving and longing in the love of Jesus.

However, it is more appropriate for angels than for men to speak of this life. It is the task of the blessed angel who watched over that desert as it was converted into a paradise, more of heaven than of earth. It is your angel, O Magdalene, and not we, who should speak of it. In recognition of our common inadequacy we should be content to furnish the veil that would hide your life, your love and your longing from mortals. For we cannot speak about it, nor can they understand anything of it.

Pièce 891:
A Letter on the Priesthood[20]

[*CB* 3, pp. 617–18]

To a Priest of the Oratory

Father,

The grace of Jesus be with you forever.

I feel obliged to speak to you a bit at length about the subject of which you wrote me so that, when appropriate, you can instruct those people of note who might wish to understand it. You should know that the church is divided into two parts and both of them are holy, if we consider its institution and origin. One is the people, and the other is the clergy. One receives holiness, and the other brings it about. In the period closer to its birth these two parts brought forth many virgins, confessors and martyrs who blessed the church, filled the earth, populated heaven and diffused everywhere the odor of the sanctity of Jesus.

This holy body, animated by a holy Spirit and governed by holy laws, has lost its fervor and diminished in holiness through the corruption of the ages. This slackening began in its weakest part, the people. Then, from among the people, some withdrew to preserve in themselves the holiness proper to the whole body. These were the monks who, according to Saint Denis, constitute the highest and most perfect part of the people. They were governed by priests in the early church, receiving from them direction and perfect holiness, to which they aspired in an extraordinary way.

At that time holiness dwelt in the clergy as in its fortress, and it struck down idols and worldly impieties. At that time the clergy, composed of prelates and priests, radiated only holy things and dealt only with holy things, leaving worldly things to the worldly. At that time the clergy bore nobly the mark of God's authority, holiness and light: three beautiful jewels in the priestly crown, joined together by God's design for his anointed ones, his priests and his church. The first priests were indeed both saints and doctors of the church. God preserved within this same order authority, holiness and doctrine, uniting these three perfections in the priestly order in honor and imitation of the holy Trinity, in which we adore the authority of the Father, the light of the Son and the sanctity of the Holy Spirit, divinely united in the unity of their Essence.

However, time, which corrupts all things, brought about laxity in most of the clergy. These three qualities, authority, holiness and doctrine, which the Spirit had joined together, were separated by the human spirit and the spirit of the world. Authority has remained in prelates, holiness in religious and doctrine in the schools. In this separation God preserved in different segments of his church what he had joined in the clerical state. Such is the plan of God and the institution of his Son, Jesus. Such is the excellence of our state. Such is the power, light and holiness of the priestly condition.

However, alas! We have fallen from it. The evil of the world in which we live has demoted us from this dignity. It has passed into foreign hands, and we can rightly utter these words of lamentation: *Our inheritance has been handed over to strangers* (Lam 5:2). For no matter how much they are at home in grace and in the unity of the body of Jesus, they are foreign to the ministry; and God, in his original, primary plan did not choose them for it.

It is the prelates and priests who are called to it. It is them that Jesus, in the gospel, refers to as the salt of the earth. It is to them that these three attributes apply. He gives ordinary people faith, hope and love, but he gives also to public persons these three other gifts: holiness, authority and doctrine. This is the core of the inheritance of the tribe of Levi, that is, the clergy, whose name in Greek means "inheritance," in order to show that they have no possession on earth and that the only wealth Jesus Christ has left them is this possession of heaven and this sharing in himself, that is to say, in his holiness, light and authority, adoring and receiving authority from the Father, light from the Son and holiness from the Holy Spirit. But we have reason to lament this loss of which we have been guilty. Also we have reason to praise the goodness of God, who gives us the means to unite once again holiness and doctrine with the authority of the clerical state, without prejudice to those who received it and made such holy use of it in our absence.

It is God's will and plan for us. This is what he has called us to. This is why we are gathered together; in order to reclaim our inheritance, to recover once again our rights, to enjoy our legitimate succession, to have the Son of God as our portion, to share in his Spirit, and through his Spirit to share in his light, holiness and authority, which are communicated to prelates by Jesus Christ and through them to priests.

NOTES

1. The *Grandeurs,* dedicated to King Louis XIII, is composed of twelve discourses, to which has been added a *Narré* dealing mainly with the "vows" of servitude.

2. "This school" refers to Bérulle's earlier statement that "the divine Word . . . having been sent to the world, wished to establish here a holy academy, a state of grace, a divine assembly, conducted and animated by his Spirit, in order to speak to earth the language of heaven . . . and to introduce [men] to an exalted and sublime knowledge of God . . . which human understanding could never teach them" (*G* 1, 1, pp. 161–62).

3. In the technical language of the French School of spirituality the term *religion* evokes a sense of reverence, adoration and love in union with God the Father.

4. In the margin the name *Eudoxe* was written, no doubt referring to Eudoxus of Cnidus, a fourth-century B.C. mathematician and astronomer. It is not clear who wrote the marginal references in the *editio princeps.* The volume was edited by François Bourgoing (1585–1662), the third superior general of the Oratory. In his preface he thanks his fellow Oratorian, Guillaume Gibieuf (c. 1580–1650) for compiling Bérulle's works and providing summaries of the material. Either of these men could have added the marginal notes, which are often vague and not always accurate.

5. The marginal reference is to Nicolaus Copernicus.

6. At this point Bérulle introduces a lengthy theological and spiritually enthusiastic prayer to the Trinity.

7. The word *état* (state) or *estat* (an older spelling for *état*) is a technical term of the French School. It refers to the permanent conditions and aspects of the life and mysteries of Jesus. While his actions were transitory, his inner dispositions are stable and remain available to us for adoration and communion. In this paragraph Bérulle is referring to the state of the Incarnation, which exists forever. See the Introduction to this volume, pp. 37–38.

8. This prayer of praise to the sacred humanity of Jesus Christ is the continuation of the prayer to the Trinity referred to in note 6 above.

9. The marginal note refers to Jerome's commentary on the gospel of Matthew 8:26 [in Book 1, n. 26].

10. "Servitude" refers to an act of total personal consecration, which was at various times and in different circumstances directed toward Jesus or

Mary or the people of God. See the Introduction to this volume, pp. 14–16 for a history of the controversy surrounding Bérulle's use of the vows of servitude.

11. The reference here is not clear. Bérulle could be referring to Plato's *Timaeus,* 90b, where the philosopher speaks of us being rooted from above in heaven rather than from below like earthly plants. He could also have been thinking of this line from the Rhineland mystic, John Ruusbroec: ". . . the tree of faith which grows downward from above, since its roots are in the Godhead" (*The Spiritual Espousals,* book 1, part 4, section D [*The Spiritual Espousals and Other Works,* p. 70]). The editor adds in a footnote to this text that this image is also found in the first Vision of Ruusbroec's Flemish predecessor, the thirteenth-century beguine Hadewijch of Antwerp.

12. The marginal reference is to Tertullian's *Adversus Praxean.* However, the quotation, *a matrice excessit, non recessit,* is not found in that treatise. Some of the thought seems contained in the last part of chap. 8, esp. n. 45.

13. The marginal reference is to Pherecydes of Syros, a sixth-century B.C. Greek writer said to have been the teacher of Pythagoras.

14. The marginal note refers to Saint Leo's letter #10 to Flavian [Archbishop of Constantinople]. However, it is listed as #28 in Migne's *Patrologiae Cursus Completus* (volume 54, column 763).

15. The note mentions Daniel 9. However there is no reference in that chapter or in the book of Daniel to the Holy of Holies [*au Sainct des Saincts*].

16. The French word, *Orient,* is used symbolically in this context to refer to any source from which the light and hope of a new day or era breaks forth. From this perspective Jesus' Incarnation is the Orient of all Orients. I chose to keep the term to respect that allusion.

17. The authors of the French School were so struck by the humiliation and sublime grandeur of Jesus living in Mary's womb that they counted his time on earth from the moment of conception. See p. 171 where Bérulle implies that Nazareth and not Bethlehem is where the "first birth" of Jesus occurs. It is fascinating to note that, although he intended to write about all of Jesus' thirty-four years on earth, Bérulle's *Life of Jesus,* through its thirty chapters, never moves beyond the nine months of gestation. It, too, was dedicated to King Louis XIII.

18. The French expression here is *hostie,* which in the usage of the period evoked both the sacrifices of the ancient Hebrews and the host at Mass, which is the body of Christ and the sacrifice of the new covenant. This play on words is intentional for Bérulle and the authors of the French School. This is why I have translated it as host-victim to capture the double meaning.

19. This *elevation* is composed of twenty chapters, to which are added

some observations on Luke's view of the favors accorded to Magdalene. It was a consolation for Queen Henriette (a princess of France), the wife of England's Charles I (an Anglican), to whom it was dedicated.

20.   There is much in this view of priesthood that seems antithetical to our contemporary theology of ministry. It might help the reader to recall that this hierarchical model was the accepted view of that period and that it continued into our own age until the current renewal. When Bérulle and the other authors of the French School wrote texts like this letter, it was primarily to invite the priests and bishops of their day to conversion. They were challenging them to live up to the dignity that was theirs by virtue of their calling. It was not the evocation of an elitist attitude, but rather a call to base their lives on the spirit and values of the gospel that they preached and the sacraments that they celebrated. See the Introduction to this volume, pp. 54–58; 60–66; 87–88.

MADELEINE DE SAINT-JOSEPH

The Spiritual Letters of Madeleine de Saint-Joseph

Unknown Correspondent, 1628–34

Since you believe that I am in possession of both great and ordinary realities all at once, I want to speak about that freely with you. I have none of these subtleties, but it is true that I, like the others, may have some of this and some graces in prayer. However, in my experience these things are more like something toward which I reach, rather than something I have achieved. I am amazed at those souls who have immediately accomplished everything. For my part, I am fifty years old, but I do not seem to have yet begun. Those other souls are in the divine essence. They no longer exist. They have lost their being in Jesus Christ. They are intimately with God, to hear them tell it. Indeed there is nothing more beautiful in the world. My approach is quite different. One of the greatest sorrows I bear is to see that the evil spirit has been able to detach so many good souls from the blessed person of our Lord Jesus Christ on the pretext of attaining more sublime realities and thus leading them along paths of illusion. O my God, what is more sublime than Jesus Christ? Is he not the splendor of the Father and the image of his substance? Is he not his beloved Son in whom he is well-pleased? Is he not the one in whom the fullness of the divinity resides? Has not the Father commanded that everyone should honor Jesus Christ as himself and offer him the same homage? What better thing can we do than to honor his holy person and all the mysteries of our salvation he has accomplished? Why have we been created, if not for that? Our blessed father[1] and our blessed Sister

191

Marie of the Incarnation, when I first knew them thirty years ago, expressed great sorrow to see the beginning of this development. They told me that it was one of the great problems of the church.

LETTER 42

To Father Gibieuf of the Oratory, 2 October 1629

✝ Jesus Maria
Dear Reverend Father,
May the love of Jesus Christ fill your soul.

Humbly I beg you and all the Reverend Fathers of your house to please do us the favor of giving us the heart of Monsignor, the very renowned and very revered Cardinal de Bérulle, our Reverend Father Superior and Visitor. I am sending you an act of our chapter by which all the sisters and I make this request with all the power of our hearts and minds. For it is the heart of the one, after God, to whom we owe all that we are in Jesus Christ, our Lord. I know that such was his will, and that he desired this for the union of these two Orders and for the glory of the Son of God and of his holy Mother. We desire it for the same reasons, and also, that in this union we may be worthy to receive together, as children of this holy Father, his blessings.

> We desire very much these blessings for you and we remain, Reverend Father,
> Your very humble, affectionate and grateful servants in Jesus Christ,
> Sister Madeleine de Saint-Joseph
> Sister Marie de Jésus
> Sister Marie de Jésus
> Sister Marie de Saint-Jérôme

LETTER 45

To a Friend in the Monastery,
Shortly after Cardinal Bérulle's Death,
2 October 1629

Sir,
May our Lord grant you his holy graces.

I am very grateful to you for making the effort to let me know what is happening with you. I was deeply touched. Since you want me to send you something about the virtues of our blessed Father Cardinal de Bérulle, I will do it willingly to satisfy you and, in this way, to do my small part to honor his memory as I should, since I have been graced by his confidence in me. He is a saint known only to God but whom I hope we will know in eternity. Nevertheless he is a very great saint and particularly outstanding in humility. For the humility with which he stood before God is inconceivable. He believed that no novice or soul existed who was not more initiated in the ways of God, more interior and more advanced than he was.

I think he spoke more than five-hundred times of his dispositions, but it was always in simple, ordinary terms, which indicated on the one hand how much he valued the grace and on the other how much he despised himself. When he spoke of others he used terms that were appropriate to what he wanted to say, but for himself he only used the lowest and most common terms, in keeping with the humble opinion he had of himself. He said that lofty things were not for him, and most often he spoke only of his poverty and indigence. However, this very humble, holy man, who thought so little of himself, who spoke of himself only with such fear and so little esteem, never stopped believing that the person of our Lord Jesus Christ dwelt in him in a special way and that he was present in such an extraordinary manner that it could be easier believed than articulated. This truth was repeated to him so often that he could not doubt it, and its effects in his life and in his death give obvious witness to this presence.

It seemed that he could act only for Jesus Christ, thinking and speaking only of him and his mysteries. He was so filled and so continuously occupied by him that, in order to believe what he was like, you needed to see the holy and great actions this grace produced in him. He seemed to have been born only to love the Son of God, to honor him and make him honored by others. We can say that there has been no one in this century who can be compared to him on this point. As a result of this very great and holy gift, which the Son of God made to him of himself, he gave him a number of great privileges. He received a very great and extraordinary grace to inspire the souls entrusted to him. His repeated influence on them was so powerful that it seemed to flow from an angel rather than from a man. Our Lord gave him such an ardent, loving desire to help them and comfort them in the trials that occur on the path toward virtue that we can not express what he offered to God in this matter nor the effort he expended through prayer, penance and the word. He was more affected by their needs than his own, and above all he experienced incredible sorrow when he had in his care a soul who was unfaithful to Jesus Christ.

A book rather than a letter would be needed to tell you, sir, the effects of the love of this great servant of God. Even an entire book would be insufficient. For I boldly assure you that all we could say would be nothing in comparison to the reality, which I have seen. I assure you this is equally true for his other virtues.

His faith was very strong, his hope and confidence in God unshakable. His courage in undertaking projects for his service, as well as his perseverance in seeing them through to the end, no matter what difficulties he encountered, was marvelous. However his profound humility never noticed these many gifts. Even though he received sublime insights from God both regarding what he owed to him and to his mysteries, he never saw them as anything special, but rather as the effects of the faith offered to every Christian. The insights we have on earth are transitory and do not last forever. Therefore once those he received had disappeared, he only remembered them when they might produce results.

When the pope made him a cardinal, it would be impossible to express the interior and exterior humility with which he received this honor. He would never have accepted it, if the Holy Father had not ordered him to do so under penalty of disobedience.

He was a most solitary and withdrawn soul who fled, as much as he could, from involvement in public affairs and communication with the important people of the world. However, our Lord often obliged him to get involved and gave him such zeal and such admirable courage for both his works and the public good that he always said what he believed useful, even though that often exposed him to great danger. He once said to one of the leaders of the state: "If you destroy the peace, God will destroy you as he has destroyed others."[2] Once he was consulted by the confessor of an important person wanting to know if he was obliged to tell him his opinion on a matter concerning the church's welfare, even though he knew it would not be followed. He responded that to relieve his conscience and fulfill before God the obligation he had for the salvation of that soul, for whom he would have to answer on judgment day, he should speak sincerely to him, even though he was sure that his words would have no effect. He further added, with a powerful and admirable zeal:

"What good did it do for Saint John to say to Herod that it was not permitted to take his brother's wife, except to have his head taken off? He knew it only too well. Yet he did not stop saying it so as to render to God what he owed him."

Among the gifts that Jesus Christ gave this great man, power over evil spirits was one of the most remarkable. It became clear in several subjects and especially in a number of exorcisms. Demons feared him so much that even when he was absent his name subjected them to the exorcists and terrified them.

But none of this was surprising, since he was so filled with our Lord Jesus Christ and so outstanding in the love of his Blessed Mother. He belonged in a special way to this Queen of men and angels. Since nothing is dearer or closer to the Son of God than his Blessed Mother, he could never have been so devoted to our Lord unless he belonged to the Virgin. He never spoke of him without speaking of her, and he told me that he could not speak of the Son without thinking of the Mother.

It should be very consoling to you, sir, to have been known and loved by such a great servant of God, as it is for us to be the daughters of so virtuous a father and such a great saint. I beg you to ask him through his paternal care for us that he give us a share in his virtues, especially in his unshakable faith and burning love for our Lord Jesus Christ and his Blessed Mother. I will make this same prayer for you, in whom I remain, in their Majesties . . .

LETTER 128

To a Former Prioress

My dearest Mother,

May the holy soul of Jesus Christ fill your soul.

I received your letter on the vigil of the blessed Trinity, to whom I offered you fervently to each of the divine persons, asking them to give you love and strength in the faith. I ask the same blessed Trinity to give you the entire share of the life of grace and glory it has destined for you from all eternity. With all my heart I offer, in a special way, your soul to the person of the Son, so that he might communicate to it an emanation and special part of the love he has for his Father; that he might initiate it into his strength, his power, and clothe it completely with himself and his holy and divine attributes, according to everything that is part of his plan and design for you. In whom I am forever yours . . .

LETTER 129

To a Carmelite Prioress

May the love of Jesus Christ fill your soul.

I received your letter and I am very glad to write and implore you to lift your spirit mightily to God during this time of grace and sanctification, when he gives the Holy Spirit on earth so that you may welcome all the most holy and splendid results he wishes to produce in each one of us, provided he finds us disposed for them.

I pray to the same Holy Spirit that he give you his light and his love, for he is light and love. Quite often what we consider to be light, in the ways of God, is not. However, the Holy Spirit gives us the true light, which causes us to progress in the ways of the Son of God, in the ways of humiliation, strength, justice, penance, submission, patience and poverty. For since the Son of God and the Holy Spirit are but one essence, they accomplish the same work. Jesus Christ begins it, and the Holy Spirit finishes it. He comes to initiate souls into the states through which Jesus Christ passed and bring them to imitate all the virtues he practiced during his most holy life. You see what he tells us in the gospel: *The Holy Spirit whom the Father will send you in my name will teach you all things and will call to your mind everything I said to you* (Jn 14:26).

Now the disposition we should have in order to welcome him is a very great and profound humility, as these words from scripture teach us: *Upon whom will my spirit rest, if not the humble?*[3] This is why we must work with very great care to acquire this virtue. It is so necessary and so valued by God because it makes us worthy to have his Spirit dwelling within us. Even if we have all the other virtues, if we do not have humility, we have nothing. It is the one he looks for and hopes to find in us so he can give us his graces. Thus, let us ask him for his Spirit with profound self-abasement. Few souls are worthy of asking and receiving it because there are so few who are truly humble. This is why even though we ask frequently, we are seldom heard. I beg Jesus Christ to make us worthy of asking and receiving, as daughters of God, as daughters of grace and sanctification.

In his divine Majesty, I am yours . . .

LETTER 138

To an unknown person

. . . We are born into this world, not for the world, nor for all that is in the world, wealth, honors, pleasures, nor for ourselves, nor to follow the inclinations of our senses, nor to do our wills, but rather for God and for Jesus Christ, his only Son, to know, love and serve the Father in his Son and the Son for the love of his Father and to accomplish the Father's will so that every tongue confess him and every knee bend before his name, both in heaven and on earth and even in hell, as Saint Paul says (Phil 2:10–11), and that every creature submit itself to the sovereign power that he gave him, as he himself has taught us.

LETTER 139

To a Carmelite Prioress

My good Mother,

May the love of Jesus Christ fill your soul.

Since you wish to know the explanation of the words by which the Son of God teaches us that he is the door, and the others which follow them, I am satisfied that you are not in any way interested in leaving him.[4] This is a leave taking I would wish on no one. I fear it for myself and for those whom I love in our Lord, not simply as I would fear death, but rather eternal death. For Jesus is life and life eternal.

Previously, good Mother, I experienced at times the same difficulty with these words of the gospel. I asked for an interpretation from our blessed Father Cardinal Bérulle. He helped me understand it and I was overjoyed. He said to me that it was not a question here of leaving Jesus Christ, which he could not approve. Also let us note that when he asks his apostles if they wish to leave him, Saint Peter answers: *Lord, to whom shall we go? You have the words of eternal life*

(Jn 6:68). Rather, it is a manner of speaking which means that whoever unites himself perfectly to our Lord Jesus Christ as the way by which we go to God and the only way to get there, placing all his confidence in him alone without relying on himself or even other creatures, this person will live in perfect freedom. He will go and come freely and nothing will prevent him, as the same Son of God says in Saint John: *You will see heavens open and the angels ascending and descending on the Son of Man* (Jn 1:51); that is, serving him in his every command and accomplishing perfectly his every will. Scripture teaches us that because of this they are powerful (Ps 103:20).

To enter then and leave through this door who is Jesus Christ is a manner of speaking that means to accomplish freely everything God asks of us, entering into the divinity and going out into the humanity of Jesus Christ. We enter into his interior life where he is occupied with his Father. We go out into his exterior life where he lives familiarly with men. We ascend in imitation of the angels through attention and contemplation of his grandeurs, in which *he is in all things equal to his Father* (Jn 10:30). We descend through love and the imitation of his humiliation, by which he says through his prophet *that he is a worm, not a man, a disgrace among men and the scorn of the people* (Ps 22:7). We enter with Mary and go out with Martha. At times we remain recollected within ourselves and occupied solely in adoring him in spirit and truth, listening in silence to the words of life he speaks to our heart. At other times we go out through the practice of charity and all the exterior virtues of which he gave us such a perfect example.

Without doubt, my dear Mother, in these holy reflections we will find a pasture quite capable of nourishing our souls, capable of sustaining them and causing them to grow in this holy union with Jesus Christ and with God, which his own Son wished for us, asked for us and acquired for us at such a great price. I beg him to make us worthy of it and believe me that I am yours in him . . .

LETTER 142

To a Carmelite Prioress

My good Mother,
  Peace in Jesus Christ.
  You ask me what the life of Carmelites should be like. I answer

198

you that we should desire that it conform to the life of the saints in heaven. The saints contemplate always the face of God and that of Jesus Christ, his Son whom he sent. Eternal life consists in this, as the same Son teaches us. Were it possible, we should do the same thing on earth. But because the corruption of the body, which weighs down the soul, does not permit it, we should at least try to approximate it as much as possible. We should unceasingly contemplate our Lord Jesus Christ, and even though we cannot see him in his glory and in his grandeurs as the saints see him in heaven, we should contemplate and adore him in his humiliation and in the mysteries of his holy humanity.

You will find that they are all there in him who is the summary of his marvels and in whom he chose to enclose himself in order to keep us company faithfully until the end of the world, to unite us to all that he offers there to his Father, to receive the homage we owe his most holy person and all his states,[5] and to produce in our souls the effects of grace, which are appropriate to them and which will make us worthy of honoring them authentically. For as you know, Mother, we cannot honor God, or Jesus Christ, who is God like his Father, in an authentic manner worthy of his acceptance, except through what we receive from him. Therefore, ask the Father to draw you to his Son and ask the Son to give you a share in himself, which will inspire your spirit, your heart and all that you are unceasingly to contemplate him, love him, imitate him and adore his Father with him and as a part of him, in spirit and truth according to what he asks of us.

In this way you will satisfy the plan of the eternal Father, who wants everyone to honor his Son as himself. You will obey what our rule commands us, to meditate day and night on the law of God. Not only will you meditate, but also you will obey that holy and sanctifying law, that law of grace and love that he substituted for that of severity and terror. He did not give it to slaves, but to children, for it is in Jesus Christ that he has given us that holy law. It is through this divine legislator that he has given us his commandments and that he has made known to us his will. It is in his life and all his actions that he has placed before our eyes a most perfect exemplar on which he wants us to model our own [life]. Finally, it is through the grace that he has enclosed in him for us that he gives us the will and strength to accomplish what he commands us and that he makes us accomplish it, in fact, in a manner worthy of him and worthy of the reward he promises to those who observe perfectly his law, that is, the eternal possession of himself.

In him, I am forever . . .

LETTER 144

To a Carmelite Prioress

My good Mother,

May the love of Jesus Christ fill your soul.

I have been thinking about what you asked me for a long time, but since I received your letter I have applied myself more to the question and I continue to have the same thought that I had: to prefer the act of adoration to that of thanksgiving, because it is more extensive and it exposes us less to the danger of too much self-preoccupation even under the pretext of thanking God for the blessings he has given us, especially when they are unique to us. Moreover, the respect toward the majesty of God that adoration creates in us moderates the excesses of sensibility many good souls experience easily in their devotional exercises.

It is not that I fail to recognize that thanksgiving is very good and even a strict obligation for every soul, for a creature has nothing except what it receives from the infinite generosity of God. Nevertheless, I find that this act of thanksgiving is included in that of adoration, and my thought is that it is generally more useful to souls for the reasons I have just given.

Adoration is what God looked for from the beginning in his creatures, in the angels in heaven and in men on earth, because adoration is a duty and a respect that the lesser owes to the greater, the subject owes to the sovereign Lord. Through it the creature experiences its nothingness in order to offer homage to its Creator. However, since angels and men failed in this and rebelled against his majesty, he wanted to choose a worshiper as great as himself and as little capable of failing as he would be. Thus he decided upon the mystery of the Incarnation, where a God would adore God. Also let us note that the first state that his Son took on as soon as he clothed himself with our nature was the state of lamb and victim for God, which is a state of adoration, for it is through sacrifice that adoration is offered.

The first act or disposition of his holy soul, according to the teaching of the great theologians, was the oblation he made of himself to his Father in that moment, blessed for all times, when he placed his body and his soul in the hands of this Lord, who, while being his Father, became his God in the temporal order. This is what Saint Paul teaches us when he portrays the Son of God's entrance into the world and into our nature. The words that he attributes to him at that moment are words by which he consecrates to his Father the body he gave him to be sacrificed to him in place of all the former victims and by which he continues to assure him that he welcomes his law and places it in the center of his heart. Subsequently, during all of his most holy life, he continued with this same disposition and what he did in dying was to consummate this great sacrifice, immolating to his own Father with the shedding of his blood this holy victim he had continually offered him since his Incarnation.

Upon entering the world, Saint Paul tell us, *he first appeared as a host through his sacrifice,*[6] which teaches us that he is in his state as host-victim[7] forever. Saint John confirms the same thing for us in his Apocalypse, where he says that he saw the Lamb slain (that is, sacrificed) (Rv 5:6). He shows us all the angels and saints offering him their homage as Lamb. Their greatest glory is to adore God with him, united to his adoration, which is the adoration of eternity. Finally, on earth, in the blessed sacrament, where he has chosen to dwell as long as the church remains, he is there in a state of adoration and immolation, which is why we call it the holy host. What he does there is nothing other than offer homage to his Father and adore him in the name of us all as our high priest. It is true that he is there also as bread come down from heaven, as bread that gives eternal life, but what he does as bread is to transform us into himself to make us capable of adoring with him. He makes us what he is so that we may do now what he does and will do eternally, which is to adore his Father.

You should not be surprised, dear Mother, if I elaborate so much on this subject, since it is so extensive that it surpasses greatly what I might say about it. For adoration is a definite duty by which the creature proclaims the supreme grandeur and the infinite excellence of the being of God and by which we recognize that he is the author of our being and of all the good that is in us and could be in us. It is not only from him and through him, but even more for him that we receive without ceasing, through the gift of conservation, everything of which he is the goal as well as the source. Recognizing that these things belong to him because of so many claims, we protest that we never want to use them except in relation to him. Moreover, we give him power over them, being glad for him to dispose of them himself according to his will and that he makes use of them in every way he wishes for his glory.

What is most important to understand is that not only is adoration imperfect without love, but that it does not even deserve to be called adoration, nor is it welcomed by God as such, if love is not its soul and its life, if we can speak thus. Otherwise it is only a pretense of adoration and the kind of cult practiced by [some] Jews about which God complained a long time ago when he said through one of his prophets that this people honored him with their lips, but that their hearts were far from him (Is 29:13). Now just as adoration cannot be perfect without love, so that the creature is fully possessed by its Creator, it is likewise true that love cannot be perfect unless it is accompanied by adoration. These are the two obligations that must be necessarily linked together in order to offer God what we owe him and what he asks of us. It seems to me that it is truer to say that it is one and the same duty, to which we give two different names because of the different effects that it produces.

I do not know, Mother, if you have noticed something on this topic that is very important. It is in the first article of the law of God. After he presented himself to his people as the Lord their God who took them out of Egypt and who forbade them to have any other god or to make idols and offer them the adoration and service owed to him alone, he adds that he, the Lord their God, is mighty and jealous, inflicting punishment for the iniquity of fathers on their children through the third and fourth generation on those who hate him, and that he is merciful for a thousand generations to those who love him and who keep his commandments, which is the true proof of love (Ex 20:4–6). What God says in that place shows us clearly, if we know how to understand it, that he does not see adoration and love as two different duties, but as one and the same. Jesus Christ witnesses to this as well in the gospel when he is asked what is the first and the greatest of the commandments of the law. For although he knows that it begins with the adoration of God, and he knows quite perfectly the meaning of everything in the law since he and his Father are its author, he answers with these words from Deuteronomy: *You will love the Lord your God with all your heart, all your soul and all your strength* (Dt 6:5), adding that this is the first and greatest commandment. Also he says to the Samaritan: *True worshipers will worship his Father in spirit and in truth* (Jn 4:23–24). The fact that he is looking for such people to adore him and that, since God is spirit, those who adore him must adore him in spirit and truth, all of this, I say, expresses quite profoundly this most important truth. I believe that you will easily understand it even with little time spent before God, if you have not already done it.

We must further notice clearly that, as the Son of God gives us in his own person the example of all the virtues that he teaches with his sacred lips, he does it most particularly in this matter, which deals with our first duty toward God. We see from the words of Saint Paul, which we have already mentioned, that from the moment he took on our nature, he humbled himself before God his Father. He recognized his supreme authority over him; he submitted to his will. He offered himself to him as a perpetual victim. When he said that his law was in the center of his heart, that shows the burning love with which he fulfilled his duty. Thus it is only in as much as we conform to this divine model and unite ourselves to his holy dispositions that we can accomplish perfectly the first and greatest commandment of the law, which contains all the others. Since it is not in our power to give God the final and most important proof of our love, which is to sacrifice ourselves to him physically, not being permitted to take our lives (and God does not ask it of us), Jesus Christ, our head, on his part makes up for what is lacking in us. He remains continually on our altars and deigns to come into our souls and even our bodies through holy communion, so that becoming one with him, we can, through this union, offer him to his Father and offer ourselves as well as a holy and acceptable sacrifice in the eyes of his majesty.

You are no doubt astonished at the length of this letter, since you are not used to it from me. Furthermore, I have written it several times. The importance of the subject and the great desire you have shown to be enlightened obliged me to try to satisfy you as well as I could. You will pardon me, I hope, if I have not done better. You know that ignorance is proper to our sex and particularly to me who is yours . . .[8]

MADELEINE DE SAINT-JOSEPH

LETTER 147

To a Mistress of Novices

My good Mother,
    May the love of Jesus Christ fill your soul.
    You want me to tell how we must begin prayer, continue it and finish it. I tell you wholeheartedly that we must always begin, always continue and never end. All our actions in the service of God are only beginnings, being so weak, so impoverished and so insignificant. Our concern must be to begin well and continue well always, rather than finish, at least in the present state, since finishing can only be done at the moment of our death when Jesus Christ, through his infinite kindness, will bring to fulfillment his grace in us. For the way to finish well then is to begin well and continue well now.
    You know well, my dear Mother, that prayer is a communication of the soul with God, that it is what Saint Paul calls, *The fellowship of Christians in heaven* (Phil 3:20) whose treasure, which is our Lord Jesus Christ, is in heaven. They have nothing on earth except what they must leave. They must not seek this fellowship on earth, but only in heaven. Their spirit must be in heaven where their true Father is; *their heart must be in heaven where their treasure is* (Mt 6:21). They must live as creatures risen from death to life, having no more taste or affection for anything but eternal goods and not for things that will pass with this present world. It is said that Noah walked with God. All his fellowship was with God during the pilgrimage of the present life. Also our Father Elijah said ordinarily, as you know, my good Mother, *long live God in whose presence I am* (1 Kg 17:1), which indicates to us that he experienced God as always present and that he accomplished his every action in the awareness of that divine presence. And further, what is said of Moses, *that he conversed as intimately with God as one friend speaks with another* (Ex 33:11). Now, if even then the fellowship of the saints was continually with God, how much more should it be so now that God has become a man, our brother and our companion, and become available so that we can freely address him, approach him and keep him company, which are the graces and advantages we have through the mystery of the Incarnation? This mystery creates a holy and divine fellowship among God and Jesus Christ, his only Son, and us. Therefore, Saint

204

John says *that we have fellowship together and our fellowship is with the Father and his Son Jesus Christ* (1 Jn 1:3).

Let us recognize then the graces that are offered to us. Let us make use of our rights, for we are invited to share in a privilege that we could not have hoped for, fellowship with God and with Jesus Christ his Son. Let us be careful not to neglect it or to take advantage of it without the care and gratitude that we owe. Let us live always in God's presence. Let us use everything that happens to us in life to lift ourselves to him and to unite ourselves to his will and his most holy plans for us. Let us adore the Son as our God, obeying him as our king and our sovereign Lord, honoring him, loving him as our Father, going to him in our every need with confidence as to a Father who has begotten us in his blood and who has given us life through his own death.

Let us approach him, joining with him as a brother, since that is what he willingly humbled himself enough to be. His word teaches us *that he was not at all ashamed to call us his brothers* (Heb 2:11). Bring all our concerns to him as to our best, truest and most intimate friend, who has not spared his own life to rescue us from an infinite misfortune and make it possible for us to rejoice eternally with his very own happiness. Let us offer him continual gratitude as a benefactor who was so generous that he gave himself to us with all his riches and never ceases to be good to us. Let us unite ourselves to him as our head, since we are honored to be his members. Let us follow his movements, unite ourselves with his intentions, his thoughts and his activities. Let us adore his Father with him and with his own adoration. Let us love God with him and with his own love. Let us praise God with him and with his own praise. And on every occasion let us practice the virtues, humility, gentleness, kindness and the others with him, by sharing in his own virtues, which he will not fail to give if we ask him for them humbly and with perseverance and if we are faithfully disposed to receive them.

Finally, let us be with one another as if we were with God and with Jesus Christ, for that is what the beloved disciple teaches us, *that the fellowship we have together is with Jesus Christ and with his Father* (1 Jn 1:3). We should live together united with God and with Jesus Christ. Every bond we have with one another should be through the same Spirit, which unites God with Jesus Christ. Oh, how great these things are! How holy they are! How divine they are! Yet they are our rights and privileges. However, they do ask of us a continual detachment from ourselves without which we will never achieve such a great and precious reality.

I think at times that we should blush to be so cold and weak about surrendering ourselves to this divine fellowship in the midst of all the help we have been given since the coming of our Lord Jesus Christ. Look at how perfect the saints of old were in this matter, without having seen what we see nor having received what we receive.

I beg his divine Majesty to give you the grace to make a more perfect use of this every day, and I beg you to obtain for me by your prayers the grace to begin to leave my misery behind and render to him what I owe him.

I am yours in him . . .

LETTER 174

To a Carmelite Prioress

My good Mother,
    Peace in Jesus Christ.
    I rejoice at the blessings with which his divine hand inundates your soul, and especially because he unites you to himself suffering and nailed to the wood of the cross, where I behold you in a way that I cannot explain. I beg his infinite goodness to make you worthy of adoring his agony and sharing his interior and exterior sufferings.

Ask the blessed Virgin to admit you into fellowship with her as she did those holy women who followed Jesus on the way to the cross. Consider their patience in suffering so much disgrace, so many blows, so many insulting words in order to approach him. And above all, see their great strength and constancy as they watched him suffer, he whom they knew to be the only Son of God and the life of their life. These holy women did not look to themselves or think of themselves, but they were completely filled with the Son of God and his extreme sufferings. In the same way, good Mother, never separate yourself from Jesus Christ and beg him to make you worthy of following him perfectly, for he is the way that leads us to his Father.

I ask him with all my heart that he stay with you until he has established you in his bosom with himself, in whom I am yours . . .

MADELEINE DE SAINT-JOSEPH

LETTER 207

To a Carmelite Prioress

My good Mother,

May the love of Jesus Christ fill your soul.

I have been meaning to write to you for a long time, but various occupations prevented me from doing so. His divine Majesty permitted this so that I might write now on this day of the great Saint Magdalene, to whom we offered you devoutly, desiring that you be numbered among those souls of whom she takes special care.

Reflecting this morning on those phenomenal things that God produced in that soul, I felt a great desire to honor her thirty-year solitude in that cave, where she experienced so many things known only to God and angels and unknown to men. It seemed to me that since our Order is a solitary one, we should all look intently to her so as to learn from her example what we should do in our seclusion.[9]

If we try to discover what occupied her seclusion, we will find that the Son of God was the only focus of her attention. He was her life and her all and nothing but him had any part in her. Thus if we wish to live in authentic solitude, let us banish from our minds, in imitation of her, all esteem, all love and all desire for the earth and the present age, in order to be taken up solely with him who totally fulfilled that soul, which was so rare and outstanding in grace and love. Let us contemplate him in his grandeurs and in his humiliations. Let us adore his holy person. Let us consider his mysteries. Let us reverence his wisdom. Let us submit ourselves to his power. Let us admire and love his infinite goodness and charity. Let us acknowledge his blessings. Let us listen to his words of grace and eternal life. Let us show him our misery. Let us open to him the depth of our hearts, desiring that he fill them, take total possession of them and that he operate in them according to his divine plans. Since he has deigned to lower himself to the very vile and miserable thing that we are and to live closely with us, let us ask that he might be gracious enough to teach us also how to live closely with him and that he not allow that we or any other creature occupy the place in us that he alone should fill.

I ask him with all my heart to grant you this grace, good Mother, and I beg you to ask it also for me, who am yours in him forever . . .

MADELEINE DE SAINT-JOSEPH

LETTER 236

To a Cleric

Sir,

Peace in Jesus Christ.

I received your letter, filled with expressions of your kindness toward us, for which I am most obliged. I thank our Lord for his care in inspiring you to offer us to him in your holy sacrifices. I am in great need of that for my soul and my body, both of which are filled with misery.

I beg his divine Majesty to make me worthy of acknowledging this charity in his holy presence, according to his desire, and to be able to give you a little of what you ask of us. However, I feel very powerless and I do not know why you approach me to give you advice about such important things. Nevertheless, since you wish, I will ignore my littleness to satisfy your humility.

First then, I will tell you this, sir, about the direction of souls. It is very dangerous to meddle in it. One must be constrained and called to it by God. As far as the qualities of those that his divine majesty chooses for this most worthy activity, you see what Jesus Christ asks of Saint Peter, which is to love him more than all the others (Jn 21:15). Also Saint Paul wishes that bishops be irreproachable, so that they might teach grace and virtue by their lives as well as by their words (1 Tm 3:2). Finally, directors should be filled with Jesus Christ, and they should continually strive to form him in souls. They must not guide them according to their inclinations, but rather with very great submission to the Spirit of God in them and with benevolence and charity. Also, it seems to me, it is good to treat them with respect, like souls for whom Jesus Christ died. We should offer them often to him, to whom they belong and on whom they and we depend absolutely.

There are directors who, when they undertake the care of a soul, totally turn it upside down in order to form it in their mode. This is not my approach. Rather, it seems to me that if we find a soul who has made some progress in grace, we should simply follow what we see God has done for it, since there is no question of leading everyone along the same path.

Concerning what you ask me, sir, whether we should give souls as much time as they wish, I will tell you that I do not agree with that, especially when they have been leading a devout life for a long time. Our blessed sister Marie of the Incarnation told me on several occasions that it was sufficient to talk a quarter of an hour with souls and that anything beyond that was useless because, as she said, a quarter of an hour is enough to learn their needs and to respond to them. The rest is for our own satisfaction. It seems to me that what is most useful for these advanced souls is that, according to their needs, we give them some words from sacred scripture, particularly from Jesus Christ, either to strengthen them if they have some difficulty or weakness, or to confirm them in what God is doing in them. For souls who are new to piety it is necessary that we speak more with them for several years to instruct them about many things they do not know. Also, it is possible at times to find in the others certain needs that require more communication, but we must be careful to give them only the necessary time.

I believe, sir, that you do not have much need for this advice, being drawn to solitude as you are. However, I am saying everything to you that comes to mind since you are a person with whom I can be completely free.

It is necessary at times to listen to the little difficulties that souls can experience in order to unburden them without spending much time on them. On the contrary, we must even use this occasion so that they can be lifted up to Jesus Christ, so that they can resort to his holy person and especially his states and mysteries, according to their diverse dispositions. For it is Jesus Christ and all that he is in himself that should fill souls and not what they have or what they suffer. It is even good to teach them to seek the Son of God on their own in their difficulties and to work at offering him the homage he asks of them in each state, without waiting always for us to be with them. Once we have told them several times what they must do, if they do not apply themselves to it faithfully, then their effort is not genuine and lasts no longer than our urging. On the contrary, souls that give themselves over to what we say to them for love of Jesus Christ remain steadfast in his ways. He is their strength and their exemplar in all kinds of labors and dispositions.

I beg you to continue including me in your holy prayers and to believe that I am yours . . .

MADELEINE DE SAINT-JOSEPH

LETTER 253

Probably to a Carmelite Prioress

. . . Concerning those good souls about whom you spoke to me, some of whom are devoted to the divine Essence and others to the eternal Persons, I think that you can let them follow their dispositions, since you have reason to believe that they are of God and you see that these souls approach this in an authentic and solid way. However, you should introduce these souls to other exercises of homage to our Lord Jesus Christ and his mysteries in order to enrich and fill out their spiritual lives, because sometimes the most exalted pathways can be very sterile. And it happens that when these souls have produced a naked and partially formed act,[10] they remain often with nothing to do. Now if they are devoted to our Lord Jesus Christ and his states, they are much richer and can more easily persevere in their contemplation of God.

LETTER 284

To a Woman

Madam,

I beg our Lord to give you his holy graces.

Since I have never believed myself worthy to give witness to the virtue of blessed Catherine of Genoa, I will only be able to say a few things about what you want and what I would desire as well to contribute to the honor due such a great servant of our Lord Jesus Christ.

All that I can write you is that she has been of great assistance to most of the souls whom I know whose piety has been outstanding. The late most illustrious and most reverend Cardinal de Bérulle had a great devotion to her and always carried her image on him. He honored infinitely the grandeur and purity of her love and desired greatly that both the Carmelites and the Fathers of the Oratory have a special confidence in her.

Our late, good Sister Catherine of Jesus, whom you know was a soul of rare grace and holiness, received a number of very noteworthy graces from her, particularly during an illness when she was quite

nauseated and could not take any nourishment without great difficulty or retain it without experiencing extreme pain. That summer
she had recourse to Saint Catherine of Genoa whose image she had
on her bed. She gave her so much strength that while she did not
remove the problem, she was able to take whatever was deemed
necessary for her without any apparent difficulty. After that illness
she always asked for her blessing when she wanted to take
something.

That good saint helped her quite a bit as well in life and death,
having helped her greatly in the interior pathways where God was
leading her, especially in the desire she had to disappear completely
for God. For one day when she was suffering very much, and it
seemed that she was experiencing some of the most painful inter-
ventions of God, Saint Magdalene and the blessed Catherine of
Genoa appeared to her all covered with thorns as a way of comfort-
ing her and showing her that they themselves had also suffered.
Another time this good sister was shown how that saint had been
totally consumed by love and that God would give her some share in
that same grace. However, a handwritten paper from the day of the
Exaltation of the Holy Cross, which was found in her cell after her
death, will help you know her dispositions and the merits of the great
Saint Catherine of Genoa better than anything I could write you. It
contained these words, which I believe I should copy for you here
since this letter is meant to be a deposition.

"O holy and lovable cross! O interior and greatly desired cross! O
blessed Catherine of Genoa, how well you were able to exalt it! O
great God, you who dispose souls and wish that they cooperate with
you, did you not find this soul to your liking? Yes, my God, but what
did you want to do, having found her thus disposed, if not leave her
all day, that is, all her life, in a blessed torment that you, her love,
created in her? Oh, the great faithfulness of that holy soul! O my
God, it seems that you wanted this holy soul to exalt your interior
cross so that she might become the mother and protectress of the
souls you have chosen for that blessing. Thus, once the day had been
spent in this way, you took her to yourself. Oh, my God, please give
us a share in your love!"

I regret infinitely, madam, that I have not indicated all the very
great graces and the special favors that the Son of God was pleased to
pour forth on the souls of our Order through the prayers of this saint.
You can see that we must certainly ask God, as we do with all our

heart, that soon this great saint will be publicly honored and invoked in the church, to the glory of the Son of God himself.

I beg him to give you the blessings you desire. I am yours . . .

LETTER 296

To an Unknown Correspondent

Since it was by these spiritual paths[11] that this soul was so greatly deceived, she must definitely detach herself from them, moreso than another who had no such attachment. For the latter, it is enough to let it pass and leave it as it is, while not settling in there, but for the former these things constitute another sort of danger, and she must distance herself much more from them. She does not need to do herself in in order to remove it from her mind, but she must consider it suspect, mistrust it and ask God at once to deliver her from all these things that have placed her in such great danger. While she awaits this mercy, she should suffer gently and patiently what she cannot remove. She must strive mightily to achieve profound humility with great obedience, perfect charity and all the other authentic virtues. If she believes me, I would advise her, in order to establish a good and lasting foundation, to detach herself to the core from all these things and to set herself anew on another approach. She says that she adores the unity of God. If someone else told me that perhaps I would leave them there, knowing their dispositions and that it would not do them any harm. However, in her case, it is something harmful and she needs to heed the basic counsel, which is that by ourselves and through our own choosing we should always take the simpler way.

NOTES

1. She is referring to Cardinal Bérulle.

2. This allusion here is no doubt to Cardinal Richelieu (1585–1642). Bérulle was an outspoken opponent of some of the prime minister's political decisions. Finally he fell from grace at the French court in 1629 shortly before his death. See the Introduction to this volume, pp. 4–5.

3. Mother Madeleine appears to be alluding from memory to Isaiah 11:2 and 66:2.

4. In John 10:1–17, where Jesus speaks of himself as the Good Shepherd, he also says that he is the door through whom those who believe will go in and *go out* (v. 9). This seems to be the textual point to which she is referring here. However the deeper theological issue is a belief of abstract mysticism that the mature spiritual person can pass beyond Jesus' human mediation. See the Introduction, pp. 24–25; cf pp. 10–11.

5. The word state (*état* or *estat*, an older spelling for *état*) is a technical term of the French School. It refers to the permanent conditions and aspects of the life and mysteries of Jesus. While his actions were transitory, his inner dispositions are stable and remain available to us for adoration and communion. See the Introduction, pp. 37–38.

6. The reference here is probably to the thought developed in Hebrews, chaps. 9 and 10. It is not clear what the exact text is.

7. The French expression Mother Madeleine uses is *hostie*, which in the usage of the period evoked both the sacrifices of the ancient Hebrews and the host at Mass, which is the body of Christ and the sacrifice of the new covenant. Since the play on words is intentional with the authors of the French School, I have translated it as host-victim to respect that double meaning.

8. This appears to be an indication of a misogyny that the French School did not always transcend. See the Introduction, pp. 25–26.

9. In his footnote to this letter Pierre Serouet cites Ribadeneira's *Les fleurs des vies des saints* 2, trans. and ed. René Gauthier (Rouen, 1645), page 72, which offers us this context for Magdalene's solitude: "Magdalene, after having preached with her own lips and converted many souls, withdrew to the desert to weep for her sins. She remained in this solitude for thirty years, eating herbs and tree roots. . . . She led a life that was more angelic than human and the angels lifted her up seven times a day so she could hear their heavenly music" (my translation). See above, pp. 179–82.

NOTES

10.   She is probably referring again to a form of abstract mysticism. See the Introduction, pp. 24–25.

11.   See note 10.

JEAN-JACQUES OLIER

Introduction to the
Christian Life and Virtues

The Religion[2] of Jesus Christ

Our Lord Jesus Christ came into this world to bring love and respect for his Father and to establish his reign and his religion. He never asked anything else of him during his lifetime. In the thirty-three years that he lived on earth, he laid these foundations. His incessant desire was to open the minds and hearts of the faithful to this religion. He foresaw that they had been destined to be the ones in whom he would instill his own religion in order to honor his Father through them as he honored him in himself.

He requested this grace for men and he merited it for them during his life. Through his death he not only continued this prayer, but also gave clear witness to the respect and love he had for his Father, which are the two realities that constitute the virtue of religion. He experienced his Father to be so pure and holy that he could see nothing that deserved to live or even exist in his presence. This was what he affirmed by the death that he suffered in order to witness to this truth and bring it to light.

He died not only out of reverence but also from love. For he accepted his death most willingly and joyfully because he saw that the Father was both satisfied and pleased by it. He had understood that no worthy reparation had been offered to God for the sins committed against him. He died then to satisfy him completely and to leave nothing for which he was not abundantly satisfied.

In this way he gives an example to Christians who commit themselves to Jesus' own religion, respect and love. He shows them that they must spare nothing to bear witness to genuine sentiments of religion, which will on occasion call for sacrifice. This will make their sacrifice more authentic than simply being content with a mere inner inclination, which can often be deceptive.

By all sorts of loving strategies, our Lord has continued after his death to procure for men this religion toward his Father. He gave them his own Spirit, the Spirit of God dwelling within him, so that he might plant within them the very sentiments of his own soul. In this way Jesus dilates[3] his holy religion so that he and all Christians might become one religious of God.[4]

Reigning in heaven, Jesus lives in the hearts and the pens of the evangelists in order to inculcate everywhere a sense of disdain for creatures and a respect for God alone. He lives in the hearts and mouths of his apostles and his disciples to proclaim everywhere the kingdom of God, thus obtaining an adoration worthy of his holy name and offering him perfectly obedient subjects and worshipers who respect him in spirit and truth (Jn 4:23).

The Spirit of God also fulfills his particular role in priests[5] by continuing in them what he accomplished in Jesus Christ. Through their words, writings and example as well as in all other possible ways, the Spirit gives birth to the holy religion of God to whom we owe all adoration and respect while we hold all else in contempt. Everything outside of him is nothing but vanity and mere symbol. For all of created reality is only a flimsy shell of the being that is hidden in him but becomes visible in some way through the appearance of all that is visible. Every reflection will pass away (1 Cor 7:31) on that day when God will no longer reveal himself through his reflections, but rather will plainly show forth all that he is. Once our spiritual sight is awakened and strengthened by the light of glory, then the world will no longer please us. We look beyond a shadow once the body that has cast it appears. We are no longer interested in a portrait once the actual person arrives. A mask loses its appeal when the face is uncovered. In the same way, all will seem to us mere appearance, mask and nothingness when God will reveal himself fully to our souls.

May God be adored in himself and may everything else perish before him in our spirit; for everything else is as nothing in his presence. In this spirit of religion let us anticipate the abnegation[6] and universal sacrifice of all manner of being which is called to perish on God's behalf as a witness to his grandeur and holiness. May our faith be the light and the torch of our religion so that we may sacrifice every existing thing before God. For if Jesus Christ himself desired to be sacrificed because of the great respect and esteem he had for God and his holiness, how much more ought we to sacrifice everything for God and disdain all things. In this way we will value and see only the One who is true, the One who alone deserves to be esteemed and revered.

In the presence of the true God, no idols are to be adored. Everything must be reduced to ashes. Thus may all creation perish before my God. In his sacrifice our Lord claimed to annihilate everything and to sacrifice all things in himself because he had brought everything together in his person. Therefore, it is right that we condemn and sacrifice all things that are outside of him, since they are less holy for being less closely related to him. It is the true sign of our religion to offer everything in sacrifice to God and thus to testify how vile and despicable all things are in his presence. In this way we value and respect nothing other than him alone.

Finally our Lord comes to us in order to dilate his holy religion toward God and to multiply it in our souls. He remains on earth in the hands of priests as a host of praise so that we might commune in this spirit of host-victim,[7] giving ourselves over to praising him and communing inwardly in the sentiments of his religion. He fills us with himself. He invades every part of us and anoints our soul, filling it with the interior dispositions of his religious spirit. Thus his soul and ours become one. He breathes into our souls a similar spirit of respect, love and praise; a spirit of the interior and exterior sacrifice of all things to the glory of God his Father. This is how he brings about our soul's communion in his religion so that we may be, as we said earlier, true religious of his Father.

Similarly, so that he might render our state more perfect and bring us to the most pure and holy spirit of religion, he draws us to communicate in his state of host-victim so as to be a victim with him. Thus we are religious not only in spirit but in truth as well, that is to say, in reality. We have sacrificed within ourselves everything that is of the flesh with all its sentiments. We have not only made this sacrifice as Jesus Christ did on the cross through mortification and interior crucifixion (2 Cor 4:10), but we have consumed everything interiorly with Jesus Christ, consumed on the altar. This is the height of perfection to which he calls us in this life. For by his intimate presence in us and through his fire, which devours us, he brings us to communicate in the most perfect state of his religion, which is to be a host consumed for the glory of God. Such a host no longer lives through its own life and the life of the flesh, but lives totally through the divine life and the life of one consumed in God.

This is the very state of the risen life to which we are called in imitation of our Lord. He was exteriorly consumed into his Father on the day of the resurrection and wishes that we may be interiorly resurrected and consumed in him as well. That is why he says that he has communicated to men the clarity that the Father had given him (Jn 17:22). That clarity is the resurrected state, which he already possessed in the host at the Last Supper: *That they may be one, as we are one. I in them and you in me* (Jn 17:21). I am in them, producing the same effect that you, my Father, who dwells in me, produces in me. I give them life as you give me life. I consume them as you consume me. Thus he calls us to be living hosts, holy and acceptable to God (Rom 12:1). This is why Saint Paul prays most insistently that Christians be brought to that perfect consummation in Jesus Christ in accord with that Spirit which renders them interiorly totally like him. I pray to God with all my heart that he may bring you to consummation, which I wish you to have by the power of the Spirit of Jesus Christ, who consumes you interiorly with him (2 Cor 13:9).

This is the work of the Holy Spirit, who comes into this world as a witness to the truth in our hearts. The Spirit accomplishes this much better than Saint John, who was only his spokesman. For the Spirit is the spirit of truth (Jn 16:13).

It is he who will begin to show us interiorly through faith the falsehood and the deceit of all created reality, of all that is not God. He will lead us to despise it as nothing in the presence of this All who is so great, magnificent and worthy of admiration. He will give us a distaste for it and thus lead us to total detachment. He will offer us to God with ardor and unite us to him so intimately that he will make us all one in him, consuming us perfectly and thus bringing us to resemble Jesus Christ, who is consumed in his Father.

CHAPTER TWO

Concerning the First Way
We Must Conform to Jesus Christ

We must all be conformed to Jesus Christ. Saint Paul teaches us this when he says that God predestined us to be conformed to the image of his Son (Rom 8:29).

This conformity consists in being like him; first in his exterior mysteries, which were like sacraments of the interior mysteries he was to bring about in souls. Therefore, just as our Lord was exteriorly crucified, we are called to be interiorly crucified. As he died in exterior reality, we must die interiorly. As he was buried exteriorly, we must be buried interiorly. Everyone should have within him the interior life that the exterior mysteries represent as well as the grace acquired by these same mysteries, because they have been merited for everyone. That is why Saint Paul, speaking about all of us, said: *You have died* (Col 3:3).

It is true that God has chosen certain souls to express through them these very mysteries even in an exterior way. We see this in certain holy religious whom he sent to earth in order to renew the life of Jesus Christ. They were so thoroughly filled with his Spirit and the grace of these mysteries that they expressed visibly his external state. Such was Saint Francis, to whom the Spirit of our Lord Jesus Christ crucified was so fully given that it overflowed into his flesh, thus manifesting externally the mystery of the crucifix through the wounds of his body. He allows this to continue in his children who mortify their flesh continually. Such was the case of Saint Benedict, who symbolized the burial of Jesus Christ by hiding himself in a cave and leaving his children in tombs. In a similar way several other saints, who have appeared in the holy church, have borne certain exterior manifestations of these mysteries. But the remainder of Christians, to whom they left the example of their devotion by placing these mysteries in a concrete form before their eyes, must have within themselves these graces and this spirit even if they do not conform externally to these same mysteries.

The spirit of these holy mysteries is given to us through baptism, which activates within us graces and sentiments that are in relation and conformity to the mysteries of Jesus Christ. We have only to allow him to operate in us, and through the power of his graces and lights, to work on us and others in conformity to these holy mysteries.

For example, we have in us the Spirit of Jesus Christ crucified, which offers us the light and grace to crucify us interiorly and to mortify us at those times when our flesh seeks its own pleasure and satisfaction. Thus, through this Spirit we will be conformed interiorly to Jesus Christ crucified.

Thus, this same Spirit gives us the grace so that we might share in and become like Jesus Christ risen from the dead. Interiorly we have a life hidden in God just as he did exteriorly. First of all, he was exteriorly removed from everyday human life, having withdrawn into his Father where he lived and prayed. He was not seen among men nor did he become involved with them. In the same way our soul should be interiorly withdrawn from contact and communication with creatures. It should be detached from futile worldly pleasures, having no more interior interest, or thoughts or affection for them. Thus, withdrawing from things of the world and attending to God, the soul leaves behind all those attachments by which it had been immersed in the world and in visible creatures. It begins to enter into God in order to live with him in solitude and interior retreat. It is by this means that the soul enters into the very state of the resurrection.

Second, our Lord was hidden in God by his holy resurrection, so that his life, that is his fleshly life, his human life, his life of weakness, was lost in God. For since he was consumed in God, like wood in the fire, there was nothing that appeared in him besides God, in whom he was lost, buried and totally engulfed.

This risen life and this life of God in God is the hidden life that all Christians should aspire to and participate in because of the nature of the intimate union to which they are called even in this life. This union is with the God, who, like a devouring fire and an ardent furnace, engulfs the soul, absorbing it, annihilating it and destroying it. It is thus that he hides the soul in himself. This is how we share in the mystery of the resurrection. This is the risen life, which according to Saint Paul is given to all Christians by baptism: *So just as Christ rose from the dead through the glory of the Father, so we might also live a new life* (Rom 6:4). Jesus Christ entered into the life of God through his resurrection so that he no longer lived the life of the flesh. The soul no longer gave life to his body in the crude way it enlivened it before, that is to say, in order to meet its needs and the demands of life in the world. Rather, his soul, totally transformed into God, was completely devoured, lost and absorbed in God. Everything that was earthy and crude in his flesh was wholly consumed in glory. In the same way, the Christian life bears within it a movement of our whole soul into God, so that afterward it only thinks of loving him, seeing him, remembering him, serving him with all its strength, so that it brings to God and to his service all its life and power.

Therefore, in this state of resurrection and divine life the soul no longer feels attached to the flesh in order to serve it and to follow its inclinations and its movements. Rather, it is in such a breathless pursuit of God that only a very small part of it actually enlivens the flesh. For this reason the soul's least concern is to give life to the body, which is half-dead and without energy, since the soul has been caught up in God and only lives for him. The soul borrows the qualities of God and his being. It is much more appropriate that God should consume us than enliven us, since he is ablaze in himself. Also he is the fullness of being for which all things were made, and he was made for no other thing. Therefore it follows that the soul exists much more for him than for the body. Thus, it loses itself much more so in him than it would ever be capable of drawing him to enliven the body and to have God become its form.

Thus, since the soul is in God where it loses itself, being annihilated in his love and uniting itself to him, it shares in the life of God himself and is thus resurrected in spirit. It inwardly shares in the resurrection of the Son of God, who was outwardly hidden in God. The power of that divine life overwhelmed him and annihilated all the life and weakness of the flesh that had been in him previously. This is the first conformity to which the Spirit of Jesus Christ calls us, once he has told us to follow him, by making us like him (Mt 16:24).

CHAPTER THREE

*Concerning the Second Way
We Must Conform to Jesus Christ*

The second way in which we should conform to Jesus Christ is to his interior[8] through his mysteries. In this way our souls, in their interior sentiments and dispositions, will become conformed not only to

JEAN-JACQUES OLIER

the outer aspects of the mysteries, as we have seen, but also to the interior dispositions and sentiments that our Lord had in these mysteries.

Christian life strictly speaking is the Christian person living interiorly, through the operation of the Spirit, in the same way Jesus Christ lived. Without this there can be neither the unity nor the perfect conformity to which our Lord does call us. He wishes that, through the operation of the Holy Spirit, we live with him a life that is truly one, just as the Father and Son live with one another. For they have only one life, one sentiment, one desire, one love, one light, because they are but one God living in the two persons.

This is why the Spirit of God is poured forth in Christians, as in the members of the same body, to enliven them with the same life and to have in them the same operations he produced in Jesus Christ, thus dilating his occupations, dispositions, loves and movements. It is like a drop of oil on a piece of white satin, which at first covers only a small corner of the material, but spreads out quickly over the whole piece. In the same way the Spirit of God, who lived in the heart of Jesus Christ, with time and the passage of the years during which the faithful have been united to Jesus Christ, has spread out in all, guaranteeing that everyone is made to share in the same taste and the same smell and finally in the same sentiments.

It is the same Spirit in all, producing the same effects in everyone. Having been transformed and reformed in this way by the Spirit in Jesus Christ at the depth of their souls, they are no longer distinct by the individual sentiments of their flesh and their self-love, which normally rule in everyone differently according to their various temperaments and distinct caprices. Rather, they are all one through the unity of the same Spirit, who rules in them and penetrates their hearts. They are no longer distinct through the diversity of religions: *There is no Gentile nor Jew, circumcised nor uncircumcised* (Col 3:11); no Jew nor Greek (Gal 3:28) nor through the distinction of climates, nations, nor the opposition of temperaments and barbaric customs: *Barbarian nor Scythian* (Col 3:11); nor through the distinction of social condition: Slave nor freeman (ibid.); nor through sexual distinction: *Neither male nor female,* because they are all the same in Jesus Christ: *You are all the same in Christ Jesus* (Gal 3:28); and Jesus Christ is all things in all, *Sed omnia et in omnibus Christus* (Col 3:11).

Furthermore, the Spirit fills them not only with the general dispositions of his heart, such as a horror for sin, self-annihilation, profound adoration and reverence for his Father, and perfect love of neighbor, but also with the particular dispositions that he had in his mysteries. Because every holy disposition in the soul of Jesus pleased the Father and caused him joy, thus the Holy Spirit, who seeks only to please the Father in everything, gladly pours himself out in the same way through his holy operations in those souls prepared to let him act in them.

This is what he accomplishes for the glory of God, especially in those souls who, because they are at peace and emptied of all things, give him the opportunity. And above all he desires to do this in those souls who are chosen to represent Jesus Christ on earth and to continue his life as Head and Shepherd for others, his life as a supplement for others, which is the life of the priest. It is the priest who takes the place of Jesus Christ in order to make up what is lacking in the religion of men, and therefore to be the universal religious of the church, praying, praising, loving on behalf of everyone, accepting and fulfilling the duties of all, the one who makes amends for the omissions of all.

This, then, was the plan of the Son of God, as he came on earth. He wished to continue in Christians the holiness of both his exterior and interior mysteries and establish in them these two conformities, which create a perfect likeness between the members and the head.

God's way of carrying out this very sublime work is in accord with the way he acts in the natural order, where nothing changes suddenly. In fact, each thing grows little by little and achieves imperceptibly the perfection to which the holy providence of God wishes to elevate it in the natural order. Thus we must be children before we become fully adults. Trees must have buds, leaves and flowers before bringing forth fruit. It is the same in the spiritual life. First we must begin, then advance before being brought to completion. For the height of the Christian state consists in the participation and the blessed communion in Jesus Christ, our Lord, risen, ascended in heaven and consumed in God his Father. Moreover, we must first pass through his first state, which is that of mortification, suffering, the cross, humiliation and death to everything.

In order for Christians to live their true vocation, which is to reproduce Jesus Christ in themselves, they must express all these holy states in their life in the same order in which they occurred in Jesus Christ. Therefore, as our sacred model Jesus Christ first suffered all sorts of disgrace, scourgings and gibbets, then died and was buried before rising and entering into his glory: *It was necessary for the Christ to suffer and then enter into his glory* (Lk 24:26), in the same way Christians must bear in their lives all these states of humiliation before being able to share in his grandeur and state of exaltation.

Christian life has two parts: death and life. The first is the foundation for the second. This is repeated in the writings of Saint Paul and especially in the sixth chapter to the Romans: *Are you not aware that having been baptized in Christ Jesus, we were also baptized into his death? For we were buried with him in death through baptism, so that, as he is risen from the dead, we might also walk in the newness of life* (vv. 3–4). And afterward he adds: *Consider yourselves dead to sin and living for God in Jesus Christ* (v. 11). And in a thousand other places he repeats these two elements of the Christian life. Therefore, as we have said, death must always precede life. This death is nothing other than our complete downfall, so that as everything in us opposed to God is destroyed, his Spirit may dwell in us in the purity and holiness of his ways.

It is therefore through death that we enter into the Christian life. But we must know how this death comes about and how the Spirit of God works in us. To do this we must be aware of the difference between the Spirit of God and the Spirit of Jesus Christ. Even though the Spirit of God and that of Jesus Christ is one, nevertheless, due to the diverse operations that the Spirit produces, at times he is called Spirit of God and other times Spirit of Jesus Christ.

When the Holy Spirit acts in us and establishes within us the virtues of fortitude, vigor and power and gives us a share in the perfections and attributes of God, which contain in themselves no abasement, then this divine Spirit is called Spirit of God, because God as God has only grandeur and majesty in him. However, when this same Spirit produces in us the virtues of Jesus Christ, which are the Christian virtues containing abasement and humiliation, such as love of the cross, of humility, of poverty, of disdain, then this holy Spirit is called the Spirit of Jesus Christ. We have pointed out this difference so that, in what follows, the reader can distinguish between these ways of speaking. Thus it is this Spirit of Jesus Christ who introduces us into death to sin. By sin I mean all the life of the flesh, which Saint Paul normally calls sin. He brings about this death in us by placing in the depth of our soul the virtues of Jesus Christ; that is, the virtues that he produced in Jesus Christ in his first state, which was one of abasement and humiliation.

Thus it is by these holy virtues that the Spirit of Jesus Christ crucifies our flesh and causes it to die to itself; knowing full well that if anyone tried to build the spiritual life on any other foundation, it would be only an illusion and a deceit. It would never be solid, but constantly wavering and would fall with the first wind of temptation and contradiction. Holy mortification, which flows from an authentic practice of virtues, is the firm rock on which we should build and without which there can be no guarantee.

Let us work seriously at this first part so that we may be worthy to share in the second. In this regard we will speak later about several Christian virtues that are most essential in order to ground us in this death.

CHAPTER FOUR

Concerning the Practice of the Virtues

In order to begin the practice of the virtues of our Lord, we can at times, without any specific insight or understanding, simply give ourselves over to the unique Spirit of Jesus Christ, who is the source of all virtue, and thus imbibe them from him. But it is a great grace when he gives a clear insight into them, when he reveals in particular their nature and inclinations, and when he brings us into the spirit of those we should practice on certain occasions. Even though this insight seems less simple, nevertheless, because it is more developed, it gives a better understanding of the virtues, which exist in him in an eminent and simple way, and a more general grace for their acquisition. This is very helpful for our perfection and as we come to resemble Jesus Christ.

God's way of advancing a soul is first to point out faults that are contrary to the virtues as well as its powerlessness to protect itself and to preserve itself from them without the help of Jesus Christ.

Second, he places before its eyes adept people who are committed to the study and practice of the purity of the virtues. They become for the soul living models and supplements of the presence of Jesus Christ. He then gives it the desire to imitate them.

Third, this good master of souls gives, through his Spirit, the grace to tame the flesh, which is opposed to virtue. He also even brings it, despite its resistance, to an interior exercise of the virtues.

Fourth, he shows the soul the purity of the virtues and the holy way in which our Lord himself practiced them, grounding it with a disposition toward these virtues through Jesus Christ, who is the one and only master of them. And this becomes so natural to the soul, which is thus grounded, that it is only in this divine exercise that it experiences joy and freedom.

Now the best disposition by which we can be prepared to allow the Spirit to possess us and to be grounded by him in these virtues is interior annihilation. So much so that as soon as we allow ourselves to be annihilated by this divine Spirit throughout our whole being, we will experience ourselves as established by him with a disposition toward every virtue as well as with a readiness and inclination to practice all of them when needed. Also, we will live continually in this disposition. I pray to Jesus Christ, our beloved, if it is for the glory of his Father, to graciously grant us this grace to perceive ourselves always as annihilated, insignificant, the least of men, poor insignificant slaves and servants of all, even though we are unworthy; admitting that we are even more unworthy than we can express or imagine and seeing others as incomparably superior to ourselves.

Now the quickest way to experience this annihilation and to attract within us the Holy Spirit, who implants the virtues, is to come before God often as poor beggars, insignificant, annihilated and stripped of everything, but at the same time desiring deeply our perfection. There is no better way to do this than by prayer. Therefore we believe that we should offer a method here to facilitate this exercise.

A Way of Meditating on the Virtues[9]

The method that our Lord teaches his disciples is given only when the more individual attentions of the Spirit, who guides his children in prayer, are absent.

Whenever he abandons them, and they do not know which path to follow, they can become quite hindered in such a period if they are not sustained and directed by some holy method to guide them.

We are suggesting an easy method here, which also is in keeping with the very plan of God the Father, expressed formerly in the Law. It consists in having our Lord before our eyes, in our heart and in our hands. Following the command of God, this is the way in which the Jews were supposed to carry the Law with them. *Let these words be in your heart. Bind them to your hand as a sign and let them hang and swing between your eyes* (Dt 6:6,8).

Christianity consists in these three points, and the whole method of prayer is contained therein; that is, to look at Jesus, to unite ourselves to Jesus, and to act in Jesus. The first point leads us to acts of respect and religion. The second leads to union and unity with him. The third leads to action, which is not isolated but rather united to the power of Jesus Christ, whom we have drawn to us through prayer. The first is called adoration; the second, communion; the third, cooperation.

So that you can easily apply this exercise to any virtue, we will give now an example of this method applied to the virtue of penance.

FIRST POINT

Let Us Place Our Lord Before Our Eyes

That is to say, let us respectfully look at Jesus Christ, doing penance for our sins. Let us honor in him the holy Spirit of penance, which animated him all the days of his life and which subsequently filled the hearts of all those who have done penance in the church.

Let us remain reverent and respectful before such a holy and divine reality. After our heart has expressed freely its love, praise and other duties, let us remain for a while in silence before him, with these same dispositions and religious sentiments in the depth of our soul.

SECOND POINT

Let Us Have Our Lord In Our Hearts

After having considered in this way Jesus Christ and his holy Spirit of penance, we will spend some time longing for this divine Spirit. We will pray to this Spirit, who alone can create a new heart and fashion a penitential soul. We will ask him to please come into us. Using all the wiles of love we will plead with him to enter our soul to make us like Jesus Christ, the penitent one. We are called to carry on in ourselves the same penitential spirit that the Spirit began in him. We need to experience the amount of suffering appropriate for a body, such as ours, which is filled with sins.

We will give ourselves over to him in order to be possessed and enlivened by his power. After this we will spend some time with him in silence to allow ourselves to be saturated interiorly with his divine balm, so that he may bring us, when appropriate, to whatever practice of mortification is pleasing to him.

THIRD POINT

Let Us Hold Our Lord In Our Hands

The third point of this prayer is to have our Lord in our hands, that is to say, to wish that his divine will may be accomplished in us, who are his members. We must be submissive to him who is our head and should experience no other movement than that prompted in us by Jesus Christ, who is our life and our all. Filling our soul with his Spirit, his power and his strength, he should be accomplishing all that he desires in and through us.

In pastors, he is *the* Pastor; in priests, *the* Priest; in religious, *the* Religious; in penitents, *the* Penitent. Through them he accomplishes the works of their vocation. Thus he should produce in us the effects of penance. We should always dwell in that Spirit, in faithful cooperation with all that he wants to do in us and accomplish through us. Thus, in this third point, we will give ourselves over to this Spirit, whom we have drawn to ourselves in the second point. This is so that we may produce through him all day long the works of penance, wishing to live in him constantly, since this is the reason we have sought him in our prayer. We will give ourselves over to that divine Spirit in order to produce through him works of penance, since without this union with him there can be none. Furthermore, we will abandon ourselves completely to him so that he can accomplish in us and with us all that he wishes in order to satisfy God.

In order to further clarify this method and so that it may be used more easily for the other virtues, of which we should say the same things as we have with penance, we should know that it is only through our Lord that we can do penance, for he is the one and only

Penitent in the whole church. He is poured out in the souls and hearts of all penitents, who must groan and suffer in this world in order to atone to the Father.

Thus we must open our heart to the Spirit of the penitent Son of God, so that we may do penance in his person and in his power. We must ask him for the Spirit, who gives us the interior dispositions of penance toward God, such as humiliation, true contrition, condemnation of sin, and horror of the world and its maxims. He also gives us a consuming zeal to make satisfaction in ourselves and upon ourselves for the punishment due to sin. Thus we will not be content simply to behold penance in others or to feel it in our heart, but rather we will desire and ask for the strength to do penance in our bodies, because, since all have sinned, all must offer retribution to God.

Thus we must ask God for his strength and power in order to accomplish the satisfaction he desires, abandoning ourselves to everything he wishes to impose on us himself or through his ministers. We must participate in the interior penance of Jesus Christ, which is boundless in himself and in his members, wishing, if it pleases God, to suffer all that he bore in his flesh and all that his members have suffered in theirs. We should want only those limits that his wisdom imposes on us and that he makes known to us through our superiors, who take his place.

Thus we must lose ourselves in this Spirit of contrition of Jesus Christ, in this boundless sea, in this ocean of penance, so that we can be present in spirit to all that it has produced in him and to all that holy penitents of the church accomplish. For they only express what he contains in his interior and what he would have wished to bear in his body, if he could have endured, in the weakness of his flesh, all that they have suffered.

Our Lord has dilated himself by dilating the body of his church. Furthermore, he bears the suffering of his members since he is inserted and enfleshed in them through his Spirit. He gives life to their souls. He gives strength to their spirits and to their hearts by his presence and his power. Thus he is more the penitent in them than they are in themselves. It is the Spirit of Jesus Christ, the penitent, in their souls that makes penitents of them.

This is the second effect of prayer and the second intention of God and of Jesus Christ in prayer. The first is to make holy the name of God: *Hallowed be your name*. This is why our first occupation is to honor and respect the Spirit of God in him. The second is to bring his kingdom to us: *Your kingdom come*. Now the kingdom of God comes in us when, in prayer, we invoke his Spirit upon us and then he, through his power, subjects us entirely to him. The third is to desire that his holy will be done in us: *Your will be done*, which is accomplished by faithfully cooperating with the movements of this same Spirit.

CHAPTER FIVE

The Virtue of Humility

Humility is the virtue that is the foundation for all the others. It must be presupposed in every work of piety. Without it, we will never make any progress. Pride, which is the opposite of this virtue, is the vice that displeases God the most. This is the horrible and damnable sin that God insists so often in the scriptures that he wants to resist: *God resists the proud* (Js 4:6).

God resists pride because it injures him in a strange way. It takes from him what is most precious: the glory and honor that are due to him and that he reserves for himself. It attributes it instead to a nothing and a worm. There is nothing of which God is more jealous. He shares with us his divine being, his nature and all his gifts, but only on the condition that we do not steal from him what he does not wish to share with any creature: *I will not give my glory to any other* (Is 42:8).

God has such revulsion and hatred for pride that, as soon as a soul is so unfortunate as to open itself up to it, at that very moment God pulls back and leaves the soul to itself. He removes his grace and assistance. Likewise, he will not come close again until the soul empties itself of pride and all self-love. This is why we say that holy humility is the basis for all the virtues, because they cannot be acquired without grace and divine assistance, which are given only to the humble: *However he gives his grace to the humble* (Js 4:6).

Therefore we will begin with humility and see first of all in what it consists.

232

JEAN-JACQUES OLIER

FIRST SECTION

The Nature of Humility

Humility has three parts. The first is to take pleasure in self-knowledge. For there are many people to whom God makes known their own misery and failings. He even gives them some experience of this, making them aware of their stupidity, their superficiality, their uselessness and their inability to do anything. But they are saddened by this vision. They cannot bear it. They look for something in themselves that is flattering. They try to discover some perfection and some virtue that would shelter them from this awareness. This is a result of pride. At times we find ourselves in such a state that we are greatly discouraged to see ourselves as we are, that is to say, nothing without grace, and nothing in nature, useless for any good purpose, unbearable to ourselves and to all others. If all this brings about interior discouragement, it is a sign of false humility.

On the other hand, our Lord gives this same experience to those holy persons whom he cherishes and loves and who are rooted in true humility, so as to further deepen this virtue in them and to prepare a broader base to welcome his grace and his love. But these souls, who are already humble, rejoice to know who they are. Provided that they do not adhere to the wickedness of their flesh, they are content. But sometimes they do not know, and God does not permit them to distinguish between the attacks of the flesh, that is, covetousness and consent, which at times causes them to suffer. On certain occasions, they will feel unfavorable toward the poor and to offering them charity. At other times they will feel opposed to God and his holy Word. Sometimes they will feel other movements that originate from the malicious depth of the flesh, which generally we refer to as our corrupt nature. And being unsure whether they have consented to these movements, they are most distressed and greatly humiliated in this state and also in the thought that they have not worked hard enough to triumph over themselves.

Now these trials in the lives of saints are not so much a question of pain and discouragement as they are of confusion and humiliation. And even this serves as a reminder to them of who they are, reminding them of the flesh they carry and what their nature is like; a nature of sin, a terrain of inexhaustible malice, on which they are the laborers. For having consented with Adam to sin, and having acquired, through the multitude of their own sins, many vicious habits, they have altered the purity of their nature. They have so ruined it that there remains in it nothing of value. A new source is needed. Another generation is needed to give us a second life and a second spirit to maintain it. It is the Holy Spirit himself who creates in us movements for good and who invites us to good works, just as our flesh draws us toward bad ones. Thus the spirit and the flesh are in perpetual conflict. Saint Paul says, *The flesh fights against the spirit and the spirit fights against the flesh* (Gal 5:17).

In this way the saints, who are truly humble, recognize very well what they are by themselves and what in them is of God. They know where the good comes from and who causes it. They offer unceasing praise and glory to God for the good things that he accomplishes in their souls and humiliate themselves just as unceasingly for the evil that they do and that they experience in themselves, recognizing their poverty, their misery and their vileness. They even condemn themselves as the cause of the evil they experience. This insight humiliates them, but does not at all crush them or discourage them because of any sadness they may feel about it.

This, then, is the first aspect of the virtue of humility: to know and to love one's own vileness and misery. For the knowledge of this vileness and misery is not a part of the virtue of humility, but rather a foundation and presupposition for it. This is why even though self-knowledge by itself existed in pagans, nevertheless they possessed nothing of this Christian virtue, of which the first step is the pleasure and the joy that one experiences in knowing oneself.

What then is this humility? It is the love of one's own degradation, so that little by little one becomes so enamored of vileness, littleness and baseness, that one loves it everywhere and in all things.

For example, someone recognizes in himself his nothingness, which makes him vile and abject. He recognizes his weakness, his defects and even his sins. He should take pleasure in his vileness, in his own degradation and in the scorn he will receive. He should take pleasure in what is vile, abject and humiliating in himself.

The vileness and the degradation that result from sin are quite distinct from opposition to God. If the soul is humble, it should love the vileness to which it is reduced through sin, but should despise its sin inasmuch as it is opposed to God. The soul should be so enamored of its vileness and baseness that it should love it everywhere it is found or where it might be encountered. It should find its charms so delectable that it could find nothing else so lovable. It should be our queen, our one and only beloved. Our happiness and our only peace consist in the love of littleness, the love of baseness and the love of degradation.

This type of humility has its source in God himself, who, although incapable by nature of being abased, due to his infinite perfections, nevertheless has in himself an inclination toward little things. For in himself he loves what is lowly. David says, *He looks upon what is lowly* (Ps 112:6). The blessed Virgin states: *He has looked upon the lowliness and the littleness of his handmaiden* (Lk 1:48); that is, he is pleased by this and takes pleasure in it.

The immense power of the Godhead first filled the soul of Jesus Christ with its inclinations and placed in him an infinite tendency toward baseness, which is continually at work in him, but is never fulfilled or satisfied. All the scorn, abasement and degradation that exists is like nothing to his soul before this immense thirst that engulfs him.

This is what constitutes the humility of God and that of Jesus Christ, in which we should commune and which he pours forth in the heart of Christians, to whom he gives the same tendency and the same inclination toward lowly things. This is true Christian humility.

We should look at what the prophet says about the heart of Jesus Christ, which he notes was overwhelmed with humiliation. This was caused by the immensity of God working in the depth of his soul through his infinite power.

We should not only consider him in the humiliations that he bore himself, of which he said on the cross, *I am thirsty* (Jn 19:28) but also in the humiliations and the scorn he desires to suffer in his Mystical Body and in his members. Beholding them he said also, *Sitio, I am thirsty.* I am languishing and dying of desire for more sufferings and new scorn. Since I must extend myself throughout my whole church and in her satisfy my thirst, then the more scorn I suffer in her, the more joy and consolation I will experience and the more I will satisfy my immense desire to enter into littleness.

It is my Father, infinite in his desires, who causes this yearning and this immense desire in me, before which I am nothing and I am unable to satisfy it. Therefore, I am continually looking for someone on earth to satisfy the pain and the desire that I have to drink deeply of shame and scorn at all times and in all places. This means that when someone suffers and welcomes this with love and joy, then it amounts to satisfying my thirst.

It seems to me that it would be right to give such joy to Jesus Christ in us and to work at satisfying him and making him happy in this way. We should fully realize how little opportunity we give to the power and fruitfulness of God's activity in our heart, because of the aversion we have to shame.

God is immense in himself. The infinite weight of his being should humiliate everything under him, leading us to the love of scorn and vileness. Nevertheless, we discover that our heart resists him so strongly and exercises such control over him that, instead of tending toward littleness, we tend only toward greatness, looking only for praise, esteem and applause. God, who is so powerful in all things and especially in the soul of his Son, finds himself powerless in us.

Let us study how to renounce our inner core, how to condemn it and how to surrender it to God, so that he can imprint in us what he wants and insert in us his inclinations, his sentiments and even his dispositions. We must pray much to the majesty of God that he exercise his power and immense strength in us, so that he may humiliate us in him and offer us a share in his inclinations and desires.

The most important humility is the interior one, which concerns primarily the spirit. It consists in always submitting the powers of the soul to God in complete dependence on him, so that the spirit of the Christian would never be so insolent and so proud as to exalt itself in the presence of its king and God, but rather would remain always in submission and reverence before him, waiting upon his light and his orders with patience. And thus it will never be so bold as to act or reason about things on its own and in itself, but rather it will always submit itself to God, waiting with faith upon his guidance and his command.

It is the same with our will, which being in sinful flesh and in the present state of disorder, needs, even more than our understanding, much like a queen who commands and rules, to depend on the Holy Spirit, who wishes to be king and master in us.

Our will is more affected by sin than the rest of us. Therefore it is more haughty and arrogant. It is always ready to give orders and rarely disposed to obey. It takes great effort and continuous attention to keep it in subjection and submission. It gives commands in every situation and pays no attention to the orders, movements and guidance of the Holy Spirit and to his love, which alone should rule over us and lead us smoothly toward those things that God desires.

Therefore, true and perfect interior humility consists in the submission of the will to God, along with our understanding, which should act as if it were dead and wait very faithfully, submitting itself to the divine impressions and to those lights that God promises to his children. Thus the soul will be truly humble in spirit and truth, in deed and in perfect sacrifice. For the soul in this state protests that it is worth nothing, that it cannot act in justice and holiness, but that everything comes from God and depends on him and that everything in us should be accomplished by him.

To be aware that we are worth nothing, that we know nothing and that we can do nothing, and to take pleasure in this insight and knowledge, is the first point of humility.

The second is to love one's vileness, littleness and nothingness in other people's awareness as well as in our own. In other words, it is to love being known as vile, abject, nothingness and sin and to want to be seen in this way by everyone. For the heart of humility is to allow ourselves to experience the love, joy and pleasure of being known and valued by everyone for what we are. Otherwise we remain hypocritical and dishonest, desiring to appear to be something we are not, even doing and saying many things to excuse the defects that people notice in us.

It is this defect in humility that causes the pain and shame we have experienced when people have discovered our imperfections. This causes the struggle that we feel and the anxiety that prods us to succeed in our undertakings so that we might acquire a reputation and pass for something of value in the eyes of other people. We can never tolerate what Jesus Christ wishes to accomplish in us through his spirit of humility, that is, to love being known for what we are: nothingness and sin. We are nothing more than this in ourselves and of ourselves. All else comes from God, and we are stealing from him everything that we wish to attribute to ourselves besides nothingness and sin.

We are so totally and truly nothingness that if God does not communicate existence to us at all times, then there is nothing in us. Only nothingness remains. This is our core and our true reality. So much so that if there is something in us which is not sin, that is to say, not corrupted by sin in our faculties, we should give thanks to God, who has accomplished this in us by his goodness to which belongs all honor. For it is we who have committed sin with Adam, having consented with him to his fault. For we were contained in him, as if he were our procurator, holding our will in his hands. God had chosen him for us with great kindness as the most perfect man in the world and the one to whom, quite appropriately, we gave the power to deal with God for us and in our name. For Adam dealt with God for the whole human race. Thus it was that our will was in this way united and in agreement with his.

So there is this first fault, which is our doing and which is the root cause of the evil that pollutes every day and every hour. It also causes that corruption in us which Saint Paul calls sin, because it comes from sin and draws us toward it, thus making us sin. Besides this first sin to which we consented in Adam; besides this disordered desire that inclines us unceasingly toward sin, we have also committed a thousand crimes, which have totally blackened us. This is why truly we are sin in ourselves and nothing but that. This core of malice, with which we are filled, is a horror to God. Therefore, in that part of us we are accursed children, and we cannot conceal what we are in the sight of heaven and earth. Thus we should want to be seen as such in the minds of everyone.

Thus humility is that virtue which gives us this pleasure and this satisfaction of appearing as we are, of being seen as people who are nothing and who are accursed sinners in everyone's eyes. For in ourselves we are nothing but that. For if there are graces in us or any gifts, these do not come from us, but from God. If we wish to be appreciated and esteemed for that, then we unjustly steal what does not belong to us, and we claim for ourselves what belongs to God alone.

Humility must make us take a good look at what we are and what is ours, so that we might leave for God and return faithfully to him all that belongs to him and all that comes from him. The devil concentrates all his efforts here and works especially on this point, trying to blur these two distinct insights, which teach us so clearly what is of us and what is of God. He works to make us believe that what is in us is from us, that it belongs to us and that, because of it, we can value ourselves and seek to be valued by others.

However, the truly humble soul, who skillfully wards off the wiles of the evil one, works at never forgetting what it is and what it produces. It sees itself as nothingness and sin and wishes to be seen as such in the sight of every creature. Thus, it is dead to esteem and is no longer concerned about what people think of it. When it does receive some honor and praise, inwardly it laughs at itself and makes light of those who value it, considering them to be blind people who speak unknowingly. At times it experiences such disgust and such horror at these things that it would much rather suffer a thousand insults than a single word of praise. For the former is based on the truth and the latter on a lie. Thus, it is very surprised when people appreciate it in some way other than what it sees and experiences continually in itself.

Saint Bernard says that the second degree of humility is to know not only that we are nothing, but that even what appears in others is nothing. All being, goodness and truth exist in God and, through participation, in creatures, whose depth and intrinsic reality is nothing. Flowing from the nothingness that we are as creatures, our proper activity is a tendency toward nothingness. The essence of nothing is to tend toward nothing. This is what man is and how he should want to appear. Otherwise he is robbing and stealing from the supreme Being, desiring to take his place and to claim for himself what belongs to God.

The third point of humility is to not only want to be known in this way, but also to be treated as vile, abject and contemptible. It is to welcome with joy all possible scorn and shame, never getting enough insults, but on the contrary hoping for more of them with an insatiable desire. In other words, it is to desire to be treated according to one's merit. Since we think of ourselves as only insignificant nothingness and accursed sinners, and we do not want to be thought of differently by other people, therefore humility gives us the desire to be treated as nothingness, as accursed creatures and unfortunate sinners, which are two of the most scornful titles imaginable.

If we try to imagine all possible scorn, it would be nothing compared to what is due us. This is why the truly humble soul cannot be scorned. No matter what anyone says or does against it, it cannot be shamed and even less take offense, because all of that is nothing compared to what it has merited. What scorn does nothingness deserve? It has nothing in itself to recommend it. It possesses nothing to capture our thoughts or actions. For nothingness speaks of the privation of all being and all perfection, which are the only bases for our esteem and appreciation. Moreover, what scorn should we not have for sin, which is not in the least attractive and tolerable, but on the contrary, of its very nature, speaks of alienation from the true good, who is God and therefore is the privation of every good?

It is clear that an insult is an honor to a humble soul. For since it is nothingness, it does not merit being noticed or being thought of. It is not worthy of the scorn and the consideration of others. Since it is nothingness, who would speak to it in order to insult it? We do not insult ghosts, because they do not exist and are not worthy of insult. Therefore, the one who knows that in himself he is only nothingness, and much less than a ghost, thinks himself quite honored that anyone has thought of him and spoken some insult to him. Therefore, if others forget him and despise him, the humble person is not astonished and does not think that they should act any differently. An affront does not surprise him at all, and he would be quite astonished if he were treated in any other way. Even if God despises the soul interiorly, it should not be astonished, for it does not deserve anything else.

This is the true touchstone to recognize authentic humility: that in interior dryness, aridity, abandonment and rejection by God, the soul takes God's side and approves of his prosecution of itself; that it humiliates itself and annihilates itself in prayer, condemning itself and saying that it deserves no other treatment. We should admit that he is right to reject our works and our very selves. When we see some evidence of this, if this bothers us, it is a lack of humility. It is a sign that we are not thoroughly convinced of how totally useless we are.

Our nothingness, which is clothed with a being corrupted by sin, can do nothing of its own self but sin. It can only spoil everything it does, which is a source of great shame, making us admit that God, who is fairness, perfect integrity and true justice, has every right to reject us and all that is part of us. For our good works and all that is holy and acceptable to God in our activities proceeds from his Son, in whom all his pleasure resides through the work of the Holy Spirit.

To be despised and rejected by God, mistreated by our superiors, our peers and even our subordinates, in other words, by all creatures, this is our due and should make us rejoice. It is the most appropriate response, which we should love more than anything, being the best, most advantageous thing for us and the most in conformity to the desire of Jesus Christ.

Thus we should love littleness, no matter where it comes from and no matter where we find it. We must love it not only in this world, but also in the other, not only on earth, but also in heaven. For example, we should love having the lowest place, as our Lord recommends. It is a sign of the love of littleness. We should so love the lowest place that we even desire it in paradise.

It is not that we should desire to be the least in the love of God, nor the most negligent about growing in perfection, nor should we say, as do the least committed, that just to begin is enough for them. They say that they do not care about being great saints, and by this they risk never achieving it. On the contrary, we should strive to love God as much as he desires and be faithful enough to attain the degree of glory and beatitude, which he prepares for us.

Thus anyone who would commit a fault that is sinful in order to be humiliated would be doing nothing of value. In the same way, anyone who omits doing good in order to be little in heaven would be very wrong. I am speaking specifically only about littleness in itself. It should be always so attractive to our spirit that we would love it everywhere. We should perform no action with the intention of being great and of protecting us against littleness.

Our pride is so subtle that when we close one door to it, it opens another one for itself. When we deaden the desire for greatness in this world, then it desires it in the other. When we have eliminated it in the base things of the earth, it goes looking for it in the things of spirit and grace. As soon as we have renounced the love of being great, excelling in the honor and richness of the world to which pride was leading us, then right away, it seeks to be great and outstanding in grace. It desires to excel in the spirit, it seeks and desires great gifts and superior lights, spectacular graces, in other words, extraordinary talents. Thus it always seeks greatness.

And if we manage to remove this desire and recognize this subtle pride, then it seeks to excel in another way, that is, in glory. It hopes for an exalted place in heaven, which, in fact, is fine when it does not come from a spirit of pride. However, frequently we can even love littleness on earth through proud desire, hoping, by this means, for greatness in paradise. Because humility on earth is the seed of exaltation in heaven, we accomplish our actions with this intention of being great and consoling ourselves in our humiliations through this insight. The spirit of pride is strange, always looking for excellence and greatness, in this moment and the next, in one thing and another.

On the contrary, true humility desires to be nothing, neither in its own eyes nor in anyone's mind. It is careful to not stand out in anything. It creates a great desire to be hidden and to love being unknown, passing for nothingness. Only Jesus Christ should stand out in all things and we should not stand out at all. We should destroy our own being in order to be clothed with Jesus Christ, so that we are noticed only under him and in him. This produces a desire and a holy inclination to accomplish nothing by ourselves and makes us faithful in denying ourselves interiorly; working to mortify our own spirit and will, at all times, so that we come to live in this spirit of interior death. Neither our spirit nor our will act any more by themselves, but rather, both exist in simple cooperation with the Holy Spirit, who animates our interior and gives life to our faculties.

Thus we live in authentic annihilation and we have nothing but God living and reigning in us. This is why God loves humble souls so much and why he establishes his throne and his domain in them in such an absolute fashion. For there exists in the annihilated person a total freedom for him to do what he pleases. He takes supreme pleasure in the religious sacrifice of all one's intrinsic being, which immolates itself and is divinely consumed.

CHAPTER NINE

On Patience

Patience is a virtue that causes us to bear difficulties and sufferings in peace and gives us joy in the tribulations that God chooses to send us.

For patience to be Christian, it must, through the eyes of faith, see God as the author of all the sufferings and persecutions that happen to us.

It must even bear affliction and abandonment with the power of the Spirit of God, who first dwelt fully in Jesus Christ and then was transmitted to us through baptism and the other sacraments.

JEAN-JACQUES OLIER

FIRST SECTION

The Degrees of Patience

Patience has three degrees, which our Lord indicates to us in the gospel and of which he wished to offer us the example.

The first is to suffer the trials that come to us with resignation and complete surrender to the orders of God. Thus Job, in the midst of his sufferings and trials said with perfect tranquility and total abandonment to the divine will: God *has given it to me*, God *has taken it away: blessed be his holy name* (Jb 1:21).

Patience never murmurs against God or against its neighbor. It is not interiorly anxious in pain, and it offers us the same dispositions as the souls in purgatory, who suffer the violence of the flames and the torments in sublime peace.

This first degree is indicated to us by these words: *Blessed are they who suffer persecution for justice* (Mt 5:10) and who suffer it in peace and in surrender to the holy decrees of divine Providence. He gave us an example of this when he submitted voluntarily to so many trials and in the midst of all these sufferings experienced the tranquility of a lamb being led to the slaughterhouse.

The second degree is to desire passionately to suffer. We see this in the martyrs whose hearts, inflamed with this desire, even indicated externally the great love that they had for suffering.

Thus Saint Andrew, when he saw the torments prepared for him, cried out: *O good cross, how long and passionately have I desired you!* In the same way Saint Lawrence showed how he suffered with difficulty the delay of his martyrdom. Similarly, Saint Teresa, transported by love, cried out: *Either to suffer or to die.*[10]

Our Lord expresses this second degree with these words: *Blessed are those who hunger and thirst for justice* (Mt 5:6) and who desire ardently to suffer in order to fulfill in themselves the plan of God, who wishes that all Christians suffer with Jesus Christ and that they appease in him and with him his divine justice.

Thus he wished to achieve this and show us how much he loved suffering, when he said: *I have desired passionately to eat this Passover with you* (Lk 22:15). He considered the Passover sacrifice to be the same sacrifice as that of the cross in which all suffering is contained and enclosed. With this in mind, he showed what a great desire he experienced.

The third degree is to suffer with pleasure and joy. Thus the apostles and the first Christians went forth rejoicing, because they had been found worthy to suffer for Jesus Christ (Acts 5:41).

Saint Paul in his epistles tells the faithful that he wants them to share the joy he has in his afflictions and difficulties. He is not content just to share his joy with them, but he tells them that he is victorious in his weakness and that he glories in his sufferings (2 Cor 12:9). Saint James tells us that our hearts should be filled with joy when various difficulties and temptations come to us (Js 1:2).

Our Lord expresses again this third degree when he says that *we are blessed when men persecute us and make us suffer all sorts of misfortune and calamity and that in those moments, we should rejoice* (Mt 5:11–12). He gave us the example himself, for it says that *he carried his cross with joy* (Heb 12:2).

SECOND SECTION

Motives for Patience

We are obliged to be patient. First, in our condition as creatures; for God, sovereign master of life and death, on whom our existence depends absolutely, has the right to dispose of us as he chooses.

Saint Paul says that the potter has the right to do whatever he wishes with his pot (Rom 9:21) since it is the work of his hands. He shatters it, he breaks it, he refashions it, he molds it, he bends it, he compresses it and shapes it as he wills.

This is how we are in the hands of God. Since we are the work of his hands, he can do with us anything he wishes. Whether he shatters, breaks, kills, mortifies, plunges us to the depth of hell and takes us out again, this is totally in his hands and we should suffer it in peace, adoring his desires, his judgments and his designs for his handiwork and remaining completely abandoned to his good pleasure.

Second, as sinners. For in this condition, we must bear with the effects of his justice and wrath toward us. All the punishments that he carries out in this world are nothing compared to what we deserve and what he would make us suffer if he did not choose to be merciful toward us and to treat us with gentleness and clemency in this life.

The punishments that God meted out to sinners, as we see in the holy scripture, even the torments of the damned and the penalties the demons suffer and will suffer eternally for one sin, should cause us not only to be at peace, but to rejoice in our sufferings.

In fact, what is there in hell that we do not deserve? What torments do they suffer there that we do not merit as well and a thousand times more? For mercy is even found in hell and we are not worthy of it. Should not this insight compel us to bear patiently all the difficulties and tribulations of this life, especially since our Lord says that these are signs of his love? *I reprove and I chastise those whom I love* (Rv 3:19).

Third, as Christians. For as such we should bear with many difficulties and sufferings. This is why we are initiated into the church. For our Lord only admitted us into it to continue his life, which is a life of opposition, contradiction and condemnation toward the flesh.

He must then humiliate it and subdue it in us, using the ways he knows and judges to be most useful, so as to win a complete victory. He first achieved victory in his own flesh, and he wishes to continue it in ours in order to show forth in us a sample of the universal triumph that he had achieved over it in his own person.

The church and Christians are only a handful of flesh compared to the whole world. Nevertheless, he still desires to be victorious in them to proclaim his triumph and to give definite signs of his victory. Thus, from this perspective, the Christian should be very faithful to the Spirit and completely abandoned to him in order to overcome the flesh and to destroy it completely.

There will be no lack of opportunities in this life, for he must suffer: first, the attacks of the world through scorn, calumny and persecution; second, the violent onslaughts of the flesh in its uprisings and its revolts; third, the battles with the devil in the temptations he sends us; finally, the ordeals from God through dryness, desolation, abandonment and other interior difficulties, which he afflicts on him in order to initiate him into the perfect crucifixion of the flesh.

Fourth, as clerics. For clerics should participate in the fulfillment of Christianity. This cannot exist without patience.

Patience is a sign that the soul is intimately united to God and that it is rooted in perfection. For it must be very much in God and fully possessed by him in order to bear difficulties and torments with peace, tranquility and even joy and beatitude in one's heart.

It must be quite profoundly immersed in him and remain quite powerfully and strongly united to him, so that the flesh has no power at all to attract it to itself and share with him the feelings and aversions that it has toward suffering and endurance.

In this state the soul experiences the perfection attainable in this life, since it conforms to our Lord's perfect submission to God during his sufferings. For although his flesh experienced aversion and revulsion for the cross, he paid no attention to it with his will. Rather, he always adhered perfectly to the wishes of his Father.

Therefore clerics, being perfect Christians chosen from the midst of the church to assist before the tabernacle of God, should pay particular attention to this virtue. This is their very nature. It is the sign by which they can be identified. This is what predisposes them for the honorable rank that they possess. This is how they are recognized as domestics and servants of God.

Finally, priests and pastors should have a very high degree of patience because, in Jesus Christ and with Jesus Christ, they are both priests and victims for the sins of the world. Jesus Christ the priest wished to be the victim of his sacrifice. He became the host-victim for all people. Since priests are like sacraments and representations of him who lives in them to continue his priesthood and whom he clothes with his external conduct and his interior dispositions, as well as with his power and his person, he wishes furthermore that they be interiorly rooted in the spirit and dispositions of a host-victim in order to suffer, endure, do penance, in short, to immolate themselves for the glory of God and the salvation of the people.

In imitation of our Lord, priests should not only be victims for sin through persecution, penance, internal and external sufferings, but also they should be like the victims of a holocaust. This is their true vocation. For they should not merely suffer, as he did, all sorts of difficulties both for their own sins and the sins of the people entrusted to them, but even more they should be entirely consumed with him through love.

The spirit of love strengthens and empowers us to endure affliction and suffering, no matter how great they are. Since he is infinite, he gives us as much as we need to endure those that can occur in our vocation.

All the torments of the world are nothing to a generous soul filled with the power of a God, who is able to shoulder countless sufferings more violent than all those that the world and the devil might afflict us with. It is with this Spirit that Saint Paul said: *I can do all things in him who strengthens me* (Phil 4:13). Everything he saw seemed little to do or suffer because of the God who dwelled in him.

It is through this same eternal, immense and all-powerful Spirit that he called his sufferings light and momentary, because Jesus Christ who suffered and bore them in himself and allowed him to see and experience something of his eternity through his presence, caused him to look upon the entire duration of this life as but a moment. This is how our Lord, who allows us to experience interiorly that his power and his strength could support a thousand worlds, leads us to call his burden light.

However, it is not as if he does not occasionally withdraw his tangible strength from us so that we might experience the burden of tribulation in the weakness of our flesh and in the frailty to which it is reduced because of his absence. However, he makes us endure this abandonment in order to produce two wonderful effects in our souls.

The first is to mistrust ourselves and the weaknesses of the flesh. The second is to appreciate God and his strength. For in this state we are necessarily forced to turn to God and to dwell in him so that we might be strengthened and sustained in order to accomplish and to suffer all that he wishes for his glory.

Chapter Eleven

On Poverty

Poverty exists not only to separate man from the external realities of the world, but it has another goal and more important purpose, which is to return the whole interior man to his original state.

This detachment from external things exists among Christians only in imitation of Jesus Christ our Lord, who was the first to desire to detach himself from them, in order to make the holy and heroic virtue of poverty accessible to men, who fear it so much that they are afraid of being poor even in the midst of wealth and riches.

It exists as well to punish men for the misuse they have made of all things, both in Adam and in themselves. To make satisfaction for this God has desired to deprive them as well as to undergo penance himself as an example for his church.

FIRST SECTION

On the Nature of Poverty

If we are to understand the nature of poverty in its purpose and in the intention of Jesus Christ, who offers reparation for the human race, we must know that man was formed by God to be his temple, in which he alone wished to be loved, praised and adored. His intention then, in satisfying God his Father, is to restore man to his original state, to the original perfection and holiness in which he was created.

His first commandment is the expression of the original state of man and of his original designs for him, when from the first moment of his creation, he imprinted in his heart the same law he later etched in stone, obliging him to use his whole soul, his whole heart and all his strength to love him. It is for this reason, then, that in this first commandment he speaks thus, *You will love your God with all your heart,* and so on (Dt 6:5). It is also for this reason that he created the human heart empty of any object, as a pure capacity for him and for his love.

However, the work of the devil was to fill the human heart with idols, facsimiles and illusions, to occupy his thoughts and fill his desires with the love of these things so that turning away from true worship and from the unique and pure love of God, he might fall into idolatry.

Saint Paul says that avarice and the love of worldly things is an idolatry and once it is implanted in the human heart, we can say that it is the abomination of desolation in the holy place.

What could be more horrible or be a greater desolation than to see the human heart, which is the temple of God and a holy place, which he has consecrated in a special way to himself, filled with so many unclean and impure things and to see in the niches of this temple, as in the one Ezechiel saw (Ez 8), snakes, crocodiles and the other abominable things that fill it?

This is such an abomination before God that formerly he abandoned his people to the wrath of his enemies in order to punish the greed of only one person who had kept a scarlet mantle and a bar of gold, and had taken them from Jericho, a place of anathema, condemned to fire by a judgment pronounced by the mouth of God (Jos 7:20–21).

The intention of Jesus Christ, as he comes into our heart to sanctify it and to restore it to its original state of emptiness, is to banish from his temple all that fills it. He cannot tolerate there anything but his Father and his divine perfections. With the lashes of a whip he drives from it, through persecutions and through crosses, all the buyers and sellers.

Our Lord becomes zealous and furious when he finds his Father's house, this house of prayer, which should be decorated with holiness, filled with merchants. Merchants here symbolize the greedy, because they risk their life using all their time and their energy in dealing and negotiating for earthly things, instead of using it for God, who desires all the mind, all the heart, all the time and all the strength of his weak creatures.

This is why Jesus Christ came into the world. He wanted to purify the human heart, empty it of every creature and thus make reparation for the original misfortune and disorder into which we had fallen through the misery of sin and the goading of the devil. Thus it follows that he has established, as the major foundation of our salvation, holy poverty, which tends by its nature to empty the human heart of everything that could fill it, other than God.

This is why he said in his first sermon and established as his first maxim, *Blessed are the poor* (Mt 5:3), in order to teach Christians that the virtue of poverty is necessary to them in the most basic and important way.

And to teach them what this poverty is, he says, *Blessed are the poor in spirit*, that is, whose core is empty of any hold on creatures and who have nothing in their heart that takes and fills the place of God, who alone wants to fill them and occupy them.

Outside of God, everything is an illusion, everything is imaginary, nothing but a husk and surface. God alone is the authentic good, and he alone is the entire fundamental and incorruptible life of our souls.

JEAN-JACQUES OLIER

Divisions of Poverty

There are two kinds of poverty, one interior and one exterior. One concerns the stripping of the heart, which should be emptied of all desire and all love for creatures. The other concerns exterior stripping.

Exterior stripping without the interior is no virtue at all. But the interior stripping disposed to an exterior stripping is the virtue of poverty of which our Lord speaks in the gospel when he says: *Blessed are the poor in spirit.*

In this way he wishes to teach Christians that they must exist in poverty, in the stripping and deprivation of spirit, in order to be disposed for the pure love of God. For he cannot co-exist with the love of creatures. He cannot tolerate the slightest attachment to them. He desires a heart that is not full, that is detached from everything and whose entire capacity has been emptied.

THIRD SECTION

Exterior Poverty

There are three kinds of poverty, of which the first two were much in use in the beginning of the church of God.

The first was to leave everything behind and to sell it. Our Lord suggested this to certain individuals in the gospel (Mt 19:21). And also he chose to renew this in recent centuries with Saint Francis and several other saints who practiced this type of poverty.

The second was to place all one's goods in common, which was normal among the early Christians. Each person stripped himself of all he possessed and gave it to God, so that everyone could take according to his needs and, everything being shared equally, the poor person was cared for as well as the rich.

The third is to strip ourselves of the usage of the goods God has given us while remaining in actual possession of them. This poverty can be practiced to great advantage. For, first of all, in this way, we remain in the state of life where divine Providence has placed us. Second, we can use well what he has chosen to give us, utilizing it for his glory. Third, we have the advantage of poverty, which means we have nothing that prevents us from devoting our attention to God alone. It is about this poverty and these poor that it is said, *Blessed are the poor in spirit, for the reign of God belongs to them* (Mt 5:3).

FOURTH SECTION

Interior Poverty

Interior poverty does not include merely detachment from bodily goods, from which the spirit should be separated, interiorly detached and even quite distant. It strips the spirit not only of all honors, all riches and all the goods of the world, but it detaches it as well from the spiritual gifts of God, in the midst of which it should exist as if naked.

It should always consider them as belonging to and attached to God, just like rays to the sun or as diamonds and pearls would be attached to a garment. Since the master has put them there only to make his garment more striking and more precious, he is always empowered to remove them when he wishes. From this perspective, then, the soul should be perfectly detached from them. It should exist in the midst of all things without at all touching them and without its heart ever participating in them.

Poverty of spirit has three parts. The first is to see ourselves destitute before God, begging for all his gifts, being naked in ourselves without any grace, living in spirit as a beggar, so that we may be clothed with his goods.

The second is not to claim as our own the gifts and graces of God, considering them to be ours and as something that has become part of our nature, once we are in possession of them. We must look at them as a man looks at the garment he wears. He knows that his body is naked in itself and lacking in itself those things that are necessary to protect it from the discomfort of the seasons. This is why he has a constant need to clothe himself and to look outside himself for this help and comfort.

The truly poor soul, even though it might be clothed and enriched with the gifts of God, thinks of itself as always totally naked before him. For firmly rooted in the knowledge of what it is, even though it is possessed by and clothed with God, it sees itself all the same as naked in itself. Thus it never becomes complacent about what it is.

251

For being always the same in its core, it does not think any more of itself with all its gifts than it did before being filled with them.

The soul should see the gifts of God as emanating from him alone, as belonging to him, as his possessions and his property and as his rays, which he shines on us in order to hide our lowliness from his eyes and to make our misery more tolerable.

God is glorious in us through what belongs to him and he alone should be appreciated for what is good in us. He alone should take satisfaction from it. And if in our depth we think well of ourselves because of the gifts in us, for which the glory should be given to God alone, we attract and deflect toward ourselves the glory that is due to him only. This is a very great injustice. For to him alone belongs the praise that the gifts, by their very nature and with their whole being, offer to his divine majesty.

The third degree of spiritual poverty is to carry within us the gifts of God and to keep his treasures in the coffers of our hearts without daring to touch them and without using them for ourselves, letting God be the one to place his valuables in our hands as he takes from these coffers what he chooses and directs us to dispense them as he wills, so that he himself will be the author and the manager of the distribution of his graces.

Not only should we take care not to use the gifts of God for our own temporal and vulgar interests or in order to acquire honor and esteem, which would be a terrible sacrilege, but we must also abstain from touching these sacred gifts. He deposited them in our souls and we should leave to him the choice of taking us by the hand, directing us to withdraw what he wishes and distributing them in his name.

The humble soul, hidden and faithful, to whom our Lord has confided his wealth, is a treasure sealed with seven seals, which the Lamb alone can open. He alone can search in the coffers where he has enclosed his treasures. He alone can open them and through the splendor of his rays, through the clarity of his divine lights; in short, by the power of his grace, direct the soul to use them as it should.

Unlike earthly kings he does not delegate the care of his finances to treasurers who hold the key in their hands and to whom he gives the authority to dispense them as they will. He himself has the key to these coffers in his hands so that he may open them when he wishes.

He is the universal bursar. He is the general distributor. He is everything in us. He does not need to add anything to his presence or his power. For he is everywhere. He is capable of all things. He sees everything. He dispenses his goods in us always, in keeping with his wisdom and love.

He wishes then that the soul, present to his treasures, exercise this kind of restraint, touching nothing in its depth that God had placed there and that he had locked with a key, certainly not forcing the locks when the coffers are closed, that is, not looking for something through an effort of memory or with violence.

However, even when God leaves the coffers open, that is, when we are present to all God's lights and all his truths, it is not up to us to put our hand in them or to take from them what we want according to our liking.

We must look with reverence upon these gifts and treasures, which he has placed within us because of his infinite mercy, as belonging to him. There is nothing in us that gave us reason to hope for this grace. Our inner depth, in its impurity, was not worthy of his favors. Nevertheless, through his infinite grace and love, he chose to deposit them in this notorious place. Since he did it only because he wished to, then it is also up to him alone to use them in us as he chooses.

God works in the soul like a master in his field, who has piles of rocks brought to his land and has materials placed here and there so that he may build according to his idea and plan. He has unloaded more in one spot than in another because of the size of the building, of the pavilion or the structure that he wants to erect. It is necessary that he use them according to his plan.

He needs to use the materials and to direct his masons and laborers to build and work according to the design, which often he hides from them. Without revealing anything to them, he shapes his building little by little. He executes and accomplishes it according to the idea he has in his mind and in his wisdom, which surpasses theirs.

This is the way God uses his gifts. They are materials that he dumps in us as in a blind field, which knows nothing of the building that the great architect and the master craftsman wants to build there. It is up to us to tolerate his gifts and his presents. It is up to him to put them to work and to use our faculties, which should cooperate faithfully with his grace in this construction, based on his power and his adorable designs, which are unknown to them.

JEAN-JACQUES OLIER

FIFTH SECTION

The Foundations of Poverty

We are called to share in the life of God in Jesus Christ. Our life, like his, is hidden in God. It is he who places it in us as he did in his Son and allows us to share in his dispositions, in his sentiments and in his virtues.

God dwells in his Son with his divine splendor. He lives in him with his majesty, so that nothing equals his glory. He is clothed with brilliance of divine riches, next to which all things are but mud and muck.

All the riches of the earth are but rags compared to the glory of God. For this reason we see that our Lord, after returning to heaven, where he entered perfectly into the grandeur of God his Father, is infintely more removed from natural assistance than he was during his earthly life, when he tolerated his disciples having some money to sustain him, preserve his life and help the poor.

Our Lord, living in God and dwelling interiorly in the splendor of his divine glory, never could have any desire or love for the wealth of this world. Since in his interior he shared in the being of his Father and was in his essence rich with this divine wealth, he could not tolerate that of the earth. Everything seemed to him insignificant and unworthy of his appreciation.

Thus a soul, withdrawn into God and clothed with the dispositions of Jesus Christ, discovering in him such great wealth, cannot desire earthly goods. If it did have the slightest appreciation of them, it would be like a king who, not being satisfied with his glory and majesty, would go looking for wealth and splendor in the sackcloth of a peasant.

We are called to poverty and detachment from all the world's goods because of the immense and infinite riches that we find in God. Next to them, all those of the earth are nothing, and in possessing God, we possess all earthly riches in an eminent way.

God contains everything in himself. He is the source and origin of all goods. He possesses them all, freed from the imperfection and lowliness of creatures. He is, par excellence, all wealth, all greatness, all beauty and all splendor. This is why the one who is in God is removed from everything and possesses everything.

Thus the saints who leave the world and who after the resurrection dwell body and soul in God, will possess everything in him. Without the use of any creature they will discover in him their world. He will no longer give himself through the multiplication of vulgar realities, which man collects to maintain and preserve himself in this life. Rather, then he will be himself the fulfillment of their need. He will envelop them, embrace them and saturate them with himself.

This is the advantage God lets us taste in this life when we possess him perfectly. A sponge filled with water is so thoroughly penetrated with its substance that all the empty places are filled with it. In the same way God fills all the needs and the desires of the man who is in this state. He can no longer desire anything else because he possesses a God who is everything to him.

Riches exist in this world only as the shadow and the image of God. In their way they contain all creatures in an eminent way and make them available to man for his needs. In fact, it is with gold and silver that we draw everything to ourselves. These metals, which through divine providence have an unbelievable value in the eyes of men, allow us to acquire, beckon and draw all things to ourselves.

This is why the one who exists in God, even in this life, and who begins to taste him, to nourish himself with him and to behold some of the brilliance of his glory and his divine splendor, can no longer experience any appreciation, taste, joy, desire or love for all the vileness of worldly things, because they are only image and illusion. We can easily leave the image when we possess the truth.

Our Lord enjoyed and possessed God in this world. He was saturated and satiated in his soul by what God is in himself. And since he enjoyed in himself true wealth, he could have no desire for what was only its shell and surface.

He discovered in God his Father the one who fulfilled all his desires. Thus he could desire nothing from all this vile and vulgar world. This is the state and disposition in which Christians can share even in this life and which Saint Paul wished for the faithful with these words: *May God fulfill gloriously all your desires in Jesus Christ, our Lord, according to the fullness of his divine riches* (Phil 4:19).

However, this is not to say that our Lord did not sometimes use worldly goods for his necessities and to meet his needs. But when he did it, it was to sanctify their use and to teach men, all of whom need to own individually some of these goods in order to preserve themselves in this life since sin has taken away the common use of them, how to possess in a holy way what Providence has mercifully placed in their hands.

This is why, although silver and gold are in themselves something quite vile, quite abject and quite vulgar, nevertheless God created man, in this miserable state to which he is reduced, to have a natural love and inclination to own them, so that always having some for his use, he could thus respond to the neediness in which God has left him as a result of sin.

It is part of the design of God's Providence to leave this inclination and desire in men, just as he leaves in them the appetite to drink and eat in order to preserve their life. This desire for wealth is a tyrannical, famished, annoying and unsettling desire because it exists in man as a result of sin.

Thus graced souls, united securely to God, who enjoy all things in him, lose their desire for this world. If they experience it at all for their needs, it is a peaceful desire and frequently it is even so dead in them that they do not think of it in the slightest.

Apostolic souls who live in God through community have the advantage of being able to easily free themselves of these desires and cares, because they experience God present in their midst, furnishing adequately what is needed and assuring for them what is necessary to meet their needs. Their concern is for God himself, who is everything for them, as they are completely given to him and live only for him.

Oh, how happy in this world is the soul thus devoted to God and living without concern! It is a servant of God, living for God, devoted to God alone, for whom it labors unceasingly. God as well, on his part, is looking after its needs and its life. Oh, the soul who serves God in this way and who seeks his kingdom and his justice possesses marvelous guarantees!

There is nothing more certain than the Word of God. It is worth more than a thousand contracts. It can never be falsified, or altered, or disputed. It is preferable to any revenue, any possession, any treasure, which could be stolen from us. Everything perishes. Heaven and earth will pass away, but the Word of God will never pass away.

O blessed soul who is able to grasp the truth of God and his holy Word! O apostolic soul, living in the Holy Spirit, who grounds you in the Word of your powerful, ever vigilant and all loving God! Why concern yourself with anything other than God? Does not God know your needs?

The Gentiles, who know nothing at all about a universal intelligence that is attentive to the needs of all and whose love cannot tolerate any poverty in his children, can well struggle and work hard to provide for themselves. However, we see that our Father lives in us, sees the needs of his family, and senses the affliction and neediness of his children. Why then so much worry and frenzy?

He is good, tender and filled with love. He does not at all exhaust himself when he gives us his goods. The generosity he shows us comes only from him. He is not like those fathers who, whether they be misers or poor, whether they might become even poorer in giving, and whether they are mainly untouched by the misery of their children, would nevertheless be unable to refuse the help requested of them. Why should we not have perfect confidence in God? Why would we not be like our Lord, who lived peacefully and quietly relying on the Providence of his Father?

Our Lord in this world lived in constant poverty because he led a life of penance. If he kept in his disciples' care the alms that people gave him, it was a sign of his penance. For retaining thus the charity and mercy that God his Father gave him through others, he believed that he should safeguard with respect these precious presents, of which he felt unworthy, since he was burdened with our sins. He did not want to squander them, like something God his Father should not at all have furnished to his state, and which therefore he should use without expecting others that were not in the least due him.

From this penitential perspective the least thing he received was a great treasure for him. He did not look upon any good, any revenue or alms as guaranteed to him. Seeing himself very unworthy of the slightest kindness from God toward him as a public penitent, he lived in continual dependence on divine mercy.

In this condition, since he was taking the place of all sinners, everything should have been taken away from him. Nothing was due him. Thus he should have received the least possessions as very great graces, with very profound feelings of his unworthiness and with a great appreciation and reverence for the mercy of God his Father.

He should have been deprived of all help and all wealth since he was doing penance for so many greedy, money-hungry people and for the luxury and excesses committed by everyone. His nudity and the shameful stripping of all his clothes was the punishment for these overly rich and sumptuous garments with which people adorn themselves with excess and vanity. His crib, his stable, his straw and his dung heap were a punishment for the very rich houses, excessively gilded, decorated and so superbly furnished. And the blessed harshness of the cross, where he lay in death, was a punishment for the many luxurious beds that fill the world with scenes of so much sensuality and impurity.

Penances exist in the church to continue the holy penance of Jesus Christ. The holy souls who are called to this, in a special way, should be victims for the sins of the world, making satisfaction to God through the very Spirit of Jesus Christ.

They should be poor with him, doing penance for the sins that prevail on earth. They should oppose luxury and for that reason groan on wood and straw, being content with the poorest rooms and furniture and with the most mediocre clothes, to give an example to the world through the power of Jesus Christ, who, through us, can enlighten it and reveal its duty and life.

SIXTH SECTION

Motives for Poverty

1. The heart that is filled with creatures, and especially with wealth, is always anxious. This is why the Son of God compares, in the gospel, wealth to thorns, which torment it and never leave it in peace.

2. The heart filled with this love is pulled down to the earth and turned away from heaven.

3. God does not fill it with himself. He even burdens and disgusts it.

4. As Saint Paul says: *It falls into the traps of the devil* (1 Tm 6:9; see also 3:6–7). By giving in to its own desires, it is fixated in its attachments, which will hasten it toward certain ruin.

5. Sooner or later the soul will be detached and separated from everything. The justice of God will force it to leave some day what it has not chosen to leave now out of love.

6. Christians should be dead to all the desires of the world, and they should no longer follow its inclinations, acting as if they did not

have any of them. Thus they must smother all these vulgar desires for the external realities of this world and all the affection they might have for the riches of the earth.

7. Christians should live the life of heaven. For in heaven we are freed from all the dispositions of Adam's flesh. We live only according to the inclinations and dispositions of the Spirit. We are freed from any attachment to creatures. In short, with Jesus Christ and all the saints, we are hidden in God and separated from everything.

God, in himself, in Jesus Christ and in his saints is the model of our life for he is perfectly holy and separated from everything. This is what Christians need to do if they wish to be lifted up into God, even in this lifetime, as they will be in paradise. They must detach themselves by a holy life from themselves and from every creature.

The Spirit needs to be separated from the soul, which in itself is drawn and inclined by its fleshly life toward all creatures, so that our superior faculties, in which all the principal operations of the interior and divine Spirit reside, will not be pulled down by the weight and inclination of the inferior part, which is saturated by flesh and its vulgar, animalistic and earthly life. In this way, these faculties will rise toward God without resistance or impediment.

Therefore our spirit and will need to be healed of every attachment to any creature whatsoever and must in this way be free, devoid and detached from everything.

To attain this we must be equipped with the wings of the contemplation of the divine truths and of the holy love of God, which lift us up and cause us to fly, in order to prevent, through this divine movement, the downfall the weight of the flesh would cause in us. Since in this life we always have this miserable weight drawing us down, we must as well always lift ourselves to God through the power of the Holy Spirit.

SEVENTH SECTION

Other Motives for Poverty

1. God is our true and only good. He is the universal good in himself, fulfilling and satisfying all the desires of those who possess him.

The adorable Persons of the Blessed Trinity are infintely rich and happy in the possession of the divine Essence. The angels and saints of heaven, with their immense capacity, are perfectly satisfied, in their desires, with the possession of God. The same is true for the just on earth, who, being filled with the superabundance of God, are totally content and fully satisfied by the enjoyment of him.

God is our good to such an extent that he is our total good. The least possession of him satisfies us more and makes us more content than all the goods of the world. These goods are not substantial enough to fill the human heart. For since it is born for God, who alone is its true good, it finds nothing but emptiness, vanity and falsehood outside of him. He alone can satisfy it perfectly.

God is so perfect and contains in himself, with such fullness and superiority, all the advantages of creatures, that the slightest possession and enjoyment of him allows us to taste all kinds of goods. So much so, that those who possess him, whether on earth or in heaven, discover in him all their joy, contentment, peace and beatitude.

This is what our Lord wants us to understand in the gospel when he says that if we are poor in heart, that is, detached from everything, then to us belongs the kingdom of God, which is God himself, containing in himself the fullness of all goods.

The Son of God did not come down from heaven and come to earth simply to detach us from the goods of the world, but rather to obtain for us true wealth by depriving us of those [goods] that only appear worthwhile.

This is why the children of the faith can no longer attach themselves to or even look lovingly at the visible things of this world. Because faith, which is the source of their conduct and life, leads them toward invisible realities and toward the love of them alone.

The children of faith are dead to the senses and to the generation of their original father. They can no longer attach themselves to the earth. They can no longer relish creatures. They can no longer love this world, which has been made for Adam and destined for his children.

Faith causes them to perceive God as the only, unique and ultimate good hidden in everything visible. It causes them to see everything in its truth and in its core, which is God alone. It obliges them to say to every creature, You are only a lie; and to God, You are all my truth, who will one day destroy every symbol so that you alone will be revealed as the world of believers.

God is not only the true and unique good, who can adorn and

JEAN-JACQUES OLIER

enrich people, but he wishes as well to give himself to Christians who are detached from everything. At one time he gave himself to Adam through creatures, but seeing that they distracted him and that that was dangerous for humanity, he stripped himself and shed everything in order to offer himself as the sole possession of Christian souls.

This is why he wishes that Christians be satisfied with him alone and that they come to him as he gives himself to them, in perfect nakedness, having nothing but faith, which helps them to embrace and possess him.

This is the holiest state possible, that is, to possess God as he is in himself, with no distractions and no intermediary that can stop us, or that can impede us or lead us astray. God fills us completely in this state and satisfies us, leaving no aversion or void.

In heaven God allows the saints to possess him without intermediary or image. In the same way he wishes that the Christian soul be emptied of everything and stripped of every created being so that it might be disposed to receive him in interior nakedness and in poverty of spirit. Oh, how blessed is the soul that knows and tastes God in this state! Oh, how blessed is the condition of Christians, who are all called to this grace!

2. Christians are not of this world. Since baptism places them in another generation, it also transplants them into a different world. It makes them citizens of another city. It places them in another kingdom.

This kingdom is the kingdom of God into which we are introduced by faith, which shows us other riches to possess, another King to serve and honor, other pleasures to enjoy, another earth to inhabit, another air to breathe, and another light to guide us.

Now the first point and the first condition required to enter this kingdom is poverty. *Blessed are the poor in spirit, for the kingdom of heaven belongs to them* (Mt 5:3).

The great King of this new world is Jesus Christ, who is poor. The princes of his court, the holy apostles, are poor. The mistress and queen, the blessed Virgin, is poor. All the courtiers and all the bourgeois there are poor. Even the angels are all naked. What would it be like to see a rich person in the midst of so many poor people?

If at court, where everyone is rich, there appeared a poor person, he would be found repulsive and would be driven away. Likewise in the kingdom of Jesus, where all the courtiers are poor, a rich person cannot enter or show up at the door without being driven away or shamefully rejected.

Our Lord drives away from his banquet the one who did not have on a wedding garment and threw him, with feet and hands bound, into hell. The wedding garment and holy poverty are the livery of the bridegroom.

He himself declares that the rich cannot be welcomed or admitted into his banquet or into his kingdom: *Oh, how difficult it is for the rich to enter the kingdom of heaven* (Lk 18:24)! The rich man mentioned in the gospel cannot be admitted, but the poor are welcomed with Lazarus. For the kingdom of heaven is theirs.

The kingdom of Jesus Christ is not of this world. Here we think highly of the rich: Blessed are the people who have possessions; but in the kingdom of Jesus Christ, *Beati pauperes, Blessed are the poor.* The kingdom of the world is a staged kingdom, but the one belonging to Jesus Christ is authentic and its reign is forever.

EIGHTH SECTION

The evils of self-centeredness[11]

There is nothing more opposed to Christianity than self-centeredness. For Christianity has its source in Jesus Christ, who fashions his members after himself. As a human being he is grounded and transplanted in the substance of the Word.

This is why the Christian spirit desires that Christians be transplanted and transferred from the stalk of Adam onto the incarnate Word and that, being enlivened by him and sustained by him, they no longer exist for themselves, no longer live their own life and no longer act except through him alone.

We should hold nothing more in horror than self-centeredness, which deprives us of the fullness of the Word, his life, his activity and which makes us, in this admirable body, like useless members who cannot lay claim to any substantial or true good. On the contrary, if we abnegate ourselves and then ground ourselves in Jesus Christ, we are all things and can do all things in God.

This is why our Lord put abnegation in his gospel as the first step we must take in the Christian life! *If someone wishes to come after me, let him renounce himself* (Mt 16:24), because self-centeredness, being filled with the self, blocks Jesus Christ and the fullness of his divine life from entering us. It is the inexhaustible source of every evil and every sin.

In the state of innocence Adam did not belong to himself, but totally to God. By sin he became self-centered and the father of all sin. Thus having transmitted to men both the sin and the self-centeredness, they find in the latter the origin of all their vices and all their deformities.

Self-centeredness is a horrible monster and the hideous ocean of all sin, just as abnegation is the summary of perfection and the source of the Christian life and virtues.

The person who lives in self-denial holds onto nothing. He no longer possesses human prudence or false wisdom. He no longer has any desires or will of his own. He is flexible, pliable and docile to the law of the Spirit. He has surrendered to his holy guidance and to his divine movement. In short, he is entering the reign and domination of God.

NINTH SECTION

The Effects of Self-centeredness and Annihilation

Self-centeredness	Abnegation
1. The self-centered person dwells in himself.	1. The Christian goes out of himself.
2. The self-centered person is full of himself.	2. The Christian is empty of himself.
3. The self-centered person places his trust in himself and relies on himself.	3. The Christian mistrusts himself and relies on Jesus Christ.
4. The self-centered person is always preoccupied with himself.	4. The Christian always forgets himself.
5. The self-centered person thinks highly of himself.	5. The Christian despises himself.
6. The self-centered person wishes to make an impression and show off.	6. The Christian withdraws and hides himself.

7. The self-centered person loves praise and seeks it.

7. The Christian is confused by praise and flees it.

8. The self-centered person speaks about himself.

8. The Christian never speaks about himself.

9. The self-centered person has difficulty tolerating any praise given to his neighbor. He never speaks of another's perfections, or if he does, he diminishes them.

9. The Christian rejoices in praise given to his neighbor. He describes with delight another's perfections and extols them.

10. The self-centered person cannot tolerate being contradicted and gives in to no one.

10. The Christian gives in easily to his brother and submits himself freely to all.

11. The self-centered person is obsessed with his own opinion and judgment. He despises all advice and has respect only for his own.

11. The Christian always mistrusts his own judgment. He honors the opinions of others and defers to them.

12. The self-centered person acts on his own and with his own power, without paying any attention to his weakness.

12. The Christian acts in light of his nothingness, by uniting himself to the power of Jesus Christ.

13. The self-centered person acts independently and always follows his own will.

13. The Christian acts dependently and follows the will of Jesus Christ in his superiors.

14. The self-centered person sees, desires and draws everything to himself and wills good only for himself.

14. The Christian desires nothing for himself and only desires the good of his neighbor.

15. The self-centered person acts in all things for himself.

15. The Christian acts in all things for God.

16. The self-centered person values his own pleasure and satisfaction in everything and seeks it everywhere.

16. The Christian values detachment from himself in everything and seeks it everywhere.

17. The self-centered person is attached to everything.
18. The self-centered person stands out in everything.

19. The self-centered person gets along with no one.
20. The self-centered person, seeing himself as better than the rest, withdraws from everyone, and is happy to remain by himself and with those who esteem and approve him.

21. The self-centered person draws the world to himself and becomes more possessive, uniting all others to himself and detaching them from everyone else out of love for himself.
22. The self-centered person wants to fill the heart and mind of every creature with himself.
23. The self-centered person is willing to be devout in consolation, abundance and praise, but he abandons all in desolation, dryness and scorn.

24. The self-centered person always wants to be in charge and speaks to his brothers arrogantly and generally in a loud voice.

17. The Christian is free and liberated from everything.
18. The Christian is ordinary in both his exterior and his interior.
19. The Christian gets along with everyone.
20. The Christian, seeing himself as inferior to all, is delighted to live with everyone, as the least of all, without wondering if anyone sees him, appreciates him or loves him.
21. The Christian is detached from everything and seeks to offer and lead everyone to Jesus Christ, respecting the social order.

22. The Christian wants to fill everyone with the love and the knowledge of Jesus Christ.
23. The Christian is the same in dryness and abundance, in scorn and praise. In whatever state he is in, all his thought and devotion are for the service of Jesus Christ.
24. The Christian always wants to obey. He speaks with respect and gentleness to everyone, whom he regards as his superior.

25. The self-centered person wants the very best for himself in clothes, food, lodging, and so forth.

26. The self-centered person wants to pass for the author of everything and wishes that the glory be given only to him.

27. The self-centered person wants to appear involved in everything. He works and searches in his mind for ways to prove it in order to win the admiration of others.

28. The self-centered person is always agitated, troubled and anxious, always frustrated and hindered, always timid, frivolous and unstable.

29. The self-centered person is generally sad, closed, lost in reverie and withdrawn.

30. The self-centered person becomes upset by the most insignificant statement. He gets angry at everything and suspects that everything is done and said in relation to him.

31. The self-centered person becomes exceedingly joyful when his self-love and pride succeed. He changes and is unrecognizable whenever various mishaps occur to him.

25. The Christian only desires the least and the simplest of everything.

26. The Christian does not want to pass for the author of the good he does and deflects the glory on to others.

27. The Christian always works to open people's eyes to show them that God is the author of every good. Thus he tries to abnegate himself everywhere in his presence.

28. The Christian is always even-tempered and calm, always peaceful, courageous and constant, always free and ready to do anything.

29. The Christian is joyous, open and his mind is free of all daydreaming.

30. The Christian never gets angry. He endures everything without his heart ever changing. He never thinks that anyone pays any attention to him or intends to hurt him.

31. The Christian, who does not look at reality in relation to himself but to God, remains united to him in everything and therefore is always the same in any kind of occurrence.

JEAN-JACQUES OLIER

CHAPTER FOURTEEN

Charity Toward the Neighbor

God, in creating man in his image and likeness, not only gave him a share in his being, his life and his divine perfections, but also wanted him to be like him in his activities.

Thus, as God loves himself with all that he is and to the full extent of who he is and what he is capable of, so that he cannot love himself more, in the same way he gave man an explicit commandment to love him with all his heart, all his soul, all his mind and all his strength.

God wishes that man use his whole self to love him and that he be completely lost and consumed in his love. Just as God is the fullness of love in himself and all that he does outside himself, he does for the love of himself, likewise he wishes that man use all his strength and do everything only for the love of God.

Not only did God create man in his image and likeness, but also he modeled human society after the society of the Persons in the most holy Trinity. For this reason, just as in that adorable society, the Father loves his Son as himself, and loves himself in his Son, and the same is true for the love of the Son toward the Father and toward the Holy Spirit, and for the love of the Holy Spirit toward the Father and the Son, he also wants man to love his neighbor as himself.

This is why he gave this second commandment: *You will love your neighbor as yourself* (Dt 6:5), which Jesus Christ said was like the first (Mt 22:39), because it also conforms to the divine and eternal life of the Persons in the most holy Trinity.

This is how our Lord has loved us. For, speaking of the love he has for humanity, he says that it is like the love that his Father has for him: *As my Father has loved me, so I have loved you* (Jn 15:9). The same love he has for me, I have for you. This shows us that the love he has for his neighbor is drawn from the love his Father has for him and that it is an imitation of the love that one divine Person has for another, loving him as another self.

This is the way our Lord wants men to love one another. This is why he says to his disciples: *Love one another as I have loved you* (Jn 15:12). As I have modeled my love that I have for you on that which my Father has for me, in the same way, I want you to model the love you should have for one another on the love I have for you, so that yours may be found to conform totally to and resemble fully that of my Father.

Conditions for the Love of Neighbor

The qualities and conditions of the love of neighbor should resemble those of the love that God has for himself in his Son and those with which his Son loves humanity.

This is why the external examples of his love toward humanity should be the model for what charity obliges us to do externally for our neighbor; and his interior Spirit, which is given to us, should govern us and activate us interiorly in that same love. For we can never carry out or accomplish perfectly this holy command except through this Spirit who is God himself.

God, who is in us, loves himself through his Spirit in the neighbor where he dwells. And thus he causes us to love him as he loves himself. For he is totally in the other and loving himself everywhere, as he deserves, he loves himself infinitely in the neighbor.

He animates our heart, fills it with his own love, establishes us in his life, in his movements and in his own inclinations. This is why the soul, following the sentiments and interior dispositions of his divine Spirit, loves its God in its neighbor with the same love and the same passion with which it loves God in itself.

The soul should never love itself except in God, that is, only because God animates it and fills it. It should love itself in God, as God loves himself, because it shares in the life of God. Thus it should love its God and love itself with the same love. And since God is also in the neighbor, it should love God with the same love with which it loves him in itself.

God loves himself in his Word and gives himself infinitely to him. He gives himself so fully to him that he holds back nothing of his riches and glory. He exists fully in him. There he dwells and experiences his beatitude just as he does in himself. Even though he does this out of necessity, he never stops doing it out of love. Indeed he does it with a necessary love. For necessity in God cannot impede his love, since he is love in everything that he is.

Thus we must do the same toward our neighbor. We must love

him with our whole selves. We must share ourselves with him: from our hearts, our souls, our resources and our presence. In short, we should never have anything we are not ready to invest in him.

The first Christians lived with God's life, following the rule of love, which he had commanded for them and which the Holy Spirit caused them to follow. They possessed everything in common, as Jesus Christ shared everything in common with his Father. Just as in God there is only one Spirit, only one vital will in three Persons and a perfect unity of dispositions, thoughts and desires, in the same way, it is said of the first Christians that they had but one soul, one heart and one and the same will. This is the life of the saints in heaven, who exist in perfect unity, and it should be also that of all the faithful living in the church.

This is how our Lord showed that he was the first to follow the orders that he decreed for man and that he was fulfilling the law of his Father. For being the first-born of his brothers, he needed to be the first one to obey his Father perfectly and to be for us the model and image of how to conduct our lives perfectly.

He imitates his Father in the eternal love that his Father has for him and shows in his life that he loves us as his Father has loved him from all eternity: *I have loved you as my Father has loved me*. My Father pours all his substance into me, and I communicate mine to you in my blessed sacrament and in my communion.

My Father communicates and gives me his life. I give you mine, not only by not sparing it on the cross and giving you the very last drop of my blood, but also in giving you my Spirit, who is my life.

My Father communicates his riches and treasures to me. I give you the gifts of my Spirit.

He gives me his fecundity, so that I am able to produce a divine Person. I give you the same fecundity in order to produce and generate children for God and for eternal life.

He gave me all power in heaven and earth. He gave me power over all nature to do with it as I wish and to alter its order when it pleases me and however I choose. I have given you strength and power, through the presence of my Spirit, to do the same things and even greater ones whenever it will be necessary for the glory of God my Father and for the good of his church.

I have nothing that I have not given to you. All that I have in me, I wish you to share with me; just as all that my Father has, I share in common with him. Finally, just as my Father places in me all that he has and all that he is, in the same way, I place in you all that I have and all that I am. This is the law of true and perfect charity toward the neighbor.

SECOND SECTION

Signs of True and Perfect Love of Neighbor

True and perfect love can be recognized by the great love we have for everyone. This love would like to set everything ablaze, even to seeing itself filled with a fire, a passion and a zeal to make God known and loved everywhere.

This universal charity should not be an illusion, as in some who are ablaze with a zeal generated by a spirit of pride and self-love, which relishes great things and wants to be involved in brilliant and extraordinary works.

It should be shown toward all individuals, for whom we should want to do as much good as possible, helping them with our resources in their struggles and needs and satisfying, with Christian gentleness and cordiality, all those who come seeking some comfort.

Pure love has no external tenderness and no apparent emotional expression. It binds hearts to itself with such purity that, although it wins them all over and, by a secret operation of God, keeps them intimately united and bound to oneself, nevertheless, externally, it does not keep them bound. That is what results from the freedom of a holy and pure love, which liberates those who are united in God from any external and tangible bond.

This divine charity never exhausts itself or grows weary. The neighbor in need can always have recourse to it in any place or occurrence it may find itself without fear of rejection.

It always produces this marvelous result as well, which is one of its infallible signs. It remains bound and united to all, never attracting anyone to itself, in a way that would separate it from others, or from its duty and obligations.

Its love fosters union among all things. It becomes a center point where every line ends and comes together. Unlike false charity, which divides people who are united in order to draw them to oneself alone, true charity holds together people with the most diverse inclinations. Through its care the most polarized are maintained in relationship.

Perfect love of neighbor leads us to rejoice with him over his goods as if they were our own. Just as God rejoices in the goods of his Son and the Son rejoices as well in the goods of the Holy Spirit as if they were his own, in the same way we should rejoice over the blessings of God in the neighbor and look upon them as our own. Therefore, if love in us is perfect and if it is truly God who produces it in our heart, then it will rejoice and dilate in us as we behold the blessings that our neighbors have.

Thus our Lord rejoices interiorly, through the action of the Holy Spirit, to see the holy apostles recount the admirable effects of his Father in them. He rejoices to see his disciples clothed with the gifts and riches of his Spirit. He rejoices in advance over all the activities with which this divine Spirit will one day adorn and enrich his church through the merits of his death. This is a mystery hidden from the eyes of the wise and prudent and which was only to be known by the little ones, who, being subject to the guidance of the church and its leader, would see that a most insignificant reality of nature, that is, the son of a carpenter, a poor man, disgraced and worthless in the eyes of the world, would stir the world and overturn all nations, monarchies and empires through the power and efficacy of his finger, who is the Holy Spirit present in his gifts. For if we take into account the substance of this same Spirit, then these gifts, compared to the Holy Spirit, are only like the finger of a man compared to his whole body.

In this same way the Holy Spirit rejoices through Saint John and through Saint Elizabeth in the good fortune of the blessed Virgin, who had become Mother of the Son of God and thus the bride of the eternal Father. For she became, with him, the source of the temporal generation of the Word, accomplishing together with him in the Incarnation what he accomplishes alone in eternity.

That is the most wondrous activity and the most divine exaltation possible for a creature, to share with the eternal Father in his fecundity through the actual generation of his Son.

The highest, the most sublime and most perfect power of the Most High is his fecundity. It is this he shares with the blessed Virgin, in marrying her, in order to realize with her the temporal generation of the eternal Word.

She becomes at the same time the temple of the Holy Spirit in the purest and most abundant fullness possible. Since she was destined to be the Mother of Jesus Christ, she received the fullness of grace. The angel acknowledges that by these words: *Hail, full of grace* (Lk 1:28). This is why she is the purest, most divine and most perfect creature possible. Her maternal fecundity flows from this fullness of perfection, just as the fecundity of God originates from the exuberance of his perfect substance and his divine being. In a similar way trees only produce their fruit through the overabundance and excess of the sap in them.

However, even though this admirable Mother is filled with the perfection needed for divine fecundity, she receives further graces and gifts through a wonderful superabundance. This is what the angel says to her: *The Holy Spirit will come upon you* (Lk 1:35) to work great things, and they will surpass the fullness of blessings he has already communicated to you. This is the reason for Saint Elizabeth's joy, who rejoices in her cousin's happiness as if it were her own.

Even the blessed Virgin, in contemplating Jesus Christ, who comes to her with the fullness of his Father's divinity, rejoices in her spirit. She rejoices in the blessings of Jesus Christ. She rejoices in the fullness of God in him, who clothed him with the treasures of his wisdom and his knowledge. This was the great reason for her joy.

She rejoices also that the church is to be clothed and filled with the fullness of her Son. For it is through his divine Spirit that all the faithful come to share in his grace and his gifts.

In the same way all the saints in heaven rejoice in the gifts of God, which they possess. They rejoice for each other, each one sharing in the good fortune of everyone else and making it his own.

In fact, these gifts are all shared through the real and perfect communion in the favors of God, which exists among them, and which they communicate to one another through the common indwelling that they have with one another.

Through an admirable resemblance to the three Persons of the most holy Trinity, they are in a circumincession,[12] dwelling in each other, as the divine and eternal Persons dwell in each other through their circumincession.

This is what our Lord teaches us with these words:

As I am in my Father and my Father is in me through the sharing of his substance and his life, and yet at the same time he never ceases to remain who he is, and I remain who I am, thus it is with you. For I am likewise in you and you are totally consumed in me, as my Father and I are identified in the simplicity and the unity of the same Essence.

Just as my Father and I are distinguished by the characteristics of our Persons, even though, however, our goods are in common and individually we possess nothing of the treasures and riches of his common, divine substance, similarly, even though you are totally consumed in me, each one nevertheless remains who he is. Each one preserves his individual being. Each one is distinguished by his gifts, by his graces and by his own personality.

This is the condition of the saints who possess Jesus Christ completely. He is their common substance. For although each one possesses the whole Spirit and the whole life of Jesus Christ, nevertheless they are not indistinguishable. Each one has his own personality and his own gift.

Thus in the holy church on earth, as well as in heaven, just as each individual possesses Jesus Christ in his fullness, all share in his gifts, all communicate in his holy disposition, all share in his divine Spirit, which is a Spirit of joy, and which dilates in giving itself and pouring itself out into the hearts of the faithful, so everyone should rejoice in their common goods, as if they were their own. Also we notice that when this Spirit is given to an individual, all pure souls give thanks and rejoice.

As Saint Anthony was dying, the whole church was filled with sadness, because this same Spirit stopped sharing himself with him on earth, along with the joy and dilation that the souls of the church militant experienced when he received it. For in his time he was one of the those in whom the Spirit of God was most pleased.

Let us bless God for everything: for the gifts he has given to the church in heaven and for those he communicates to the church on earth, in which every individual participates.

CHAPTER FIFTEEN

How to Accomplish Our Works
According to the Principle of the Christian Life

The old man in us wants always to be active and therefore to be self-seeking, because flesh in us, in its present state, cannot stop looking after its own interests.

Since the flesh does not want to lift itself to God, or lead us to him, and since it is unceasingly self-seeking, it must be rejected at the beginning of every undertaking with all its plans and intentions. This is why the first disposition we should have in our works is to renounce ourselves in all self-seeking.

The second thing we must do is to adore the Spirit of Jesus Christ who lifted his soul to God with all the purity, holiness and justice possible. He lifted it to God with the holiest of intentions and the purest dispositions he could muster. For the Spirit of God in the soul of Jesus Christ rendered to God the Father all the honor, praise and glory that he was capable of receiving.

The third thing we must do is to ask this divine Spirit to pour out in us the dispositions in which he wishes to establish us for the glory of God.

Finally, we must abandon ourselves to this Spirit, so that he can lift our soul to have the dispositions that he wishes for this entire undertaking, remaining intimately united to him in all we must be about.

The interior of Jesus Christ consists in the divine Spirit filling his soul with all the intentions and dispositions by which God could be honored by him and by his whole church. This interior life must be always before our eyes as the source and model of all the interior life of our souls.

We must even offer often to God this divine interior as a supplement to our own so that it might act as a reparation to him for our faults. Our Lord himself graciously chose to offer it often to God for this intention.

For this union that we must have with the Spirit of Jesus Christ in order to live the Christian life and act in a holy manner, we must also realize that it is not essential to feel in ourselves this Spirit and to taste experientially the sentiments and the dispositions of Jesus Christ. Rather, it is enough to unite ourselves through faith, that is, through our will and a real and authentic desire. This is what the Holy Spirit gave us so that we might act according to the desire of our Lord himself, when he said *that his Father desires worshipers in spirit and truth* (Jn 4:24), that is, true religious and worshipers who are separated from themselves in truth, not seeking their own interests, and who adhere in a real way to the Spirit of Jesus Christ, the religious and worshiper of God the Father. This is what constitutes the authentic interior Christian religion.

When the Holy Spirit dwells in us through grace, and we are separated from sin, it is enough that our soul, in its purest part, that is, in that part that is called spirit, remain united to the Holy Spirit so that we might act with his life and his holiness.

We must also realize, for the consolation of pure and holy souls, that our Lord served his Father, especially during his passion, with his spirit and the superior part of his soul, without feeling anything in the inferior sensate part.

The superior part of Jesus Christ our Lord was in glory and saw, in its full light, the whole range of adorable intentions by which he could honor God the Father. He entered into these intentions. He adhered to the Spirit who showed them to him and who produced them in him. During the time his soul experienced aversion, dryness and bitterness, he experienced resistance toward that which his spirit accepted and which he willed for the glory of God.

Thus we should not become very upset over the dryness and aversion of the flesh, provided that we are doing our duty and that through the superior part of our soul, which is our spirit and our will, we adhere to the Holy Spirit, who is in us to act according to his intentions and his desires.

We must unite ourselves with a pure spirit of sacrifice and faith, that is, with an intangible and obscure yet certain knowledge that God is in us through his holy and divine spirit to help us in our infirmity, which cannot on its own lift itself to God.

When he sees our assent to the good desires that he gives us, that we wish only to act for his glory, that we give ourselves totally to him and that we seek the help of his grace, he embraces us, he elevates us, he sanctifies us and leads us to act in spirit and truth, without in any of this making himself felt by the soul, in order to wean it from the flesh and to maintain it in a greater holiness and detachment from itself.

This Spirit is the spirit of all Christian religion, which gives life to all the faithful, as well as the power to act in holiness and justice. We must lose ourselves constantly in him, separating us from ourselves, following our Lord's commandment in the introduction he gives us to the Christian life: *He who wishes to come after me must deny his very self, take up his cross and follow me* (Mt 16:24). The authentic disciple of Jesus Christ, who wants to live like him, must renounce himself. He should no more seek to please himself than did Jesus Christ. Rather, he must adhere to the divine Spirit who is in him. He must follow him and imitate the conduct of Jesus Christ, who never did his own will.

He lived in perfect adherence to the Spirit of God his Father and kept his soul, in its superior and principle part, always united to him during all the aversions, alienations and contradictions that he allowed to arise in his flesh. *Such was the contradiction that he suffered in himself against himself.*[13]

This is the third condition of those who follow our Lord: to adhere continually to the Spirit through a resolute will, which keeps us always at our duty in the middle of crosses and contradictions and which elevates us to God without pleasing ourselves, during which our flesh, wishing the complete opposite of what it should and being unable to ever subject itself to God, contradicts him unceasingly.

The flesh desires the opposite of what the spirit desires. Thus during this struggle a part of us, which is the spirit, must adhere to the Holy Spirit with which it should be totally one in its desire, its will and its divine qualities, infinitely separated from and transcending the flesh. Meanwhile, the other part of us, which is the soul in its inferior part, adheres to the flesh.

Furthermore we must hate the soul that animates the flesh and maintains within itself this struggle and this perpetual cross. *If anyone would come after me, let him deny himself daily, take up his cross and follow me* (Lk 9:23).

The Christian Day [14]

On Seeing the Sun

My God, I adore you in this beautiful star, where you dwell as in your tabernacle. *He made the sun to be his tabernacle* (Ps 19:5).

In it I adore and conceive some small idea of what you are in yourself.

In yourself you are one. You are very simple in your life and substance. Nevertheless, my God, you give life to a countless multitude of creatures, all distinct and different, which subsist and have life through you.

Have you not expressed, my God, this wonder? Have you not shown in the sun, which is unique and simple in its substance, that the lives of creatures depend on a single reality?

If it traverses the whole world, is it not to proclaim this truth: that you are the Father of every creature and the source of life in all that subsists?

When this sun brings creatures to the fullness and perfection of life, which they receive from you, you show us that you possess in yourself alone, in unity and eminent perfection, the life that is poured out in creatures. You have placed yourself in it, as in a throne, from which you enliven all the dead and all the creatures that languish in the graves of earth, where they possessed only the seed of life, which you furnish them through this star.

O my God, my possession and my life, everything depends on you. If for a moment you would cease giving existence and life to creatures, we would see everything perish.

You teach us this truth through this beautiful star, for when it undergoes an eclipse and is prevented from lavishing its effects on the earth, it leaves everything to languish.

O my God, you use the rays of the sun to bring life and energy to everything on earth. Through the absence of their effects, you make us realize that it is through them that you operate in the world.

You wish, O my possession, that while we see creatures rejoicing at its rising, turning themselves toward it and opening themselves to it in order to receive life; you wish, I was saying, that we adore you in it and that we fix our gaze on you, proclaiming with a spirit of religion that it serves only as a covering for you and as a channel to bring your life into the world, for there is nothing in us that does not come from you.

Also it is you, O my God, that all creatures behold. They give homage to you as their sovereign, and in this star they recognize you as the king and source of their life.

In it all creatures are your slaves. They all render homage to you. From them you receive adoration and the unspoken reverence of the work of your hands.

However, O great all-encompassing One, this veneration is quite lowly and very unworthy of your sovereign majesty. Jesus Christ came to offer you the homage of all creatures. He is the one who should animate them, who, through them, should adore you as the author and the source of everything and who should give you thanks for all your lavish generosity.

O Lord, O the love of our hearts, you who are yourself a sun, do for us what you do for your non-rational creatures. Thank your Father for us, since you cannot tolerate that he remain without honor and gratitude for all the good he does. Do this both for them and for us at the same time. For we are indebted to God for all the good that he does for us through them.

We are overwhelmed with blessings. Through both grace and nature, he gives us everything we could think of and more than we can understand. O my Lord, you alone understand everything. Be charitable and merciful enough to kindly thank him for everything.

It is not, my Lord, that we want to become lazy in offering our homage for his lavish gifts or that we want to remain ungrateful or silent because you are thanking your Father on our behalf. No, my Lord. For we want to lose ourselves, plunging into your Spirit and thus entering into your praise and thanksgiving to God.

Inasmuch as it is possible, we wish to share in your religion toward him. However, since we know practically nothing of the gifts he gives us, and since we have nothing in us that is pleasing or acceptable to him, we need to approach you and seek in you what we need to satisfy him.

O Lord, be our only supplement. And you, who alone are worth more than all things, be our unique offering and present to God.

ANOTHER MEDITATION

On the Sun

I greet you, image of my master Jesus Christ. You are the original emanation from my God, filled with his light and splendor.

God engenders his Word in eternity, as a light proceeding from light, a God emanating from God. In the first production of the world God creates light and attaches it to the sun, which fills the whole world with clarity. Similarly, in the creation of the new world Jesus Christ enlightens all men. *Coming into this world, he enlightened every man* (Jn 1:9). *He who said let light shine in the darkness has shone in our hearts* (2 Cor 4:6).

Jesus Christ, my sun, you fill with your power your sacraments, which are like the planets and stars that sustain the world.

O beautiful sun of justice, grant that your light will never fail us, that your church will never experience your eclipse, that your clarity and your holy influence will pour forth on us forever.

Without you, everything would perish, O my Lord Jesus, because God lives in you to enlighten and to enliven the world.

God enlightens the world in you and through you by faith, which is an obscure light, because we are pilgrims. However, in eternity, O my Jesus, God will enlighten us in you and through you with a splendor a thousand times brighter than the sun.

It is you, as Saint John says in his Apocalypse, who are the sun of paradise. He says that he no longer saw the sun shining on that city because of the light of God, which shone brilliantly in the Lamb (Rv 21:23).

O Lord, how happy I will be when I will see that splendor! It is a sun that never blinds and never dazes those who approach it. *Approach him and be enlightened: and you will not be confused* (Ps 34:6).

Lord, how strong my countenance will be! How powerful will be

279

my eyes in those beautiful days when your majesty, a hundred million times more splendid and brilliant than the light of the sun, will not weaken or blind my vision!

Then, my all, my love, my possession, my life, my God, I will see you in your light. You will be in me, sustaining me and strengthening me in my nothingness. You will see yourself in me and you will be another you in me.

Oh, how irritating and unfortunate is any other brilliance, any other light of day for us who wait for that one!

O my Master, grant that soon you will be all things to me and that I will enter into that light which permits no darkness.

PRAYERS

When We See the Earth, Plants, Flowers and Fruits

My God, how adorable you are in this spectacle of nature!

My God, you are much more beautiful and more wondrous in yourself than concealed in these beautiful things!

O my God, how happy I would be if my faith and your holy light allowed me to see what you are beneath them.

How greatly I should lament that my sin has deprived me of this light!

Adam rejoiced in his innocence because he saw you in all things. He saw what they showed him of your beauty. In their depth, he adored your hidden divinity.

The universe, my God, and even a thousand universes together could not represent you. Only your Word represents you as you are in yourself.

However, my God, since the Word can only be seen in heaven, it is quite fitting that you furnished a kind of word on earth to express yourself. It is fitting, O my All, that you caused your creatures to speak perceptibly to our eyes and ears, proclaiming what you are and teaching us something of what you keep hidden in yourself.

You have thus manifested the depth of your existence, your substance, your life, and your beauty, albeit coarsely, through these insignificant creatures. This was no doubt so that you would be adored through them. Thus, O my Love, I adore you in all you are and in all that you wish to reveal of yourself.

I do not know very clearly all that you are, but it is enough that I know that you have placed these tableaux before our eyes so that, through them, we might adore your beauty and that our faith might be aroused, since it often becomes listless when it does not have something external to awaken it.

My God, you create everything to lead us to your love, and I want to love you for all these beautiful means, which you give me.

My God, do I not see on earth, on the one hand, stones that exist without producing any fruit, and on the other, land which gives life to a thousand plants?

What does that mean, my God? From what little I can understand, it seems to me that these stones represent your being, that is your eternal being. The earth, which produces fruit abundantly, represents the fecundity of that being and that life-giving substance which, from its depth, enlivens all things.

My gentle Love, your own substance possesses every imaginable treasure in the same way that you chose the earth to carry, in its womb, mines and hidden treasures.

Your substance, beyond the beauties and perfections, which it contains in itself, is also the source of the fecundity and life in all things. It is in this way, O my All, that the earth is, so it seems to me, like the source of life for all those beautiful things, which are born in her.

My God, my All, so many diverse and admittedly coarse things exist in order to reveal that which you are in the simplicity of your being!

How perfect you are, O my possession and my God, since you contain all these things in your simplicity and without any of their corruption, their complexity and their impurity!

O Fullness of Being, how perfect you are! How pure and holy you are! When will I have the great blessing of seeing you in yourself?

One day you will draw back the irritating and unfortunate curtain from all those created things that hide you and shield you from the eyes of your lovers.

You leave this blindfold on them to create the desire to see you. Lord, you wish to train us to long for you.

Take away, my God, all these images and show us the truth. They will perish one day. For we will not be interested in the shadows once we see the light. We will see the sun of justice himself. We will see Jesus Christ, the portrait of your beauty. We will see you, O my God, who is the source of everything!

How the whole universe displeases me when it hinders me from enjoying you! However, my possession and my God, how it pleases me, in my exile and deprivation, when it speaks to me of you!

Therefore, all you creatures, speak of my love. All of you, open yourselves up, uncover your bosom and show me what you carry in yourselves of my All.

You cannot argue with me. It is clear. It is up to you, my possession, to show yourself and to reveal yourself to me in your very self.

How easy it is for my love to project rays of light from all these places where he dwells in order to reveal himself to my mind and my heart!

It is very easy for my All to reveal himself from the depth of all things and to make himself known to us through all that he is in them. My God, I desire this to the extent that it is for your glory and no more.

In the meantime, I condemn the sin of my first father and my own, which caused you to remove from all things the revelation of what you are in yourself, which you had given to us.

While awaiting, my possession, for you to choose to reveal this to me, I adore you in Jesus Christ, who is my universe and who reveals to me in himself all your perfections. Having become man, he contains them all as in a précis. He desires that we find in him our whole universe, so that nothing of you will remain hidden in him. *Quick destruction is decreed, overflowing with justice. For the Lord will execute his decree without delay in the midst of the earth. Quickly the Lord will fulfill his word on earth* (Is 10:22–23; Rom 9:28).

He became a man, visible like us, to reveal visibly and tangibly what you are in yourself. He came to make known to men your beauty and your perfections by his way of life, his words and his powerful works.

He showed men your love, your gentleness, your patience, your power, your strength, your beauty and your life.

I see clearly that these herbs, these plants and these fruits represent the life of God, but it would take thousands and millions throughout the world to reveal it to us in its infinite expanse, and even then they would do so quite imperfectly.

But you, O my Jesus, who contain in yourself all the life of God and all the forms of life that he communicated to creatures, you reveal in yourself alone, in an eminent way, what all these things show us very imperfectly.

My possession, my All, do you not possess, beyond such ordinary, natural lives, that divine life in which you wish that all might participate?

Do you not have within yourself the source of all life and all authentic life, my beloved Jesus, you who took on our life in order to offer us the fullness of your Father's life?

My Jesus, blessed be you, gentle source of my life, blessed be you above all these creatures, which perish and which are nothing but vanity, short-lived tableaux and images that last but a moment.

My possession, continuously they perish in order to give homage to the life of God, which never perishes. You never come to an end. You live forever so as to be the tableau and the eternal representation of the life of your Father. *Jesus Christ yesterday, today and forever* (Heb 13:8).

My All, these creatures represent so little of you that they need to be reborn every year through an alteration of beauty and form in order to manifest, at least by their vicissitude, their alteration and their diversity what you alone do perfectly.

My Jesus, you are unique. You were yesterday, you are today and you will be for all ages the same without change, because you alone are all the beauty of God. You are the perfect representation and the perfect universe of God, containing in yourself alone the whole universe and every distinct creature scattered throughout heaven and earth: *His plan . . . is to restore in Christ what is in heaven and on the earth* (Eph 1:10).

My God, you show us your life, not only through these plants, but even more you reveal your beauty through these flowers.

It seems to me that flowers bear within themselves the image of your Word much as plants, O eternal Father, bear that of your divine Person.

The Word, having emerged from your bosom, shows us your beauty, which you keep hidden in yourself as if in a stem.

You keep your life hidden within yourself and your beauty dwells in the secret of your essence. However, your Word brings it forth and reveals it to us.

This is why, my God, he is called the flower of the fields and the lily of the valleys (Sg 2:1). He is the lily, which is begotten in your bosom. He is also the flower of the fields, who contains in himself more than all those in the countryside and, to say it better, he is the one who is the only flower begotten in the great countryside and in the vast expanse of your essence, which is immense and infinite in itself.

A flower gives off the odor that it contains in itself. Likewise, O my God, your Son Jesus Christ came into the world to sow the sweet odor of the virtues and the perfections that you had enclosed in him. He made it possible for the earth to experience the love, sweetness and peace that you had possessed in him from all eternity. Furthermore, previous to his blessed sojourn with us on earth, they had never been experienced nor recognized by men.

Before his coming, you were, O my God, only justice and severity. You were experienced through thorns, *as a lily among the thorns* (Sg 2:2). Your gentleness was enclosed in your justice. You did not let your odor escape. You allowed the goodness of yourself to be experienced only through the loving behavior and the gentle relationship that your Son had with men.

Finally, my All and my Love, those trees laden with fruits that nourish us, represent for me your Holy Spirit, whose tasty fruits nourish the whole church. His gifts give life, strength and energy, and his sweet fruits give the soul its nourishment, its support and its food.

Therefore, O my All, may this whole coarse world perish before me, as long as I possess Jesus Christ your Son and his divine Spirit, who brings forth in me the life he has received from him and which he maintains always present in the church in order to satisfy and support it.

The tree is the image of the Father. The flowers begotten on it represent the Son, who appeared for a very short time in the world: *flowers have appeared on our earth* (Sg 2:12). But the fruits represent the Spirit, who is always living in the church and who is always suspended there to nourish souls.

O life of God, how sweet you are! How adorable you are! You are worth more than all these husks and images; more than all the pleasures and charms that gratify our senses.

My God, how I wish to live your life alone! Caring for this coarse life is so displeasing, annoying and burdensome to me!

My everlasting All, my Beloved and my only One, my God, my Jesus, my Savior, my flower, my fruit, my food, if it pleases you, may

I delight only in you. May I be dead to this exterior aspect of the world and to this coarse existence, so that I may live only in you!

It seems to me that this world was made only for the children of Adam, who need to use it in order to preserve the life that they have received from him. However, my Jesus, it seems to me that you are the world of God's children, who need to nourish themselves with you through your Holy Spirit.

Alas! My All, when I eat all these fruits, what passes through me? A bodily substance and an earthly life for the sustenance of my body.

However, O my All, when I enjoy you, when I nourish myself with your Spirit through your Blessed Sacrament or through prayer, in which the Spirit nourishes me and enlivens me interiorly, I am being nourished with your divine life. I am being nourished with the very life that God lives in himself from all eternity and that he comes to pour forth in souls through Jesus Christ and through his divine Spirit.

What an honor! What a joy! What blessing and what greater happiness than to be invited to live the life of God himself!

My God, may I cease to live the life of my own spirit so that I might live in your divine life and in you alone; knowing through your light, loving through your love and acting through your power.

Therefore, I bid farewell to the whole world. May I no longer savor you, since your author himself wishes to be my entire universe. Farewell to all images, since I see the truth. Farewell to all the treasures of the world, since I am enjoying every good thing in my God.

I desire nothing but you, O my Jesus, whom I carry in my soul and whom I contemplate within me, while withdrawing interiorly away from the sight of all these things, to contemplate through him the beauty of his Father, to hear his Word and to taste its fruit.

Upon Hearing the Birds Sing

My God, I adore you, the life of all things.

You are the life of plants and birds. The depth of your immense life pours itself out into every living thing.

Your life is expressed with some beauty in plants, but it appears much more perfect to us in your animals. You have given them a more complete and perfect level of life than the other things on the earth.

O my God, these birds express something of you in their song, which seems to me most wondrous.

Is it not true, my God, that you are sufficient unto yourself and that you experience bliss in possessing your peace and in beholding your beauty and your perfection? You experience, O my God, perpetual happiness, beatitude and jubilation.

All these birds, my God, express nothing in their song but the jubilation of their heart and the joy of their soul as they behold the beauties of nature and savor leisurely the serenity and the delightfulness of this season.

They sing neither at night nor in winter, for these times are not in any way meant to express your divine life and the beauty of your essence.

The angels in their song and the church in its song express the jubilation of your Holy Spirit in your divine life.

The operations of the Holy Spirit in us are participations in the immanent operations of God in himself, which his kindness makes tangible in us in order to express externally something of his interior life and operations. This is why souls at times find themselves sharing in this spiritual jubilation, which caused the great saints to utter canticles of joy: *Rejoicing with cymbals* (Ps 150:5). They are only slight expressions of the immense and eternal jubilation that God enjoys unceasingly in his own beatitude.

Lord, what transcendent jubilation, which expresses itself through the saints of heaven and earth, whom you possess and permeate with yourself and who participate in your operations and the effects of your blessed life!

Alas! Splendid fullness of being, should these birds enjoy your life in their own way, while men, due to their sins, are deprived of your beatitude? My God, should they be more faithful to their vocation than we are to ours?

Oh, wondrous vocation! Oh, holy vocation! We are called to share in the divine nature, *sharers in the divine nature* (2 Pt 1:4), yet we want to share only the life of animals!

God has given us a share in all the lives of nature. He has even given us the life of angels, and not satisfied with that, he wants to give us a share in his own divine life.

God wanted to give us all of these more basic lives so that we might spurn them and thus experience the excellence of the ultimate life, so as to sacrifice all the others for it.

God has rightly given us reason, which is a life he wants us to keep obedient and subject to faith. If he wants us to despise it in comparison to faith, what scorn then should we have for all the other lives and their operations in us?

My God, I am no longer concerned about anything but your holy, interior and divine life. All the rest, O my God, is nothing to me but instability and corruption. All of it is nothing but vanity, error and illusion. It is all nothing to me except as it is in you.

NOTES

1. The *Introduction to the Christian Life and Virtues* contains fifteen chapters. We have omitted the following chapters: six, "Pride"; seven, "The Virtue of Penance"; eight, "Mortification"; ten, "Gentleness"; twelve, "Chastity"; thirteen, "Obedience"; and the second through the fifth sections of chapter five.

2. In the language of the authors of the French School of spirituality the term *religion* evokes a sense of reverence, adoration and love in union with God the Father.

3. The term here is *dilatant* from the verb *dilater*, which means "to dilate" or "to expand." Father Olier uses it in a very poetic sense. Thus the living reality of the religion of Jesus Christ grows and radiates outward to penetrate and enliven more and more of the spiritual universe. To capture this special meaning, I have generally translated the term with the English word *dilate*.

4. Since we are in communion with the mysteries of Jesus Christ, we share in his religion and thus together, as the body of Christ, we express the type of loving reverence the term implies. This is not a specific reference to the state of the vowed religious.

5. The priesthood and the clerical state were of primary importance to Olier and the French School. It had become clear to him early in his parish mission work that the ongoing reform of the church depended greatly on the renewal of its leadership, which in that period was almost exclusively clerical. To accomplish this he invited bishops and priests to live as fully as possible the common baptismal commitment shared by all Christians, while not denying their particular responsibilities as leaders in the church. The reader may wish to look at the other references to the clerical state in this work and note how they are situated in a universal call to holiness addressed to all Christians (see pp. 218, 219, 225, 230, 245–46). In a section of *The Christian Day*, dealing with the spirit of sacrifice, Father Olier states: "Although priests are particularly called to this continual sacrifice . . . nevertheless all Christians are priests in faith and in the hidden life of the spirit. They are all priests in Jesus Christ. They are called to live in a spirit of sacrifice because the spirit of Jesus Christ dwells in all the faithful in order to exercise his priesthood and dilate his sacrifice" (*J*, p. 193). See also the Introduction to this volume, pp. 61–63.

NOTES

6.   The French term is *anéantissement*. For Father Olier and the other authors in this volume the foundational attitude of the authentic Christian life is to deny oneself, especially in one's inner attitudes and dispositions. In this way we commune in Christ's own *kenosis* or self-emptying (Phil 2:5–11). We claim as our own the nothingness from which we were drawn by the creative hand of God and to which the weight of our sinfulness pulls us once again. To appreciate the overall positive context of this term, we must realize that *anéantissement* and *communion* are two sides of the same movement into deeper union with God. Generally I have translated this term with the word *abnegation*.

7.   The French word is *hostie,* which in the usage of the period evoked both the sacrifices of the ancient Hebrews and the host at Mass, which is the Body of Christ and the sacrifice of the new covenant. This play on words is intentional. This is why I have translated it "host-victim," to capture the double meaning.

8.   The use of the word *interior* here reflects the great respect that the French School had for the inner world of Jesus Christ and the Christian. It refers to the sentiments, dispositions and spiritual movements that animated Jesus Christ and that will animate us if we are open to them. Clearly our authors highly valued the "interior" and saw it as primary in the ongoing conversion of the Christian life.

9.   Father Olier's method of mental prayer is very simple in its original expression, as we see here. However, what has been passed on historically as the method of Saint-Sulpice was his original structure plus the considerable additions of Louis Tronson (1622–1700), the third superior-general of Saint-Sulpice. Apparently he felt that the seminarians of his time needed more structure than M. Olier offered here.

10.   Actually the original quote of Teresa is *o morir o padecer,* "to die or to suffer." Throughout the years it has been quoted differently in various editions. This text can be found in her *Life,* chap. 40, no. 20.

11.   The French word is *propriété,* which has a sense of inappropriately clinging to the goods of the world and to oneself. As the reader will see, the term *self-centeredness* fits well in the various contexts in which M. Olier uses it.

12.   *Circumincession* is a technical term of scholastic Trinitarian theology that attempts to describe the unique way in which the Persons of the Trinity are present to one another in both their total unity and real distinctness at the same time.

13.   It is not clear to what text he is referring here. Perhaps it is Hebrews 12:3: *Consider him who endured from sinners such hostility against himself, so that you may not grow weary or fainthearted.*

14.   The *Christian Day* is a remarkable devotional work applying the principles of the Christian life to common everyday occurrences. It is a

series of reflections, meditations and prayers by which Olier seeks to help
the reader sanctify his or her entire life. It is divided into two relatively equal
parts. The first section offers thoughts and prayers for the various spiritual
exercises that make up the devout Christian's day, for example, morning
prayer, Mass, visits to the Blessed Sacrament and Marian devotions. The
second section focuses on other daily events such as waking up in the
morning, dressing, meals, work, conversations and going to bed at night.
There are also meditations and prayers for the time of sickness and recovery. We have included in this translation the last twelve pages of this work,
which will give the reader some feel for how Father Olier invited Christian
people to commune with their God in every moment of their lives. For a
contemporary theological appreciation of the *Journée,* cf. William M.
Thompson, "Olier's *La journée chrétienne* as a Guide for Today's Theology," *Bulletin de Saint-Sulpice* 14 (1988): 113–127.

JOHN EUDES

The Life and Kingdom of Jesus in Christian Souls

[2, 1–21: *OC* 1, pp. 161–204]

[THE CHRISTIAN LIFE AND ITS FOUNDATIONS]

Speaks of What We Must Do in the Whole of Our Life
to Live in a Christian and Holy Manner
and to Form, Sanctify and to Cause Jesus To Live and Rule in Us

I.

The Christian Life Must be a Continuation of
the Most Holy Life which Jesus Lived on Earth

Jesus, Son of God and Son of Man, King of angels and humanity, is not only our God, our Savior and our sovereign Lord, but he is also our head and we are *members of his body* (Eph 5:30), as St. Paul says: *bone of his bones and flesh of his flesh.*[1] Therefore, we are united with him in the most intimate union possible, that is, the union of the members with their head. We are united with him spiritually by faith and by the grace he gave us in holy baptism. We are united with him bodily in the union of his most sacred body with ours in the holy Eucharist. It follows necessarily from this that, just as bodily members are animated by the spirit of their head and live its life, in the same way we must be animated by the spirit of Jesus, and live his life and walk in his ways. We should be clothed with his sentiments and inclinations, perform all our actions with the same dispositions and intentions that he brought to his. In a word, we should continue and bring to fulfillment the life, religion and devotion with which he lived on earth.

This proposition is very well-founded. It is supported in several places by the sacred words of him who is truth itself. Do you not hear him saying in various places in his gospel: *I am life and I have come that you may have life. You do not want to come to me in order to have life. I live and you will live. In that day you will know that I am in my Father and you are in me and I am in you* (Jn 14:6; 10:10; 5:40; 14:20). This means that just as I am in my Father, living the life of my Father, which he communicates to me, you are also in me living my life and I am in you, communicating that very life to you. Therefore I live in you and you will live with me and in me.

Furthermore, does not his beloved disciple cry out to us that *God has given us eternal life and that life is in his Son; and the one who has the Son of God within him possesses life?* On the contrary, *the one who does not have the Son of God within him does not have life;* and *God sent his Son into the world so that we might live through him;* and *we are in this world as Jesus was in it* (1 Jn 5:11–12; 4:9, 17), which is to say that we are taking his place and that we should live as he lived.

Also in his Apocalypse, does he not proclaim to us that the beloved Spouse of our souls, who is Jesus, continually cries out to us saying: *Come, come to me and let the one who is thirsty come, and let him who wishes draw freely the water of life without charge* (Rv 22:17)? This means let him take, let him draw from me the water of true life. This agrees with what is narrated in the holy gospel, that one day the Son of God, standing in the midst of a great crowd of people, cried out in a loud voice: *If anyone is thirsty, let him come to me and drink* (Jn 7:37).

And what else is the holy apostle Saint Paul continuously preaching to us if not that *we are dead and our life is hidden with Jesus Christ in God; that the eternal Father has given us life with Jesus Christ and in Jesus Christ* (Col 3:3; Eph 2:5)? This means that he has brought us to life, not only with his Son, but even in his Son and with the life of his Son. *We should reveal and show forth the life of Jesus in our bodies. Jesus Christ is our life. He is in us, he is dwelling in us.* Saint Paul also says, *It is not I who live, but it is Jesus Christ who lives in me* (2 Cor 4:10–11; Col 3:4; Gal 2:20). If you consider carefully the remainder of the chapter where he says these words, you will discover that he is not only speaking of himself and in his name, but that he is speaking in the name and person of every Christian. Finally, in another place, speaking to Christians, he says that *he prays to God to make them worthy of their vocation, and to bring about powerfully in them all the desires of his goodness and the work of faith, so that the name of our Lord Jesus Christ might be glorified in them and them in him* (2 Thes 2:11–12).

All these sacred texts teach us clearly that Jesus Christ should be living in us and that we should live only in him; that his life should be our life and that our life should be a continuation and expression of his life; that we have no right to live on earth except to carry, reveal, make holy, glorify and cause to live and reign in us the name, the life, the qualities and perfections, the dispositions and inclinations, the virtues and actions of Jesus.

II.

Confirmation of the Preceding Truth

So that you might understand more clearly and establish more firmly in your soul this basic truth of Christian life, religion and devotion, please pay attention and realize that our Lord Jesus Christ possesses two types of bodies and two types of lives. His first body is his own body, which he received from the blessed Virgin. His first life is the life that he lived in this same body while he was on earth. His second body is his Mystical Body, that is, the church, which Saint Paul calls *Corpus Christi*, the body of Jesus Christ (1 Cor 12:27). His second life is the life that he has in this body and in those authentic Christians who are members of this body. The temporal, vulnerable life, which Jesus lived in his personal body, was fulfilled and came to an end with his death. But he wishes to continue this same life in his Mystical Body until the end of time so that he might glorify his Father by the actions and sufferings of a life, which is mortal, laborious and painful, not only for thirty-four years, but until the end of the world. So much so that the temporal, vulnerable life that Jesus has in his Mystical Body has not yet reached its fulfillment, but is fulfilled day by day in every true Christian. It will not have been completely fulfilled until the end of time. This is why Saint Paul says that *he fills up what is lacking in the sufferings of Jesus Christ for the sake of his body the church* (Col 1:24). What Saint Paul says about himself can be said of every true Christian, whenever he suffers something in a spirit of submission and love for God. What Saint Paul says about suffering can be said about all the other actions of a Christian on earth. For just as Saint Paul assures us that he fills up what is lacking in the sufferings of Jesus Christ, in the same way we can say that any true Christian, who is a member of Jesus Christ, and who is united to him by his grace, continues and completes, through all the actions that he carries out in the spirit of Christ, the actions that Jesus Christ accomplished during the time of his temporary life on earth. So that when a Christian prays, he continues and fulfills the prayer that Jesus Christ offered on earth. Whenever he works, he continues and fulfills the laborious life of Jesus Christ. Whenever he relates to his neighbor in a spirit of charity, then he continues and fulfills the relational life of Jesus Christ. Whenever he eats or rests in a Christian manner, he continues and fulfills the subjection that Jesus Christ wished to have to these necessities. The same can be said of any other action that is carried out in a Christian manner. It is thus that Saint Paul tells us *that the church is the fulfillment of Jesus Christ and that Jesus Christ, who is the head of the church, is fulfilled in all things in all people* (Eph 1:22–23). In another place, he teaches that *all of us are cooperating in the perfection of Jesus Christ and in the age of his fulfillment* (see Eph 4:1–13), that is, his mystical age in his church, which will never be fulfilled until the day of judgment.

Now you see what the Christian life is. It is a continuation and fulfillment of the life of Jesus. All our actions must be the continuation of the actions of Jesus. We should be like other Jesus Christs on earth, so as to continue his life and works and to accomplish and suffer all that we accomplish and suffer in a holy and divine manner, in the spirit of Jesus, that is, with the holy and divine dispositions and intentions with which this same Jesus accomplished all his actions and sufferings. This divine Jesus is our head and we are his members, united with him in a way that is incomparably more intimate, more noble and more exalted than the union between the head and members of a natural body. Therefore it follows logically that we must be enlivened by his spirit and his life more closely and more perfectly than the members of a natural body are enlivened by the spirit and life of their head.

These truths are very great, very important and quite considerable. They ask great things of us and should be thoroughly reflected upon by those who wish to live in a Christian manner. Therefore, study them often and attentively and learn from them that Christian life, religion, devotion and piety consist properly and truly in continuing the life, religion and devotion of Jesus on earth. Thus not only men and women religious, but all Christians are obliged to live a holy and divine life and to perform all their actions in a holy and divine manner. This is neither impossible nor even as difficult as some imagine. Rather, it is very pleasant and easy for those who take the time to frequently lift their minds and hearts to Jesus and to give and unite themselves to him in all that they do, following the approach of the exercises that were proposed above and that will be presented again later.

III.

What Are the Foundations of Christian Life and Holiness?

Since our only right to live in the world is to continue the holy and perfect life of our head, Jesus, there are four things that we should often consider and adore in the life Jesus lived on earth. As far as possible we should try, with the help of his grace, to express and continue in our lives the four things that are the four foundations of Christian life, piety and holiness and without which, therefore, it is impossible to be truly Christian. This is why it is necessary to tell you something here about each one of them in particular.

IV.

The First Foundation of Christian Life and Holiness, Which is Faith

Faith is the first foundation of the Christian life. For Saint Paul tells us that, *if we wish to go to God and have access to his divine majesty, the first step is to believe;* and that *without faith it is impossible to please God. Faith,* says the same apostle, *is the substance and foundation of the things we hope for* (Heb 11:6, 1). It is the cornerstone of the house and reign of Jesus Christ. It is a heavenly divine light, a participation in the inaccessible eternal light, a ray from the countenance of God. Or to speak according to scripture, faith is like a *divine character by which the light of God's face is imprinted in our souls* (Ps 4:7). It is a communication and an extension of the divine light and knowledge, which was infused into the holy soul of Jesus at the moment of his Incarnation. It is the science of salvation, the science of the saints, the science of God, which Jesus Christ drew from the bosom of his Father and brought to us on earth to dissipate our darkness, to illumine our hearts, to give us the necessary knowledge so that we might serve and love God perfectly, to submit and subject our minds to the truths that he taught us and that he continues to teach us himself and through his church. Thus he expresses, continues and fulfills in us the submission, the docility and the voluntary clear subjection of his human mind to the lights that his eternal Father communicated to him and to the truths that he taught him. Faith, then, is given us to capture and subject our minds through belief in the truths that are proclaimed to us on God's behalf. Therefore we continue and fulfill the loving and most perfect submission of the human mind of Jesus to the truths that his eternal Father proclaimed to him.

This divine light and science gives us as perfect a knowledge as is possible in this life of everything that is in God and outside of God. Reason and human science deceive us most of the time because they are too weak and limited in their lights to attain the knowledge of the infinite and incomprehensible things of God. This is also true because human science and reason are too filled with darkness and obscurity, as a result of the corruption of sin, even to attain authentic knowledge of the things that are outside of God. However, since the light of faith is a participation in the truth and light of God, it cannot deceive us. Instead it shows us things as God sees them, that is, in their truth and as they exist in the eyes of God.

Thus if we look at God with the eyes of faith, we will see him in his truth, just as he is and, in a certain manner, face to face. For even though faith is linked to obscurity, showing us God not clearly as we will see him in heaven, but obscurely as through a cloud, nevertheless it does not reduce his exalted greatness to the measure of our mind, as science does, but rather it penetrates, through its shadow and darkness, to his infinite perfections, so that we know him as he is, that is, infinite in his being and in all his divine perfections. It teaches us that everything in God and in Jesus Christ, Man-God, is infinitely great and admirable, infinitely worthy of being adored, glorified and loved for the love of himself.

It shows us that God is most authentic and faithful in his words and promises; that he is all goodness, all gentleness, all love toward those who seek him and put their trust in him. However, he is very strict, terrifying and severe toward those who abandon him, and it is frightening and horrible to fall into the hands of his justice. Faith gives us a very sure knowledge that divine Providence guides and governs everything that happens in the universe in the most holy, wise and best way possible, and that it deserves to be infinitely adored and loved for everything it decrees either through justice or mercy, whether in heaven, on earth or in hell.

If we consider the church of God in the light of faith, we will see that since Jesus Christ is its head and the Holy Spirit is its guide, it cannot in any way wander from the truth or become lost in false-hood. Thus all the ceremonies, customs and functions of the church have been most divinely instituted. Everything it prohibits and com-mands is most legitimately prohibited and commanded. Everything it teaches is most infallibly true. Therefore, we should be ready to die a thousand times rather than stray in the least from the truths it pro-claims to us. Thus we must revere and honor, in a special way, everything in the church as holy and sacred.

If we see ourselves and everything in the world with the eyes of faith, we will see very clearly that of ourselves we are nothingness, sin and abomination, and that everything in the world is only smoke, vanity and illusion.

In this way we must look at all things, neither with the vanity of our senses, nor with the eyes of flesh and blood, nor with the short-sighted and deceitful eye of reason and human science, but in the truth of God and with the eyes of Jesus Christ, that is, with that divine light, which he has drawn from the bosom of his Father and with which he sees and knows all things. He has given this to us so that we might see and know all things as he sees and knows them.

V.

Faith Should Guide All Our Actions

Just as we should look at all things in the light of faith so as to know them authentically, so also we must accomplish all our actions under the guidance of that same light, so as to do them in a holy way. For

God is guided by his divine wisdom; angels by their angelic intelligence; man, deprived of faith, by reason; the worldly by their maxims; and the voluptuous by their senses. Similarly, Christians should be guided by the same light as Jesus Christ, their head, that is, by faith, which is a participation in the science and light of Jesus Christ.

This is why we should attempt through all manner of means to thoroughly learn this divine science and never undertake anything except through this holy guidance. To achieve this, at the beginning of our actions, especially the most important, let us place ourselves at the feet of the Son of God. Let us adore him as the author and consummation of faith; as he who is the true light, enlightening everyone coming into this world; as the Father of light.

Let us realize that of ourselves we are only darkness and that every light of reason, science and even human experience is often nothing but obscurity and illusion in which we should place no confidence. Let us renounce the prudence of the flesh and worldly wisdom. Let us ask Jesus to destroy them in us as his enemies and not to allow us to follow their laws, their reasons and their maxims. Rather, may he enlighten us with his heavenly light, guide us by his divine wisdom, and show us what is most pleasing to him. May he give us the grace and strength to adhere solidly to his words and promises so that we might close our ears constantly to all the reasons and arguments of human prudence, courageously preferring the truths and maxims of faith, which he teaches us through his gospel and his church, to the reasons and arguments of men who are guided by the maxims of the world.

To this end it would be very good, with the permission of those who can give it to you, to read on your knees every day a chapter, either in French or Latin, of the life of Jesus, that is, of the New Testament. This is, to learn about the life of your Father and to note, by contemplating his actions, the virtues he practiced, the words he uttered, the rules and maxims that guided him and by which he wishes us to be guided. For Christian prudence consists in renouncing the maxims of worldly prudence and invoking the spirit of Jesus Christ, so that he might enlighten us, guide us according to his maxims and govern us according to the truths he taught us and the actions and virtues he practiced. This is what it means to be guided by the spirit of faith.

JOHN EUDES

VI.

The Second Foundation of the Christian Life: The Hatred and Flight From Sin

Just as we must continue on earth the holy and divine life of Jesus, so also we must put on the sentiments and inclinations of this same Jesus according to the teaching of his apostle: *Hoc sentite in vobis quod et in Christo Jesu,* "Have in you the sentiments of Jesus Christ" (Phil 2:5). Now Jesus Christ had two types of extremely contrasting sentiments in himself; namely, a sentiment of infinite love toward his Father and us, and a sentiment of extreme hatred toward what is contrary to the glory of his Father and our salvation, that is, toward sin. For just as he loves his Father and us with an infinite love, so he hates sin with infinite hatred. He loved his Father and us so much that he did infinitely great things, suffered extremely painful torments and sacrificed a precious life, all for the glory of his Father and our love. On the other hand, he has such horror for sin that he came down from heaven, humiliated himself taking on the form of servant, lived thirty-four years on earth with a life filled with labor, scorn and suffering, shed his blood to the last drop and died the most shameful and cruel death possible. All of this was due to his hatred for sin and his desire to destroy it in us.

Now we must continue in ourselves those same sentiments that Jesus had toward his Father and toward sin. We must pursue the war he waged against sin while he was on earth. For we should love God above all and with all our might, just as we must hate sin infinitely and with all our strength.

To motivate yourselves for this, from now on look at sin not as men see it, with carnal and blind eyes, but as God sees it, with eyes enlightened by his divine light, that is, with eyes of faith.

With this light and these eyes, you will see sin as in some way infinitely contrary and opposed to God and all his divine perfections and as a deprivation of an infinite good, which is God. Thus it contains in itself a malice, a foolishness, an ugliness and a horror as great, in a sense, as God's infinite goodness, wisdom, beauty and holiness. Therefore, sin should be hated and persecuted as much as God deserves to be sought after and loved. You will see how horrible a thing sin is and that it can be wiped away only by the blood of God.

It is so despicable that it can only be destroyed by the death and destruction of a Man-God. It is so abhorrent that it can only be annihilated by the annihilation of the only Son of God. It is so execrable before God, because of the infinite injury and dishonor that it does to him, that this injury and dishonor can only be satisfied worthily by the labors, sufferings, agonies, death and infinite merits of a God.

You will see that sin is a cruel homicide, a horrifying deicide and an incredible annihilation of all things. It is homicide because it is the unique cause of the death of both the human body and soul. It is a deicide because both sin and sinner put Jesus Christ to death on the cross and crucify him daily in ourselves. Furthermore, it is an annihilation of nature, grace and glory and all reality. For as it annihilates, as much as it can, the author of nature, grace and glory, it annihilates therefore, to the same extent, all reality.

You will see also that sin is so detestable before God that when the angel, the first, most noble and cherished of his creatures, committed a single sin, and one of thought only and a sin of a moment, he cast him from the highest heavens to the depth of hell without offering him a single moment for repentance, for he was unworthy and incapable of it. Also, when he discovers a soul in mortal sin at the hour of death, even though he is filled with goodness and love for his creature and has an extreme desire to save the whole world, having shed his blood and given his life to that end, nevertheless he is obliged by his justice to pronounce a sentence of eternal damnation against that miserable soul. But what is even more astonishing than all that is that the eternal Father, seeing his own Son, his only beloved Son, most holy and innocent, carrying the sins of others, *did not spare him,* says Saint Paul, *but handed him over for us to the cross and death* (Rom 8:32), so abominable and execrable is sin to him.

Furthermore, you will see that sin is so full of malice that it transforms the servants of God into slaves of the devil; the children of God into the children of Satan; the members of Jesus Christ into the members of Satan and those who are gods by grace and participation into devils through likeness and imitation, according to the word of truth himself, who speaking of a sinner, called him a devil: *One of you is a devil* (Jn 6:70).

Finally, you will know that sin is the worst of evils and the greatest of all misfortunes. It is the source of all the evils and misfortunes that fill the earth and overwhelm hell. In fact, there is only this single evil in the world that can be called an evil. It is the most terrible and horrible of all terrible and horrible things. It is more frightening than death, more atrocious than the devil and more horrifying than hell, because everything that is horrible, atrocious and frightening in death, the devil and hell flows from sin. O sin, how detestable you are! Oh, if men knew you! Oh, we must say that there is something about you that is infinitely more horrible than all we can say and think. For the soul that is soiled by your corruption can only be washed and purged in the blood of a God. And you can only be destroyed and annihilated by the death and annihilation of a Man-God! O great God, it does not surprise me that you hate so much this infernal monster and that you punish it so forcefully. Let those be surprised who do not know you and who do not understand the wrong that sin inflicts on you. Surely, my God, you would not be God if you did not have an infinite hatred for iniquity. For just as you have the blessed need to love yourself infinitely, for you are infinite goodness, you have also the holy obligation to hold in infinite horror that which in some way is infinitely opposed to you. O Christians, you who read these things wholly founded on the word of eternal truth, if you have left in you even the slightest spark of love and zeal for the God whom you adore, hold in horror what he holds in such horror and what is so opposed to him. Fear and avoid sin more than the plague, more than death and more than any other imaginable evil. Preserve always in yourself a powerful resolution to suffer a thousand deaths with all kinds of torments rather than to be ever separated from God by a mortal sin.

So that God may keep you from this misfortune, be careful also to avoid venial sin as much as possible. For you should remind yourself that our Lord had to shed his blood and sacrifice his life just as much for venial as for mortal sin. Those who give little importance to venial sin will soon fall into mortal sin. If you do not experience these resolutions within you, ask our Lord to place them within your soul. Do not rest until you experience this disposition. For as long as you are not resolved to die and suffer all sorts of scorn and torment rather than commit any sin, know that you are not truly Christian. For if by misfortune you should fall into sin, try to pick yourself up as soon as possible through contrition and confession and thus return to your original dispositions.

JOHN EUDES

VII.

The Third Foundation of Christian Holiness:
Detachment From the World and Worldly Things

It is not enough for a Christian to be free from vice and to hold every kind of sin in horror. Beyond that you must work with care and energy to become perfectly detached from the world and worldly things. By "world" I mean the corrupt and disordered life that people lead in the world, the damnable spirit that rules there, the perverse sentiments and inclinations that people follow and the pernicious laws and maxims that people obey. By "worldly things" I mean everything the world values, loves and seeks so ardently, that is, the honors and praises of others, vain pleasures and satisfactions, wealth and temporal comforts, friendships and affections based on flesh and blood and on self-love and self-interest.

Look at the life of our Lord Jesus Christ and you will discover that he lived on earth in the most perfect freedom, being stripped of all things. Read his gospel, listen to his word, and you will learn that *he who does not renounce all things cannot be his disciple* (Lk 14:33). This is why, if you wish to be truly Christian and a disciple of Jesus Christ, and if you wish to continue expressing in your life his holy life of detachment from all things, then you must strive to become absolutely and totally detached from the world and from worldly things.

To achieve this you must reflect often that the world has always been and will always be opposed to Jesus. It has always persecuted and crucified him, and it will persecute and crucify him incessantly until the end of the world. The sentiments, inclinations, laws, maxims, life and spirit of the world are so opposed to the sentiments, inclinations, laws, maxims, life and spirit of Jesus that it is impossible for them to exist together. For all of Jesus' sentiments and inclinations lead only to the glory of his Father and our sanctification. The sentiments and inclinations of the world lead only to sin and perdition.

The laws and maxims of Jesus are very gentle, holy and reasonable. The laws and maxims of the world and the laws and maxims of hell are totally diabolical, tyrannical and unbearable. What can be more diabolical and tyrannical than the execrable laws of those martyrs of the devil who are obliged, according to their damnable maxims, to

304

sacrifice their well-being, their soul and their salvation to Satan for a cursed point of honor? What is even more horrible is that they are bound by the mad tyranny of the abominable laws of the world when they are called as seconds, to fight at times in cold blood, without cause and reason, for the passion and foolishness of an insolent person who is nothing to them, against their closest friend, frequently introducing sword and death into his bosom and thus ripping the soul out of his body, delivering it to Satan and to eternal fires.

O God! What cruelty, what madness! Is there anything more difficult and tyrannical?

The life of Jesus is a holy life, adorned with every type of virtue. The life of the world is a depraved life, filled with disorder and every sort of vice.

The spirit of Jesus is a spirit of light, truth, devotion, love, trust, zeal and reverence toward God and the things of God. The spirit of the world is a spirit of error, disbelief, darkness, blindness, mistrust, grumbling, impiety, irreverence and hardness of heart toward God and the things of God.

The spirit of Jesus is a spirit of humility, modesty, distrust of self, mortification, self-denial, reliability and firmness among those who live with this spirit. On the contrary, the spirit of the world is a spirit of pride, presumption, disordered self-love, frivolousness and irresponsibility.

The spirit of Jesus is a spirit of mercy, charity, patience, gentleness and of unity toward our neighbor. The spirit of the world is a spirit of vengeance, envy, impatience, anger, calumny and division.

Finally, the spirit of Jesus is the spirit of God, a holy and divine spirit, a spirit of every type of grace, virtue and blessing. It is a spirit of peace and tranquility, a spirit that only seeks the interests of God and his glory. On the contrary, the spirit of the world is the spirit of Satan. For Satan is the prince and leader of the world. Thus it follows necessarily that the world is animated and governed by his spirit; an earthly, carnal and animal spirit, a spirit of every sort of sin and malediction, a spirit of unrest and anxiety, of storm and tempest, *a spirit of devastation* (Ps 10:7). It is a spirit that seeks only its own ease, satisfaction and interest. You judge now whether the spirit and life of the world are at all compatible with the Christian life and spirit, which is none other than the spirit and life of Jesus Christ.

Therefore, if you wish to be truly Christian, that is, if you wish to belong perfectly to Jesus Christ, live with his life, be animated by his spirit and be guided by his maxims, you must necessarily commit yourself to renounce the world completely and to bid it farewell forever. I do not mean that you must leave the world and shut yourself up between four walls, if God is not calling you to that. Rather you must strive to live in the world without being at all of the world, that is, you should make a public, generous and faithful profession to no longer live the life of the world and to no longer conduct yourself according to its spirit and laws. You should not be ashamed, but rather glory, in a holy way, that you are a Christian, belonging to Jesus Christ and preferring the holy maxims and truths, which he left us in his gospel, to the pernicious maxims and falsehoods that the world teaches to its disciples. You should have sufficient courage and determination to make a clean break with the laws, sentiments and inclinations of the world and to despise virtuously all its empty discourses and deceptive opinions, just as it shows a diabolically audacious and impious disregard for Christian laws and maxims and insolently attacks those who follow them. For true courage and perfect generosity consist in this. However, what the world calls courage and strength of character is nothing but cowardice and fear. This is what I mean by detaching oneself from the world, renouncing the world and living in the world as not of it.

VIII.

Continuation of the Same Subject:
Detachment from the World

In order to deepen this detachment from the world in your soul, you must not only strive to separate yourself from it, but also to hold it in horror, just as Jesus Christ held it in horror. For Jesus so held the world in horror that not only did he exhort us through his beloved disciple *to not love the world, nor the things of the world* (1 Jn 2:15), but also he tells us through his apostle Saint James that *friendship with the world is an enemy to him* (Jas 4:4), that is, that he considers as enemies all those who love the world. Furthermore, he assures us himself *that his kingdom is not of this world, no more than he is of this world and that those whom his Father has given him are not of this world just as he is not of it* (Jn 18:36; 17:12–16). What is much more overwhelming is that he solemnly protested at the very time when he manifested the greatest excesses of his goodness, that is, on the eve of his death, when he was ready to shed his blood and lay down his life for the salvation of men; he protested solemnly *that he does not pray for the world* (Jn 17:9). In this way he pronounced a dreadful anathema, curse and excommunication against the world, declaring it unworthy to participate in his prayers and mercy.

Thus he assures us *that the judgment of the world has already been made and that the prince of the world has already been judged* (Jn 12:31). In fact, as soon as the world had fallen into the corruption caused by sin, at that very moment divine justice judged it and condemned it to be ignited and consumed by fire. And even though the execution of the sentence has been deferred, nevertheless it will be carried out at the end of the world. It follows then that Jesus Christ looks upon the world as the object of his hatred and curse, as something that he intends and desires to burn on the day of his wrath.

Embrace then these sentiments and inclinations of Jesus toward the world and everything in the world. From now on look at the world as Jesus looks at it, that is, as the object of his hatred and curse. Look at it as something that he prohibits you from loving under the pain of incurring his enmity; as something he has excommunicated and cursed with his own mouth. Therefore you cannot communicate with it without sharing in its curse. It is something he wishes to burn and reduce to ashes. Look upon everything the world values and prefers, such as pleasure, honor, wealth, worldly friendships and affections and all other similar things as realities that are only passing away, according to this divine oracle: *The world passes away along with its lust* (1 Jn 2:17). They are only nothingness and smoke, deceit and illusion, vanity and affliction of spirit. Read and consider often and attentively these truths. Ask our Lord every day to imprint them in your mind.

Finally, to dispose yourself in this way, take some time each day to adore Jesus Christ in his most perfect detachment from the world and beg him to detach you from it completely, imprinting in your heart a hatred, horror and abomination for the things of the world. On your part, be careful not to engage in the futile visits and conversations that occur in the world. If you are involved in them, in the name of God leave them at any cost and flee, as you would from the plague, from the places, persons and company where they only speak of the world and worldy things. For since they speak of such things with esteem and affection, it would be very difficult for these conversations not to leave some bad impression in your mind. Besides, you will gain nothing from them except a dangerous waste of time. You will experience only a sad dissipation and affliction of your spirit. You will carry away with you only bitterness of heart, a loss of devotional fervor, estrangement from God and the countless faults you will have committed there.

And while you will be seeking and enjoying the company of the world, he who takes his delight in being with the children of men will take no delight in you. He will not give you any taste of the consolations that he communicates to those whose only delight is to spend time with him. Thus I say once more to you, flee from this world. Flee from it and abhor its life, its spirit and its maxims. As fully as possible, only make friends and spend time in the company of those people who, by their example and word, can help and inspire you to love our most beloved Jesus, to live in his spirit and to detest everything opposed to him.

IX.

Detachment from Oneself

It is a lot to have renounced the world in the way we have just mentioned, but this is not enough to achieve perfect detachment, which is one of the first foundations of the Christian life. For our Lord cried out in a loud voice *that the one who wishes to come after him must renounce himself and follow him* (Mt 16:24). Therefore if we wish to follow Jesus and belong to him, we must renounce ourselves, that is our own mind, insight, will, desires and inclinations as well as our self-love, which makes us hate and avoid everything that causes any pain or mortification to our spirit or flesh and makes us seek and enjoy everything that offers them any pleasure or satisfaction.

Two reasons make this self-denial and renunciation necessary.

1. Everything in us is so disordered and depraved, due to the corruption of sin, that there is nothing of our own in us, which is not opposed to God, which does not place obstacles in the way of his plans and which is not contrary to the love and glory that we owe him. This is why, if we wish to belong to God, we must necessarily deny ourselves, forget ourselves, hate ourselves, persecute ourselves, lose ourselves and annihilate ourselves.

2.   Our Lord Jesus Christ is our leader and exemplar. There was nothing in him that was not completely holy and divine. Nevertheless, he was so detached from himself and so abnegated in his human spirit, his own will and self-love that he never did anything according to his own insight or human spirit, but according to the guidance of his Father's spirit. He never followed his own will but that of his Father. He behaved toward himself as someone who had no love, but rather an extreme hatred toward himself. He deprived himself, in this world, of infinite glory and happiness, of all human pleasures and satisfactions, embracing instead everything that could cause him to suffer in his body and soul.

Consequently, if we are truly his members, we should embrace his sentiments and dispositions, resolving powerfully to live from now on in complete detachment, forgetfulness and hatred toward ourselves.

To this end make sure that you adore Jesus often in this detachment from himself and give yourself to him, begging him to detach you entirely from yourself, your own mind, your own will, and your self-love so that he might unite you perfectly to himself and govern you in all things according to his mind, his will and his pure love.

At the beginning of your actions, lift your heart to him in this way: "O Jesus, with all my strength, I renounce myself, my own mind, my own will and my self-love. I give myself completely to you, your holy spirit and your divine love. Free me from myself and guide me in this action according to your holy will."

In moments of disagreement, which occur all the time because of diverse opinions, even if you feel that you have reason and truth on your side, gladly renounce your point of view for the opinion of others, provided the glory of God is not at stake.

When you experience any desire and inclination toward something, abnegate it immediately at the feet of Jesus, assuring him that you have no other desires and inclinations than his own.

As soon as you notice that you have some tenderness or emotional feelings toward something, at that moment turn your heart and affections toward Jesus in this manner: "O my beloved Jesus, I give you all my heart and all my affections. O unique object of my love, grant that I never love anything except in you and for you."

When someone praises you, return it to him, who alone is worthy of every honor, in this fashion: "O my glory, I desire no other glory than yours. For to you alone is due all honor, praise and glory and to me all abjection, scorn and humiliation."

Whenever you experience something that mortifies your body or mind, or whenever there are opportunities to deprive yourself of some satisfaction (this happens all the time), embrace them willingly for the love of our Lord and bless him for giving you the chance to mortify your self-love in honor of the mortifications and deprivations which he experienced on earth.

Whenever you experience some joy or consolation, return it to him who is the source of every consolation and speak to him thus: "O Jesus, I desire no other satisfaction than your holy satisfaction. Lord, I have enough joy just knowing that you are God and that you are my God! Ah, Jesus, be always Jesus, that is, full of glory, grandeur and joy, and I shall be content. O my Jesus, never allow me to be satisfied by anything other than you alone. Rather make me say with the holy queen Esther: *You know, O Lord God, that I have never rejoiced in anything other than you.*"[2]

X.

Perfect Christian Detachment

Perfect Christian self-denial or detachment does not simply consist in being detached from the world and oneself. It obliges us to be detached even from God in a certain fashion. Do you not know that while Jesus Christ was on earth he assured his apostles that it was expedient for him to leave them so that he might go to his Father and send his Holy Spirit to them? Why was this so, if not because they were attached to the tangible consolation afforded them by the presence and visible companionship of his sacred humanity? This was an obstacle to the coming of his Holy Spirit in them. For it is essential to be detached from all things, no matter how holy and divine, so that we might be animated by the Spirit of Jesus, which is the Spirit of Christianity.

This is why I say that we must be detached from God in a certain way, that is, from the delights and consolations that ordinarily accompany the grace and love of God; from the pious plans we make for the glory of God; from our desires for greater perfection and love of God; and even from our desire to be freed from the prison of the body in order to behold God, to be united perfectly with him, and to love him purely without interruption. For when God allows us to experience the delights of his goodness in our devotions, we must be careful not to rest there and become attached. Rather we should humiliate ourselves immediately, considering ourselves very unworthy of any consolation. We should return them to him, being ready to have them stripped away and assuring him that we desire to serve and love him, not only for the consolation that he gives, whether in this world or the next, to those who love and serve him, but for love of him and for his own pleasure.

Whenever we undertake some pious plan to do some holy work for the glory of God, we should attempt with all our power to carry it out. Nevertheless, we should keep from being attached to it, so that, if by some accident we are obliged to interrupt or completely abandon this plan or deed, we would not lose our peace of soul. Rather, we would be satisfied with the divine will or permission, which guides all things and is equally loved.

Similarly, even though we should try our best to overcome our passions, vices and imperfections and to become adept in the exercise of every virtue, nevertheless we must work at it without being overly zealous and attached. Therefore when we do not experience in ourselves as much virtue and love of God as we might wish, we can remain at peace without anxiety, humbling ourselves because of the obstacle we place in the way of virtue. We will be able to love our own abjection, being content with what God chooses to give us and persevering always in the desire to make progress, having confidence in the goodness of our Lord, who will give us the graces needed to serve him with the perfection he requires of us.

In the same way, it is true that we should anticipate, desire and languish continuously for the blessed hour and moment that will separate us completely from earth, sin and imperfection in order to unite us perfectly with God and his pure love. We should labor strenuously to complete the work of God in us, so that once this has been accomplished, he can call us back to him right away. However, this desire should be without attachment and anxiety. In this way if it pleases God that we remain separated for some years to come from the sweet vision of his divine face, we might be satisfied with the vision of his most lovable will, even if he should want us to experience this painful privation until the day of judgment.

This is what I mean by being detached from God. This constitutes the perfect detachment that all Christians should have from the world, themselves and everything else. Oh, how sweet it is to be so free and detached from everything!

You might think it is very difficult to achieve this. However, everything will be easy for us if we give ourselves totally and without reservation to the Son of God, and if we place our trust and confidence, not in our own strength and resolve, but rather in the greatness of his goodness and in the power of his grace and love. For wherever this divine love is found, everything is accomplished with gentleness. It is true that we must do violence to ourselves at times and experience much suffering, bitterness, darkness and mortification. Nevertheless, on the path of sacred love there is more honey than gall, more gentleness than harshness.

O my Savior, how you glory, how you delight and how you accomplish great things in a soul that walks courageously on this path, thus abandoning all and detaching itself from everything, even from yourself in a certain manner, in order to give its whole self more perfectly to you! How strongly you unite it to you! How divinely you take possession of it! How divinely you plunge it into the abyss of your holy love! How wonderfully you transform it into yourself, clothing it with your attributes, your spirit and your love!

Oh, what satisfaction, what delight it is for the soul to be able to say truthfully: My God, here I am free and detached from everything! Who can prevent me from loving you perfectly? Now I no longer cling to anything. Draw me now closer to you, O my Jesus, *Draw me after you. We will make haste in the fragrance of your oils* (Sg 1:3,4). Ah, what a consolation it is for the soul who can say with the holy spouse: *My beloved is all mine and I am all his* (Sg 2:16); or with Jesus: *Omnia mea tua sunt, et tua mea sunt*, "Everything that is mine is yours, O my Savior, and everything that is yours is mine" (Jn 17:10).

Let us cultivate a great desire for this holy detachment. Let us give ourselves totally and without reservation to Jesus, begging him to use the power of his arm to break our bonds and to detach us completely from the world, ourselves and all things, so that, without any obstacle, he may work in us everything he desires to accomplish for his glory.

JOHN EUDES

XI.

The Fourth Foundation of Christian Life
and Holiness: Prayer

The holy exercise of prayer must be considered one of the chief foundations of Christian life and holiness because Jesus Christ's whole life was nothing but a continuous prayer, which we must continue and express in our life. It is very important and absolutely necessary because prayer is more essential for a Christian who wants to live a Christian life than are the earth which supports us, the air which we breathe, the bread which sustains us and the heart which beats in our breast necessary to us for human life. This is because:

1. The Christian life, which the Son of God calls eternal life, consists in knowing and loving God (Jn 17:3). Now, it is through prayer that we acquire this divine knowledge.

2. By ourselves we are nothing. We are capable of nothing. We possess only poverty and nothingness. This is why we have a very great need to turn to God at every moment through prayer in order to obtain and receive from him all that we lack.

Prayer is a respectful and loving elevation of our mind and heart to God. It is a delightful encounter, a holy communication and a divine conversation of the Christian soul with its God. There we consider and contemplate him in his divine perfections, in his mysteries and in his works. We adore him, bless him, love him, glorify him and give ourselves to him. We humble ourselves before him at the sight of our sins and ingratitude, ask him for mercy, learn to become like him by imitating his divine virtues and perfections, and finally we ask him for everything that we need in order to serve and love him.

Prayer is a participation in the life of the angels and saints, in the life of Jesus Christ and his blessed Mother, in the life of God himself and the three divine Persons. For the life of the angels, the saints, Jesus Christ and his blessed Mother is nothing else but a continuous exercise of prayer and contemplation, in which they are constantly given over to contemplate, glorify and love God, asking him to give us those things that we need. The life of the three divine

313

Persons is a perpetual contemplation, glorification and love of one another, which is the primary and principal object of prayer.

Prayer is the perfect delight, the highest happiness and the true paradise on earth. For through this divine exercise the Christian soul is united to its God who is its center, its goal and its highest good. In prayer it possesses him and is possessed by him. In prayer it offers him its respect, homage, adoration and love, and receives from him his light, his blessing and a thousand tokens of his unbounded love. It is in prayer that God delights in us: *My delight is to be with the children of men* (Prv 8:31). There God teaches us experientially that true delight and perfect happiness are found in God and that a hundred, even a thousand years of the false pleasures of the world do not equal one moment of the authentic delights that God allows those souls to taste, whose greatest joy is to commune with him through holy prayer.

Finally, prayer is the worthiest, noblest, most exalted, greatest and most important activity and occupation to which you can give yourself, since it is the continual work and occupation of the angels, the saints, the blessed Virgin, Jesus Christ and the holy Trinity throughout all eternity. It will also be our perpetual exercise in heaven. Indeed, it is the true and proper function of a man and a Christian. For man is created for God alone and to live with him. The Christian is on earth for the sole purpose of continuing what Jesus Christ accomplished here during his lifetime.

This is why, with all my power, I plead with you who read this and beg you in God's name, since our most beloved Jesus deigns to take delight in being and dwelling with us through the means of holy prayer, do not deprive him of his joy, but rather experience for yourselves how true are these words of the Holy Spirit: *There is no bitterness in his presence or boredom in his company, but only joy and gladness* (Wis 8:16). Consider this activity as the first, foremost, most necessary, most pressing and most important of all your occupations. Free yourselves, as much as possible, from other less essential activities so as to devote as much time as you can to prayer, especially in the morning, the evening and just before dinner, using one of the ways that I am going to now propose.

JOHN EUDES

XII.

Various Ways of Praying, Beginning with Mental Prayer

There are various ways of praying. I will indicate here the five most important ones.

The first is what we call mental or interior prayer, in which the soul converses interiorly with God, taking as a subject for this encounter one of his divine perfections or some mystery, virtue or word of the Son of God or what he has accomplished or now accomplishes in the order of glory, grace, nature or in his blessed Mother, in the saints, in his church or in the natural world. The soul begins by applying its understanding, with a gentle and firm attention and effort of the mind, to consider the truths contained in the chosen subject, and which are able to incite the soul to love God and detest its sins. After that the soul applies its heart and will to produce many acts and feelings of adoration, praise, love, humiliation, contrition, oblation as well as the resolution to flee evil and do good and other similar acts according to the promptings of the Spirit of God.

This way of praying is so holy, so helpful and so filled with blessings that words cannot explain it. Thus, if God draws you to prayer and gives you the graces for it, you should thank him indeed for giving you this very splendid gift. If he has not as yet given you this gift, pray that he gives it to you and do all that you can on your part to correspond to his grace and to cultivate this holy activity. God will instruct you in it better than all the books and all the doctors in this world, if you throw yourselves at his feet with confidence and a pure heart, in the way I will now propose.

XIII.

The Second Way of Praying: Vocal Prayer

The second way of praying is called vocal prayer. In this we use our mouth in speaking to God, either by saying the divine office, the rosary or some other vocal prayer. This means is almost as useful as the first one, provided that your lips are united to your heart. In other words, as you speak to God with your lips, you are also speaking to him with your heart and an attentive mind. For in this way, your prayer will be vocal and mental at the same time. On the contrary, if you become accustomed to reciting many vocal prayers in a routine and inattentive manner, you will leave God's presence more dissipated, colder and less fervent in his love than you were before. This is why I advise you to do little of this, except for the obligatory prayers, and to do them well with much attention and application of yourself to God, filling your mind and heart with some holy thoughts and feelings while you speak with your lips. Remind yourself that you must continue the earthly prayer of Jesus Christ. To accomplish this, give yourself to him. Unite yourself to the love, humility, purity, holiness and the very perfect attention that he brought to prayer. Beg him to imprint in you the dispositions and the holy and divine intentions with which he prayed.

You can offer your prayer to God in union with all the holy and divine prayers that have been and will be offered continually in heaven and on earth by the blessed Virgin, the angels, and all the saints of earth and heaven, uniting yourself to the love, devotion and attention they bring to this holy practice.

XIV.

The Third Way of Praying:
Performing All Your Actions in a Spirit of Prayer

The third way of praying is to accomplish all your actions in a Christian and holy manner, even the least significant, offering them to our Lord when you begin them and lifting your heart to him from time to time while you are performing them, according to the way that has been and will be proposed once more in the sixth part of this book. For in this way, we perform our actions in a spirit of prayer. We are always in a continual exercise of prayer, faithful to our Lord's command that *we pray always and without interruption* (Lk 18:1; 1 Thes 5:17). It is a very excellent and quite easy way to remain always in the presence of God.

316

JOHN EUDES

XV.

The Fourth Way of Praying:
Reading Good Books

The fourth way of praying is to read good books, not hurriedly and in haste, but in a leisurely fashion, applying your mind to what you read, stopping to consider, mull over, weigh and savor the truths that touch you most, in order to imprint them in your mind and draw from them various acts and feelings, just as I suggested for mental prayer. This exercise is very important and accomplishes in the soul the same effects as mental prayer. This is why I insist in particular that you never let a day go by without reading some holy book for half an hour.

The most appropriate are: the *New Testament*, if you have permission to read it; the *Imitation of Jesus Christ;* the life of the saints; the books of Grenada, especially the splendid *Guide for Sinners* and the *Memorial of the Christian Life;*³ the books of Saint Francis de Sales; those of the most illustrious founder of the Oratory of France, Cardinal de Bérulle; the *Spiritual Treasury* of Father Quarré.⁴ However, take care at the beginning of your reading to offer your mind and heart to our Lord. Beg him to give you the grace that will allow you to derive the fruit he expects of you and allow him to accomplish in your soul what he wishes for his glory.

XVI.

The Fifth Way of Praying:
Speaking about God.
How to Speak about God and
Listen to Others Speak of Him

It is also very useful, holy and capable of greatly inflaming our hearts with divine love to speak and converse with one another at times in an intimate way about God and the things of God. Christians should spend part of their time in this way. It should be their usual discourse and conversation. In it they should find their relaxation and delight.

The prince of the apostles exhorts us to do this when he says: *If someone speaks, let his words be like the words of God* (1 Pt 4:11).

For since we are children of God, we should delight in speaking the language of our Father, which is most holy, heavenly and divine. Since we are created for heaven, we should begin speaking on earth the language of heaven. Oh, how holy and charming this language is! Oh, how sweet it is for a soul who loves God above all else to speak and hear about what it likes most in the world! Oh, how pleasing these sacred conversations are to the one who said that *where two or three are gathered in his name, he would be in their midst* (Mt 18:20)! Oh, how different these conversations are from the usual conversations in the world! Oh, what a holy use of time this is, provided we come to it with the proper dispositions!

To this end we should follow the example and rule on this subject given us by Saint Paul in these words: *Sicut ex Deo, coram Deo, in Christo loquimur,* "We speak as from God, before God in Jesus Christ" (2 Cor 2:17). These words indicate three things we must observe in order to speak of God in a holy manner.

First we must speak *from God,* that is, we must draw from God the realities and words we are to say, giving ourselves to the Son of God at the beginning of our spiritual conversations so that he can put in our mind and on our lips the realities and words we have to say. Thus we can say what he said to his Father: *I have given them the words you have given me* (Jn 17:8).

Second, we must speak *before God,* that is, with attention and application to God, who is present everywhere and with a spirit of prayer and recollection, giving ourselves to God so that we might bring forth the fruits of what we say or hear said and use them according to his will.

Third, we must speak *in Jesus Christ,* that is, with the intentions and dispositions of Jesus Christ and in the same way he spoke while he was on earth or as he would have spoken if he were in our place. To this end we must give ourselves to him and unite ourselves to his intentions when he spoke in the world, having no other goal than the pure glory of God. We must be united as well to his dispositions of humility toward himself, of gentleness and love toward those with whom he spoke as well as love and devotion toward his Father. If we do this our conversations and encounters will be very pleasing to him. He will be in our midst. He will delight in being with us, and this time spent in such holy encounters will be a time of prayer.

JOHN EUDES

XVII.

The Dispositions and Qualities that Should Accompany Prayer

The holy apostle Saint Paul teaches us that in order to accomplish all our actions in a holy fashion, we must do them in the name of Jesus Christ. This same Jesus also assures us that whatever we ask his Father in his name, he will give us. Thus, in order to pray in a holy manner and to obtain from God what we ask of him, we must pray in the name of Jesus Christ. But what does it mean to pray in the name of Jesus Christ? I have already mentioned it in passing, but it cannot be repeated too often, so that it will be imprinted in your mind as a very important truth that can help you in all your exercises. It means that we continue the prayer of Jesus Christ on earth. For since all Christians are members of Jesus Christ and are his body, as Saint Paul says, they take his place on earth. They represent his person, and therefore they must do all that they do in his name, that is, with his spirit, his dispositions and his intentions, as he himself did while he was in the world and as he would do if he were in their place. This is like an ambassador, who takes the place of and represents the person of the king. He must act and speak in his name, that is, with his spirit, his dispositions and his intentions, acting and speaking as he would if he were present. This is why I say that praying in the name of Jesus Christ is to continue the supplication and prayer of Jesus Christ, that is, to pray with the spirit of Jesus Christ and with his dispositions and intentions, just as he prayed himself on earth and as he would pray if he were in our place. This is how Christians should pray.

To this end, when you go to pray, remember that you are going to continue the prayer of Jesus Christ; that you should continue to pray as he would if he were in your place, that is, with the dispositions with which he did pray and still does pray in heaven and on our altars where he is present in continual prayer to his Father. To this end unite yourselves to the love, humility, purity, holiness, attention and all the holy dispositions and intentions with which he prays.

Now among these dispositions, there are four in particular with which he prayed and with which we must pray if we wish to glorify God in our prayer and obtain from him all that we ask.

JOHN EUDES

XVIII.

First Disposition

The first disposition for prayer is to present ourselves before God with profound humility, recognizing that we are most unworthy to appear before his face, to comtemplate him or to be seen and heard by him. Of ourselves we are unable to produce any good thought or any act pleasing to him. This is why we must abnegate ourselves at his feet and give ourselves to our Lord Jesus Christ, asking him to annihilate us and fill us with himself so that he might pray through us. For he alone is worthy to appear before the face of God his Father to praise and love him and to obtain from him all that he asks. After this, with assurance we should ask the eternal Father for everything we seek in his Son's name, through his Son's merits and on behalf of his Son, who is in us.

XIX.

The Second Disposition for Prayer

The second disposition with which we must pray is a respectful and loving confidence, believing with full assurance that we will obtain infallibly everything we ask that is for the glory of God and for our salvation. Often we will obtain something better than we ask, provided that, relying not on the merits and the power of our prayer, we ask instead in the name of Jesus Christ, through the merits and prayers of Jesus Christ and on behalf of Jesus Christ himself, relying on his absolute goodness and the truth of these words of his: *Ask and you will receive; everything that you ask for in my name will be given to you;* and *when you ask God for something, believe and have full confidence that you will receive it and it will happen to you in this way* (Lk 11:9; Jn 16:23; Mk 11:24). For indeed, if God treated us according to our merits, he would drive us from his face and destroy us as we appeared before him. This is why, when he grants us some grace, we must not think that it is our own, or [that he gives it] because of the power of our prayers. Rather, everything he gives is to his Son Jesus, and on account of the power of his prayers and merits.

XX.

The Third Disposition for Prayer

The third disposition with which we must pray is purity of intention, assuring our Lord from the beginning that we renounce all curiosity of mind, all self-love, and that we wish to perform this action not for our own satisfaction and consolation, but only for his glory and satisfaction, for in this way he will deign to delight in dealing and conversing with us. We must assure him also that our desire is to ask him everything for this same goal.

XXI.

The Fourth Disposition for Prayer

The fourth disposition that should accompany perfect prayer is perseverance.

If you wish to glorify God in prayer and obtain from his goodness what you ask, you must persevere faithfully in this divine exercise. For there are many things we ask of God that he does not give us the first, second or third time we ask because he wants us to ask him for a long time and frequently, intending by these means to keep us in a state of humility and self-contempt as well as the appreciation of his graces. He is pleased to leave us for a long time in a matter that makes us return many times to him, so that by this means we might be with him and he with us often, because he loves us so much and because it is true that he delights in our company.

Finally, to fulfill every holy disposition, when you begin your prayer, give your mind and heart powerfully to Jesus and his Holy Spirit, praying that he place in your mind the thoughts and in your heart the sentiments and affections he wishes. Surrender yourself completely to his holy guidance so that he may direct you as he wishes in this divine exercise. Have confidence in his most splendid goodness, that he will lead you in the most appropriate manner and grant you everything you ask him. If it is not in the way you desire, it will be in some better way.

JOHN EUDES

[6, 24: *OC* 1, pp. 459–64]

An Exercise for Holy Mass

XXIV.

*What We Must Do to Assist Worthily
at the Holy Sacrifice of the Mass*

In order to assist in a holy manner and to glorify God worthily at the most holy sacrifice of the Mass, you must do four things.

I. As soon as you leave your house to go to Mass, you should realize that you are not going merely to assist or to see, but indeed you are going to perform an action that is the holiest and most divine, the greatest and the most important, the worthiest and most admirable action accomplished in heaven and on earth. Therefore it should be performed in a holy and divine manner, that is, with the most holy and divine dispositions and with very great care and attention of mind and heart, being the most important thing you have to do in the world. I said *that you are going to do*. For all Christians are one with Jesus Christ, who is the high priest. Therefore they share in his divine priesthood, which is why they are called priests in the scriptures (see 1 Pt 2:9). Therefore they have the right not only to assist at the holy sacrifice of the Mass, but to join with the priest in doing what he does, that is, to offer with him and Jesus Christ the very sacrifice that is offered to God on the altar.

II. As you enter the church you should humble yourself profoundly in your heart, seeing yourself as most unworthy of entering the house of God, of appearing before his face, of taking part in such a great mystery, which contains in itself all the mysteries and all the wonders of heaven and earth. This awareness of your nothingness and sins should create in you a spirit of penance, humiliation and contrition at the beginning of Mass. You should accuse yourself of them in a general way with the priest, asking God for pardon and praying that he will grant you perfect repentance, as well as the grace and strength to avoid them in the future. In reparation you should

322

offer him the holy sacrifice of the precious body and blood of his Son, which was offered to him on the cross and is about to be offered to him on the altar.

III. Next you should adore our Lord Jesus Christ, who makes himself present to us on the altar, so that we might offer him the homage and adoration we owe him. Pray that just as he changes the lower, earthly nature of bread and wine into his body and blood he might change and transform also the sluggishness, coldness and dryness of our earthly and arid heart into the fire, tenderness and agility of the holy, divine affections and dispositions of his divine and heavenly heart. Then you should remember that Christians are one with Jesus Christ, as members with their head, and thus they share in all his attributes. So as Jesus Christ is in this sacrifice both as priest and host at the same time, so all those who assist should be there as priests and as those who offer sacrifice in order to offer, with Jesus Christ, the High Priest, the same sacrifice he offers. They should also be there as hosts and victims, who are but one host just as they are one priest with Jesus Christ. They need to be immolated and sacrificed with the same Jesus Christ for the glory of God.

Therefore, since you share in the divine priesthood of Jesus Christ and, as Christians and members of Jesus Christ, you bear the name and attribute of priest, you should exercise this quality and use the right it gives you, which is to offer to God, with the priest and with Jesus Christ himself, the sacrifice of his body and blood offered in the holy Mass. You should offer it to him, as much as possible, with the same dispositions as Jesus Christ offers it. Oh, with what holy and divine dispositions it is offered to him by his Son Jesus! Oh, with what humility, what purity, what holiness, what detachment from self and all things, what devotion to God, what love toward men, what love for his Father! Unite yourself in desire and intention with these dispositions of Jesus. Pray that he will engrave them within you so that you may offer this divine sacrifice with him, united to the same dispositions with which he offers it.

Unite yourself to the intentions for which he offers it. There are five main ones. The first is to honor his Father with all that he is in himself and in all things and thus offer him an honor, glory and love worthy of him. The second is to offer a gratitude worthy of his kindness; for all the blessings he has ever given to creatures. The third is to make full satisfaction for all the sins of the world. The fourth is to fulfill his plan and will. The fifth is to obtain from him everything that men need for their bodies and souls. In harmony with these intentions of Jesus Christ, you should offer God the holy sacrifice of the Mass:

1. In honor of the blessed Trinity, in honor of all that Jesus Christ is in himself, in all his states, mysteries, attributes, virtues, actions and sufferings; and in honor of all that he is and performs through both mercy or justice in his blessed Mother, in all the angels and saints, in the whole church, triumphant, militant and suffering, and in every creature in heaven, on earth and in hell.

2. In thanksgiving to God for all the temporal and eternal blessings he has ever conferred on the sacred humanity of his Son, the blessed Virgin, every angel and man, every creature and especially yourself.

3. In reparation to his divine justice for all your sins, for all the sins of the world and especially for those poor souls in purgatory.

4. For the fulfillment of his every plan and will, in particular for those he has for you.

5. To obtain from his kindness all the graces that are necessary for you and all men so that he may be honored and served by all, according to the perfection he asks of each person.

This is what you must do as a priest. However, beyond that, as a host, in offering Jesus Christ to God in the holy Mass as victim, you must offer yourself also with him as a victim. More exactly, you should pray that Jesus Christ come within you and that he draw you within himself, that he unite himself to you and that he unite and incorporate you with him as host, in order to sacrifice you with him to the glory of his Father.

Since the host that is to be sacrificed must be killed and then consumed in the fire, pray that he will make you die to yourself, that is, to your passions, your self-love and everything that displeases him. Pray that he will consume you in the sacred fire of his divine love and that he will make your whole life from this moment on become a perpetual sacrifice of praise, glory and love for his Father and for himself.

IV. You should prepare yourself for communion, at least spiritual if not sacramental. You need to realize that our Lord Jesus Christ, who loves you infinitely, does not become present in this sacrifice only to be with you, to relate with you in a familiar manner and to communicate his gifts and graces to you. There is much more. He wants to be within you. He has a strong, burning desire to dwell in your heart and to give himself to you through sacramental or spiritual communion. This is why you should prepare yourself to receive him and, to that end, adopt the same dispositions you should have for sacramental communion, that is, dispositions and sentiments of humility and love. Humble yourself then before him, considering yourself most unworthy to receive him. Nevertheless, since he desires it so, desire as well to receive him. Invite him by repeated acts of love to come within you, so that he might live and rule in you perfectly.

V. Finally, after having thanked our Lord for the graces he granted you during holy Mass, go forth with a firm resolution to make good use of the day in his service. Also take this thought with you: that you should be from now on a host, dead and living at the same time; dead to everything that is not God and living in God and for God, totally consecrated and sacrificed to the pure glory and most pure love of God. Assure our Lord that this is what you desire and that you offer yourself to him to accomplish and suffer for this goal all that he wishes. Pray that he accomplish this in you through his great mercy. Pray that he give you the grace to lift your heart to him often during the day, to do everything for his glory, to die rather than offend him. To this end ask that he give you his most holy blessing.

This is the way in which you should take advantage of such a holy and divine reality, that is, the most holy sacrifice of the Mass. If you do not need all these things to occupy your mind devoutly during Mass, choose the ones that afford you greater blessing. However, in order to make these exercises easier for you to use, they have been summarized in prayer form. Use them, not hastily and on the run, but leisurely and with an attentive mind and heart, if you wish to benefit from them for the glory of God.

[There follows a series of prayers for Mass.]

The Most Admirable Heart of
the Most Sacred Mother
of God[5]

[1, 2: *OC* 6, pp. 33–40]

The Meaning of the Heart of the Blessed Virgin

Before speaking of the phenomenal supremacy and the incomparable marvels of the admirable heart of the blessed Mother of God, according to the lights that it pleases him who is light itself and the source of all light to give me through the divine scriptures and the writings of the holy Fathers, I will first state that the word *heart* has many meanings in sacred scripture.

1. It signifies this material and bodily heart, which we possess in our chest. It is the most noble part of the human body, the source of life, the first to live and the last to die, the seat of love, hatred, joy, sadness, anger, fear and all the other passions of the soul. It is of this heart that the Holy Spirit speaks when he says: *Omni custodia serva cor tuum, quia ex ipso vita procedit,* "Take good care of your heart for it is the source of life" (Prv 4:23); which is as if he said: Take great care to subdue and rule the passions of your heart. For if they are appropriately subject to reason and the Spirit of God, you will live a long and peaceful life in your body and a holy and honorable one in your soul. However if, on the contrary, they possess and govern your

326

heart as they wish, they will bring you temporal and eternal death through their dissipation.

2. The word *heart* is used in sacred scripture to signify the memory. This is the meaning of these words of our Lord to his apostles: *Ponite in cordibus vestris, non praemeditari quemadmodum respondeatis,* "Put this in your hearts," that is, remember, when they bring you before kings and judges for my name's sake, "do not worry about what you should respond" (Lk 21:14).

3. It also denotes the understanding used for meditation, which consists in the discursive reasoning of our intellect about the things of God. This tends to persuade us and convince us of the truth of Christian teaching. It is this heart that is indicated by these words: *May the meditation of my heart be always in your sight* (Ps 19:15). "My heart," that is, my understanding, "is forever devoted to meditating and reflecting on your grandeurs, your mysteries and your works."

4. It signifies the free will of the superior and reasonable part of the soul, which is the noblest of its powers, the queen of the other faculties, the root of good and evil and the mother of vice and virtue. It is this heart our Lord mentions when he says: *The good man out of the good treasure of his heart produces good, but the evil man out of the evil treasure produces evil* (Lk 6:45). "A good heart," that is, the good will of the just man, "is a rich treasure out of which can come only good; but an evil heart," that is the ill will of the wicked man, "is the source of all sorts of evil."

5. It means that highest part of the soul, which the theologians call *the point of the spirit.* This is the seat of contemplation, which consists in a most special gaze and an utterly simple vision of God, without discursive reasoning and the multiplicity of thoughts. The holy Fathers understand that these words, which the Holy Spirit inspires in the blessed Virgin, refer to this part of the soul: *Ego dormio, et cor meum vigilat:* "I sleep and my heart is awake" (Sg 5:2). According to Saint Bernardine of Siena and many others, bodily rest and sleep did not prevent her heart, that is the highest part of her spirit, from being always united to God in sublime contemplation.[6]

6. At times it signifies the whole interior of man. By this I mean all that pertains to the soul and the interior and spiritual life, according to these words of the Son of God to the faithful soul: *Pone me ut signaculum super cor tuum, ut signaculum super brachium tuum,* "Place me as a seal upon your heart and on your arm" (Sg 8:6); that is,

imprint, through perfect imitation, the image of my interior and exterior life in your interior and exterior, in your soul and your body.

7. It means the divine Spirit, the heart of the Father and the Son, which they wish to give us to be our spirit and our heart: *I will give you a new heart and I will place a new spirit in your midst* (Ez 36:26).

8. The Son of God is called the heart of the eternal Father in the sacred scriptures. For it is of this heart that the divine Father speaks to his divine spouse, the most pure Virgin, when he says to her: *You have wounded my heart, my sister, my spouse* (Sg 4:9); or in the Septuagint version, *You have ravished my heart*. Also, in the same scriptures, this same Son of God is called, *The spirit of our mouth* (Lam 4:20), "our spirit," that is, soul of our soul, heart of our heart.

All these hearts are found in the Mother of love and make up a single heart in her because all the faculties of the superior and interior part of her soul have always been perfectly united with one another. Moreover, both Jesus, who is the heart of his Father, as well as the divine Spirit, who is the heart of the Father and the Son, have been given to her to be the spirit of her spirit, the soul of her soul and the heart of her heart.

But to understand better what we mean by the heart of the blessed Virgin, we must know that just as we adore in God three hearts, which are in fact a single heart, and just as we adore in the Man-God three hearts, which are one and the same heart, so also we honor in the Mother of God three hearts, which are a single heart.

The first heart in the blessed Trinity is the Son of God, who is the heart of his Father, as we have said earlier. The second is the Holy Spirit, who is the heart of the Father and the Son. The third is divine love, one of the adorable attributes of the divine essence, which is the heart of the Father, the Son and the Holy Spirit. These three hearts are an utterly simple and unique heart with which the three eternal Persons love one another with as sublime a love as they deserve and with which they love us as well with an incomparable love.

The first heart of the Man-God is his bodily heart, which is divinized, as are all the other parts of his sacred body through their hypostatic union with the divine Person of the eternal Word. The second is his spiritual heart, that is, the superior part of his holy soul containing his memory, understanding and will, which have been divinized in a special way by the hypostatic union. The third is his divine heart, the Holy Spirit, which has always animated and enlivened his adorable humanity more than his own soul and heart ever

JOHN EUDES

did. These three hearts in this admirable Man-God are but a single
heart, because his divine heart is the soul, the heart and the life of his
spiritual and bodily heart. He grounds them in such a perfect union
with himself that these three hearts are but a single unique heart,
filled with an infinite love toward the blessed Trinity and an inconceivable love toward men.

The first heart of the Mother of God is the bodily heart enclosed
in her virginal breast. The second is her spiritual heart, the heart of
her soul, which is indicated by these words of the Holy Spirit: *Omnis
gloria Filiae Regis ab intus,* "All the glory of the King's daughter
originates from her interior" (see Ps 45:14), that is, in her heart and
in her inmost soul, of which we will speak more later. The third
heart of this divine Virgin is the one she refers to when she says: *I
sleep and my heart is awake;* that is, according to the explanation of
many holy doctors, while I give my body the needed rest, my son
Jesus, who is my heart and whom I love as my own heart, is always
watching over me and for me.

The first of these hearts is bodily, but totally spiritualized by grace
and by the Spirit of God who fills it completely.

The second is spiritual, but divinized, not by the hypostatic union
like the spiritual heart of Jesus, which we just mentioned, but by an
eminent participation in the divine perfections, as we shall see in the
following pages.

The third is divine, indeed God himself, since it is the Son of God.

These three hearts of the Mother of God are but a single heart
through the most holy and most intimate bond that ever existed or
will exist, next to the hypostatic union. Referring to these three
hearts, or rather to this unique heart, the Holy Spirit uttered twice
these divine words: *Mary kept all these things in her heart* (Lk
2:19,51).

First she preserved all the mysteries and marvels of her Son's life in
some way in her material, bodily heart, source of life and seat of love
and all the other passions, because every movement and beat of this
virginal heart, all the functions of material life that flowed from it and
all the activities of the aforementioned passions were at the service of
Jesus and everything that occurred in him. There was love to love
him; hatred to hate everything opposed to him, that is sin; joy to
rejoice in his glory and splendor; sorrow to grieve over his labors and
sufferings; and so on with the other passions.

Second, she preserved them in her heart, that is, in the noblest part of her soul, in the innermost recesses of her spirit. For all the faculties of the superior part of her soul were occupied unceasingly in contemplating and adoring everything that happened in the life of her Son down to the least detail.

Third, she preserved them in her heart, that is in her son Jesus, who was the spirit of her spirit and the heart of her heart. He preserved them for her, suggested them to her and recalled them to mind when it was opportune to serve as nourishment for her soul in contemplation and so that she might honor and adore them as they deserved and repeat them to the holy apostles and disciples, who would then preach them to the faithful.

This is what we mean by the admirable heart of the beloved of God. It is a perfect image of the adorable heart of God and of the Man-God, as we will see more clearly later.

Such is the most worthy subject, which I will treat in this book. The following three chapters will explain more in detail about the bodily heart of the Mother of the Savior, her spiritual heart and her divine heart. Throughout the remainder of the book you will find a number of things, some of which are appropriate to her bodily heart, others to her spiritual heart, others to her divine heart and others that refer to all three. All of them will be quite useful for your soul, if you read them after having given your spirit over to the Spirit of God with the intention of putting them to good use.

To this end, take care from time to time, as you read this, to lift your heart to God to praise him for all the glory he has given himself and will give himself eternally in this wondrous masterpiece of his divine love. Bless him for all the extraordinary favors he has bestowed on this most august heart. Thank him for the countless graces he has granted to men through her. Offer him your heart and beg him to make it like his own, destroying in it everything that displeases him and engraving on it an image of the most holy heart of the Mother of the saint of saints. I exhort you to give your heart often to her as well with the same intention.

O Jesus, only Son of God, only Son of Mary, you see that I am involved in a task that is infinitely beyond my grasp. However, I undertook it out of love for you and your most worthy Mother, confident in the kindness of the Son and the charity of the Mother. You know, my Savior, that I have no other intention in this than to please you and to offer you and your divine Mother some small gratitude for the numerous mercies that I have received from your paternal heart and through the intervention of her most gracious heart. Nevertheless, you see also that of myself I am nothing but an abyss of unworthiness, powerlessness, darkness, ignorance and sin. This is why I renounce with all my heart everything of my own. I give myself over to your divine spirit and holy light. I give myself over to the immense love you have for your beloved Mother. I give myself over to the burning zeal you have for your glory and her honor. Possess and animate my spirit, enlighten my darkness, enkindle my heart, guide my hand, direct my pen, bless my work and please use it for your greater glory and the honor of your blessed Mother and to imprint in the hearts of those who will read this book an authentic devotion to her most lovable heart.

[12, 6: *OC* 8, pp. 344–47]

The Three Hearts of Jesus, Which Are Only One Heart

FIRST POINT

We have three hearts to adore in our Savior, which are nevertheless only one unique heart because of the very close bond that exists between them.

The first is his divine heart, which he possesses from all eternity in the adorable bosom of his Father, which is but one heart and one love with the heart and love of his Father; and with the heart and love of his Father, it is the origin of the Holy Spirit. Therefore, when he gave us his heart, he gave us as well the heart of his Father and his adorable Spirit. Because of this, he says to us these marvelous words: *As my Father has loved me, so I have loved you,* "I love you with the same heart and the same love with which I am loved by my Father" (Jn 15:9). My Father loves me with an eternal, boundless and infinite love, and I love you also with an eternal, boundless and infinite love. My Father makes me what I am, that is, God like him and the only Son of God; and I make you, through grace and participation, what I

331

am by nature and essence, that is, gods and children of God. You have the same Father as I, a Father who loves you with the same heart and the same love with which he loves me. *You have loved them as you have loved me* (Jn 17:23). My Father makes me the universal heir of all his goods, *He appointed him heir of all things* (Heb 1:2); and I make you my co-heirs, *heirs of God and fellow heirs with Christ* (Rom 8:17). I promise you that I will give you possession of all my treasures, *He will set him over all his possessions* (Mt 24:47). My Father takes all his pleasure and delight in me. Also I take my delight and pleasure in you, *My delight is to be with the children of men* (Prv 8:31).

O goodness! O love! O excess! O God of love! How can the hearts of men be so cool and frigid toward you, who are all on fire and aflame with love of them? Oh, may all my joy and delight be in thinking of you, in speaking of you and in serving and loving you! O my All, may I be totally yours and may you alone possess everything that belongs to me, that is part of me and is within me.

SECOND POINT

The second heart of Jesus is his spiritual heart, which is the will of his holy soul. It is a purely spiritual faculty whose proper role is to love what is lovable and detest what is detestable. However, this divine Savior so completely sacrificed his human will to his Father that he never fulfilled it while he was on earth and will never do so in heaven. He accomplishes nothing but the will of his Father, according to these words of his: *I do not seek my will, but the will of him who sent me. I have come down from heaven not to do my own will, but the will of him who sent me* (Jn 5:30; 6:38). Now it was for love of us that this lovable Jesus renounced his own will in order to accomplish our salvation, through the will of his Father alone, especially when he spoke to him in the Garden of Olives: *Pater, non mea voluntas, sed tua fiat,* "Father, not my will, but yours be done" (Lk 22:42)!

O God of my heart, if out of love for me you sacrificed a most holy and divine will, how much more should I, for love of you, renounce my own will, which is totally depraved and corrupted by sin! Oh, grant that with all my heart, I renounce it now and forever. I beg of you most humbly, O adorable Redeemer, to crush it in me completely like a snake filled with poison and replace it with the rule of your will.

THIRD POINT

The third heart of Jesus is the most holy heart of his divinized body, which is a furnace of incomparable, divine love toward us. For since this sacred heart is united hypostatically to the person of the Word, it is enkindled with the flames of his infinite love toward us. This love is so ardent that the Son of God is impelled to carry us continually in his heart; to keep his eyes fixed always on us; to take such good care of the least things that pertain to us, that he counts all the hairs of our head and will not let even one perish; to ask his Father that we may dwell with him eternally in his bosom: *Father, I desire that those whom you have given me may be with me where I am* (Jn 17:24); and to assure us that, if we overcome the enemies of his glory and our salvation, he will seat us with him on his own throne and will give us possession of the same kingdom and the same glory that his Father has given him.

Oh, how abundant and enraptured is the love of Jesus for men, as ungrateful and unfaithful as we are! O Jesus, my love, either let me live no longer or let me live only to love you, to praise you and to glorify you without end! Let me die a thousand deaths rather than do anything willingly that would displease you! You have three hearts, which are one and the same heart, which is devoted to loving me continually. Oh, that I might have all the hearts of the universe in order to consume them in your holy love!

EJACULATORY PRAYER

I love you most beloved Jesus.
I love you infinite goodness.
I love you with my whole heart
and
I wish to love you more and more.

NOTES

1. He appears to be referring here to Genesis 2:23, which he has attributed inaccurately to Paul. Many of the scripture texts in this section are blended together by Saint John Eudes even though they are taken from various places. I will place the references at the end of these "textual mosaics" to make them more readable.

This entire book is a loosely related series of prayers, meditations and teachings on the spiritual life. The selections translated here illustrate the range of topics.

2. The reference given here in the French edition is to Esther 14:18. This is the numbering of the Vulgate. The reader will only find ten chapters in most contemporary versions of the Bible, where this text and other later Greek additions have been incorporated. For a reconstructed version of this text see the *Bible of Jerusalem* (Garden City, New York: Doubleday, Inc., 1968), p. 563.

3. Louis of Grenada (1505–88) was a noted Dominican preacher.

4. John Hughes Quarré (1589–1656) was a priest of the Oratory and a follower of Cardinal Bérulle.

5. For an overview of the contents of the *Coeur*, see the *Introduction* to this volume, pp. 52–54, 73–98.

6. Saint Bernardine of Siena, *Sermon 51*, art. 1, c. 2. Bernardine was a Franciscan reformer and preacher who lived in Italy from 1380 to 1444.

SELECTED BIBLIOGRAPHY

Bérulle

Primary Sources

Bérulle et le sacerdoce: étude historique et doctrinale. By Michel Dupuy. Paris: P. Lethielleux, 1969. Pages 255–430 are *textes inédits* of Bérulle's writings on the priesthood. Citations indicated by *OR.*

Collationes. Latin manuscript 18210, Paris, Bibliothèque Nationale. Citations indicated by *Coll.*

Correspondance du Bérulle. 3 vols. Edited by Jean Dagens. Paris: Desclée de Brouwer, 1937–39. Citations indicated by *CB.*

"Des nouveaux inédits de Bérulle." Edited by Michel Dupuy. *Revue d'histoire de la spiritualité* 48 (1972): 435–52; 52 (1976): 345–86; 53 (1977): 275–316; and *Revue des études augustiniennes* 26 (1980): 266–85.

Élévation sur sainte Madeleine. Foi vivante Series, 224. Introduced and edited by Joseph Beaude. Paris: Cerf, 1987. A helpful introduction, and a modernized version.

Les "Oeuvres de piété" du cardinal de Bérulle. Essai de classement des inédits et conjectures chronologiques. Edited by Jean Orcibal. *Revue d'histoire ecclésiastique* 57 (1962): 813–62. Citations indicated by *RHE.*

Oeuvres complètes. 2 vols. Edited by François Bourgoing. Villa Bethanie, Montsoult Seine-et-Oise: Maison D'Institution de L'Oratoire, 1960. Unless indicated otherwise, all citations are from this.

Oeuvres de piété. From *Les oeuvres de l'eminentissime et reverendissime*

BIBLIOGRAPHY

Pierre cardinal de Bérulle. Edited by J.-P. Migne. Paris: Ateliers catholiques, 1856. We have chosen this edition for our citations, indicated by *OP*, since this contains a more ample collection of the *OP* than the Montsoult edition (the numbering of the two editions is slightly different also). It is best to test the two editions against one another; the Montsoult edition is often considered the more "authentic."

Pierre de Bérulle: Introduction et choix de textes. Témoins de la foi Series. Edited by Michel Dupuy. Paris: Bloud et Gay, 1964.

English Translations

Bremond, Henri. *A Literary History of Religious Thought in France* 3: *The Triumph of Mysticism.* Translated by K. L. Montgomery. London: SPCK, 1936. Selections from Bérulle throughout, esp. pp. 1–222.

Secondary

Bellemare, R. *Le sens de la créature dans la doctrine de Bérulle.* Paris: Desclée de Brouwer, 1959. A fine analysis of Bérulle's relational anthropology.

Bremond, Henri. 3 (above) and *Histoire littéraire du sentiment religieux en France* 7: *La metaphysique des saints.* Paris: Bloud et Gay, 1928, pp. 5–162 (for some comparisons between Bérullian spirituality and St. Francis de Sales).

Cochois, Paul. *Bérulle et l'école française. Maîtres spirituels* Series. Paris: Seuil, 1963. Perhaps the best overview of the controversy of the vows of servitude.

Cognet, Louis. "Bérulle et la théologie de l'incarnation." *XVIIe siècle* 29 (1955): 330–52.

———. *La spiritualité moderne (Histoire de spiritualité* 3/1). Paris: Desclée de Brouwer, 1966, pp. 310–59. Indispensable.

D'Angers, Julien-Eymard. "L'exemplarisme bérullien: les rapports du naturel et du surnaturel dans l'oeuvre du cardinal de Bérulle." *Revue des sciences religieuses* 31 (1957): 122–39.

Dagens, Jean. *Bérulle et les origines de la restauration catholique*

BIBLIOGRAPHY

(1575–1611). Paris: Desclée de Brouwer, 1952. The best historical study to date.

Dupuy, Michel. *Bérulle. Une spiritualité de l'adoration*. Paris: Desclée de Brouwer, 1964. A particularly fine and sophisticated analysis, with some helpful comparisons with St. Ignatius Loyola.

Guillén Preckler, Fernando. *Bérulle aujourd'hui 1575–1975: pour une spiritualité de l'humanité du Christ. Le point théologique* Series, 25. Paris: Beauchesne, 1978. An excellent attempt to probe Bérulle's contemporary relevance, noting Bérulle's similarity to Hans Urs von Balthasar's theology, and suggesting service as a contemporary transposition of servitude.

———. *"État" chez le cardinal de Bérulle: théologie et spiritualité des "états" bérulliens. Analecta Gregoriana* Series, 197. Rome: Gregorian University, 1974. The best study of the difficult notion of *état*, and also a fine overview of Bérulle's entire thought.

Houssaye, Michel. *Le cardinal de Bérulle et le cardinal de Richelieu*. Paris: E. Plon, 1875.

———. *Les carmélites de France et le cardinal de Bérulle*. Paris: E. Plon, 1873.

———. *Le père de Bérulle et l'oratoire de Jésus*. Paris: E. Plon, 1874.

———. *M. de Bérulle et les carmélites de France*. Paris: H. Plon, 1872. (Houssaye's works are the "classic" historical sources.)

Huijben, J. "Aux sources de la spiritualité française du XVIIe siècle." *Supplément de la vie spirituelle* 25 (1930): 113–39; 26 (1931): 17–46, 75–111; 27 (1931): 20–42, 94–122. Helpful especially for the Rhineland-Flemish mystical tradition's influence on the French School.

Minton, Anne M. "Pierre de Bérulle: The Search for Unity." *The Spirituality of Western Christendom 2: The Roots of the Modern Christian Tradition*. Edited by E. Rozanne Elder. Kalamazoo, MI: Cistercian Publications, 1984, pp. 105–23.

———. "The Figure of Christ in the Writings of Pierre de Bérulle: 1575–1629." Ph.D. dissertation. New York University, 1979.

Orcibal, Jean. *Le cardinal de Bérulle: évolution d'une spiritualité*. Paris, Cerf, 1965.

Thompson, William M. "A Study of Bérulle's Christic Spirituality." In *Jesus, Lord and Savior: A Theopathic Christology and Soteriology*. New York: Paulist, 1980, pp. 226–49.

BIBLIOGRAPHY

———. "The Christic Universe of Pierre de Bérulle and the French School." *American Benedictine Review* 29 (1978): 320–47.

Vasey, Vincent R. "Mary in the Doctrine of Bérulle on the Mysteries of Christ." *Marian Studies* 36 (1985): 60–80.

Vidal, M. de. *Le cardinal de Bérulle théologien marial. La doctrine de Marie épouse.* Nicolet Quebec centre marial canadien, 1957.

Walsh, Milton Thomas. "The Sources of Pierre de Bérulle's Christocentric Spirituality." M.A. thesis. Menlo Park, CA: St. Patrick's Seminary, 1978.

Madeleine de Saint-Joseph

Primary

Lettres spirituelles. Edited by Pierre Serouet. Paris: Desclée de Brouwer, 1965. All citations from her letters are from this edition, indicated by *Lettre.*

Une mystique du XVII siècle: soeur Catherine de Jésus. Editions de la *Vie spirituelle.* Edited by Jean-Baptiste Ériau. Paris: Desclée et Cie, 1929. A fine edition of Madeleine's *La vie de soeur Catherine de Jésus.*

English Translations

Bremond, Henri. Vol. 2 (see above): *The Coming of Mysticism (1590–1620).* Translated by K. L. Montgomery. London: SPCK, 1930. Selections from the *La vie de soeur Catherine de Jésus,* pp. 227–67.

Secondary

Bremond, Henri. Vol. 2 (see above). Pp. 227–67.

Cognet, Louis. *La spiritualité moderne* (see above). Pp. 362–67.

Ériau, J.-B. *La vénérable Madeleine de St.-Joseph: première prieure française du Carmel de l'Incarnation (1578–1637): essai sur sa vie et ses lettres inédites.* Paris: L'Art catholique, 1921.

BIBLIOGRAPHY

(Louise de Jésus). *La vénérable Madeleine de Saint-Joseph: première prieure française du premier monastère des carmélites déchaussées en France (1578–1637)*. Paris/Clamart: Carmel de l'Incarnation, 1935. The best biography available, with ample selections from her writings.

Macca, Valentine. "Magdalen of St. Joseph (Magdalen du Bois de Fontaines, 1578–1637)." In *Saints of Carmel: A Compilation from Various Dictionaries*. Directed by Louis Saggi. Rome: Carmelite Institute, 1972, pp. 183–86.

Madaule, Jacques. "La première prieure française du Carmel réformé." *La vie spirituelle* 49 (1936): 499–516.

Rimaud, Elisabeth. "Présence au monde d'une carmélite: la vénérable Madeleine de St.-Joseph." *Le carmel* (1966), 48–66. A good view of Madeleine's involvement with the aristocracy.

Serouet, Pierre. "Madeleine de Saint-Joseph." *Dictionnaire de spiritualité*. Vol. 10. Edited by Marcel Viller, et al. Paris: Beauchesne, 1980, cols. 57–60.

Winowska, Maria. "Mère Madeleine de Saint-Joseph, première prieure du Carmel de France." *La vie spirituelle* 89 (1953): 57–83.

Olier

Primary

Anthologie. Edited by Michel Dupuy, et al. Paris: Compagnie de Saint Sulpice, 1987.

Catéchisme chrétien pour la vie intérieure et Journée chrétienne. Edited by François Amiot. Paris: Le Rameau, 1954. The best critical edition, from which our citations come. Citations indicated by *Cat* (for the *Catéchisme*) and *J* (for the *Journée*).

Divers écrits. Paris: Sulpician Archives.

Esprit de M. Olier. Paris: Sulpician Archives.

Introduction a la vie et aux vertus chrétiennes with the *Pietas Seminarii*. Edited by François Amiot. Paris: Le Rameau, 1954. The best critical edition, from which our citations come. Citations indicated by *I* (for the *Introduction*).

Lettres de M. Olier. 2 vols. Edited by É. Levesque. Paris: J. de Gigord,

1935. Our citations are from this, indicated by *Lettre* with the appropriate volume number.

Mémoires autographes. 8 vols. Paris: Sulpician Archives, 1642–52. Our citations are from this, indicated by *Mém* or *Mém c* (a later copy).

Oeuvres complètes de M. Olier. Edited by J.-P. Migne. Paris: Ateliers catholiques, 1856. Unless indicated otherwise, this is the source of our citations.

Traité des saints ordres. Edited by Gilles Chaillot, Michel Dupuy and Irénée Noye. Paris: St.-Sulpice, 1984. The best critical edition, arguing that the *Traité* is a touched up anthology of various works of M. Olier. Citations indicated by *T.*

Translations

Bremond, Henri. Vols. 2 and 3 (see above). Selections throughout both volumes.

Olier, Jean-Jacques. *Catechism of an Interior Life.* Translated by M.E.K. Baltimore: Metropolitan Press, 1847. I was unable to locate a copy of this translation.

Secondary

Bouchaud, Constant. "Le role de mère Agnes dans la preparation spirituelle de Jean-Jacques Olier à la fondation du Séminaire de Saint-Sulpice." *Bulletin de Saint-Sulpice* 12 (1986): 160–70.

Bremond, Henri. Vol. 3 (see above). Pp. 359–434. A very lively overview of Olier's life and spirituality. Bremond clearly has an affection for his subject, but his interpretation, especially of Olier's "great trial," sparked an ongoing controversy.

Chaillot, Gilles. "Criteria for the Spiritual Formation of Pastors: The Pedagogical Tradition Inherited from M. Olier." *Bulletin de Saint-Sulpice* 4 (1978): 24–32.

———. "L'expérience eucharistique de J.-J. Olier: témoignage des *Mémoires*." *Bulletin de Saint-Sulpice* 10 (1984): 63–106.

———. "Les premières leçons de l'expérience mystique de Monsieur Olier." *Bulletin du comité des études* 40 (1962): 501–43. An

BIBLIOGRAPHY

indispensable analysis of Olier's "great trial," this time surfacing its genuinely mystical character.

Cognet, Louis. *La spiritualité moderne* (see above). Pp. 399–406.

Dupuy, Michel. *Se laisser à l'Esprit: itinéraire spirituel de Jean-Jacques Olier*. Paris: Cerf, 1982. The most recent biography, from a psycho-historical perspective. Plentiful selections from the *Mémoires*.

Faillon, Étienne-Michel. *Abrégé de la vie de M. Olier*. Montréal: L. Perrault, 1847.

———. *Vie de M. Olier*. 3 vols. Paris: Poussièlgue Frères, and F. Wattelier et Cie, 1873. A basic historical study, upon which all others must rely.

Glendon, Lowell M. *An Annotated and Descriptive Chronology of the Important Events in the Life of Jean-Jacques Olier (1608–1657)*. Baltimore: Society of St. Sulpice, 1987.

———. "Jean-Jacques Olier's Shifting Attitude Toward the Human." *Bulletin de Saint-Sulpice* 5 (1979): 43–49.

———. "Jean-Jacques Olier's View of the Spiritual Potential of Human Nature: A Presentation and an Evaluation." Ph.D. dissertation. Fordham University, 1983. A very challenging study of how Olier's spirituality intersects with some currents in contemporary American (U.S.) theology and spirituality.

Huvelin, Abbé. "Monsieur Olier at St. Sulpice" and "Monsieur Olier and the Seminaries." *Some Spiritual Guides of the Seventeenth Century*. Introduction and translation by Joseph Leonard. New York: Benziger, 1927, pp. 63–86, 87–108. Huvelin was Baron Friedrich von Hügel's spiritual director; this work is one of the links between the Baron and the French School.

Icard, H.-J. *Doctrine de M. Olier*. Paris: Victor Lecoffre, 1891.

Johnson, Timothy K. "Jean-Jacques Olier: Spiritual Director." *Bulletin de Saint-Sulpice* 6 (1980): 287–310. A valuable study of the most important sources on this topic.

Letourneau, G. *La méthode d'oraison mentale du séminaire de Saint-Sulpice*. Paris: Victor Lecoffre, 1903. A genetic study, tracing the various accretions to Olier's approach to prayer, as well as its origins.

Monier, Frédéric. *Vie de Jean-Jacques Olier*. Paris: Poussièlgue, 1914. Unfortunately incomplete, this is a very fine historical study.

BIBLIOGRAPHY

Noye, Irénée. "Sur la prière: 'O Jesu vivens in Maria.' " *Bulletin du comité des études* 7 (1954): 8–17; 8 (1955): 10–21.

Noye, Irénée and Michel Dupuy. "Olier (Jean-Jacques)." *Dictionnaire de spiritualité*. Vol. 11. Edited by M. Viller, et al. Paris: Beauchesne, 1982, cols. 737–51.

Pourrat, Pierre. *Father Olier: Founder of Saint-Sulpice*. Translated by W. S. Reilly. Baltimore: Voice Publishing Company, 1932. For the English reader, the best biography.

Thompson, Edward Healy. *The Life of Jean-Jacques Olier: Founder of the Seminary of St. Sulpice*. London: Burns and Oates, 1885. Based upon Faillon's work.

Thompson, William M. "Olier's *La journée chrétienne* as a Guide for Today's Theology." *Bulletin de Saint-Sulpice* 14 (1988): 113–27.

Eudes

Primary

En tout la volonté de Dieu: S. Jean Eudes à travers ses lettres. By Clément Guillon. Paris: Cerf, 1981. A very helpful selection of letters by the saint, spanning his career and major concerns, with critical commentary.

Oeuvres complètes du vénérable Jean Eudes. 12 vols. Introduction and notes by Joseph Dauphin and Charles Lebrun. Vannes or Paris: P. Lethielleux, 1905–11. The critical edition; unless otherwise indicated, all our citations are from this.

Saint Jean Eudes: introduction et choix de textes. *Témoins de la foi* Series. By Paul Milcent. Paris: Bloud et Gay, 1964. This work contains a thematic selection of the saint's writings.

Translations

Bremond, Henri. Vol. 3 (see above). Esp. pp. 497–572.

Eudes, Saint John. *Letters and Shorter Works*. Translated by Ruth Hauser. New York: Kenedy, 1948.

BIBLIOGRAPHY

————. *Meditations on Various Subjects.* Introduction by Charles Lebrun. New York: Kenedy, 1947.

————. *The Admirable Heart of Mary.* Translated by Charles di Targiani and Ruth Hauser. New York: Kenedy, 1948. A nicely condensed version of the three volumes of the *Coeur.*

————. *The Life and Kingdom of Jesus in Christian Souls: A Treatise on Christian Perfection for Use by Clergy or Laity.* Translated by a Trappist of Gethsemani. Introduction by Fulton J. Sheen. New York: Kenedy, 1946.

————. *The Priest: His Dignity and Obligations.* Translated by W. Leo Murphy. Introduction by Charles Lebrun. New York: Kenedy, 1947.

————. *The Sacred Heart of Jesus.* Translated by Richard Flower. Introduction by Gerald A. Phelan. New York: Kenedy, 1946. (All the Kenedy translations are in the series *The Selected Works of St. John Eudes.* Edited by Wilfrid E. Myatt and Patrick J. Skinner.)

Milcent, Paul. *Saint John Eudes: Presentation and Texts.* Glasgow: John S. Burns, 1963. An English translation of Milcent's book (above).

Secondary

Arragain, Jacques, et al. *Le coeur du Seigneur: études sur les écrites et l'influence de saint Jean Eudes dans sa devotion au coeur de Jésus.* Paris: La Colombe, 1955.

Bremond, Henri. Vol. 3 (see above). Pp. 497–572. This includes helpful and provocative studies of the saint's relation to Marie des Vallées and of the saint's sacred heart theology in comparison with that of St. Margaret Mary Alacoque.

Herambourg, Peter. *St. John Eudes: A Spiritual Portrait.* Translated by Ruth Hauser. New York: Newman, 1960.

Lebrun, Charles. *La dévotion au coeur de Marie: étude historique et doctrinale.* Paris: P. Lethielleux, 1917.

————. *La spiritualité de saint Jean Eudes.* Paris: P. Lethielleux, 1933.

————. *Le bienheureux Jean Eudes et le culte public du coeur de Jésus.*

BIBLIOGRAPHY

Paris: P. Lethielleux, 1917. Lebrun is the premier historian of the saint.

Legaré, Clément. *La structure semantique, le lexeme du coeur dans l'oeuvre de saint Jean Eudes.* Montréal: Les Presses Universitaires du Quebec, 1976.

Milcent, Paul. "Jean Eudes (saint), 1601–1680." *Dictionnaire de spiritualité.* Vol. 8. Edited by M. Viller, et al. Paris: Beauchesne, 1972, cols. 488–501.

————. *S. Jean Eudes: un artisan de renouveau chrétien au XVIIe siècle. Semeurs* Series. Paris: Cerf, 1985. The leading historical study.

Peyrous, Bernard. "La christologie de saint Jean Eudes." *Divus Thomas* 88 (1985): 42–57.

General Studies

Aumann, Jordan. *Christian Spirituality in the Catholic Tradition.* San Francisco: Ignatius, 1985.

Balthasar, Hans Urs von. "Die Metaphysik des Oratoriums." *Herrlichkeit: Eine Theologische Ästhetik,* 3/1: *Im Raum der Metaphysik.* Einsiedeln: Johannes Verlag, 1965, pp. 471–79. Bérulle and Condren are featured.

————. "Pascal." *The Glory of the Lord: A Theological Aesthetics* 3: *Studies in Theological Style: Lay Styles.* Edited by John Riches. Translated by Andrew Louth, John Saward, Martin Simon and Rowan Williams. San Francisco: Ignatius, 1986, pp. 172–238. Sensitive to Condren's influence on Pascal.

————. "Theology and Sanctity," and "Spirituality." *Essays in Theology* 2: *Word and Redemption.* Translated by A. V. Littledale in cooperation with Alexander Dru. New York: Herder and Herder, 1965, pp. 49–108.

Bertaud, Émile. "Élévations spirituelles." *Dictionnaire de spiritualité.* Vol. 4/1. Edited by M. Viller, et al. Paris: Beauchesne, 1960, cols. 553–58.

Boisard, M. *La compagnie de Saint Sulpice: trois siècles d'histoire.* 2 vols. Paris: Compagnie de Saint-Sulpice, n.d.

Bremond, Henri. Vols. 2, 3 and 7 (see above). A great and provocative study, beginning the modern reappropriation of the French School. Controversial, but indispensable. The entire series was published under the general title of *Histoire littéraire du senti-ment religieux en France depuis la fin des guerres de religion jusqu'a nos jours.* 11 vols. Paris: Bloud et Gay, 1916–33. English translation: *A Literary History of Religious Thought in France From the Wars of Religion Down to Our Own Times.* 3 vols. Translated by K. L. Montgomery. London: SPCK, 1928–36.

Cahiers lasalliens. Rome: Casa Generalizia, 1959ff. Critical editions of the works of St. John Baptist de La Salle, and of the early biographies.

Cahill, Michael. *Francis Libermann's Commentary on the Gospel of St. John: An Investigation of the Rabbinical and French School Influ-ences.* 2 vols. in 1. Dublin and London: Paraclete Press, 1987.

Callahan, C. Annice. *Karl Rahner's Spirituality of the Pierced Heart: A Reinterpretation of Devotion to the Sacred Heart.* Lanham, MD: University Press of America, 1985. Helpful suggestions for a renewed heart theology, and for understanding St. Margaret Mary Alacoque.

Cognet, Louis. "Ecclesiastical Life in France." *History of the Church 6: The Church in the Age of Absolutism and Enlightenment.* Edited by Hubert Jedin and John Dolan. Translated by Gunther J. Holst. New York: Crossroad, 1981, pp. 3–106. The best gen-eral historical survey of our period.

———. *La spiritualité moderne* (see above). The best survey of the spirituality of the "modern" period.

———. "Libermann et la spiritualité française." *Spiritus,* Supplément, 1963, 23–30.

———. "Mysticism: E. École Française." *Sacramentum Mundi.* Vol. 4. Edited by Karl Rahner, et al. New York: Herder and Herder, 1969, pp. 151–52.

———. *Post-Reformation Spirituality.* Twentieth Century Encyclo-pedia of Catholicism. Vol. 41. Translated by P. Hepburne Scott. New York: Hawthorn, 1959.

Condren, Charles de. *Lettres du Père Charles de Condren (1588–1641).* Edited by Paul Auvray and André Jouffrey. Paris: Cerf, 1943. Essential for understanding Condren's influence over our prin-cipals.

———. *The Eternal Sacrifice.* Translated by H. J. Monteith. London: Thomas Baker, 1906. A translation of Condren's *Idée du sacer-doce et du sacrifice de Jésus-Christ.* See J. Galy (below) for theories of how much of this book comes from Condren, and how much from his disciples. In any case, Condren's theology of the "eternal sacrifice" of Jesus in heaven will be found here.

Cooke, Bernard. *Ministry to Word and Sacraments*. Philadelphia: Fortress, 1976. An excellent study, recognizing the place of the French School.

D'Angers, Julien-Eymard. *L'humanisme chrétien au XVIIe siècle: St. François de Sales et Yves de Paris*. International Archives of the History of Ideas, 31. La Haye: Martinus Nijhoff, 1970. This work attempts to clarify and critique Bremond's confusing meanings of the idea of "humanism."

Daniel-Rops, H. *History of the Church of Christ 6: The Church in the Seventeenth Century*. Translated by J. J. Buckingham. London: J. M. Dent & Sons/New York: E. P. Dutton & Co., 1963.

De Paul, Vincent. *Entrétiens spirituels aux missionaires*. Edited by André Dodin. Paris: Seuil, 1960.

Deville, Raymond. "Actualité de l'école française?" *Bulletin de Saint-Sulpice* 8 (1982): 42–54.

———. *L'école française de spiritualité*. Bibliothèque d'histoire du christianisme Series, 11. Paris: Desclée de Brouwer, 1987. An excellent introduction, with selected texts from Bérulle, Condren, Olier, Montfort and La Salle.

Dionysius (the Areopagite). *Pseudo-Dionysius: The Complete Works*. Classics of Western Spirituality Series. Translated by Colm Luibheid. Introductions by Jaroslav Pelikan, et al. New York: Paulist, 1987. Essential for the Dionysian, exemplarist horizon of the French School.

Dupuy, Michel. "Intérieur de Jésus." *Dictionnaire de spiritualité*. Vol. 7/2. Edited by M. Viller, et al. Paris: Beauchesne, 1971, cols. 1870–77.

Egan, Harvey. *Christian Mysticism: The Future of a Tradition*. New York: Pueblo, 1984. Very helpful for exploring the relation between theology and spirituality, a theme important to the "science of the saints" of the French School.

Galy, J. *Le sacrifice dans l'école française*. Paris: Nouvelles Éditions Latines, 1951. Especially good on this theme in Condren, with ample studies of Bérulle and Olier, and briefer studies of others.

Goichot, Émile. "Du 'siecle classique' au 'siecle mystique': l'apport historique de l'abbé Bremond." *La vie spirituelle* 142 (1988): 433–50.

———. *Henri Bremond historien du sentiment religieux: genèse et strategie d'une entreprise littéraire.* Paris: Éditions Ophyrys, Association de Publications près les Universités de Strasbourg, 1982.

Harang, Jean, ed. *La spiritualité bérullienne. Prières de tous les temps* Series, 32. Chambrey: C.L.D., 1983. Samples of prayers from the spectrum of the French School, with an introduction.

Kasper, Walter. *Jesus the Christ.* Translated by V. Green. New York: Paulist, 1976. Very helpful for understanding the "privation" of Jesus' human "person" (in the technical conciliar sense) by the "person of the Logos." A central theme in Bérulle and Olier especially.

Kauffman, Christopher J. *Tradition and Transformation in Catholic Culture: The Priests of Saint Sulpice in the United States from 1791 to the Present.* New York: Macmillan, 1988. An accessible entry into the Sulpician tradition for the American reader, stressing its progressive leadership in the United States.

La Salle, St. John Baptist de. *John Baptist de La Salle: The Letters.* Edited by Augustine Loes. Translated by Colman Malloy. Romeoville, IL: Christian Brothers Conference, 1988.

———. *Meditations for the Time of Retreat.* Translated by Augustine Loes. Romeoville, IL: Christian Brothers Conference, 1975. A popular entry into the saint; the influence of the French School is quickly felt by the reader.

Laurentin, René. *Dieu seul est ma tendresse: René Laurentin présente L. M. Grignion de Montfort, Le secret de Marie. La mère du Seigneur* Series. Paris: O.E.I.L., 1984. Written for the sake of the saint's becoming a "doctor of the Church." The saint's influence on Pope John Paul II is also featured.

Le Brun, Jacques. "VI. Le grand siècle de la spiritualité française et ses lendemains." *Dictionnaire de spiritualité.* Vol. 5. Edited by M. Viller, et al. Paris: Beauchesne, 1964, cols. 917–53.

———. "Marguerite–Marie Alacoque (Sainte)." *Dictionnaire de spiritualité.* Vol. 10. Edited by M. Viller, et al. Paris: Beauchesne, 1980, cols. 349–55.

Lebrun, François. *Le XVIIe siècle. Collection U. Histoire moderne* Series. Paris: A. Colin, 1967.

Marie-Thérèse de Saint-Joseph. "Marie de L'Incarnation (bienheureuse)." *Dictionnaire de spiritualité.* Vol. 10. Edited by M. Viller, et al. Paris: Beauchesne, 1980, cols. 486–87. A study of Mme. Acarie.

BIBLIOGRAPHY

Matthews, V. J. *St. Philip Neri.* Rockford, IL: Tan Books and Publishers, 1984. Helpful for the origins of the Oratory.

Mersch, Emile. *The Whole Christ: The Historical Development of the Doctrine of the Mystical Body in Scripture and Tradition.* Translated by John R. Kelly. London: Dennis Dobson, 1938. An extensive treatment of the French School's contribution is included.

Milet, Jean. *God or Christ? The Excesses of Christocentricity.* Translated by John Bowden. New York: Crossroad, 1981. Tends to view the French School as the influential factor promoting an unbalanced Christocentrism, which in turn leads, the author suggests, toward humanism. Milet seems to exaggerate the influence of the Renaissance on the French School, and misses the relational and dialogical view of God characteristic of the school.

Montfort, St. Louis-Marie (Grignion) de. *Oeuvres complètes.* Paris: Seuil, 1966. (English translation [nearly complete]: *God Alone: The Collected Writings of St. Louis Mary de Montfort.* Bayshore, NY: Montfort Publications, 1987.)

———. *The Love of Eternal Wisdom.* Translated and annotated by A. Somers. Bayshore, NY: Montfort Publications, 1960.

———. *True Devotion to Mary.* Translated by Frederick Faber. Rockford IL: Tan Books and Publishers, 1985. The influence of the French School is quickly evident to the reader.

Muto, Susan Annette. *Pathways of Spiritual Living.* Petersham, MA: St. Bede's Publications, 1984. Helpful and contemplative explorations of themes central to the French School, as well as to other great spiritual families.

O'Shea, William. "The Liturgical Tradition of the Society of St. Sulpice." *Worship* 31 (1956-7): 443-529. A good beginning; we need a solid study of the liturgical contributions of the entire French School.

Osborne, Kenan B. *Priesthood: The History of the Ordained Ministry in the Roman Catholic Church.* New York: Paulist, 1988. Includes the Olierian, Sulpician contribution at some length.

Pascal, Blaise. "Lettre de Pascal à monsieur et madame Périer, à clermont" (No. 5). *Ouevres complètes. Bibliothèque de la Pléiade* Series, 34. Edited by Jacques Chevalier. Paris: Gallimard, 1954, pp. 490-501. This illustrates the influence of Condren's views on sacrifice.

BIBLIOGRAPHY

Pourrat, Pierre. *Christian Spirituality* 3: *Later Developments: Pt. 1: From the Renaissance to Jansenism*. Translated by W. H. Mitchell. Westminster, MD: Newman, 1953.

Rahner, Karl. *On Prayer*. New York: Paulist, 1958. Turns to Bérulle to highlight the role of the Incarnation in prayer.

———. "Some Theses for a Theology of Devotion to the Sacred Heart." *Theological Investigations* 3. Translated by Karl-H. and Boniface Kruger. Baltimore: Helicon, 1967, pp. 331–52. Proposes that this devotion is an alternative to both Jansenistic rigorism and Renaissance "secularism."

———. "The Eternal Significance of the Humanity of Jesus for Our Relationship With God." Ibid., pp. 35–46. A profound study of the theological foundations of Christocentrism, a theme central to our principals.

Ruusbroec, John. *The Spiritual Espousals and Other Works*. Classics of Western Spirituality Series. Introduction and translation by James A. Wiseman. New York: Paulist, 1985. An excellent entry into the themes characteristic of Rhineland-Flemish mysticism, a major source of the French School.

Sauvage, Michel, and Miguel Campos. *St. John Baptist de La Salle: Announcing The Gospel to the Poor: The Spiritual Experience and Spiritual Teaching of St. John Baptist de La Salle*. Translated by Matthew J. O'Connell. Romeoville, IL: Christian Brothers National Office, 1981.

Saward, John. "Bérulle and the 'French School.'" *The Study of Spirituality*. Edited by Cheslyn Jones, Geoffrey Wainwright and Edward Yarnolds. New York: Oxford, 1986, pp. 386–96.

Sheppard, Lancelot. *Barbe Acarie: Wife and Mystic*. London: Burns Oates, 1953. An accessible introduction to Mme. Acarie, but biased against Bérulle.

Squire, Aelred. "The Human Condition: A Study of Some Seventeenth-Century French Writers." *Life of the Spirit* 15 (1961): 166–82.

Thompson, William M. *Fire and Light: The Saints and Theology*. New York: Paulist, 1987. An analysis of theology's relationship to mystical experience, a theme central to the "science of the saints" of the French School.

Tenailleau, Bernard. "Father Libermann's Spirituality." *Spiritans Today* 4 (1985): 49–76. Helpful in appreciating the French School's influence.

BIBLIOGRAPHY

Tracy, David. *The Analogical Imagination: Christian Theology and the Culture of Pluralism.* New York: Crossroad, 1981. Essential for appreciating the theo-literary nature of religious classics.

van Kaam, Adrian. *A Light to the Gentiles: The Life Story of the Venerable Francis Libermann.* Milwaukee: Bruce, 1959.

Walsh, Eugene A. *The Priesthood in the Writings of the French School: Bérulle, De Condren, Olier.* S.T.D dissertation. Washington, D.C.: Catholic University of America Press, 1949. Still a very fine introduction; particularly good on the theology of sacrifice in the French School.

Wright, Wendy M. *Bond of Perfection: Jeanne de Chantal and Francois de Sales.* New York: Paulist, 1985. Very helpful for appreciating male-female "spiritual" friendship during the founding period of the French School.

INDEX TO THE FOREWORD, PREFACE, AND INTRODUCTION

INDEXES

INDEXES

INDEXES

INDEXES

Marguerite du Saint-Sacrement (of Beaune), 22, 30n54, 80
Marguerite du Saint-Sacrement, 80
Marie des Vallées, 20–22
Marie of the Incarnation, Bd.: See Mme. Acarie
Marie of the Trinity, 15
Marie-Euphrasie, St., 80
Marie Thérèse, 27n2
Mariology, 25–26, 35, 47–54, 65–66, 72nn88,91, 73n93, 81–82, 86–87, 95n21
Mary, B. V., xvi, 39, 66, 78, 81; See Mariology
Mass: See Eucharist
Maurists, 8
Maximus Confessor, St., 8
Mazarin, J., 27n2
Mercier, A., 91n6
Mersch, E., 82–83, 92n12
Métézau, P., 81
Milcent, P., 20, 27n5, 28n23, 29n48, 29–30n49, 30nn51,53–54, 65, 68n9, 69nn29,31–2, 71n67, 73nn94–95,99, 74n102, 75nn134,136, 76nn140,142, 91n6, 96n23, 101n1
Ministry, 87–88; See Priesthood
Minton, A., 89n2
Monier, F., 29n47
Montfort, L.-M. Grignion de, St., 47, 81, 84
Montgomery, K., 28nn21,30, 68n13, 89n4
Morgan, D., xiii
Morland, D., 90n4
Morris, W., xiii
Mudge, L., 101n1
Morin, J., 9
Muto, S., xiii
Mystery, 70n40; See Christology
Mystical Body, 39, 60, 65
Mysticism, 9–11, 13, 44–45, 50ff., 71n60, 93n15; Abstract: 10–11, 13, 24–25, 35–36, 48, 69n27, 78, 88; Everyday: 10

Néant/Nothingness, 40–47, 77
Neoplatonism/Neoplatonic, 14, 32–33, 35, 37, 40, 55, 78, 84–85, 100; See Classical/Platonic and Dionysius
Neri, Philip, St., 74n103
Neufelder, J., 75n133
Nevers, C. de, 4
Newton, I., 6
Nicholl, D., 29n41

Nobility, the, 28n23
Nowak, S., 75n130
Noye, I., xiii, 61, 67n7, 71n57, 73n93, 91n6, 101n1; See references to Olier's T

O'Carroll, M., 95n21
O'Connell, M., 92n8
"O Jesu vivens in Maria" (prayer), 52, 73n93–94
O'Kane, P., xiii
Olier, J.-J., xi–xii, xv–xvii, 5–6, 10, 12–13, 16–19, 20, 22, 29nn36,38–40,42–43,46, 30nn50,53–54, 31n61, 34 (on God and Trinity), 37–39 and 43–45 (on Christology, soteriology, and spirituality), 51–52 (on Mary), 60–64 (on ecclesiology and pastoral work), 66 (on eschatology), 67n8, 69n25–27, 70n50–51, 71nn52–55,57–61, 72n89–91, 73nn92–93,101, 74n102, 75n121–33, 76n145, 78ff., 90–91n5, 91–92n6, 93–94n15 (beatification process), 94n16, 95n21, 95–96n23, 98 and 100 (texts of), 101n3
Oratory/Oratorians, 12–14, 16–17, 20, 23, 55, 57, 59, 61, 64, 66, 69n23, 74n103, 81, 91n6 (religious foundations associated with)
Orcibal, J., 28n30, 29n32, 30n60, 68n11, 90n5
Osborn, H., 101n2

Pascal, B., 83, 92n10
Passion (of Jesus), 10
Pastoral Renewal/Reform, 11–13, 54–65
Patristic influence on French School, 84
Paul, St./Pauline texts (in the French School), 9, 33, 39, 44–46, 71n61
Paul V, Pope, 15
Person (of Jesus), Privation of Human: See Enhypostasia
Pelletier, R.-V., 80
Petau, D., 8
Petite oeuvre, 91n6
Pius VI, Pope, 93n15, 98
Pius IX, Pope, 95n21
Pius X, Pope, St., 22, 95n21
Pius XI, Pope, 22
Platonic, 9, 34–35; See Classical/Dionysius/Neoplatonic
Prayer, 70n45, 71n58, 99–100; See Spirituality

355

INDEXES

Priesthood, the, 11–13, 54–58, 60–66
Principe, W., 91n6

Quesnel, P., 94n16
Quietism, 93n15
Quinn, E., 93n14

Rabelais, F., 5
Rademacher, W., xiii
Raffelt, A., 93n14
Rahner, K., 6, 27n7, 68n19, 70n49, 79, 83, 86, 89n1, 89–90n4, 90n5, 92–93n14
Reference, 99
Reformers/Reformation, 5, 8, 11, 55, 57–58, 73n95, 77–78, 89n2
Religion, 39, 56, 61, 75n123
Rembrandt, H., 5
Renaissance, 5–6, 38, 40, 57, 89n2, 89–90n4, 100
Reversal of Hierarchies, the Dionysian, 14
Rhineland (School)/Rheno-, xv, 10, 42, 44, 47–48, 70nn39,41
Richelieu, A., 4–5, 11, 16, 24, 27n2
Riches, J., 92n13
Ricoeur, P., 101n1
Rodriquez, O., 89n2
Rolle, R., xv
Romaillon, J., 91n6
Roquette, P., 29n41
Rousseau, M., 19, 22
Rubens, P., 5
Ruether, R., 25, 31n65
Ruusbroec, J., Bd., xv, 7, 10, 73n78

Sacred Heart (of Mary and Jesus), 6, 19–21, 38–39, 46–47, 52–54, 61, 65–66, 73nn99,101, 73–74n102, 86–87, 90n5; Feasts of: 22, 54, 96n23
Sacrifice, 37, 60–61, 63–65, 68–69n23, 86; See Condren/Host-Victim/Immolation
Saints, 66
Saint-Cyran (Duvergier de Hauranne), 90–91n5
Saint Sulpice, Company (Society) of: See Sulpicians
Sales, F. de, St., 10, 16, 35, 39–40, 67n9, 83, 93n15
Sauvage, M., 92n8
Schillebeeckx, E., 87, 95n21
Science of the Saints (in the French School), xi, 32, 99
Scott, R., 28n21

Scotus, D., 47, 68n20
Séguenot, C., 81
Seminary Reform/Seminaries, 11–12, 20
Serouet, P., 97–98, 101n1; See references to the *Lettres* of Madeleine de Saint-Joseph
Servants of Jesus the High Priest, 91n6
Servants of Mary Immaculate, 91n6
Servitude/Service, 26, 41–50, 70n39, 85–87, 92n9, 99; See Kenosis
Servitude, Vows of, 14–16, 23, 29n32, 38, 41, 48, 51, 68n19, 81
Seton, E., St., 91–92n6
Seward, J., 92n13
Shakespeare, W., 5
Simon, M., 92n13
Simon, R., 8–9
Sin: See Evil/Soteriology
Sisters of Charity of Nazareth, 91–92n6
Sisters of Providence of Evreux, 91n6
Sisters of the Good Savior, 91n6
Society of the Heart of the Admirable Mother, 91n6
Soteriology, 35–47
Solemnity of Jesus, Feast of the, 14, 54
Spalding, C., 91–92n6
Spiritans: See Congregation of the Holy Spirit (Ghost)
Spiritual Direction, 54–55, 58–60, 63–65, 75n133, 76n142
Spirituality, 35–47, 65; See Prayer
State (*État*), 37–39, 41, 72n81, 78–79, 85
Substance (of the mysteries), 36, 41
Sullivan, J., xiii
Sulpicians, 12–13, 19–20, 55, 61–62, 64, 74n103, 80–82, 91–92n6 (religious foundations associated with), 93–94n15, 94n19
Surin, J.-J., 29n41, 81
Suso, H., Bd., xv

Tauler, J., xv
Tenailleau, B., 92n10
Teresa of Avila, St./Teresian, 10, 22, 24, 36, 38, 50, 59, 68n23, 83, 89n2, 93n14, 94n18
Theology, 6ff
Thérèse of Lisieux, St., xvii, 29n41, 50, 72n82, 92n9
Thomassin, L., 8
Thomistic; See St. Thomas Aquinas
Thompson, E., 74n103
Thompson, P., xiii

356

INDEXES

Thompson, W., 68n19
Tillard, J., 92n10
Tracy, D., 84, 89n3, 93n15, 94n16, 101n1
Trinity, the Holy, 33–35, 85; See Bérulle, John Eudes, Madeleine de Saint-Joseph, and J.-J. Olier
Trinitarians of St.-Marin-en-Haut, 91n6

Unity, the Divine, 33–35
Urban VIII, Pope, 16
Ursulines, 91n6

Vasey, V., 95n20
Velázquez, D., 5
Victim: See Host-Victim
Vidal, M. de, 71–72n76
Vincentians, 20

Vinci, Leonardo da, 5
Voegelin, E., 101n1
Vows of Host-Victim and Servitude: See Host-Victim and Servitude, vows of

Wakefield, G., 94n16
Walsh, E., 75n130
Webb, E., 101n1
Whelan, J., 95n19
Williams, R., 92n13
Winston, C., 92n9
Winston, R., 92n9
Wiseman, J., 72n78
Women: See Feminist Theology

Zamet, S., 9, 17, 24

357

INDEX TO TEXTS

INDEXES

359

INDEXES

Other Volumes in this Series